After Before

This is a Shane alert. The story that I have written for you actually begins after this introduction. It is not like I reveal the surprise ending or anything like that, it is just your choice as to whether you want to read this before or after the story. Assuming you will have made up your mind before getting to the next paragraph, I will proceed on that basis.

Over a year ago, I began writing a diary of my mind for my grandson, Shane. It ended up taking up a year of my life, from October 31, 2011 to the following Halloween. At the time this began, Shane was soon to turn three and when it ended a year later, he was several months away from smashing through the four year barrier.

While it wasn't my motivation in the first place, this exercise became a way of kicking mortality right in the nuts. The vast majority of us come and go with not a whole lot of fanfare. Sure, there are usually at least several people to mourn your loss and in many cases there are actually hundreds who come to pay their respects. After a while, the vast majority of attendees go about their own lives and your demise gradually diminishes in significance. Yes, there are a small number that have this red, hot branding iron on their heart and it has other's names on it. Believe me, having lost my father when I was extremely young and my mother when I was much older, I am well aware of loss' ability to mark us forever.

I finished the actual writing of this story around a month ago and spent a majority of that time rereading the manuscript, a term very, very loosely used and without an ounce of seriousness. You will have to believe me that when I began this haphazard journal, I wasn't even sure I would sit down a second time and pick up the thread wherever it happened to be dropped. Much to my surprise, it quickly developed into a fairly strict discipline and one I was conscious of regardless of what happened to be going on in my life or my memory during the year. It became the story of that year and my life, long before the year began.

Now, I have a serious problem. The story to Shane is finished and I am not, which leaves me feeling like a painter with a pallette full of paint and a bare assed, naked canvas. Well, I knew this venture required some kind of forward, in the off chance that anyone else reads this thing. The range of potential readers runs the gamut from people revealed in this story to someone who picks up a bottle with the entire manuscript in it. Now, I know you are going to think I am full of shit, but as Buddha is my witness, I will get a manuscript printed out and I will cork it in a bottle large enough to hold this diary of my mind. It is the other side of this effort, which began with writing to my grandson, who will not be able to understand much of this for many, many years to come. Setting it afloat is the absolute antithesis, left completely to chance. I am so glad we just thought of this, no shit.

Having just referred to “we” in the above entry, let me ‘splain this to you, Lucy. (As I do throughout the story to Shane, I simply tell him to look a word or phrase up.). After completing this year long discipline, I have been feeling a bit lost. Writing had become a complete part of my life and evolved into sort of an impatient urge. Every story usually requires some kind of preface and absolutely nothing came to mind, beyond the need to continue writing. You will never guess what happened? This evening, I decided to keep writing and put it on the front of my story to Shane. If you happen to be one of the two or three people actually reading this, you might want to start with my Halloween in Portland story to Shane and come back to this. In the interest of confusing you, it drove me nuts during my writing that I was doing this in the absolute present moment to someone who would actually be reading it fresh in a whole bunch of years from the moment it was written. Time became what it actually is, something we cling to in order to hold on to sanity in a senseless world.

It is definitely safe to say that anyone coming upon this between now and then will simply take it for what is worth in the moment. Seriously, though, Shane will read all of this years from its being written and it will be brand, spanking new for him. Somewhere along the way, I decided that my story would be published by yours truly. Personally, I think it pretty much sucks, but Shane will undoubtedly find it impactful because I am his Grandpa Larry and God only knows how our connection will evolve on this earth and relocate to a more ethereal location after that. The rest of you, if there are any, have no excuse at all.

Aside from trying to be honest, the only other thing I care about is what is written about anyone else. I promised myself and Shane when I began that I would not go back and rewrite anything because the intent was to capture the moment. As God is my witness, I only wrote about people I love, warts and all. Being a recovering asshole, anything that is felt to be even remotely critical or judgemental is not worth the paper it is written upon. I am not in any position to cast judgment on anyone at all. Every single woman I wrote about, at one time or another, I loved with every ounce of juice I had in me. Their demise had nothing at all to do with any perceived deficiencies on their part. In every instance, if I behaved differently, the outcome may have been different. There is no bullshit in here and it is truly heartfelt. Trust me, I am no lothario, but I have been over the moon with every woman written in this story. The guys are a slightly different story, but not that big a deal either. Every man written about in this is an asshole, so let’s level the playing field

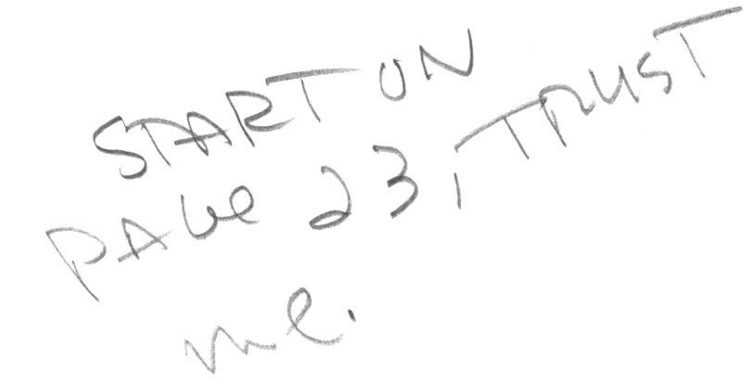

HALLOWEEN IN PORTLAND

Diary of a Mind

Larry Feinstein

NORA -
HAVE REALLY ENJOYED GETTING TO KNOW YOU, AT LEAST A LITTLE. AS A RESULT, YOU WILL NOW HAVE TO SUFFER MY ENTIRE LIFE, LAID BARE IN THESE PAGES.
BEING CONTRARY BY NATURE, I CONSIDER MYSELF THE ANTI-WRITER, OBSERVING NONE OF THE RULES. THE STORY IS REPETITIOUS AT TIMES AND IT IS FLAWED WITH SOME TYPOS. THE BOOK IS NO MORE IMPERFECT THAN OUR LIVES. LARRY

ISBN: 978-0-9721162-1-3

Kauaian Press

with the boys. However, I didn't waste a critical thought or word on anyone else and it is because these men made a difference in my life, a life I am very happy to be living.

Next, I want to address the writing thing. I am not a writer and this is not a book. Clearly, there is some demented need to communicate, but that doesn't mean in any way that I am a professional. Admittedly, the path of my life has nurtured an inner dialogue and some limited ability to communicate it to others. Yes, especially at my age, I know the difference between a colon and semicolon, but have forgotten whatever was taught me about grammar and syntax, etc. because form was not my forte. If I was some old guy writing a letter to his grandson, there would be no judgment about obeying the rules of the real writer. Sorry to disappoint you few readers, but I completely suck at all that stuff and wouldn't dream of having anyone touch any of this, no more than I would want anyone to proof read a letter to my grandson.

My excuse for not laying this tale to rest is that I am waiting for a message from my friend, Eiju. He is an Argentinian Zen Buddhist priest, with whom I have had the privilege of being with and communicating with now for a number of years. A few people have known about this private effort of mine and he is certainly one of them. With the exception of a handful of quotes from the likes of Albert Einstein, the Dalai Lama and a gifted journalist by the name of Chris Hedges, there isn't anyone involved in this other than myself. If you can believe it, no one will have read this prior to it being published because this is all mine, warts and all. Getting back to Eiju, because he embodies so much that draws me to Zen, I asked him if he would write something to Shane, anything at all. My words start the story to my grandson and his will bookend this monologue.

If you are not completely turned off by this post prequel, you will find that my story is continually interrupted by music and some accompanying explanation for Shane. I was born in 1945 and you can do the math in figuring what music meant to someone like me, growing up during a time when we took over ownership of this powerful force. It started with Doo Wop in the mid fifties and I would sit on the stoop of my home in Flushing, Queens and listen to this music on my little transistor radio. The music we listen to today began with the enslaved African Americans all over this country. African chants melded with church music and that chain is still unbroken, with many jewels added along the way. In the Sixties music became very important and it moved a generation, pretty much my generation. To this day, I will wait to do something if there is music I want to listen to. If the music is really good, you don't turn your back and walk away from it, you wait for it to end.

Like every other musical side road in my tale, it was always because of something I was listening to at the moment. Right now, I am listening to some very fine Ray Charles tunes and am reminded of a time when I saw him. Back in the mid-sixties, I was a page at NBC and I went with one of my page friends to see a midnight concert of Ray Charles at Carnegie Hall. It was incredible and being in that elegant venue with fans of his music was something else. Within this story, there are a number of musical highlights and I want my little one to appreciate how special music is and what it has meant to me after all these years. The roots of our contemporary music are incredibly rich and the good stuff rubs off on you. Shane, I know you will be reading this, so add Mr. Charles to your list. Somewhere in the body of this tale is a whole explanation of the page thing and I am not going to waste our time here.

So, the truth is we are killing time until Eiju delivers the goods and I hope you don't mind.

I have been single for a couple of years now and the last time I was naked with a woman was around a year ago and that didn't work out all that well either. The few of you who read this will hopefully be adults and might appreciate the dilemma of being with a partner or being alone. Each one has its sacrifices and I guess it is just a matter of what you want to do without in return for what you get. There are so many people unhappy in relationships and just as many who are miserable in their solitude. Personally, after all these years and a handful of strong relationships, I haven't figured out the path to take. As I encroach upon my late sixties, I am feeling increasingly adverse to unnecessary drama and personal sacrifice for the sake of partnership. At the same time, there is nothing like embracing the naked body of a loving partner and stripping your own self bare in the presence of another.

So many of us get married when we are in our twenties and how in God's name can we possibly know what we want from a relationship at that age, let alone when what we simply want for ourselves. Hindsight provides such spectacular clarity, but last time I checked, we can't go back and change a damn thing. However, the past is our own special School of Life and so many of us just end up getting left back, year after year. Maybe, when you get to be an old fart like me, you might actually be able to appreciate that there are choices you can make anytime at all, as long as you take responsibility for them. Believe me, I am not looking for a president of my very small fan club, rather I am looking for someone who understands what is truly important, particularly in light of the pressing nature of our remaining time here. Trivia devours couples because their basic foundations sucks from the get go. For me, it's like, "Don't you get it, we are all on borrowed time and what the fuck truly matters in the glaring light of that undeniable truth." Right now, I answer to no one and it ain't half bad. There are no phone calls in the middle of the day, asking me to do this or that and pressing for an answer.

When you actually believe that each day is gift, priorities get reordered, assuming you really appreciate the privilege of being given a ticket to ride. We get lost in the minutia of the moment and it is a really shitty habit. A good deal of this story deals with women in my life and women in general. I am enamored with the gender because they can be beautiful in very different ways than guys, at least for me. I am a huge fan and hope I have an opportunity to bury myself once again in the belly of the feminine. In the interim, I got to tell you that solo ain't half bad.

This project of mine, while possible with a woman in my life, would have been completely different and I rather like the singularly confessional dimension of this tale. This has been my secret and it has been easy to maintain that secrecy without any intrusion, a horrible way to refer to a relationship. It seems our lives are these perfect accidents and seat belts are of no use at all. Everything on these pages happened just as it happened and I sure hope there has been no tampering on my part, which I am pretty sure I have avoided even during the sparse re-reads. While this may be my life because it is in my name, this is about all of our lives and I have completely busted my chops to stay as close to the ground as possible. We think everybody's life is so much more interesting than our own and this is a story of an ordinary life and an attempt to share it with my grandson. This has been quite an exercise and anything but easy. If you really care, it is hard to call it easy because it requires your true presence, a test of your deep seated ethics.

Again, I mentioned earlier that I am simply spilling time until I get my epilogue from Eiju and the idea of not sitting here and writing someone about something is pretty much impossible. There are these moments when all I want to do is sit and write something. You know, it just dawned on me that I will feel like a complete schmuck if I don't publish all of this in some form or other. Here I am, talking to you as if this is a book that you are reading. So, I am either a delusional fool or someone who will make sure this message in a bottle gets a chance to float out there. The other side of this is that this exercise has been such an incredible gift to me that if Shane is the only other person to read this, I have achieved whatever the hell I was thinking when this began.

Being of the rock 'n roll generation, wanted to let you I am listening to some Cream and when I sign off here right here, I am likely to ferret out some Buffalo Springfield. This reminds me to let you know that I will just write one paragraph after another, without any consideration for the passage of time. In the story itself, I pretty much defined where I was when I began most entries. All we are doing is killing some time, if you don't mind. Don't blame me, it is all Eiju's fault.

With the accumulation of advantage miles that are very different than the airlines, I have continually attempted to redefine myself in this world and I never quite get it, but I don't really give a shit. Most of the people I have encountered along my journey are not necessarily as maniacally committed to shining the light inside as I think I have been. If we have the opportunity to be present for our departure, it is likely all we take with us when we cross over into anything ranging from nothing to a corridor of bright lights with Hobbitt people all dressed in white, is our sense of the life we have led. I know I mentioned somewhere in the story that the irony is as our time remaining shortens, our appreciation for that diminishing time ought to increase, but it doesn't seem to work that way either. Listen, I am no fucken hero and I will likely misbehave at the end if I am given the privilege. At the same time, I have burrowed into myself a fair amount and honestly hope this little story at least affirms that much. I know this is no masterpiece, rather it is just me and my life and my opinions.

Oh, I just sent a bonsai Jade tree to Shane for his fourth birthday on December 13th. As we say here, that boy is "choke" with stuff and his upcoming birthday will dramatically increase the inventory. A couple of years ago, I had a hunch to send him a ukulele and he connected with it in an unusual manner. He seems to enjoy music, but that could vanish in a day or a week or a month. It seemed like it would be cool to give him something that is alive and requires a little caring, a good lesson if he is old enough to sort of get it.

You will be happy to know it was a very big hit and I am pleased and hope he shows it one hundredth the attention he shows to his accumulation of guitars. Apparently, he wants to continually water the little tree, while a good sign, it would clearly spell the demise of this mini-Jade tree, which is already considerably older than he is.

I wonder if many other people are tempted to do this kind of thing and I have a feeling there aren't all that many. To those of you who want to do it, but think you can't write, I would like this effort to give you the confidence to move ahead and share your life experience with others. Seriously, I am not concerned about editorial inconsistencies, typo's or grammatic disasters. We all have stories to tell and the untold ones perish when we do. I am not about to let form fuck with what I have to say and I also think there is an inherent fear in appearing stupid because the rules of the page are a pain in the ass to follow. We are all free to share, simply for the sake of sharing.

I shut off the machine and just turned it on for a quick second. As I have said, I am just going to slap paragraphs together and ignore the time thing. Dave Brubeck died this week and that matters. I think he was a guy who lived for self-expression and in his case it was Jazz. Trust me, not writing this very epitaph because he was my musical God. After all, I sure as shit hope I am talking about celebrating life and it feels right to recognize the passage of a talent who touched so many. Shane, all you need to do is sit in a real comfortable spot without anything going on and listen to Take Five.

I have always had a crush on music, more than any other art form. It is so easy to love listening to music. You don't have to do anything at all in order to enjoy it. You can now easily have it wherever you happen to be, with whatever you happen to be doing at the time. Most evenings in the past year of writing, there has always been just me and the music.

Many of my extended writing sessions occurred on Sunday afternoon, when I got home from a good motorcycle ride with the Sons of Kauai. There is plenty of bike stuff in the story and no need for me to tell it now, considering I have already written about it in great detail. The only reason why I mentioned any of this is because it is Sunday afternoon once again and I am back from a glorious bike ride to the end of the road in Kokee, with a breathtaking view of the Kalalau Valley unfolding below. It is a site to behold and I am certain there are riding stories about it included further down the road of this tale.

I feel bad about doing all this writing, when I know you are dying to get to the beginning of my story to my grandson. Believe me, I am not to blame and it rests squarely on the robed shoulders of Eiju. Well, that is not completely true either. For some reason, I started thinking about a Hawaiian musician and spirit by the name of Keale, who appears further into this story. I asked him if he could provide a Hawaiian blessing for a young child in both Hawaiian and English. Don't ask me where the idea came from because it was really spontaneous and didn't make complete sense after that. So, in the interest of full disclosure, we are now waiting on both Eiju and Keale. It might be a while, but I will do my best to push this along. When Eiju comes in, we are good to go.

A day of riding a bike on this beautiful island, in the company of many other two wheel soldiers, is very exhilirating and I always find myself operating at a higher energy level when I get back to the tranquil setting of my space. For the year of my writing, I always looked forward to Sunday because I knew it would be a productive monologue and very often I knew what I wanted to write about before hand. There is nothing in any of this that would make me uncomfortable in sharing with a possible partner, but this story became my partner in a very intimate way. For better or worse, here I am.

The curtain on center stage will be going up shortly, at least I think so. I just got Eiju's translation in English and it needs a good deal of work. As a devoted Zen priest, it is not shocking that the message to Shane is Zen related and that can be hard to translate. I think about some of my passages in this story and it would be a nightmare to translate them, unless you actually know the person. Eiju and I think about these kinds of things in a similar manner, so I ought to be able to do a decent job. Of course, it will be sent to him so he can make any changes. Maybe, we have a bit more time than I am figuring. Well, I will just continue writing until I stop and move this thing along in its gestation. Once I stop writing, it can become more like an object I am dealing with because it will be done. It has been so deeply personal and it will be interesting to deal with it as an object, something outside of myself.

I have been away for a handful of days, but don't think you weren't on my mind. Telling my story to my grandson was quite an exercise and now attempting to give you the Cliff Notes is yet another challenge. In the course of telling my story to Shane, we developed a kind of style and if you read this after reading the story, you would know what I mean. Of course, in my case, I wrote all the stuff before and now this postscript for the story you haven't even read yet and you think you're confused?

The truth is I haven't wanted to waste your time in this sequence because I tried not to do that at any point from the beginning to the end of this effort. Today is December 14, 2012 and something awful happened today. A twenty year old man shot twenty little chlldren, some very close to Shane's age. In addition, he blew his mother's face off and killed six other adults. This occurred at an elementary school in Newton, CT. I am not sure if violence in Amerika could stoop any lower or if anything could be more depraved than this particular act. Little babies shot for no reason, because there is no reason imaginable, even in hell.

Right now, I am crying my eyes out and the keypad looks like a puddle. Why do we do these terrible things? What sense is to be made of horrid acts like this? The fact that people are allowed to buy and conceal howitzers is probably a viable direction to explore, but I am not so sure gun control is the magic pill to prevent the devil from doing his evil deeds. In addition, there are millions of weapons in the hands of millions of Americans and they are not about to surrender them. Mental illness is more dangerous than any weapon and it will find the tools necessary for its awful expression. Something happened to that demented assassin before he carried out his carnage and I think we need to look in that direction, while we also argue the Constitutional justification for an armed citizenry.

Throughout this story of mine, I have continually bowed down to the ongoing inevitability of change. It is probably safe to say that I am not one of the Founding Fathers and not nearly as visionary as they were and there is nothing but profound respect for those guys. Do you mean to tell me these brave and brilliant men thought they were writing a political bible to be taken at its word forever and ever? Let me say bullshit to that idea. We are not supposed to hide behind these powdered wigs, we are supposed to get in front of them and carry on the fight for democracy. We have confused moving forward spiritually and intellectually with pure, unadulterated, material acquisition. The soul of Amerika is shattering before my eyes. We are no different than those who have come before us to grab the reins of power. We are following in the tracks of empire, leading us up the mountain and then down the other side.

Our humanity is in a state of decay. The American Dream has become the Global Nightmare. There is a selfish quality to the dream and in this instance it is not the good kind of selfish. The selfish I believe in is making sure you are doing what you do to make certain you become the person you are meant to become. The other selfish is comfortable with stepping on the necks of those with less skin in the game. Unfortunately, we have a culture that rewards the bad selfish, which is just as easily defined as considering human beings and all sentient beings as pawns in their game, a game fixated on power and profit.

A terrible divisiveness is gripping Amerika by the short hairs. It has to do with God, technology and the wealth/power disease. Unfortunately, religion has been used to promote hierarchies that suit its needs, dogma, etc. When God says something is right or wrong, it is absolutely a big deal to all of those who feel She speaks directly to them. Going on the naïve assumption that worship is supposed to bring out the best in each of us, I am not feeling all that good about the results. With all its blessings, technology has been the wedge that now separates each of us from the other. It is like some weird condom, preventing any real contact between social media fornicators. Last, but not least to add to this cocktail of crisis, we have those folks who inherit and/or earn vast sums of money. They have been given a free pass when it comes to promoting and protecting their interests. Huge corporations control our policy and when they mate with our lawmakers, the off spring is a cold, self-serving sociopath that draws its breath from any obstacle in its mission to dominate.

There is no longer any compass for this society and I am not sure there ever was one. In many ways, we appear to be decaying. Mass shootings are no longer some unimaginable possibility, but seem to be an inevitability. My God, what kind of people are we becoming? I feel very, very sad this evening. Muddy Waters has kept me company for this entry and there has been nothing but harmony. Good night and you know I'll be back for more of this.

Hey, I'm back and it is the next evening, following the news of that awful massacre in Connecticut. There is nothing to really say about something for which there are no words. I will leave my sadness right here because mine is not yours and it doesn't serve our budding relationship.

I left the keyboard to get an appropriately filled glass of red wine, which you never fill to the top like you would a beer. I think the wine needs room to breathe in the glass. During my visit to the cellar, I was hit very hard by the idea that anyone other than myself and Shane, who are reading this, must be doing it by choice, which is honestly kind of mind blowing to me. I hope you believe I am on the safe side of vanity because it would bother me if anyone felt it was otherwise. So, let me take this opportunity to thank you for taking this ride with Shane and I (not sure, is it "me"?). He is kind of stuck with having to read this because I am his grandfather and I would wring his fucken neck if he didn't. However, anyone else reading this, I truly appreciate your taking the time.

Periodically through the story to Shane, I would always make sure to ask how he was doing? The same goes for anyone of you others who are foolish enough to be reading these ramblings of a mad man. Seriously, you really have to value your time here and you need to take it to the max. In recent years, I have begun to appreciate our dance with time, knowing the music could stop at any moment. The only way to deal with that inevitability is to keep dancing as best you can until there is silence. I wouldn't mind my story being the rhythm section for some of Shane's own dances in the key of life. Hope you are in good spirits at this moment and if you are not, the good news is that it will pass because we live in a continued state of transition. If you don't clutch the good and shun the bad, things flow with much less effort.

No need to worry, I am not going to advocate walking on molten, hot embers in your bare feet in order to get in touch with your empowerment. On the contrary, sit back and have a glass of wine, a lung load of cannabis or a cup of cammamille tea and allow yourself to be entertained by tales told by a fool. This is a privilege people and one not to be squandered.

All of a sudden, I am thinking about my total inability to deal with punctuation. I love commas because they feel like the pauses you make in your conversations. Sometimes those hesitations scream for a comma and other times it is a period or no punctuation at all. Our cadence when we speak is not always in lock step with how we write. This thing I am doing with you guys is really a conversation. Sitting at the keyboard, I feel I am speaking freely and I simply try and have my fingers move as quickly as they can to keep up. Truthfully, this is what I have attempted to set out to capture. Don't accuse me of bragging, but I know I have accomplished it and you will come out wherever you feel like in that regard.

Crosby, Stills, Nash and Young have provided the music for the above entry this evening. Let me tell you something, the sixties and seventies produced some incredible music and the vast majority was rooted in the classic music of Gospel, the Blues and Jazz, likely with a dash of the elegance of Classical music (Emerson, Lake and Palmer come to mind on the Classical side). This was and still is my music. I have become even more conscious of music during this storytelling to Shane, because I have not written in silence. Shit, I think I already wrote about this. There are so many stories worth sharing more than once, at least that is how I rationalize having episodic brain farts.

Listen, thanks very much for spending several hours of this evening with me. Now it is time for Grandpa Larry to go wandering from this conversation to a state of mind requiring minimal attention. Be well and I will be back on in a while. Good evening.

At least a couple of days have passed, while I completely understand it is just the next paragraph for you. It is kind of interesting that while you only blinked, a bundle of time has passed for me, with all that happens over the course of the days. Bear with me if it feels like a considerable amount of time has elapsed because it has.

First and foremost, need to get you up to date on some important issues relating to this page burner. After a couple of back and forths, Eiju and I have completed his epilogue for the story you haven't read yet. It is pretty good, but a little obtuse, which is the nature of Zen anyway. I know some value has been lost in moving from Spanish to English, but what are going to do? I included his initial communication to me in Spanish because that is his Truth and I didn't even like having to sort of force him into the translating thing.

The completion of the epilogue kind of shit cans my excuse for continuing to write about a story that already ended nearly two months ago. Yes, I am busted for getting a certain indefinable pleasure from this process and don't seem to be terribly interested in giving it up. Here is the deal, I am going to continue this introduction until either December 31, 2012 or New Years Day 2013. Shane, as you know I am a man of my word, having ended our extended conversation on the day that was promised. The rest of you, if there are any of you, will simply have to take my word for it and it won't take very long to find out if I am full of shit or not. I can tell you right now, no need to waste your time wondering because the plan is officially set in stone. It probably won't be that many pages anyway.

Upon completion of the recently prolonged intro, I decided I would read this in its entirety one more time. Aside from stupid errors, I am still a little concerned that some comments about others in the story may have no place in here. God knows, I am up to my butt in imperfection and have done some remarkably dumb things throughout my life. I need to be very careful about how others are portrayed, not because they are misunderstood saints, merely because they are human.

After that final reading, we are going to press, baby. One of the guests in this one man show is a guy by the name of Ken. If I spent any time on the details of our connection, we would be deep into the story. For the moment, let's say he is an actor I met many years ago and our re-connection has been a pure delight. I am afraid he gives me far more credit than I deserve in terms of my humor and my way of communicating. Of course, he thinks Halloween in Portland will be a best seller, launching me into the stratosphere of great chroniclers of untold tales. For me, we go from bestseller to a book that has some value for its only intended reader, my sweet Shane.

My commitment hasn't moved off the dime from that initial perfect moment when I found a place to be. Christ! I am crying yet again because the truth always makes me cry. The decision to do this has been such a blessing, there are no words. Imagine taking a year to think about what your life has been about and trying to write it down, while you also can't help talking about what is going on with you at the moment you are writing.

Somewhere early in this confession to follow, I told Shane my style of expression is best described as Zen Gonzo journalism. Shane is quite young right now, but maybe one of you interlopers knows something about Hunter S. Thompson and the Buddha. Imagine if they were hybridized into one being and then started writing. For the record, I am light years from either one of these guys, especially the B Man. Mr. Thompson had his excesses, as do I, but the Buddha perfected the Middle Path. The idea of Zen is somewhere bouncing around between believing we are all the Buddha already, to it being some unachievable goal that we always aspire to attain, until we realize there is nothing to attain.

I just placed the Epilogue at the end of this story and please, you are not allowed to flip to the end at this time. It may take you a while to get used to the bending of time in this story. Putting Eiju's message at the back, I had to insert a paragraph explaining a little to Shane and you, whomever (whoever?) you are. I wrote my story to Shane and then I decided to write an introduction of sorts, which was subsequently followed by Eiju's message to be attached to the end of my story. Writing all this, I am bouncing around between tenses and timelines. We will pop this particular pimple in a little less than two weeks, which will put us on January 1, 2013. For the record, the story to Shane is complete and so is the Epilogue, OK?

As the only vain man in the entire Universe, I want to let you that I am growing my hair out. It has been buzz cut at Mr. Larry's Salon for Men for a bunch of years. The attachment was always the #5 and the hair length in centimeters beats the shit out of me.

My mother was gracious enough to provide me with genetic, rock star hair and it has been extremely cool to have it all these years. Listen, I know I am the only one who gives a shit about this, but it is all part of my story. It used to be plenty black and wavy when it was shoulder length and now it is silver and a little too short to detect any waves. Shane, the hair timeline is pretty simple. I was a dedicated #5 until shortly after our story was completed and haven't chopped my hair since starting this introduction, which, as you know, is being written after our Halloween finale. Got it?

The reason for letting the locks lengthen is a pretty dumb one, but typical for us stupid men. I hadn't buzzed my head for an extra week or two passed the monthly deadline and my neighbor told me my hair looked good longer. At that moment, the bird dropped on Groucho Marx's You Bet Your Life and that was all I needed because I am many things and easy is definitely one of them.

For those of you who don't have the investment that Shane does, you need to know there is plenty of trivial shit like me letting my hair grow in the story that follows this brief trailer to my word movie, feature presentation. Of course, you can get out anytime, while I am saddled with riding this horse into the sunset. Let me tell you something, if I can ride off into the sunset, I will be one happy cowboy. However, I am in no hurry at this time, thank you. Done for now and whatever is next will come after this evening.

It is the next evening and the date likely matters because it is December 20, 2012, the day before the expiration of the Mayan calendar. Somehow or other, the ancient Mayan calendar ended on that date, at least a number of people believe it to be so. By the way, if you asked a Mayan peasant in Guatemala about its significance, they wouldn't know what the fuck you were talking about. Most of this explanation is for Shane and the fact that he will be reading it quite some time after you do, assuming there is anyone reading this at all before he does. This planet has been here a long fucken time and it has survived some really awful stuff and it will survive us as well. Come to think of it, if we acted like we were part of some spiritual progression of sentient beings, we might act a little less heavy handed. What do you think? This is something that comes up periodically throughout the story to Shane, so no need to whip it here.

When I sat down this evening to write, I put on some Tony Bennett music, primarily duets he did not all that long ago. Sit yourself down one evening and listen to him, whether you have a partner or not. He has such impeccable style and it rubs off on you when you listen because it is beyond infectious. I absolutely can't stand 99% of the Christmas music that spews forth endlessly and then abruptly ends the day after Jesus' birthday. Tony Bennett singing The Christmas Song almost makes it tolerable. It has been terrific having him for company while I write to the many millions who will be reading this in the decades to come. OK, so maybe Shane is the only one to read this and do you want to make something of it?

It just dawned on me that if anyone else is reading this, we will have survived 12/21/12. Personally, I will be very relieved because this book represents a shit load of work and I wouldn't want it to vanish before Shane gets a chance to read it. Shane, you don't mind if I call you, Shane? I didn't think so. If, for any reason, we don't talk tomorrow, there is no need to worry. I am feeling pretty good about making it through to the other side of this cataclism.

Well, it was a close call, but December 21, 2012 has pretty much gone into the record books as a day like any other, which doesn't necessarily make it a noteworthy one. However, the National Rife Association has recommended placing armed guards in every public school across the country. This is their response to the massacre at Newton, Ct. Imagine a six year old, who has never seen a real gun before, reacting to having armed guards in his school and for the rest of his time in school? I say repeatedly throughout the story that violence will be the death of us all. As long as it is the solution, it will always remain the problem. We seem to be so much more comfortable resorting to violence because we feel this need to defend our enduring self from all threats, real or imagined. Eiju talks about the myth of the enduring self and I probably do as well. Neither one of us puts much stock in the idea, so I wonder what is it that we must protect?

You see the end of that last paragraph? It is that kind of stuff that makes me nervous. I look at it and think it should be deleted because philandering our own ideas isn't that much different from objecting to the ideas of others. Here, we do not edit already written material because it may suck, we simply move on. We make mistakes all the time and there is nothing to be embarrassed about, it is part of the deal.

We have comfortably made it to the Day After and it was a pretty good one. Cleaned my motorcycle this morning, in anticipation of the ride tomorrow morning with the Sons of Kauai. Drove to a local farmer's market for a cup of coffee and then went to see The Life Of Pi. Shane, it is a very unusual story and worth reading. A very tough book to translate to film, but it worked pretty well. It is fun when a film can make you fly inside. Speaking of flying, I am completely committed to seeing my first real 3D film and it is the first tale of The Hobbitt.

I am into a four day weekend and it has been quite a while since I have had anything more than a weekend off for around a year and a half. Every six months, I fly to see my children and our Shane, which is not a vacation in the way I envision one. Being on vacation is about being in a place you want to be and not having as much control as you are accustomed to, kind of going with the flow. There are few places as beautiful as Kauai, which takes care of the location issue. Having some extra time off is the other piece that makes these next few days a mini-vacation without leaving home. It is a little late for you to be offended, Shane, but how many times do you have to see Hoboken, especially if you fly half way across the Pacific Ocean and then the entire breadth of the continental US?

I know this is beginning to sound like a goddamn diary and that is the last thing I am interested in doing. I have pretty much mined my past in the story that follows this pregnant greeting, so every know and then I will bring you up to date until we pull the plug, so to speak. In order to tell you almost any story at all at this point, I would have to rewrite what has already been written in the pages that follow this and that would be a terrible waste of time and energy.

Part of the reason for continuing to write about this commitment I made has to do with my saying goodbye to the story, which is something I never believed I could pull off in the beginning and doubts have followed me all along this path. Now, you are reading my published story and how is that for a leap? Actually, if you are reading this, I must tell that I already put the book in a bottle and set it afloat at some undisclosed location I haven't thought of yet. This was sort mentioned earlier. At this point, I haven't figured out how the fuck I am going to get a softcover book into the small opening of a bottle. I have actually transgressed by bringing up something from the story to Shane. I can't even follow my own damn rules! In sitting down and writing this story and knowing it wouldn't be read by its intended audience for quite a number of years, it struck me as being like a message in a bottle that you miraculously find in your life, just when you are supposed to. Imagine Shane finding this bottle, washed up on the shore of a Chilean beach where he has been surfing? Of course, he fell in love with surfing because of his repeated visits to see me on Kauai.

I think our dreams are such an important part of our lives and they are why we live on. I dream for Shane and my own dreams are still in good shape as well. If you are not careful, life can beat you down and compromise you all the way to the crapper. Our dreams are our life preservor in the stormy waters we inevitably encounter on our voyage.

It's kind of nice to have a Sunday evening without thinking about going back to work. Had a good motorycle ride with the bruddahs and our climb up and down Koke'e. So, I stand before you fairly relaxed. Truthfully, I didn't think I would get so involved with this introductory thing, but it now seems to have taken on its own life. I know I had a good reason in writing my story to Shane, but this after the story piece doesn't seem to have much of a reason. In spite of that, this has been and continues to be something I feel invested in. If only one person finds a single nugget in any of this, I will be a happy guy. The truth is, I am playing with a marked deck because Shane is likely to find some serious bullion amidst all the bullshit.

During the next week or so, I have to figure out how to say goodbye to you. Of course, you will keep in mind that the story we are leading into has already been written and there is a goodbye at the end of it. I am not sure if I have been actually introducing the real story to come or kind of killing time for no particular reason. If you can believe me, I simply wanted to keep writing and maintain this connection to the story I have told.

For those non-Shane readers, I want you to smile occasionally as you traverse my life's travails. While I likely suffer from having been alone for extended periods in my life, I have also had ample time to get a grip on myself and then let go, a recycling kind of thing. Maybe the great gift we can actually give ourselves is the gift of the True Self. At the risk of sounding Oprah-like, make yourself happy as often as you can. Our legacy is how we live our lives and the people we touch along the way. In my worst Zen, I sometimes think about what I will leave behind, in direct conflict with the transient nature of all things. The only effort that will survive me is this book and you better fucken believe I gave it eight fuel injected cylinders screaming to the finish line with flames rocketing from the pipes. OK, so that's a little dramatic, but you have to simply appreciate how dangerous a deviant mind can be. Instead of leaving a smoldering trail of rubber, I am leaving this and it will have to do. Hopefully, it won't smell as bad and it will last longer.

We have only a week left and then it will be New Years Day 2013. Truthfully, feeling less inclined to write at this point. During all this time, I have been writing directly to Shane and that was an easy voice for me to have. The story itself really doesn't require an introduction, but we have been over that already. My talking to Shane is filled with love and a full heart because he is my little boy. I have gotten a little stuck in this introduction, because it has gotten off course with my concern about writing to anyone else who happens to be reading this. I don't think I want to do that anymore and for the last and final week of this effort it will be directed to Shane and you are obviously free to hang in with it.

Shane, I have had a chance to finish my story to you and look forward to your getting to the heading that begins with "In the beginning….. " The decision to make a book of this felt like it should have an introduction. You didn't need one because it is right there in the beginning of our monologue. Honestly, it wouldn't faze me at all if you are the only one to read this or if anyone reads this and thinks it sucks.

Got a quick story for you, buddy. It is Christmas Day and I am going over to friends for dinner. I have never tasted a piece of barbecued beef any better than Jimmy G's. He is an investor in the company I am involved with, plus he is opening a microbrewery in Lihue. While he pays the bills with a software business he started many years ago, he loves making beer and food. We are pretty good friends and I like him a great deal. He lost his wife and life partner a couple of years ago and he is a very brave man. Jim's son and daughter will be at dinner this evening. This is the really cool part, Jim's daughter's in-laws are good friends with the woman who is directly responsible for this entire story being started in the first place.

Our story begins with me returning from a trip to Portland, OR, where I spent the weekend with Josette. I first saw her at the wedding of Jim's daughter several months before Halloween of last year. The wedding was here, but it took many emails and several phone conversations to get myself invited to Portland. I just looked at a photograph of the two of us in Portland and I kind of forgot what a good looking lady she is. The weekend together is what precipitated this effort and my gratitude is never ending. It will be very entertaining to tell Jim's son-in-law that his parent's friend is completely responsible for this entire story. In many ways, my gift to you is a direct result of having attended that wedding. I can guarantee I will definitely have fun with it this evening.

I just got back from dinner and most importantly, the side of beef and trimmings were sensational. When I first arrived, I sat down with Jim and told him about why this was so unusual for me because of the book and its genesis. He has known about my writing since the time I began this journey and thought he would enjoy my reminding him how it all began. His kids were great and they remembered the story and I guess read one of my emails to Josette in the very beginning. His daughter was very complimentary about what I had written and while it was sweet to hear, it is also a little embarrassing as well. I did take up some of the evening recounting the story and how it began at the wedding. I sold at least seven books at dinner!

I had no intention of writing tonight. The last paragraph happened on Christmas Day and it is now three days later. It is Friday night and the start of yet another four day break, which works very well for me. I am particularly excited because the whales are finally here and this begins my season of solo kayaking out in the Pacific for some up close and personal episodes with these behemoths of the sea. The story spends plenty of time with this particular nautical adventure from the prior whale season, so no need here. I've already loaded the kayak in the back of my faded red, geriatric truck for a late morning cruise. I really like the idea that something like this still gets me feeling fresh and exuberant.

Shane, I got a card from your Mom and Dad and it has a sweet picture of you and your guitar and the back has two other adorable photos. Sent your folks a message: "Joy Joy Joy! Having this card in front of me for the long weekend will guarantee a smile during the change of years" We are also firming up my Spring trip and it is looking like early April when you are out of school. Your Mom said they were going to rent a farm house in the Hudson Valley for the time I am in. Uncle Danny, that would be your father's brother and my son, will undoubtedly join us for the festivities. For the rest of you, give me a break here, I am talking to my grandson.

Now, here is something that requires no elaboration because we have already spoken briefly about Josette and the dinner at Jimmy G's on Christmas Day. After telling my story at the dinner, when I got home, I wrote a very sweet note to Josette. The entire experience with her made this monumental effort possible. Believe me, I am not confusing the term "monumental" with having anything to do with something of great importance and/or genius. Imagine, if most everyday, you came home and got in front the computer to continue telling a totally intimate story of your life and feelings. While doing this, you need to bring on your best game each time because that is what a pro does. Believe me, I know I've got the writing jones and I would never want anything published that didn't hold itself to some standard of personal ethics.

While I was thinking about writing to Josette, I found a photograph of the two of us, taken in the wine country of Oregon. It also involves my friend, Michael, but he comes along a little later in this narrative, but pretty close to the beginning. I looked at her and understood what got me going on that particular adventure in the first place. Shoot me, I like pretty women and they only have to be pretty to me. If a partner is not a turn on in the beginning, the likelihood of it happening down the line are pretty slim. I could care less how you define a turn on, regardless of my own filthy definition.

I hope the rest of you who read this can appreciate the inherent time warp in this narrative. You will read this long before Shane ever does. Shit, did I already write something like this above? I apologize if I did, but it is a recurring thing for me because I am really writing to Shane and no matter how many people read this before him, he will still be the first one to read it all. I also get to write a whole new ending for this introduction, after having slaved over an ending for the story itself. I will try and do what I can to make it a memorable closing.

Hold on there, we are not having a monumental closing just yet, although it is a mere thirty hours until we flip over into 2013. I wonder how long it will take for people to talk about dates and automatically not put the two thousand before the year. When I was growing up, it was always nineteen hundred and you never had to say it. We are definitely not there yet when it comes to the two thousand thing. You realize Seinfeld could easily do a half hour on this. I am serious. I throw away all these jewels and what do have to show for it, absolutely nothing!

Today was just one of those beautiful days here on Kauai. Observed the Sunday ritual of riding with the Sons of Kauai. We had a pretty good turn out, nearly thirty bikes and everyone was smiling. We always get together in a circle before we leave for the ride and

I requested a minute from Paula, who is the Queen of the group and she leads the congregation each Sunday. I told everyone that for weeks and weeks I have been wanting to say something to everyone. I told them how much it meant to me to ride with them every week and how what we do is the definition of aloha and it is a precious thing. I don't know if it is a combination of writing this book and the inexorable march of time, but I am much less shy about what happens to be on my mind.

While riding today, I thought about this writer thing and that for some reason or other I very often behave like one. If there is a way to embellish an inane response or to initiate communication with someone, I try to do it like a writer. It is no longer possible for me to say very little, however I do keep an eye on the tonnage because keeping interest is more important than unloading verbiage. I sure as shit hope I am not guilty of attempting to be a show off, because that would make me want to pick up a rock and throw at myself. Not to worry, I am a lousy shot and couldn't hit myself with a rock even if I was so inclined.

There is a certain joy that comes with trying to show yourself to others, absent any concern with judgment, etc. This has been my passion since seeing Rum Diaries with Josette on Halloween weekend in Portland, well over a year ago. Everything I have written may completely suck in someone else's eyes, but you couldn't convince me of that in a million years. When you really try to be honest in whatever you do, that is the reward and it is everything.

In the interest of honesty, I confess to listening to Bob Marley and being high at the same time, if you could imagine such a feat? It comes up more than once in my story to you, Shane. I was already twenty three during the Summer of Love, a little old by flower power standards and slightly ahead of it, if you don't mind. I was just a bit too old to be a part of the world that was tripping the light fantastic, but it was close enough for me to embrace. My introduction to and ongoing relationship with smoking pot wafts its way throughout this story, so get over it if it's a problem, OK? Actually, the very first time is a precious story and one of my favorites to recount up ahead. Once again, I am writing to you, Shane and you will read this in fifteen years or so, but those select few reading it now will have no better idea about legalization than I do. It seems to be crawling in that direction, but your guess is as good as mine regarding the future. Personally, I would be more concerned with the plethora of assault weapons in the hands of lunatics than I would be about pot.

Back to the road, I peeled off from the bruddahs in the early afternoon because I wanted to get back out on the kayak as soon as possible. Today was a weather perfect day, but no whale sightings, in spite of spending several hours out there suffering in a very calm sea with the Hawaiian sun gently baking deeper into my genetically receptive, desert skin.

Spent a beautiful couple of hours out there and the whales we will be around the next time. When I take my kayak out and head straight for the horizon, at some point I turn around to look back at the island. This is one beautiful place, believe me. When you go out on the ocean and look at its mind boggling expanse, it cuts you down to size pretty goddamn fast. This afternoon was perfect, in spite of the blatantly obvious absence of the whale beings. I did have a couple of run ins yesterday when I was out, which was a good way to inaugurate the season. This has come full cycle now because several months into my story, the whales made their annual pilgrimage to Hawaiian waters with whale tales told. These repetitions are one of many signs that it is time to move on and leave the rest for you to read.

Today is the last day of this year, 2012. It has been an interesting year for me and much of it appears in the following pages. When I began this in the last few months of 2011, it took a while for it to become what I did. A lot of stuff went on for me this year, but this book is far out ahead of anything else. Some times, I was simply happy because an event, personal or otherwise, provided me with more material to share. Everything got itself filtered through an appraisal of whether it was worth sharing in this story.

Somewhere toward the end of the book, I am pretty sure I apologize to Shane for having so much damn Zen stuff, which was never my intention. For anyone else, please, I am not promoting anything at all. Yes, I keep telling Shane how to be and then I will tell him to ignore any sales pitch. However, you have to keep in mind he is my grandson and I have a vested interest in how he turns out, while the rest of you are completely on your own.

I will tell you what is most unusual for me about 2012 and that is there is a written record of the year's events, riding on the surf of my history with occasional high minded winds of reckless and feckless opinions. Not sure how it will feel to read this entire thing and then put it aside for the last time before it gets set in stone. At this point, I definitely don't remember half of what has been written, which is probably good in terms of providing me with an almost fresh read this last time. As soon as I thought about even one pair of eyeballs other than Shane's reading this, I needed to up the ante because there is no free ride with anyone else. On the other hand, I am not so sure that is true. This story for my Shane had to be as good as I could make it, even if he found the beached message years from now and his were the first eyes other than mine to read it.

For me, this is one of many New Year's Eves spent on my own and that's just been part of the deal. There are plenty of us who do it and there ain't no shame, just in case you're thinking there is. Again, no need for me to reflect because it's in the book. After I figure out a way to say goodbye tomorrow, I will read all about 2012 and then maybe someone other than Shane will come upon it sooner than he will. This is so incredibly personal, I haven't really thought about what it means for me. Honestly, at this point in my life, why should I care about how I am judged by those who take a certain relish in holding themselves above others? There is nothing, but love on these pages and a heart that is full.

Good morning, it is the first day of 2013 and I will be saying aloha to this effort. Currently, listening to Bruddah Iz, Israel Kamakawiwo'ole and feeling like I belong right here, right now. The coming year will bring whatever it brings and my resolution, as always, is to take what comes with grace and give of myself with humility. Iz is singing, Somewhere Over The Rainbow, as if on cue. Shane, I hope that at this time of year, your regrets are few and your dreams are strong. ....My heart has busted open again and I am crying, hope you don't mind.............. It's funny, I am sitting here all alone, but feeling the company of my spirit and this magnificent island of Kauai, my home.

Hate to do this to you, but a bunch of hours have passed between the last paragraph and this one. Don't worry, it is still January 1st and I am not about to back out on my promise. This session with you is my last. There isn't a single reason for me to put down anything at all any later than today. Similarly, when I do the reread thing before going to press, I may clarify something already written, but I will not update it because that is cheating, ladies and gentlemen.

In my cheap imitation of a Star Wars prequel, the story actually ended two months ago and it has taken me this long to do a full read through and this never ending introduction. I am going to check just one thing and then I'll be right back. I want to see how I actually ended the story two months ago..................... I am not surprised with how I closed, but try not to go there until you get there. I get to go through another kind of gut wrenching experience with this second goodbye. It is seriously like that and I could explain it to you if you were here, but you'are not. Yes, you don't have to tell me that nothing at all prevents me from continuing to do this kind of thing, but this was very, very special for me.

Finally ending this has that empty feeling you are suffocated by when you say goodbye to a lover for the last time. There are precious memories and moments and then the silence engulfs you. Just reread the first two sentences and am making a mid-course correction. I was going to make a point of how creating a book and saying goodbye is a different scenario than the finality of leaving a partner. I am glad I caught it in time because that is bullshit. While the book has not directly involved sex, it is the most intimate relationship I am capable of having and I have now had it. The perfect time to roll over and light up a cigarette, stare silently at the ceiling than say something brilliant, like "I'll call you". The bed is empty Jackson, so that closing line doesn't work very well.

I am really conflicted with having pulled this off and the fact that the life of this story is coming to an end. Please, do not confuse the story coming to an end with me ending as well. This is not the last you have heard from me, Shane, plus the three other people reading this for reasons that completely escape me. If you happen to be one of the special people mentioned in the tale to come, please believe that I mean no harm with any comments. It is safe to say that on a grand scale your anonymity will be safe within the covers of this sparsely read journal. Anyway, I get a free pass because I am one of you and have hopefully provided ample proof in what you have already read so far. It gets worse after this and I know that because I have already read it. Playing with a full deck is not my strong suit, if you get my drift.

For those of you who are getting up there in age and Shane, being in your teens doesn't count, maybe you can appreciate the fantasy of unscrewing your head and putting it on the shoulders of a much younger version of yourself. Unless medicine and metaphysics make quantum leaps in the near term, the transplant idea is pretty fucken dumb. So, what is a person to do? The best I could come up with was putting my head on paper and screwing it onto Shane's (just being literary) shoulders. Maybe, just once, you will do one thing microscopically different because of me and feel enriched by it. The last sentence is for you, Shane because it is a blood thing. The rest of you will just have to figure out if there is anything you want others to know and how badly you want them to know. I guess this is an accomplishment of sorts, but not sure exactly why.

It is likely that Shane will be the last carrying my blood line forward, so it was very easy to figure out who to leave this for in a tribal sense. This is me in here kid and there are no additives. We will see what the coming year brings for us. On my end, I would like to see my business venture take hold, move into my yurt and find a lady that can read all of this and want to spend even more time with me because of it. Shane, you will be sliding into five at the end of this year and I am not sure what to wish for. Things like improving your language skills, learning how to dribble and getting the idea of the connection between your fingers and guitar strings are some of the things that come to mind. I certainly hope both of our worlds continue to expand during the coming year and beyond. The rest of you are off the hook and pretty much on your own, which is what we all have in common last time I checked.

I guess it is okay to talk to the rest of you now. I want to thank you for taking the time to read this little journey of my mind. You know, there are still monks living in caves and just sitting. This is certainly true to day and will hopefully be true in years to come. I feel a little like a monk who has spent a year in a cave and when he is asked what he has to show for it, he quietly produces his labor of love. Yes, I know I am not a monk sitting in a cave and that I am a hopeless degenerate, but it is still a labor of love and I will have to hurt anyone who disagrees.

In the story I have already written, I repeatedly state that whenever it feels like I am simply stretching a session for no particular reason, it is time to stop. We are getting dangerously close to that line with this very last entry. However, when it ends for me, it hasn't even begun for you. I say goodbye and you say hello.

In the beginning......

Today is Monday, October 31, 2011, a very momentous day for me and hopefully for you as well. Let me introduce myself to you, Shane, I am your father's father, which of course makes me your grandfather. My name is Larry Feinstein. Right now, I am wedged into my seat on an airplane traveling from San Francisco to Oahu, Hawaii. I will get back to the plane ride business in just a moment.

I want to lay out some rules in an effort to make sense of what may end up being quite a long story. At this very moment, you are a little over a month away from your third birthday. You are still shitting yourself and being spoon fed by your Dad, who we shall call Andy, and your Mom, who we will call Andrea. Andy and Andrea always struck me as a funny name combination. If it weren't for the fact that it is actually their names, I would have accused them of making up the matching monikers. You started an early version of school several months ago. You are learning invaluable information like "A" for apple and meeting your local fireman, policeman and postman. You are living in a spacious home in Hoboken, NJ with lots of stairs and so far, it would be safe to say you have been enjoying a comfortable life.

Clearly, at this time, you are absolutely incapable of understanding any of this. The obvious question has to be why the hell am I writing to you at this time in your life? Actually, the answer is quite simple. It is probably a good idea for me to write to you while I am alive because dead people are pretty fucken useless.

Michael, who is a long time friend of mine from my days in Santa Fe, NM, gave me a great idea nearly a year ago. When he was temporarily living on the Big Island out here, he had an artist friend of his make a Hawaiian fishing hook for your first birthday. They are traditionally carved from bone and many local people wear them around their necks. As a one year old, you would have likely choked on the necklace or stabbed yourself in the eye with the very sharp end of the upturned hook. I felt it was the gesture that counted most under the circumstances, what with me being your Hawaiian, Buddhist, Jewish grandfather. I knew that I would immediately ask your father for it back so I could frame it for you, which would prevent it from being lost or misplaced under the relentlessly growing pile of your accumulated tribute, which appear to mark milestones in your life, or things you receive on a random basis as acts of love and adoration from your relatives.

I guess I got it back from your Dad one or two visits ago, which, of course, you couldn't possibly remember. Amongst other things, Michael is a talented artist, although at the moment he continues to punish his body doing construction. I called Michael asking him if he would build a small frame for the hook. During this conversation, while I don't exactly remember how it came up, he suggested that I write something to you and seal it in the back of the frame, kind of like a written time capsule.

The idea really resonated with me and it was for a number of reasons. I have been told for many, many years that I am a good writer, which is very unnerving for me. While I likely have a way with turning feelings and thoughts into some decent stories, accusations of being a writer only make me feel self-conscious about the whole thing. As far as I am concerned, I am trying to be a mediocre writer and it is this idea that makes me try hard at the craft. The second reason is that my father, who we shall call Daniel, like your favorite uncle and my other son, died when I was only nine years old. I had no idea who the hell he was and never even had the opportunity for him to share any of his own stories with me. His parents died long before I was born. While I hope all of us are around in your life for quite some time to come, you just never know what tomorrow has in store.

Yes, I know I am your grandfather and for obvious chronological disparities between us it behooves me even more to let you get a glimpse of who I am and what I am about, using this kind of permanent medium. We will assume Andy is around long enough and that your relationship is strong enough for this kind of dialogue to take place in person. Knowing where you came from helps you immeasurably in knowing who you are. Knowing who you are is the internal road map for your future. Don't get nervous, it takes a long time to get any of this shit, so you can relax. You should be as inquisitive as you like with your parents and don't hold back anything. My generation grew up in homes where feelings weren't shown much and certainly not talked about. I think it has eased up some, but there is still this incredible reticence for parents to be honest with their children. This is a device used by the parents to avoid any of their own personal discomfort. Don't allow that to control your communication with your parents or anyone else for that matter.

Now, back to that idea about writing you a secret note, to be opened by you when your parents felt you were old enough. The reason for this is rather simple; I am not going to hold back even an inch from giving it to you as straight as I possibly can. I am certainly hoping you get to start reading this before you are my ripened age of sixty-six. So, I am not writing a children's story, one that talks down to you or patronizes you in anyway whatsoever.

Just a second, the stewardess has come by and I feel like having a Bloody Mary. Aside from the fact these little bottles of alcohol now cost seven bucks, you can't even pay with cash any more. You have to reach into your fucken pocket for plastic. A lady just leaned over to me and asked me if two single dollars lying on the floor close to me were mine. I said no, but split it with her anyway. I think it is a sign, an affirmation I should be writing to you. Either way, I just slipped a free dollar into my pocket.

Before I get back to the so-called narrative, I want to explain why I just interrupted us with the Bloody Mary story. While the idea of writing a note to you was very appealing on a number of levels, I had no idea where I would begin, what I would say or how I would say it. Yesterday, I saw a movie in Portland, OR, entitled, "The Rum Diaries". It is a fiction piece written by a guy by the name of Hunter S. Thompson, a writer who coined and embodied a style of writing called gonzo journalism. Simply stated, it is a pretty raw narrative and always somewhat autobiographical. He had a way of inserting himself into everything he wrote, whether it was fact based journalism or fictional storytelling. Hunter was an extraordinarily colorful character, who drank and did drugs to excess. He lived recklessly and his writing personified his life style. You may want to read some of his stuff. He wrote endlessly in Rolling Stone magazine and one of his books is Fear and Loathing in Las Vegas.

I was in Portland, visiting with a woman I had briefly met on Kauai at the wedding of a friend's daughter. I may return to the Ballad of Josette and Larry at a later time, but this is not the time. The leading actor in this film was Johnny Depp, one of my favorite actors. He was the Thompsonesque character, playing a failed novelist, who took a writing gig with an English language newspaper in 1960 Puerto Rico. He repeatedly stated throughout the film that he had not found his voice as a writer. There was something about his admission within the context of this gonzo journalism style that resonated within me and gave me my own voice and the one that will inhabit this story to you.

My voice is in the key of Zen Gonzo. It is where the idea of extraordinarily perfect Zen recklessly collides with the totally undisciplined Gonzo. It is an in the moment kind of self-expression, easily interrupted by most anything at all. Actually, when you think about it, that is how our minds work anyway. We live in a constant state of change and everything is disrupted on a moment-to-moment basis. At this point, my quickly put together plan is to write to you whenever I feel like and tell you some stories. While they will all be true, or as true as my ever changing perspective will allow, they will always be as sincere and honest as I can possibly be at that precise moment when it falls out of my mind through my fingers and on to the imaginary page.

I will admit to being very excited to have found that incredibly elusive voice I have been unable to hear until this moment. In order of importance, I owe it to your birth, my friend Michael, the Hawaiian fishing hook, my so-called Zen practice and Hunter S.Thompson.

At least one other thing belongs in this prologue. I am not going to waste a moment of my imagination trying to think about what your world will be like whenever you are allowed to take this journey with me. I don't know when the hell George Orwell wrote 1984, but I was obviously around for that year and he missed by miles. It is inconceivable to me what your world will be like whenever you are allowed to read this. Incidentally, you can share this with Andy and Andrea because there are no secrets in here, no code words between you and I that are somehow meant to secretly influence you in anyway at all. I have terrific stories to tell and every now and then a semi-interesting idea or opinion. My guess is your parents will have read this long before you do.

I am going to give you complete credit for understanding everything I will be sharing with you. Time will not be unnecessarily wasted on continually providing back-story and context for whatever is being shared. You can Google it or use whatever technology exists for you whenever you hit a roadblock in my communication. I will have my hands full simply weaving these disparate stories into a quilt of my life and I have neither the time nor the inclination to be a sociologist or anthropologist or even an apologist for that matter.

Shit, this is going as well as I expected. I know I haven't told you all that much, but we have got to begin someplace and here I am, sitting on a plane, traveling to Oahu and then ultimately on to Kauai, where I have been living for a little over eight years.

I am on my way home from the longest commute and most expensive first date of my life. I might as well tell you the story behind the Ballad of Josette and Larry. As I have already mentioned, I saw fair Josette at a wedding on Kauai. Being a hopeless romantic, a theme that will inevitably weave itself throughout this narrative without end, I was very captivated by this graceful mirage of a woman. I was left with little choice, but to somehow approach her and make conversation, a tall order for yours truly, even after these many years. While I have been fortunate to have had a series of wonderful relationships over my life, some of whom you will likely meet as I unfurl the flag of my existence, I am intensely shy and small talk is a language I have great difficulty speaking, which has certainly been an impediment for me in the social world because small talk is usually how it begins. My preference is intimate and honest dialog. However, it can often take a long time to get there and you don't often get a chance.

Well, I put a metaphorical gun to my head and left myself with no choice. We spoke briefly and even danced for several minutes, a tremendous challenge for me, coupling my shitty sense of rhythm made even worse by the nervous disconnect between my brain and my mouth. This brief meeting precipitated a series of emails to be sent and phone calls to be made. True to my Lothario leanings, I was able to win fair Josette over and within a month a trip was arranged for me to spend a weekend in Portland.

Have to stop here for just another second. I had to take a leak after the Bloody Mary had worked its way through my system. This idea that I have about writing is to share my history, but to do so in the moment. Our minds are elusive buggers and while you can force them to focus, they are happiest when they bounce all over the place. I will likely go in and out of any story I am sharing with you, but who knows because this tale has barely begun. Now remember, I am still flying and I will let you know when I have changed locations.

Josette was absolutely as beautiful as I remembered and seeing her at the airport completed my mission, regardless of outcome. The very first sign of difficulty was a comment she made about getting a new wallet, which came out to pay for our lunch . It is decades old and on its last legs, held together by some duct tape. Her comment regarding my wallet was tinged with a hint of judgment, an immediate sign of difficulty. Judgment is a tricky business and frequently disallows uniqueness, fostering conformity to some arbitrary norm. She was a lovely woman and treated me like a royal guest, which is not exactly what I had in mind, although I didn't mind being cared for by another. She or maybe we decided that our differences fostered an incompatability, rendering our future consummation moot. One of the reasons I thought going to a Sunday matinee was a good idea was because it would create a pleasant diversion from any continued dialogue about why getting together was a failed fable of my Cyrano heart. Now, you and I have Josette and "Rum Diaries" to thank for unleashing this pending torrent of tales in your direction.

Another made up factoid of this exercise is that I will try very hard not to go backwards whenever I restart the motor. My plan is to have each of these nuggets play out as a diuretic release of consonants and vowels that make perfect sense to me and me only at the time of their being expunged from my dwindling grey matter. As a result, there is a possibility that I will repeat some of these tales and possibly change the facts along the way.

This is a very big deal to me and I am trying hard not to load myself up with too much expectation. If this exercise is able to somehow mutate to a second sit down, we might possibly be on our way. In spite of a number of long-term relationships and some good friends thrown in, no one knows my story. I suppose the vast majority of us live our lives in varying degrees of anonymity and our tombstones and urns embody our disappearance and the winds of time quickly fill in our footprints. Maybe, I can get to live a little longer through you and that idea appeals to me. In addition, this exercise, if it continues, could turn out to be a gift for me as well.

Listen, the battery in my computer is running low and if I don't sign off, this could all go straight into the shitter and I would be seriously pissed, plus the idea of starting at the beginning twice.....................

Well, it went dead in the middle of the last sentence and I had to wait until the plane landed in Oahu and then I caught a bus shuttle to the Hawaiian Airlines terminal for my flight to Kauai. I just inhaled some lousy, airport Chinese food and I am now sitting in an immobile, pay for play, massage chair, the one that is closest to an outlet to bring my computer back to life.

Nothing has been lost and I am picking up where I left off. Just as I have no idea what tomorrow has in store for me, I have no idea what form this will take, other than allowing it to grow organically. We are breaking new ground here with my Zen Gonzo launch. Hopefully, I will communicate whenever I have the time and the inclination. I've got lots of stories to tell about places I have lived, jobs I have had, women I have loved and an endless number of experiences along the way. Plus, I am an opinionated son of a bitch and getting worse as my remaining time decreases and my clarity increases.

Getting a little tired now and I never want this to feel forced. When I start looking around, as I am doing right now, searching for something to say, it is time to bring the episode to a close. We'll talk again soon.

Home Again

This doesn't count as an official entry, but I wanted you to know I am pretty certain I am going to make a go of this idea. It is the day after my initial note to you. I am home from Portland and the time with Josette and my buddy, Michael, who now happens to live close by in beautiful wine country. Can't do much right now. I am heating my Gourmet Meals for Single Dummies and have a laundry coming out of the drier and I want to watch a ridiculous TV series called, " Sons of Anarchy" about a motorcycle gang somewhere in southern California. They blatantly break every conceivable law and there are no consequences. Christ, you are really not going to give a shit about 20 year old TV shows!

I will eventually tell you about the Gourmet Meal for Single Dummies, which is a good story. Got to go.

Sloppy Seconds

Now, this is a big deal! Like I told you, if I sit down one more time after the introductory salvo, then we may be on to something. To be clear, I am not writing a journal or a chronologically oriented diary, although I would call it a diary of the mind. Wherever I happen to be is where we are for the moment. I think I need to consider this a little more work than pleasure, pretending I am actually a writer and providing the time and focus for it. This is an interesting marriage of my deeply felt need to write and the desire to tell you my story.

There are a number of other things I want to share with you at this birthing of a tome moment. I am not going to bullshit you about anything. I am and will continue to be absolutely truthful with you about everything I put in this extended tone poem in the key of life. I might be forced to hold back a little every now and then, especially if it involves people who were and are close to you. Frankly, everyone else is pretty much incidental because this is about you and me. I will try and be respectful of the privacy of others and write as if they will read it.

Secondly, I have no interest in creating confusion between the two of us. This is my story and not yours. Whenever you do get to read this, the last thing I am politicking for is that you in any way emulate even an ounce of my behavior. If anything, I would be the one totally encouraging you to find your own way in the world and to be a bona fide individual. I have an endless number of stories to share with you and their purpose is a simple one, I am giving you this diary of my mind, so at least one person is the custodian of my time here.

Your Mother sent several photos of you in your Halloween (2011) astronaut costume and they arrived in between my introductory entry and this second stab. I wrote to your Mom that in these photographs I was beginning to see the face you will be wearing as you mature into a young man, admittedly about fourteen years from now. So far, you are coming along magnificently. You're a good kid, pretty joyful and comfortable in new situations.

I am playing a hunch you are going to understand a great deal of what I have to say upon first reading and that you will catch up with other stuff as your own life continues to educate you.

I have to go back to the writing thing for just a second. In the brief time I have been sitting in front of the keyboard and putting these words together, I am feeling just a little bit like a writer. I am not communicating in the conventional sense of a written conversation. This is a monologue to be read at sometime in the future by you and maybe some others. I think this is what writing feels like; at least it does for me.

Got some Blues winding up in the background, a glass of cheap red wine and enjoying the effects of some pot I just smoked. When you begin reading a contemporary history of this country, you will read about the Sixties, the Summer of Love, Woodstock, The Beatles, the Stones and a veritable Pandora's box containing all sorts of interesting energy turned loose and galloping around the world at the speed of light. If you do the math, it is easy to determine that having been born in 1945, I was a young guy in his early twenties when this social and political phenomenon made its way across the country, carried in clouds of marijuana smoke. I have a terrific story about the first time I got high in 1966, but that one is too good and will definitely be a stand-alone entry. In the spirit of truth I just mentioned, I have been indulging in this ritual for forty-five years or so and you might as well know that. There is even a distinct possibility, like this evening, when I will be under its spell. Occasionally, I'll let you know, just in case there are lapses, creating some disorder in moving from one sentence to the next. Frankly, it is unlikely because I will be policing these paragraphs as they build and rereading everything before I sew on the covers and close the book. I am seriously focused doing this thing. Hell, it will be legal by the time your get this.

I don't want to feel like I am in some sort of hurry to tell you as much as I possibly can in as short a time as possible. We will just see what is on my mind at any give moment and that is where we will travel on that trip, no map required. I have a never-ending repertoire of stories for you and I like some more than others. I will try and play the A side of this melody of the mind. In addition, I have no idea how long to make this, especially since there are so many stories in between here and there. It is kind of an arbitrary thing how long I spend in anyone place. I think next time, I will tell you a story from start to finish, which could be "real" or imagined. Then again, who knows what will happen when I pick up what I am now dropping off into the ether of this moment?

Stunning

You have no idea what is going on for me in this process of writing to you and how could you? I have never felt the continuity of concentration to be able to write more than a couple of pages about anything. I have already shattered that record and it is amazing to me. Obviously, we don't have much of a relationship at this point, primarily because of your age and only slightly impacted by my distance from your home. Not having any idea when you will read this and how much of it you will actually understand the first time or two, I am basically writing to entertain myself, which means I really can't miss as long as I please yours truly.

Frankly, I have a secret hope this may end up being a book. Having just begun the process, it is impossible for me to have any idea whether this project will have any merit, beyond my trying to riff a little bit about my life and share it with you.

You are going to Disney World this coming weekend and your parents have arranged for breakfast with Mickey. I feel I can share this with you now because this heads up will not get to you for quite some time. I think you are lucky to have such wonderful parents. I am wild about your Dad and value our time together. Your Mother is a terrific lady and I take great joy from our relationship.

Any classic stories I get into are going to take some time to tell. I will need a handful of relaxed hours for each of them. As you can probably tell by now, I am not that disciplined in my writing and it will be interesting to see if I can tell a story with out interrupting my history with some spontaneous occurrence. The truth is I am still perfecting this idea and making up the rules as I go along. I think I am a little tired right now and don't want to launch into a story and have to break it off because of fatigue. My stories need to be told in a single sitting. I do think it is time and we'll have to figure out a good first story to tell you. We don't count that very first bit about traveling from Portland home to Kauai because that was purely a prologue, a brief encounter, plus my initial rules of the road for this trip of ours.

Promise

I guess I promised to tell a story. You know, some of my stories are so long; they could go on forever. Part of the reason for that is many of them are ongoing and account for decades of connection.

Oh, by the way, you didn't go to Disney World for breakfast with Mickey because you came down with a viral infection and the trip has been postponed until some time in December. We will talk about it later because your Dad is really a good guy and he gives me all of the details of your various escapades. Both your parents have been great about sharing your life with me and I am always thrilled when I hear about your latest Nobel Prize worthy accomplishment.

Sitting here in a towel because that is always my outfit upon my return from my run. I started running when I was around thirty-two. I was still living with your grandmother, Andy and Danny in Glen Cove, Long Island. At the time, I was following a well-worn path of getting married, having babies and finally moving out of the City to a suburban home slightly beyond my means. At some point, I will likely tell you about my life during that time and how circumstances, both within and without my control, caused a major upheaval in our precariously held together nuclear family. That one will be a tough one to explore because while honesty is paramount, the feelings of others close to you is not a territory I need to intrude upon.

OK, let's get back to the towel and my running. As the domestic discomfort in Glen Cove grew exponentially, I decided running might be a good release for so much unwanted energy I was beginning to carry. You do the math, I have been running ever since and never imagined I would become so dedicated to the discipline. I used to take your father and uncle to a nearby park out there and I would run around the track, while they played on the gigantic infield.

I was never into distance and was never terribly speedy. I have always run between a half hour and an hour and in recent decades definitely on the half hour side. I guess in my prime conditioned days an eight-minute mile was about the best I could do. My crowning achievement was running in the 1982 NYC Marathon and I have the damn finish line photo to prove it, with a 3:42:43 elapsed time. The marathon tale is a stand-alone piece because of the details leading up to it and the entire experience.

Since some time in the summer of 1977, I have been running nearly every day, except most Sundays. My running shoes and shorts go everywhere I do. In New York and New Mexico, my fifteen-year home before the move to Kauai over eight years ago, running always happened regardless of weather. Detailing my moving around at this point would take us way off my rhapsody on running. However, I have run in most of the major U.S. cities, in addition to Belize, Costa Rica, Honduras, Guatemala, Israel, England and other locations.

When I come to visit you in Hoboken, regardless of season, I always go running along the Hudson River. Sometimes, your Dad will run with me. When I first started running at the track I mentioned, both my boys would run along with me for short periods. They started running with me when they were in their teens and we would sometimes run on our weekends or vacation time together.

My father was not even remotely athletic and America was not his place of birth. Immigrants from Eastern Europe began flooding into this country in the early 1900's. Jews have been coming here for years and long before that time. There are loads of stories about our tribe in the early days of US history, dating back to the Wild West of the 1800's.You should check out stories of the crypto Jews, who moved to the Southwest during the Inquisition days. I learned all about this when I lived out there. Back to my father, Daniel. His death when I was nine left me without the traditional source for all things manly. I was a really lousy athlete my entire life, with the exception of swimming, but it was an affinity left unnurtured. When I belatedly started running, it didn't take me too long to become a dedicated runner and I am still.

I encouraged both Andy and Danny in athletics, partially due to my own sensitivity about not having a Dad to do it with me. Very early, it became apparent that your father was a pretty decent athlete. He partially compensated for his height disadvantage by being a very smart player, regardless of sport. For reasons that still blow my mind, your short, Jewish father decided to focus his athleticism on basketball. He was pretty damn good in the backcourt, but his ability was hampered by his verticality. Soccer should have been the discipline he focused his attention on because he was a player for sure. I loved watching him compete because he was seriously into it and I admit to getting a vicarious thrill and having the fatherly pride thing, especially since it was not part of my own childhood.

Running, your mind does all sorts of stuff while your body and breath are pushed to exertion. Sometimes, there are great bursts of mental activity and other times you use all your energy on keeping the run going. Over these many years, it has certainly added its own special impact on my consciousness. When you run, you are completely alone; it is your mind, your breath and your body. On top of that, keeping the machine well oiled through movement and exertion makes for a better overall run around the track of life in my opinion.

I have three disciplines that have been an integral part of my life for many years and they are running, Zen meditation and yoga. Like running, which I have been doing for nearly thirty-five years now, Zen and yoga came closely packaged together time wise when I was living in New Mexico.

Like everything I write to you, running will find its way back into this narrative somewhere else. I am still not taking this writing thing for granted and even though it is beginning to develop into a pattern, realizing how easy it would be to just stop keeps enough of a flame under my ass to keep me at it and aren't you the lucky one?

Sundays on Kauai

As you know, this endlessly convoluted tale began last weekend when I was on a plane, flying home from my weekend in Portland. This is my first Sunday back and I have taken part in my Sunday ritual of riding with the Sons of Kauai, something I have been doing for nearly as long as I have been living here.

I decided this morning that after my usual motorcycle ride with the bruddahs, I would tell you the story of the Tangerine Dream and the group of people I ride with each week However, I need to take a very brief detour due to some breaking news. There was an email message from your Dad waiting upon my return from riding. November 6, 2011 is a very big day. I have just received word that you pooped in the toilet. Hopefully, when you are finally permitted to read this, taking a shit will be something you take for granted. Let me tell you something, it is a great day for parents when their child takes a crap for the first time and you don't have to clean up after. It is cute for a while when parents and others marvel at how you are growing and losing your baby fat, but after a couple of years it is a bit more of an ordeal to do the clean up the butt thing.

Let's get back to the Tangerine Dream and the need to tell at least some of the story now. The reason for giving this story a slight priority is that I generally find myself at home every Sunday afternoon after a ride with the Sons and it is a perfect time to get some more stuff down. From this day forward, I won't really have to go into the history of my rides and the Sons of Kauai adventures.

Before I left New Mexico to come here in 2003, I promised myself I would get a kayak, a tattoo and a motorcycle. Needless to say, each one of those is a story on its own and we will stick with the bike thing for now, but all have been accomplished with ease.

I had motorcycles twice before in my life. I got one when I was living in the East Village in the late sixties and that is one of the many episodes from my past that you have got to learn about. The second one came into my life when I was living in New Mexico, which has beautiful roads and spectacular country for biking. I wasn't as comfortable on the bike as I am now and therefore didn't take advantage of it the way I could have. It was a 550 cc Honda, I think. The NYC machine was a small 250cc Honda.

After about three months here, I bought a 2003 Honda Ace Shadow Classic in a tangerine color with some very cool decals along the sides of both fenders. It carries a 750 cc engine, which felt gigantic in the beginning and now after eight years on the Dream, I could do with a larger engine, but have no complaints.

Let me share a couple of observations about motorcycling in general. Leaning into curves, accelerating unnecessarily fast, the wind in your face and hair, the biker slouch, everything about it is this immaculate experience, silently shared by all serious riders. It also doesn't hurt to be riding on one of the most beautiful locations ever created by God. There are times when I ride, especially on a particularly singular day, and I am just gloriously happy, without a thought in my head and any weight on my heart. There is no helmet law here and I don't wear one. I know, don't tell me how irresponsible that is because I don't have a mature response.

So, I was riding alone for maybe a month or so and perfectly happy getting acclimated to the bike and the roads. On one particular Sunday, I took a back road down to Nawiliwili and encountered a very local guy with wild Hawaiian, Einstein hair. Harry flagged me down and began gesturing in a very animated manner and speaking a language I had never really heard before. I think Native people all around the world develop a bastardized language that consists of their own tongue and the language of whatever dominant society has chosen to take advantage of all the natural and human resources they can get their greedy hands on. Harry was speaking to me in local pidgin' and I was able to get just enough to understand there was a group of bikers at a specific location because of some kind of motorcycle show.

Whenever I have had to deal with a new situation, particularly when I made big moves like going to New Mexico and now being on Kauai, I always tread lightly and choose to never impose myself on any new circumstance. With that in mind, I felt a little uncomfortable about following Harry's direction and I didn't. It was a beautiful day and my ride continued on its non-descript two-wheel exploration. Lo and behold! Several hours later, I round a turn and there is wild Harry waving for me to come over to a group of bikers he is with. Keep in mind; this was a group of seriously local guys, all riding Harleys and wearing biker gear with black as the dominant color theme.

I wheeled my tangerine Honda around to where they were sitting. You would have to know something about the contemporary bike culture to understand how a tangerine colored, Japanese manufactured motorcycle is likely to be perceived by the men wearing black. Their bikes of choice were Harleys and various custom choppers. There were at least a half dozen guys, sitting under a shade tree on benches around a picnic table. They asked me if I wanted a beer and the rest was easy. An invitation to ride with them was genuinely offered and my acceptance was immediate.

Now, we cut to the present and find that I am now considered one of the very early members of the Sons of Kauai, a diverse group of riders, who get together every Sunday morning at 9AM at the 7/11 in Lihue. This ongoing experience has been by far one of the greatest gifts I have been given by Kauai.

On any given Sunday, there could be anywhere from six to sixty plus bikes, depending upon weather and scheduling of special events. For me, this has been the equivalent of cracking open a hard-shelled coconut, only to find sweetness and substance within. The majority of the riders are blue-collar workers or retirees and many are working their asses off six days a week. You couldn't find a more generous, embracing group of people. It has been and continues to be a tremendous privilege to be allowed in to their circle and to be accepted without judgment.

There is this weird chivalry that comes with being a Knight of the Cycle. We visit local families where there is illness or a recent death or a birthday celebration. The rumbling sound of the motorcycles approaching and departing has a very clear impact on any proceedings. Once, I rode at the head of the group to rescue a damsel in distress and it was a goose bump moment. The damsel thing is a whole other story and will likely appear when I talk about my mermaid relationship, which falls under the Ladies In My Life category.

Most of the conversations on biker Sunday are about motorcycles, whether about their pedigree or their moving parts, leaving me to look around and simply admire the surroundings and being grateful for the privilege, occasionally nodding in approval about a carburetor or the angle of someone's front forks.

Every Sunday morning, as soon as you have gotten off your bike, you go around to everyone already there and power shake with a shoulder grab. Every new person is embraced with Aloha and each person who approaches the group brings that same beautiful Aloha. Living in paradise can totally fuck you over and put a smile on your face and call it normal. Being with these people has really helped to anchor my life on this small island.

I love riding with this group of people and some time down the road, I may introduce them to you in a bit of detail. Now you know that if I am writing to you on a Sunday afternoon, it is likely after a ride with the Sons, so I can now just move forward without any back story on the Sons of Kauai. It is not all that different from my running thing. Riding a bike and running are some ongoing parts of my life and help define who I am.

Remind me to tell you about my forever relationship with Rock n' Roll, the Blues, Blue Grass and Reggae. I have even happily made room for Jazz and Classical. Music has been an unbelievably important part of my life. Reminded of it now because while I wait for my Gourmet Meals for Single Dummies to heat up, I am listening to some Blues on a radio show hosted by Dan Aykroyd. That's it, just wanted to briefly crank it up before dinner time and thought I'd mention the music thing.

Stop the music

This is a very interesting sort of experiment. I am not only writing to a three year old, I am writing as a sixty six year old man, trying to recount my history, while the world around me continues to generate even more stories to tell. This is an endless proposition and I will just continue to humor myself with whatever pops up at the moment I sit down. I could rush the process in order to make sure I get it all out there, but I will never be able to do that completely as long as I can feel and think and have a desire to express myself, thereby creating an endless process.

As this sentence begins, I am not sure where to take it because the choices are nearly limitless. I have been talking to myself for years and this monologue has been a silent one, located somewhere in the brain, deep behind the third eye. This process has honed some good stories down to their essence, especially the older ones where memory simply stages a walk out and the nuggets remain. I particularly like where the internal monologue has taken me, especially since crossing over into my sixties. My life clock is certainly closer to midnight than the first rays of dawn. It is a perspective that would serve us all much better if we could get at it sooner during the course of our day here. When you truly appreciate the limits we live within, like mortality, it tends to re-scramble priorities.

I am going to bust my chops to go light on the advice stuff. You know, sharing some incredible secrets with you that will allow you to change the course of your life forever. Even if I had the power, I would always want you to live the life that has been written for you already. Your only obligation is to live fully the life that has been inscribed on your behalf in The Book of Life. Looking over the shoulder of time, I would say a life well spent is one spent in the moment. I have already told you there is nothing in here I want you to emulate. Over time, I think it would be extremely cool if this thing I am writing for you could every now and then nudge you closer to your own journey.

It is already 7:44 and I think I can write for a little over an hour more. I need to keep that in mind because I don't want to rush something to squeeze it into the remaining time.

I feel compelled to tell you what is going on in the world right now. Keep in mind, this is toward the end of 2011, so you can find whatever distortions are written about it some time after this, like when you actually read these words. We are bleeding the world dry of its natural resources. We are killing one species off after another. Governments over the world are having their very solvency challenged. The gap between rich and poor has never been greater. All sides use terrorism, called by many different names. In the sacred memory of 9/11, our very freedoms have been sacrificed in the defense against terrorism, while terrorizing virtually every American. Basic freedoms are our birthright as Americans. Naïve or not, this country was founded as a bastion of freedom for all who would call it home.

Now, what does all of this have to do with cheap oil you ask? We have had a great ride on cheap oil; in fact, the entire world has come along on this trip of excess. I have no idea what will replace cheap oil in the future. Right now, the world is totally screwed.

This readily available energy potion blurred the geographic borders of nations and replaced them with economic ones. There is not a single country right now capable of self-sufficiency. The co-mingled world sits on a flimsy foundation, only made possible by a cheap source of energy and as it gradually disappears, the foundation will turn to powder.

We have been riding the horse of capitalism for a while now and we are being forced to whip this ailing nag. When you build a society with the mantra of more as its battle cry, you are going to inevitably reach some limits. This gluttony is unsustainable and it is catching up with us.

Our entire system has been corrupted by money, influence and power. There is an elite citizenry that walks in a rarefied atmosphere. Private interests shape our public policy. We have millions of people who have lost their homes because the mortgage system was a scam to artificially create this unrealistic, ever expanding bubble that would somehow never burst. It ruptured in 2008 and there is no sign of this royal fucking ever ending. The perfect storm that is shredding our world might possibly be enough to challenge the global oligarchy that is strangling us and level the playing field just a bit so we can at least give the appearance of civility. The alternative is to simply throw away the keys to the kingdom because the locks will have been changed and we will not be allowed in.

Oh by the way, I am not a whacked out, pinko, glue sniffing, Jew who believes in the tooth fairy. Trust me, I do not have a horse in this race. Every empire, every dominant society has had its run and there is a reason why they can't seem to get it right because none of these cultures ever acted with humility and compassion toward their own, let alone the countries depending upon the largesse of the empire of the day. Our history is strewn with wars of all kinds for reasons of all kinds. Violence is the greatest crime we can commit toward one another, whether its between two people or two countries. Humility is a steady diet for those with nothing and it would go along way if those with power could embrace by choice what the poor are force fed every day of their lives.

Personally, I am hoping I get to book end my adult life with my time in the Sixties, which anchored the start of my own trip and this time around, addressing some very basic survival issues for all of us. While I don't profess to be optimistic because the deck is stacked, it is still exciting to hear people calling truth to power. The current times will always be a backdrop for whatever I write and it made sense to get some of it out in the open right now. I am following the developments with a bit of a fiendish sense because I have such low expectations of our species, myself included. At the same time, I get up many mornings here, filled with hope and gratitude for this privilege of participating in and witnessing the events of my life.

Stuck in Time

I was thinking about this budding monologue and how it is stuck in the present. No matter what I write about, it reflects my place in time. It would be excellent if I could share with you some of my thoughts and experiences from my teens on forward to now. The problem is we are kind of screwed in that I am at a point in my life where my memories and opinions have been morphing as they percolate through my everyday experiences. Whether we like it or not, we are this specific bundle of genetics in a forever changing body, with an ever mutating awareness and perspective. This is a very Zen state of being and we will leave that story for another time.

Fuck it; let me take a whack at it now. Zen is one of the ongoing streams of my life that empties into the ocean of an ever changing self-called Larry.

From the time I was nine years old, when my father died, a sense of mortality has been ever present with me, even when I was unconscious to its power over all of us. Not speaking for others, I have always been one to have this ongoing discussion with an approving audience of one and that would be me. I am fairly introspective without being terribly neurotic. As I got older, this mortality thing began to make increasing sense and the more I was aware of it, the more it impacted on my choices.

I dabbled with some Eastern stuff when I was in my thirties. It kind of started when I began having difficulty in my marriage to Andy's mom, Ingrid. I know I have already said that the only story staying privately with me are the issues relating to the demise of our marriage. Very few things in this treatise are close to home, but that is one of the few I will keep to myself. Your Dad has some idea and if he ever chooses to tell you that is just fine, but not my place. It was the time when I also began running. I was also seeing a shrink back ten and was pretty much shrunken for around ten years, early thirties to early forties. It was the very beginning of my time of getting in touch with the invisible, trafficking in the transcendent.

For two summers, I rented a farmhouse in Honesdale, PA. Andy and Danny had a great time during those summers. It was an old house, sitting on the land of a dairy farmer, whose entire family really embraced the boys. Those summers are a great story that will likely come up in full detail later on. The place was sort of a refuge for me from all the noise of the City, especially when I was there alone or with Norma, who will reappear down the road just apiece. There was a large spiritual center nearby and I spent some

time around the place. I was also dabbling in meditation and yoga back then.
Now, travel with me to Santa Fe, NM sometime in 1987 and we find yours truly running out in the middle of nowhere, down a dirt road that led to another dirt road and so on. There were some neighbors out there and I would see one particular woman on many of the mornings. Other than shorts and shoes, my uniform consisted of a Superman shirt that I had gotten as a perk many years before that, but it was my superstitious shirt of choice for my runs out in the flats of Cerrillos, NM.

One day, I am walking in down town Santa Fe and I hear a woman shouting several times, "Hey Superman!" It was Sandy, now called Sandia and presently involved with a community in northern India. This is a lady from the flat country of Texas and a world class broad. We became very good friends and I visited with her often and she was a salty joy to be around.

One day, Sandy tells me I ought to come with her to a Zen temple she attended in town. She quickly added that I was already a Zen practitioner, whether I knew it or not. She was absolutely right. The place was run by a rather ego driven woman and while I resonated with the feeling, this was not going to be my deal. She then introduced me to a terrific couple, who had a Zendo a little south of the city. They were very down to earth people and we became good friends.

It is funny; friendships are often chapters in our lives because they can spring up unpredictably and dissipate just as quickly, something you will experience as you journey through your own life.

Off subject again, so shoot me. Their names were David and Linda. He was a gifted, artisan engraver and she was a stone cold horse lady. The cowgirl is a breed of woman I hope is still around when you begin experiencing life. Anyway, I began to "sit" with them and started doing some Zen rituals of the prayer practice. You had to bow a shit load of times and there is just one thing I want to tell you about bowing. There is nothing in the world better than starting your day bowing on your knees with your forehead on the ground. Humility is elemental in growing true compassion in us all.

My Zen time out there in Santa Fe with these folks was a time of tremendous internal growth. David and Linda were terrific people and provided me a place to explore this new practice. I had passed through to my forties, slowly peeling away another petal of baggage and gradually exposing my True Nature, one petal at a time. Personally, I think the emphasis on change in all the therapies, involves adding layers of petals, as opposed to stripping them away on a journey of discovering who you were before all those damn petals grew from the core. Zen is about the core.

Sorry for all the serious shit, but the meaning of life can play out differently for each of us. It all depends upon on how you place yourself in this world of shifting sands and ever changing perceptions. Zen appealed to me because it cut to the marrow of life. If this practice has a role or purpose, it is to drive you to a place where you give up looking for answers to the never-ending questions. Basically, life is a question and its vocabulary is an internal dialogue that provides no real answers, or at least ones that can be understood and communicated. My own feeling is that the more you talk about Zen, the less Zen you actually are. It is really about the world that exists internally just before you start thinking and speaking.

Zen would maintain that our world is ever changing and there is nothing stable to hold on to. We like to think that Shane is a person who is unchanged from day to day or moment-to-moment. This little ditty that most everyone holds on to goes right down the drain in Zen. Every conceivable moment, a cell within us dies and we are no longer that earlier person. Using this rate of change as your currency of perception, you would be bankrupt within mili-seconds. On top of that, if you accept the inevitable truth that we are all interconnected on some multi-dimensional web of affect, the rate of change is simply unquantifiable, period. When I use the word "we", it is all inclusive and takes into account all kinds of sentient beings, an infinite number that moves too quickly to even try and put your mind around.

Let me give you a quickie Buddha lesson, understanding I am a piss poor example of this practice. The Big Man said that all life is suffering. Now, why the hell would this guy go knocking around the Indian countryside laying down some very unpleasant shit? He would say the reason for this suffering is our inability to accept the true impermanence of this very moment, let alone our convoluted constructions built to deny our inevitability. Taking it one step further, if you are somehow able to understand the true nature of all things and their impermanence, the awareness liberates you from the life of suffering.

A discussion of Zen could go on forever and it would make sense because Zen incorporates every thing that has ever occurred or will ever occur. I believe that at its core, Zen is experiential and impossible to communicate because it speaks to each of us in its unique, invisible voice. Hopefully, your parents will let you read this whole thing before you are even remotely close to understanding any of this Zen shit. I think one can only get to contemplate this kind of business until they have some serious emotional mileage.

I keep putting off all the stories and I apologize, but it is hard to get me out of the way.

Just a quick one

The absolute magnificence of being alive is something we all take for granted and that is too bad. It is unbelievable to think we are here in this time and place and we are alive. The stronger this sensibility becomes in your life, the more you will appreciate every moment. Whenever you read this short paragraph, it will apply to you right at that time you are slogging through all of this mental baggage from your grandpa on Kauai. It has taken me many, many years to distill the beehive activity into quiet breaths of unexplainable joy and humility for this blessing of life I have been given.

May take you to the beach tomorrow and tell you some more stories, but I am not sure enough to give you my word.

On the Beach

Being a man of my word, I am at the Kukuiula Small Boat Harbor on the south side of the island. It is one of my favorite haunts and I get on the Tangerine Dream and ride on over there to eat a take out lunch and/or a cold beer. There are covered areas with tables and benches and coming over here to stare out at the Pacific Ocean is about as good as it gets.

I realize that the majority of the home for these stories is Kauai and there isn't much I can do about that. Now that the telling of tales has begun, I am stuck with having to recreate the past, including where I have been and traveled. Moving from this point forward will be easy because I can share what happens as it happens.

I could not have done any of this before because it took this long to be comfortable with my voice and to have you as my audience, whether you like it or not.

When you grow up in an urban world as I did and you most likely will, experiencing the majesty of nature is a stone called revelation whenever it happens to engulf you. When I left New York City in my early forties, the world literally opened up for me on many levels. The American Southwest, heading up towards the Four Corners area, is some of the most spectacular country I have ever seen. The sky, the colors and the vistas are beyond compare. So much of my own journey has been about finding the voice to share these experiences. When you see things like the high desert bloom and its countless flowers and colors, you just don't have words inside. Camping in the foothills of the Rockies and waking up early in the morning, surrounded by nature's mountain majesty, you are overwhelmed and mute because there are just no words. There is a spontaneity in those moments that burns right through you and then they are gone and so are you.

Sitting here, in this sub-tropical paradise, I am reminded of the countless moments I have had when I have been simply overwhelmed by what I have seen. I think all artistic expression comes from our efforts to describe the indescribable and we always fall short. Shane, you experience as much as you possibly can during your lifetime. Experience is the currency that builds character through the discovery of our place in the world we live in.

The trade winds are blowing pretty hard today and the palm trees and other greenery appear to be running away from the them. The sunlight is playing on the ever moving sea and parts of it glows like liquid diamonds caught in the direct rays of the sun.

For reasons that escape me, we are expected to compartmentalize our lives and seek an unattainable unity. When we go on vacations, the idea is to get away from our daily lives and enjoy a brief stay in a forbidden location, only available to us for weeks at a time. Some thought ought to be given to flipping this process on its ear. Why shouldn't you live in a place where you would be happy to vacation? I am not sure why we are expected to make sacrifices and concessions through out our lives. Personally, I think it is a very fucked up formula that somehow implies that joy is a rare gift and the everyday is arduous. Imagine if you set out as your life's goal to be joyful and to spread joy to others? Regardless of when an effort like this is undertaken, it certainly runs against the demented ideas most of us hold on to, leaving you alone with the simple truth that it is your nature and a reward unto itself.

I had to leave the beach without saying goodbye because the weather was growing a little unpleasant and it was starting to distract from my focus, rather than sharpening it. There will be plenty of opportunities to take this show on the road. This effort would be worthless if it was in any way regimented by time or place because life doesn't work that way; it never goes according to plan.

You know, I really don't have any great expectations in terms of the impact of this work. I know at least one person will read this from beginning to end and that is you. I know it will affect you because I am your grandfather. With that in mind, I would be gloriously happy if it jump-started your own journey of self-discovery and a greater awareness of the world you inhabit.

It feels like I am closing in on the story telling of my past experiences. I have had my fair share and there are fine tales to be told. Probably, the best way to begin is to simply do that and see where it takes us. Maybe, we will make chapters out of them, letting each one stand alone, or maybe I will start and get distracted. We won't know until we give it a go. I will think about that for a while and we'll see what is worth recalling and what context I want to present them in.

Occupy

Forgive me for being so self-absorbed. I don't think I have once asked you how you are doing? How old are you and where are you living? Have you done reasonably well in school? Are you a decent athlete? Did your clear interest in music as a little person mutate into becoming something resembling a musician?

Whenever you read this, I hope you have happily lost your virginity and that girls are already driving you crazy. How tall are you? There is a genetic confrontation regarding height issues. I am nearly 5'10" and both Andy and Danny caught the shorter piece of the DNA daisy chain. I wonder where you you will come out in the land of verticality.

For the purpose of this communication, I am going to assume you are heterosexual, even though I really don't give a shit one way or the other. I have one of my very best stories about a trip cross-country in the Sixties with a friend and person we had recently met. He was a tall, palms up, arm swinging, hip swiveling, homosexual. I promise to get to this one, but I have something else I need to get to right now.

I had thought about what to write next and had come up with the idea for a heading, entitled, "Getting Fired and the Mafia. Your mother recently lost her job and it took her by surprise, which reminded me of this past experience. Now, I don't want to give you a case of retro-anxiety, wondering how the three of you were going to survive in Hoboken. Of course, I have no idea how this will end up shaking out because it only happened a few weeks ago. What I do know is that your mother is an exceptional woman. Aside from being hysterically competent, she comes from the heart. The Universe embraces people who open their hearts. If you are someone who is looking for proof before you take the chance, guaranteed nothing will come of it.

Just like the allusion to my cross-country saga, the Mafia moment will be coming up before you know it.

Anyway, I feel compelled to share with you the making of a phenomenon. The reason why I want to do it now and not later is because I want to catch it while it is still raw. There is a term called "tipping point" and it means something actually starts happening before the realization takes hold in the mass consciousness.

I am definitely not a scholar and like to say that my entire knowledge base has come from hearsay. Somewhere around the post Depression rise of government services and regulations until the Reagan era of strong conservatism, the country was probably slightly left of center. Communism did ultimately put a line in the sand and the witch hunts under McCarthy with his House UnAmerican Activities Committee put a governor on the engine driving the Left. Communism was our enemy for years and the more something smacked of this evil system in America, the more the red flag loomed large and panic buttons were pushed everywhere. That experience made the Left a little nervous and self-conscious, long after the demise of the Red Threat. The timidity of the left caused a giant opening for those with different views regarding the role of government.

Around the time of Reagan and flourishing during the second Bush, the Christian God began to hold much more sway and this rampant righteousness pretty much became the heart of the Republican Party. In its extreme it was a conservative theocracy threatening to make over this American bastion of freedom in its own image. Let me tell you, there is plenty of money out there supporting this movement. It completely blows my mind that there are still legislative fights throughout the country over contraception and abortion. The cruel joke about these "right to lifers" is that they really don't give a shit what happens to you after you are born because their government is not responsible for caring for its people. We are supposed to be able to simply take care of ourselves because we are real Americans.

When electronic journalism first began in both radio and television, it was newspaper people who migrated to these new media and they brought with them an integrity and lack of bias, which was so much a part of the lore of the newspaper newsroom. I was a page at NBC in the mid-sixties and I spent time around the news department during election coverage and space launches. The page story is definitely another gem and I don't want to go there right now, but I will definitely come back to it, along with the Mafia tale and the cross-country odyssey.

Profit slowly became a corporate expectation and the less regulation in place, the easier it was to make a buck. The bottom line and obeisance to the powerful advertisers, who could not be offended, kidnapped the once highly held principle of truth in news.

Now, we throw in a very healthy dose of technology and access to endless information, along with the advent of social media like FaceBook and Twitter and a plethora of weird, fucken named enterprises doing all sorts of things that somehow became indispensable over night. Suddenly, everything was true because it appeared somewhere buried in the never-ending toilet flush of so-called facts.

The Right did a brilliant job of taking advantage of this confluence of beliefs, freeing us from government, promoting profitability over responsibility and continually painting itself as a victim of the ever present liberal bias in media and in your closet and under your bed. They were angry and their rhetoric consistently reflected their feeling of powerlessness and they did this even when they were running the White House and Congress during some of that time.

Greed had us by the balls and it was infectious, spreading to many countries around the world. Deaf to anything other than the mantra of endless profitability, our economy kept expanding and accountability was on a permanent paid holiday.

For well over twenty years, regular working people have been getting screwed. Social services have shrunken while our penchant for preemptively striking countries has increased dramatically. We will only interfere with a sovereign entity when our economic interest is at stake. We enter countries and destroy them, exiting before the brooms and dustpans come out to remove the dead and the rubble. The interests of the powerful have always trumped the needs of the people.

The liberal voices found themselves marginalized and ostracized by the God fearing, money wielding mob and they were far too polite and insecure in facing the conservative taunts. Those who speak the loudest are the ones you hear and it would not be a stretch to think the majority of the country has veered to the right. By the way, there is no one at all to blame in this scenario. Everyone who put their immediate needs and desires ahead of their brothers and sisters shares the guilt. Compassion and civility are kissing cousins, yet no society has risked losing its virginity by having sex with our own highest purpose.

In the spring of 2011, something completely unimagined began happening in the Arab world. It is called the Arab Spring, and it was a completely organic uprising of regular people against the machines that had enslaved them for decades. Our political ties are exclusively based on expedience. We supported tyrants and ignored others in the Middle East. Some guy set himself on fire in Tunisia and that tribute to the true incandescence of the human spirit spread throughout the region and is still continuing today. These happenings were detonated by social media, which until now are one of the last fortresses for freedom of expression. The future is not my bailiwick, so I have absolutely no idea what will happen when the sand castles are flooded by the people in the streets.

The aforementioned is a less than a complete backdrop for the living theatre that calls itself "Occupy Wall Street" and the hundreds of derivative movements around the country and the world. It seems that there are a whole lot of people who feel that they have been screwed long enough by the system. I have no idea how it actually began here, but depending upon its lifespan and significance, there will likely be books and movies about it, mythologizing for purposes of entertainment.

Right now, all over the country and the world, there are people camping out in peaceful protest against the absurd accumulation of power and wealth in the hands of very few people. Most government's political systems are fiendish for money from these relatively few people and corporations, in return for favorable policies.

Unions, labor's savior, empowering people against power, are now an impediment to the bottom line. The brave veterans, returning from the shit wars in Iraq, Afghanistan, Pakistan and wherever else power needs to sacrifice them, are being treated like crap when they get home and that is deplorable. It is one thing to commit this country to conflict, but its polar opposite of not caring for our heroes when they return is criminal.

People could no longer afford their homes because their value fell off a cliff and these folks were on the hook for deals that were purposely created to screw them. The government chose to spend our money in making the banks whole, while the mortgages were burying these hard working folks, duped by the promise of a free lunch.

Young people are being crushed by student loans and there are no jobs for them or the kids without access to that education opportunity.

The Occupy movement is confusing the shit out of all the soothsayers and political pabulum spitters. Personally, I am thrilled that this movement is impossible to put in a box because it keeps it free to draw more and more disenfranchised, disappointed people. There are great individuals who proved how powerful the streets are. Gandhi and Dr. King marched on their streets and the results were staggering.

As I have gotten older, my perspective about so many things has changed. I am definitely not any smarter, but I have been around to witness my own process of self-discovery. This Occupy thing may be just a blip on the radar screen of historic events, but you can rest assured there were many, many people who felt so passionately about something that they endured some pretty serious challenges and there is no act more commendable in a compassionate, civilized world. Tension is slowly increasing between the occupiers and the various impacted local governments, not to mention the ever-fearful threat of loss of control by the plutocracy pulling the strings. Once you get well above the radar, like the Occupy Wall Street movement, powerful forces immediately coalesce to crush any hint of revolution. These forces will likely prevail once again.

I really should be able to tell you one of the three stories I have already mentioned. I don't want to reread any of this right now, so I can't go backwards a page or two to recall those promises. I will likely cheat next time around and make sure I eventually cover all of them.

Getting Fired and the Mafia

Let's dig deep into the vaults of memory and resuscitate a story from sometime in 1977. I actually had to check the dates on my professional resume, which is carved on several tablets of stone because it goes back to a prehistoric time, certainly for you. As I mentioned already, this tale of old is just a little more timely now because your Mom got canned from a very sweet gig at a hedge fund. Every now and then, it is good to break up the spider webs of habit by getting flipped on your ass. Trust me, it sucks when it happens, but your Mom is number one on my list and something good will come from her shattered professional view plane.

My own tale of woe begins around the end of 1977. Somehow, I mistakenly found myself in the broadcast advertising business. When I accidentally became a page at NBC, which I have already mentioned, I was really captivated by the creative power of this medium. I don't think I have bothered to explain that a page was like an usher at a theatre, who also worked behind the scenes in a variety of functions. Had I dared to think of myself as someone with artistic tendencies, my life would likely have turned out quite differently. This is an issue I will talk about at a later time. It is of primal consequence and I am not in the mind set right now to address crucial turns in my life that have taken me on the journey I am sharing with you right now.

After the page chapter, I found myself on the business side of broadcast advertising. Jobs and work will be an ongoing thread in this sloppily weaved tapestry I am calling my life.

During that time, I confess to being somewhat intoxicated by playing the role of a grown up, wearing a suit and carrying an attaché case and feeling that what I was doing was very important. It is fucken ironic, when you are a kid, you want to be a grownup and when you are a grownup you want to be a kid. Before I get back to the story, do me a favor and don't be in a hurry to be someone else, rather, take the time to get to know your self. It is easy to get wrapped in a straight jacket of externals and abandoni the only voyage worth taking, the Voyage of the HMS Shane.

Back then, I was feeling pretty good about myself in terms of work. We had moved to a home in Glen Cove, Long Island that we could not afford, relying on the support of your grandmother's parents and my mother. Personally, I was in so deep, there was no thought of escape. Let me also say that no matter what was going in my work world, my personal life or my travels, I loved your father and uncle with all my heart. Choosing to separate from them was one of the most awful decisions I could imagine. I loved taking care of them and being a Daddy.

I was good at what I did and never imagined having the rug pulled out from under me. I was working at an advertising called Doyle, Dane, Bernbach and pretty comfortable about my work world. The economy was going through a period of adjustment back then and advertising budgets were being cut, but I never imagined being a casualty. One morning, I got kicked in the nuts. I am told Personnel wants to see me and I go there almost as naively as the Jews to the showers. They are all dressed in black, funereal clothing and I am given a brief, apologetic explanation of why I am now totally fucked. I was mortgaged to my ass and had no savings because the house and the two boys gobbled it all up.

I was in my early thirties and way over my head. Getting shit canned was devastating on a number of levels, including self-worth and net worth. I was a name and some numbers on a piece of paper and of no real importance to the folks who pulled the strings. I suppose it is good to know nothing has changed in that realm for the past thirty plus years. For what it's worth, the fledgling Occupy movement today has to do with that same disconnect between money and humanity, amongst other things.

You probably want to know about the Mafia business by now. Well, I was officially out of work and had sent my appropriate resume to everyone I could think of. We were heading into the holiday season and nothing was going to happen until early in 1978. I met some guy at a party and I don't remember his name or much of the circumstance. Your grandmother and I had befriended a couple by the name of Albie and Joanne. They were easy going, hippies from the Bronx and we enjoyed their company, which for me was a happy change of pace from the Martian media life I found myself enmeshed in, plus feeling terribly awkward in my suburban life style.

A guy at the party tells me I can make some really fast money by buying albums and eight tracks (look it up) from someone he knew. Still being stupid enough to believe there is such a thing as easy money, I told this character to count me in.

We now cut to an evening meeting at exit 46 or 47 on the Long Island Expressway. I drive there from my suburban enclave and wait. The meeting place is a gravel-covered parking lot with a bunch of trailers, looking strangely decapitated without their truck heads. There are headlights and dust and Mario appears. Mario is part of a very successful trucking family business with an Italian last name. He has a couple of guys with him in his Cadillac. We meet and then walk over to the back of one of those trailers and Mario unlocks it and opens it to reveal a huge pile of LP's and Eight Tracks. He tells us the price is $8,500 and it was clearly not something to be negotiated. We thanked him for his time and split.

Of course, what I didn't realize is that the deal was consummated the moment we met and he showed us the contents of the trailer. The viewing occurred at the start of a weekend, so we told him we would talk with him after that. I became the person who spoke with Mario because the other guy was basically useless. When I called Mario, much to my surprise, he simply wanted to know when he was going to get his money and when we would pick up the merchandise.

This unexpected news from Mario precipitated a flurry of family activity and required sharing this embarrassing interlude with your Grandmother, plus her parents and my mother. Bless them, they came up with the money and I brought it to Mario at his plastic wrapped couch house somewhere in the look alike homes on Long Island. The stolen product was stored in the garage of my antiseptic homestead and I don't believe the neighbors were informed, but I don't remember.

In the process of actually selling this hot music to stores in lower Manhattan, I ended up speaking with Mario quite a bit. You also need to keep in mind that the Godfather movie had recently come out and I identified with the Al Pacino character, a quiet force that wielded considerable power. When you are selling stolen property, you are likely to deal with unsavory characters. I literally had to tell one of those guys that I could have him killed if he kept pursuing a certain course. It was definitely a Pacino moment, but it was actually true. Mario would have made sure this person never bother me again. It is a very weird feeling, but I confess to having moments when I thought it was pretty fucken cool that I could actually have someone killed.

One day, I get a call from the Nassau County District Attorney's office asking me if I could please pay them a visit. It seemed they were tapping Mario's phone and my conversations with him were very different than the ones he had with his cronies. He was a tough guy and he dealt with tough guys, but I stood out like a sore thumb from all those people. I visited with them and they wanted to know if I had seen any cocaine or guns being transported by Mario as a result of the family business. I answered honestly and the truth was I had never seen anything like that, nor were there any conversations about anything other than the damn hot music I was stuck with.

After that meeting, I called Mario and told him to call me back from a pay phone, which would not be tapped. He did and I told him what transpired with the DA. He asked me to meet him out at the parking lot later that same evening. I went and when the big Caddy pulled up, two very large gorillas got out of the back seat and told me to get in. I got in the back seat, book ended by two extremely spacious humans. Mario is in the front with a driver and he leans over and tells me that if he didn't like me, he would kill me. I don't think that is how I learned the value of sincerity, but I will be a son of a bitch if it doesn't always pay off. I was always straight up with him and was no threat at all.

Aside from miraculously making the money back to pay off family, the story pretty much ends right there. It was an incredible experience, although pretty tough to be around for your grandmother. Not a shining moment in my life, but awfully fucken colorful, if I do say so myself. I learned a little bit about the code of the criminal and it is very real and you don't mess with it. There may still be movies about it when you are old enough to go, whether there are or not, it is authentic and dangerous to outsiders, let alone their own kind.

It was one of those amazing experiences for me and I wouldn't trade it for the world. A colorful life is filled with adventures and my Mafia escapade is one of my favorites. If I told you this same story ten minutes from now, it would undoubtedly come out completely different. It will suffice for now and I don't think I want to waste time going back over stories I have already shared. Now, I can check this off the list and see what is next in the long line of my personal exhalations.

I love you, Shane. Back soon.

An Injustice to Rock 'n Roll

I was driving in my severely faded, red, '93 Toyota truck this afternoon on a logging road, following a trailer carrying about seven really large de-barked logs, weighing well over a thousand pounds each and measuring at least 35 ft. A Crosby, Stills and Nash song came on my radio and I began singing at the top of my longs, window rolled down and elbow bent and resting on the open window. I could never do justice to the importance of music in my life. It is a very large subject for me and I am only able to share a fraction at a time because it is completely integrated into my life.

I was a young kid in the mid-fifties, living in Queens, NY, listening to 78's, 45's or the flimsy sounds coming through my transistor radio. I am not sure when I first got bitten on the ass by the strong connection to music. I know I listened to a lot of black groups like the Cleftones, the Shirelles and Clyde McPhatter, singing " The Treasure of Love." I was around ten when Elvis appeared on the Ed Sullivan Show. For some reason that I no longer remember, the crude television went out in my house and I shot like a hound over to my neighbors to make sure I didn't miss a thing.

I really grew up with Rock 'n Roll and followed all of its permutations and combinations. Favorite songs had and still have the power to transport me on a mind journey, temporarily disconnecting the world from myself. There was a musical revolution going on all around me when I was young and it was impossible to avoid. In my life, music has always had a seat at the table.

Music and love leave me feeling terribly inadequate in terms of my ability to communicate how they have both been the breath of my life.

I saw the Beatles at Shea Stadium and was in front of the stage during the Concert for Bangladesh. When Simon and Garfunkel got together in Central Park, I was one of a half a million people that night. As a page, I saw every imaginable musician from the pre-Rock era because the Tonight Show at that time was very conservative. In the broadcast advertising business, I was one of the few "adults" who would take advantage of NBC's readily available Sky Box at Madison Square Garden. I saw the Grateful Dead, Bruce Springsteen, Kiss, the Rolling Stones, Prince, the Allman Brothers and an endless list of the great names in that genre of music.

I am sure music has been important in virtually all civilizations, but in this so-called technological age, owing much of its roots to Thomas Edison, music became accessible to so many people at one time. Don't bust my chops if Edison isn't quite right, I really didn't want to stop the roll to see who developed the first recorded music. The fact that music had to be live and with a limited audience before then definitely cut down any bootlegging. This means I had the benefit of being around for both an explosion in musical creativity and the ability to communicate it to an infinitely large audience. Music has always been a very powerful force in all cultures because it is a part of who we are, but the trajectory created by the explosion of Rock 'n Roll is unmatched, until this evening at least.

I always preferred slow dances with girls because you didn't really have to dance very well and you could rub up against them. To me, music is associated with every time in my life. I don't have favorite songs or songs marking personal milestones. When you are listening to something very strong that gets you going, the music can create its own moment for you.

When I called Andrea a couple of days ago, you were there in the background and you wanted to know my favorite song. Apparently, you have continued to show a genuine pleasure being around music, which is just thrilling to me because I love music. I told her my favorite song is actually, "Rhapsody in Blue" by George Gershwin and performed by Leonard Bernstein with the NY Philharmonic.

Right now, Crosby, Stills and Nash are on the radio, singing a song recorded live at the Occupy Wall Street demonstration. The power of music is beyond belief. I think it is as close as we can get to flying. It is so overwhelming to try and get my arms around how much music has been a part of my life. It started when I was a kid and heard music that said things I wanted to say or wish for things I wished for. It adds such an incredible dimension to our being and if music were banished from my life, I really don't think I could get by.

I just thought of one outrageous musical story from my past. I met some British guy who had a radio series and I was in the broadcast advertising business at the time. I shit you not; he and I met with some high echelon administrator at the UN about having a Beatles reunion at the UN. The details are sketchy beyond that meeting, but it was not crazy for me to think about doing anything I wanted to. As long as you are not attached to outcome, being true to your dreams is all that matters.

You're gonna love this, I promoted a major, outdoor concert series called Music In the Pines in the summer of 1989 in Santa Fe. Trust me, this is a story unto itself and we will see if I come back to it down the road.

Be right back, but it is getting late and I am hungry. It is not like I am ever going to finish this story because it is ongoing, so interrupting it is no big deal. I am starving, be back soon and I want to go on a little longer about music.

Dinner is warming and there is no reason to avoid getting back while I wait. In addition to my concert promoter experience, which is quite a story, I helped launch an excellent radio station in Santa Fe and it was great fun to create a social institution in a community and to do it with music and attitude. I will have to cover this a little later. Both the promoter experience and the radio life are just great stories.

Only because I made a thing about dinner, just wanted you to know I have finished.

While I was eating, it became even clearer that music is an integral part of who I am. I grew up during a time when music became a voice for young people, something their parents would never understand. Back then; it defined a generation of people who just went wild over the power unleashed by some terrific artists. Today, musicians are more of a passing fad than a lasting influence. Believe it or not, I am listening to men and women who are even older than I am and they are still kicking ass.

I got into music before it was really big business. Radio stations began popping up and these FM wonders were being incredibly creative with their musical choices and were often referred to as "free form". There was plenty of music before then, but this was a rare confluence of circumstances, bringing together huge numbers of people to listen to this music. It was a revolutionary time for music and I got to hear so much of it, some live and mostly on radio or whatever technological format happened to be in vogue at the time.

I have a great story about my drive cross country to Santa Fe, NM, when I left the boys and set up shop in the Southwest. Music was an integral part of the journey and I will definitely share that one along way. That drive was a very powerful time in life and I have vivid memories of it.

In addition to my above-mentioned musical escapades in Santa Fe, I actually worked with a guy who had New Mexico roots, but lived in England and was quite a character. I worked with him to launch Run River Records, a British record label here in the States. Again, another long story. I am sorry to do this to you, but that is what happens when you try and live a life. I am not making anything up, although the facts are meant to be imprecise and part of this mosaic of my life, narrated by yours truly. Got no close for the music score that has enriched my life, just appreciation.

More Music

I think music grew in importance as its audience grew. All the kids born after the Second World War began to hit their teens in the late 50's and it is no coincidence that music began to explode around that time. There are some exceptions to that, including Gospel, Blues and Jazz. African Americans carried this music on their backs as slaves and in their souls as mistreated human beings, who refused to be broken.

I almost forgot to mention I was in the Gospel music business for a couple of years and it began in Santa Fe and briefly carried over to Kauai. Another guy, Pete, and myself, secured long form videos from Gospel record labels around the country. We put them on a cable network, Black Entertainment Television (BET) and sold these videos to the TV audience. There were some really fine people in that business and a church full of great musicians who just happened to believe in Christ and they played their hearts out for him.

Before I get back to my never ending riff on music and me, I realize I am mentioning a bunch of different things I have done and they are only briefly described before getting back to whatever the business at hand happens to be. All of these throw aways are long stories, filled with great characters and a breadth of knowledge and experience that begins to vaguely resemble wisdom as the years go by. When you consider experiences as part of your education and you accumulate them and learn from them, every now and then you might actually say something that is of some real value to another and occasionally of some significance to your self as well. I wouldn't trade any of my adventures for a different life than the one I have been living all these years.

During all those years, music was very close by. I even thought Pat Boone was cool when he sang "Tuity Fruity", originally done by a far more exciting performer, Little Richard. Through my teens, music was important, but when the British invaded in the mid-Sixties and hippies took over the youth culture, the sounds of that time turned me hard in its direction. I can't describe what it was like. These gifted musicians broke all the rules and crafted a genre that spoke to young people everywhere. A decade earlier, music was stirring it up with politicized folk songs and outspoken artists like Pete Seeger. Then, rock 'n roll energized a generation and several more since then. It was down right explosive.

Re-calibrate

I felt myself straining a little last night in trying to amplify music's impact on my life and that is not the idea behind this. While I have been thinking about this effort for around a year, it is only around three weeks old in terms of my putting down the first words and thoughts to share with you. I don't mean to pontificate about all sorts of shit; it is just that I am fairly opinionated in my dotage. It has taken decades to believe there is no such thing as the truth, some lasting, impenetrable expression of what transpired any time behind this very moment and even that gets kind of lost somewhere between occurrence and awareness. This is kind of a Zen way of viewing the world and where we fit into it all.

In this test of my memory and clarity, it is probably a good idea to go back to that moment with the idea about finding my voice, so I could let you know a little about me in terms of the facts, seasoned with a fair dose of character. It would be easy to lay out the facts and you would garner some information, without having any idea about who I am. It would be particularly cool if I am actually around when you get your first reading of this mini-saga of a life, but that is unfortunately out of my control. This is my insurance policy against the inevitability of my no longer being a part of your life. There is no defying mortality, but I can get to live longer through these words.

Have I told you yet that being alive is a miracle and a blessing without peer? I think our appreciation grows as the time left diminishes. Obviously, I would be thrilled if all of this affects you very deeply. You will likely be a young man when you get to see this for the first time and much of it will probably not make sense. Hell, I am sixty-six years old and my vocabulary is a reflection of all that has happened until this very moment, while you get to this after a considerable gap in time. I never imagined this journey when I was much younger and I probably would have thought it a load bullshit if I had seen it all through a crystal ball. What kind of world you will be living in is absolutely impossible for me to imagine. As you have easily guessed by now, I have no compunction about sharing perceptions of my past and present surroundings.

So far, the majority of this writing has taken place in my little ohana in Koloa. Ohana is a Hawaiian word for family and true to their spirit of aloha, it includes all loved ones. It also describes a secondary dwelling for family. I sit above a large two-car garage and I see the Pacific off in the distance. I won't be in the space too much longer and you will undoubtedly transition with me to the yurt I am putting up on the land where I am working.

Anyway, writing from this familiar place is very grounding, allowing me to focus on my internal world. While we will go on location and already have, the bulk of this will be written from wherever I am living. Aside from the two huge moves to Santa Fe and Kauai, I have always moved around within those places, including my forty plus years in New York City. In order to tell you about the yurt, I have to preface it with the work I am doing now.

You know, in keeping with this diary of the mind idea, directions of thought are unpredictable. On top of that, we continually revisit old, finger printed, grey matter and find it is continually changing, depending on an infinite number of variables. I figure if I keep chipping away in the present, I will inevitably revisit the past along the way and share it with you.

Hey Kid

Hey Kid. How are you doing? I hope at least some of this stuff is interesting. This is a later time than I have been accustomed to writing and as a result, I am likely over two glasses of wine and some pipefuls of ganja. Once again, this is shared in the spirit of honesty. I am basically asking you to take a ride with me and I am not passing out a counterfeit ticket. I suspect you will find that many artists, of which I am not, have indulged in all sorts of silk pillows to makes themselves just a little more comfortable with the wrenching exertion of self-expression. This is hard work, but it is my choice to draw it out from deep within and this little project has taken on a very curious level of importance in my life. Who knows what lies ahead in this adventure that I have chosen to take you along on?

Let me tell you about today. I met up with a guy by the name of Keale. He has an Anglo name, but it doesn't matter. In all native cultures, bloodlines are important and while it is not quite all out tribalism, these people know where they have come from, often in great detail. My friend is from a family of very powerful, revered Hawaiian musicians and this family extends throughout the islands and that is the way it is here.

I heard a CD of his music a number of years ago and got in touch with him. One of the many things I haven't yet had a chance to mention is that I have this uncanny ability to cross the barriers of Six Degrees of Separation (look it up) and connect with anyone I want to and the reason doesn't matter. I sent him some messages and we got together around four years ago when he was here performing. We connected beautifully and it was strong. I have seen him several times since and we got together today. We spent a number of hours talking about the timeless bond between his people and these islands of Hawaii. His people were here for hundreds of years, migrating from islands much further west. The first people to any place on this earth have their entire cultures inexorably linked to these special destinations as the stage and setting for their beliefs and practices.

I have no idea if native people will have survived when you actually read this, although I suspect they will be where they have always been. Their existence is threatened throughout the world right now. In many ways, the faces of indigenous people are a reminder of the crimes committed by the fashionable dominant society of the time in their clashes with these First People. Their mistreatment has been unconscionable and it is something that I was total unaware of while living in New York City.

When I moved to Santa Fe in '87, I had never seen a Native American or really gave much of a shit about them. Over time, Indians became normal to me and I befriended a few and was fortunate enough to be invited into their homes during special celebrations. They are different than you or I. Time is a big one. To them, time is not meant to be terribly precise. They didn't grow up with watches on their wrists and time couldn't be specific. If you can relax and allow things to unfold at their own pace, you are likely half way to crossing the bridge between us and them. They are also very respectful of the spirit world, where the invisible is normal. For me, it is a quiet privilege to be allowed into any culture beyond the predictably familiar of my own.

I hope you have an opportunity to spend some time around native people, regardless of location. You will learn a lot and it will help to open up your interior world to the outside.

Generally, their music is very special and that is certainly the case here. It is amazing how many people play ukulele and sing. Music and hula are deeply embedded in their genes.

I know I haven't told you what I am presently doing work- wise and how it came about, but I will. I got side tracked by Keale and wanted to share it while it was fresh. I know I got off a bit on the native thing, but in our world, which is predicated on continual change, we need to know there are people around us who understand the importance of their timeless symbols and practices and how they are anchored to a never changing spirit place.

Oh Crap!

I had really pretty much decided to tell you about the kind of work I am doing now and why, which I will, just not right now.

I want to get back to this Occupy thing that is going on at the moment. If I were a sociologist, this would be a fascinating study. Technology has had the effect of a tsunami on every human in its wake. Shane, you have no idea what this revolution has done to people all over the world and how lives were turned upside down and no one paid any attention. We all hoisted anchor and the winds of astronomical change took us all to this very strange place called technology. One of the really shitty things about this new world is the terrible disconnection from the old ways.

Let me use something as off the wall as dating. You can now have mental sex about banging a chick, who has posted her pictures, along with her desires in a mate. I am from the school of Cyrano and want to see a woman and have lightening strike me right in the chest. Life is meant to be lived physically and emotionally and not technologically, only my opinion.

The Occupy business is about many of those people who have lived in the ether of x's and o's and have now come together the old fashioned way; gathering in public places and creating a theatre for the expression of many people's paralyzing frustration with their mistreatment at the hands of the powerful public and private institutions of government and commerce.

You know, I am thinking now about what I always fall back on when I am feeling the heat to write and it has to do with compassion, pure and simple. The younger you are able to incorporate true compassion in your heart, the more you will enjoy the adventure. Caring is a remarkable accomplishment and it is an effort well worth its reward.

As long as this Occupy effort goes on, I will go on including it in our talk. It is totally fascinating to witness spontaneity in any society because society's mission is to stifle any individuality. The greatest nightmare is to have citizens in the streets and parks protesting government policy. Personally, I don't think there is any way out of this shit storm, so I go along my merry way, spreading joy wherever I can. Now, I am actually serious about this, my boy. I decided that the greatest contribution I can make in this world is to bring joy into people's lives. I shit you not.

I don't think there is enough time this time to tell you what I am doing here at the moment. I will just tease you and say that it is remarkable at this point in my life to be doing what I am doing, especially considering the decades of life preceding this and the unbelievable variety of things I've done.

Before I go, I just want to thank you for making all this possible. Frankly, I wouldn't have given a damn about my voice unless I wanted to talk to you. This has really changed my personal priorities. There seems to be this need to continue the story to you and I am amazed at how it has become a very important part of my practice, which is now added to Zen meditation, yoga and running. It totally blows my mind to be doing this. Whether I like it or not or ever intended to be doing it or not, seems to be irrelevant. I just want you to know I have been here. Shoot me!

Memories and Dreams

Today is November 22, 2011, the anniversary of the assassination of John F. Kennedy. If I weren't writing this to you, it would still cause me to reflect on that time and the legacy of his murder, because it always does. I was a freshman at Queens College and still living at home. I was taking a mid-term exam in my first year in college and we were told to leave because the President had been killed, but I don't recall when we came back or specifically what transpired on campus.

I was all of eighteen years old and just starting my training for life as a grown up. Plenty has been written about Kennedy and there will likely be more to come. The facts will always be subject to change, but its impact on most everyone at the time was very powerful. Whether you agreed with his politics or not, it was a very glamorous time in Washington, DC and millions were affected by the fairy tale aspects of this man's world. We were still naïve enough to believe in the purity of intention and not to look behind the curtain. In his case, you apparently didn't have to look any further than the bedroom, owing to his wandering ways.

It felt like the world as I knew it became unglued. My God, how could this happen and what does it means? The loss was devastating for many, many of us, regardless of age or politics. When you look to other people to fulfill your dreams, you're setting up a pretty lousy outcome. However, this was an exceptional circumstance. This guy was young, energetic, handsome, intelligent and straight out of central casting. Jacqueline Kennedy was mesmerizingly beautiful and her poise was never seen before in the White House. They even had little children. This was a guy that young people connected with because he wasn't like their parents, he was somewhere in between.

People were glued to their televisions as this deadly drama unfolded. The sight of John Kennedy Jr, saluting his Dad as the horse driven hearse drove by brought me and everyone else to tears. Seeing his killer, Lee Harvey Oswald, gunned down by Jack Ruby on live television was to say the least, surreal.

His life and death laid the groundwork for the Sixties. Young people took a hard fall when he was killed. Whether it was well founded or not, there was hope and hope is a risky business, especially when it is crushed right in your face. You add drugs, music, sex and the draft hitched to an unpopular war and you've got a lethal mix of social disruption on your hands. When Dr. King and Robert Kennedy were killed, there was no longer anything left to lose and the consequences were seismic. Once again, you will likely read about this from a variety of sources and perspectives. It was a time when America was alive and kicking, not socially castrated by today's technology. Don't get me wrong about technology, I would be a moron to say it hasn't had an extraordinarily positive impact on many parts of our lives. It is an information resource beyond compare. It has allowed us to gather knowledge at an incomprehensible rate. My concerns are about what it does to our humanity, those abilities we have that are so unique to our species.

Today, I think about the Occupy movement and how inspiring it is. You can dream for things to be better or you can live that dream. This idea is something I internalized and have no idea when it became my life. It probably began the morning I left New York for New Mexico. I know I definitely remember the gut wrenching feeling I had while I saw your Dad and Uncle slowly get smaller in my rear view mirror as I began my trip west. When that moment subsided, as they always do, my journey officially began. To me, the dream is the true journey and to make it manifest is a goal never achieved, because it is only the effort that is worth a damn.

My journey continues to be about my heart and realizing the dreams of my heart. I needed more adventure. I needed to get into the river and learn to navigate, honoring the path I was destined to be taking, while having no idea where it would take me. I am happy to report that as of this moment, I still have no idea, but the water is fine.

Something else about writing whatever it is I happen to be writing about is I don't give a flying fuck what anyone thinks about any of this. I suppose it has to include you as well in the mix. This is me writing when I want to write, about whatever I want to write about at the time. My plan as of today is to read this from the beginning whenever it gets to a point where I think I am done, completing whatever it is I imagined I would be writing to you. At that point, I don't think I would be open to any changes being made, whether for grammar or clarity or whatever. The truth is, when I am done, I will likely share it with some better writers than myself and see if they think it has any merit beyond your two eyes. Honest to God, I don't give a shit whether it does or not because this is all for you, my grandson.

I will try and get back to the history stuff, but it is so much more fun to write about what is fresh and imbued with life right now. Besides, the idea is to share who I am and not what I have done, although I wouldn't be who I am without having done all the stuff I have done in my life. I hope you are enjoying your process as much as I am enjoying mine. I got a free pass on this word trip and I can say anything at all and there is nothing anyone can do about it. It is a great power to have, but not a good enough reason to be overly self-indulgent either. Everything about this is intended to be small; it is just between the two of us. Their will be some ego ooze, but nothing too serious.

You will have to forgive me this entire transgression because it is the anniversary of the senseless death of JFK. We were both born on May 29th and that has always been a very, very quiet connection for me. His special gift was inspiring people to dream and that idea of a dream has stayed with me all these years.

No Precedent

I keep getting stuck in the quick sand of my mind about this writing thing to you. Do I have to write every day? Do I have to link each new entry with the last? Do I need to deal in dates and times and events? There are an endless number of questions I ask myself, but I always come out in the same place. I can do whatever I want and it doesn't matter what anyone else thinks, a recurring theme for me.

Right now, my days are spent hammering nails, measuring for drill holes and carrying shit that weighs more than I do; OK, nearly a quarter of my weight. I am wearing work boots and come home each day covered in dirt and my hands are pretty beaten up. So, you maybe ask yourself, what the hell is grandpa doing? Well, I am glad you asked.

My story of how I got to Kauai is for another time, but what I am doing these days is easy enough and I can actually remember the details. After I was here for no more than six months, I made a presentation to the Kauai County Farm Bureau. As a city boy, you will likely be absolutely clueless about farming and the entire agrarian way of life, but who the fuck knows where you will be in fifteen years or so? I was looking for a gig and had made indirect contacts with their farm bureau before leaving New Mexico.

My idea was to create a Grow Kauai concept and support the idea of local growing by doing a series of interviews with people who were making a difference in the world of agriculture. One of these people was a guy by the name of Bill and he was growing trees on the south side of the island. He was a tall guy who clearly enjoyed his character and the attention. In the process of talking with him about the story, we connected on a very soulful level, although he would not necessarily use that vocabulary. Bill was a Marine helicopter pilot in Vietnam and most of those guys came home dead or at least badly maimed, but he was somehow blessed and while he was a reckless man, the Gods have given him a free pass and he continues to walk under ladders and cross the paths of black cats.

We found that we had some core beliefs in common and that was very surprising considering our serious political differences. He is a very politically conservative person and I am at least as liberal as he is conservative. We both believed the world was totally overextended in terms of its use and abuse of our natural resources. We believed that the system was bankrupt and likely beyond repair. Neither one of us had a high opinion of human behavior under stress. We believed that Kauai was a canary in the coal mine. It would likely be the first to get hit by the shrapnel of an imploding system and we were also in the best position to survive. We currently import around 90% of our fuel and food and I am not shitting you. Several times a week, barges pull into our port with fuel and/or food for the week. Our survival is on a very thin, very long string. At the same time, the island is endowed with ample sun, water and land to grow the food and create the energy we would need when the barges never leave Oahu for here.

Anyway, Bill and I talked about his business and it was very intriguing to me. He had what we call long-term leases on over six square miles of land and was growing trees on much of the land. He had a slew of ideas as to what could be done with this resource and I understood exactly what he was talking about. We became friends very quickly and he is one of the special people who inhabit my world.

Back then, I told him I would commit myself to making something happen. While some things came up in between then and now, I was steadfast in my support and we spent hours and days together, trying to figure out how we could create a package that would be interesting to a potential investor. Along the way, we ran across a number of people who were going to write a check and then disappeared into the land of bullshit where they came from.

During this time, I was dedicated to doing something called, walking the walk. You will likely run across a lot of people who can talk a terrific story, but can they shut their fucken mouths and just do it? As I have told you, I committed to walking the walk when I saw your Dad in the rear view mirror, on my way to Santa Fe. Living the dream and walking it are one and the same. At some point, you just stop worrying about outcome and throw yourself to the mercy of the endless dreamers who have come before. Basically, you do a swan dive into an empty swimming pool, believing it will miraculously fill with water before your head shatters on the concrete bottom.

Well, Big Harry came along and invested in one of the businesses that was part of our overall plan for responsibly maximizing the resources we had at our disposal. As of about six months ago, I became part of company dedicated to creating a locally grown horse and cattle feed. I will handle the marketing, promotion and sales of this business, which I named, Paniolo Feed Company. There is a wild growing grass called guinea grass and it grows under our Albizia trees, which are very potent nitrogen fixing trees. This is going to be the basis for the feed. You can look up all this shit because I don't want this to be a textbook of detailed factoids.

At this time, we are fabricating various pieces of equipment we will need in order to manufacture this feed. So, for the next couple of months that is the backdrop for this pleasurable confession. Its progression will unavoidably be a part of this monologue, but at least now you have some small idea of what I am doing at this time to put gefilte fish on the table.

For some reason, I am much more comfortable writing about less factual things than what I am doing or what I have done. For me, learning and continuing to learn is what appeals to my literary vocabulary. You dance to whatever rhythm captures your attention and never worry about the music ending because it won't, until it does.

Long before the time I got together with Bill, I was completely committed to living life, confident I would be taken care of if my intentions were good. This way of being undoubtedly made me a less than comforting partner and has definitely contributed to my long-term bachelorhood. I guess my journey has been somewhat singular, although I hope I have had the ability to impact on others through my actions. Certainly, this is being written to have an impact on you and I hope one that encourages you to keep growing internally, long after you have supposedly stopped growing.

Tomorrow is Thanksgiving and I will try and get in touch with your parents and find out what you are doing for the holiday. By the way, I will be coming in to see you on January

19th and that will be great fun for me, especially now that I will write to you about it at the same time. Later, kid.

Ridiculous, Conspicuous Consumption

America has entered the perennial holiday season, a ritual of gluttony and delusion. The present state of things makes this rite of consumption even more ridiculous. The retail industry has been in the toilet, along with most every other business. The country is in the midst of a financial crisis, with threats to most social programs, while the super rich continue to be immune from any responsibility for those with less. We are more screwed up now than I can ever remember. In case you haven't guessed, it is one of the ongoing mantras in this experiment of ours.

If you are a large business and faced with these challenges, you do the obvious, which is to go after your customer even more aggressively than ever. The day after Thanksgiving has traditionally meant the start of the holiday season and people go nuts to get to their favorite super stores even before the doors open on Friday. This year, they opened at the stroke of midnight, just as Thanksgiving day ended. As if that weren't enough, the cyber world of retail has now created Cyber Monday, the techno counterpart to Black Friday.

So many people, who are already broke and in hock, will bang thousands of dollars on their credit cards for an abundance of gifts, in many cases for children who are so young they will have absolutely no recollection of this ludicrous largesse.

This culture of ours is based on externals exclusively. You must have a new car, the latest gadgets and every conceivable trapping of success. If you are really wealthy, you have to have several homes and they all must be very large. If you are poor and can't afford the real stuff, you go into debt to at least to make sure you've got some of the goods. America likes to show off and I am not sure what happened to the humility that ought to come with being as blessed as we are in comparison to virtually the entire rest of the world.

As a young man, you will likely think that many of my riffs are a bunch of shit and of no particular interest to you. I guess I would react much the same if I were the one on the receiving end of a long letter from my grandfather. In my case, it would have been easier for me to cast it aside because it would have been written in Yiddish about life in Czarist Russia. So, you are at least getting off easy in that regard.

I don't know how I would react to reading even what has been written so far. In my case, I am writing backwards in time, so there is much more context and familiarity.

Hell, I have no idea at all where you will be when you first read this. I could be this mythical figure you have been told stories about or I could be the babbling, hunched over prune that visits you periodically and someone you feel absolutely no connection with. There is room in between these bookends of possibility for all sorts of unpredictability. At least, it would be good if you believed that whatever you are reading was how I sincerely felt at the time. During the course of this endless diatribe, I will likely back track on many of my statements, because time has a way of changing most everything. We live in a perpetual state of flux and today is not necessarily tomorrow and yesterday will change today.

Let us get back to the retail rant of America's rampant and poisoned consumerism. There is no substitute and nothing more precious than the gift of love and compassion. The better you understand your true self, the clearer the value of this gift becomes. What we have to give is who we are. For most of us, the material gifts are a free pass from having to truly share our hearts with those closest to us. Believe me, I am not telling you to return all gifts or to refuse to give them to others. If you can become a heartfelt, compassionate man, you are in fat city, my boy. The more open and giving you are, the more you receive in return, but it can only start with you.

You will have to pardon the occasional lecture because you are my grandson, after all. There is nothing much I can do regarding the paths you choose. Every now and then if I can throw this writing at you and make it serve as a mirror for you to explore yourself, I will have succeeded beyond my wildest dreams. May you spend the rest of your life on this journey of self-exploration and see where it takes you. This gift of life is one we get to repay based on the choices we make. I love you, Shane. I am now crying, something I don't think I have done until this point with you............ I just think about my life and this effort to share it with you and it just makes me weep. Bless you.

Ear Plugs & My Gay Road Trip

It is a bunch of hours after my last entry and I am now in a completely different space. Made a trip to a local farmer's market and picked up a couple of videos, along with my coffee and wine fix. The trades are blowing pretty hard and it is kind of overcast. So, what are the choices in the middle of a Saturday afternoon? Unlike before, I now have this place where I can go and carry on a conversation with you. Just as I am sitting down at the computer, the neighbor's gardener cranked up a machine that puts out high-pressure water, which he uses to clean the driveway, etc. Having no choice, I cranked up the rock station and put my sleeping earplugs in. Yes, I use earplugs when I sleep because my sleep regimen is pretty poor and anything that helps is welcome. I was never a world-class sleeper, even as a kid. Sleeping eight hours has never been my world.

The intrusion of noise is one of many reasons why I am moving into a yurt on the land where we will be harvesting the grass, which I talked about a little earlier.

I cheated and scanned up to see where I had mentioned the yurt, which I am certain I did, but I couldn't find it without reading too much and I don't want to color the present with any of the past writings. However, I found a couple of loose references that I might as well clear up, along with the yurt story.

Gourmet Meals for Single Dummies is my name for a deal I made with a gourmet chef here. She prepares ten entrees for me every two weeks. Frankly, I am not sure how I have made it to this point in my life based on my horrific cooking skills. Recently, I decided it was time to treat myself well and at least for now, I have great dinners most every night.

I know I am missing other stuff I have mentioned, like the drive cross country, but if this becomes too much like homework, it will totally fuck up the immediacy of the communication. I know I have already pre-apologized for any repetition and I am inclined to leave them undisturbed. I have an endless supply of stories and ever changing opinions, which I don't have the energy to keep track of. Actually, going backwards just now into the 30 plus pages nearly gave me a nosebleed. Speaking of pages, I have no idea how this will end up getting numbered, so I am merely going off the count on my screen.

Now, let's get back to the yurt blurb. I recently purchased a 24 ft. diameter yurt, which will be mounted on a deck. They are fascinating structures and feel quite special inside. I intend to decorate it very sparsely in a Zen like manner and keep things low to the ground. The bathroom will be in a small outside structure, along with an outdoor shower, which is a must for this part of the world. The location will be very secluded and I won't want to hear any other noises other than the ones I make. It will probably take around six months to get it up the way I want and I will keep you posted on developments.

So, are you ready for grandpa's road trip to Hollywood? It is directly related to a job I had in the summer of my sophomore year in college, 1964. My employment history began when I was twelve years old and I got a job in the sixth grade as a waiter at a delicatessen that was in walking distance from my elementary school. I would rush out at lunchtime and get ready to serve the kids hot dogs, fries and sodas. My salary was 50 cents a day and it was a fortune. I have never even tried to count the number of jobs I have had over the years, but it is mind boggling by most people's standards.

Let's get back to the road trip, which is without question one of my classics. In the summer of '64, I got a job with Greyhound at the World's Fair, staged at Flushing Meadow Park, the scene of a much earlier World's Fair. I think it started some time in the spring and was to continue until basically the start of the next school year. I drove a contraption called an Escorter, which was like a golf cart with a couch in the front. These were essentially private taxis for wealthy visitors to the Fair, who would often rent us for the day and keep the meter running. World's Fairs are like Disney parks, but there are corporate and country exhibits as the theme. I suspect we have seen the last of that extravagance. I would leave school and go to work and the hours were pretty long. It was a terrific adventure for a nineteen year old.

Business started slowing down toward the end of the summer and many workers, including yours truly, were laid off. I had made a fair amount of money and school wasn't going to gear up for around six weeks. One of my college friends, Neil, was working with me at Greyhound and we decided to transport a car cross-country. Considering this adventure will have taken place at least sixty years before your exposure to this devil's work, the concept of transporting a car will be something you would need to research. I will save you the trouble because it is integral to the story. Way back then, you could hire a company to drive your car cross country if you were moving or had more than one car or who knows what other reasons.

We quickly learned that you needed to be over twenty-five to sign the paper work and Neil was one year ahead of me and too young as well. We decided to put an ad in one of the local papers, looking for someone over twenty-five who would drive a car with us to California. I think we only got one phone call and it was from Stanley. We agreed to meet at his place. Stanley lived up near Columbia University in a borderline neighborhood walk up. We knocked on the door and a somewhat effeminate sounding voice came from within, saying he would be right there.

The opened door revealed Stanley in all his plumage. He was well over six feet and wore his pants very high and his walk was something between a glide and a prance. Our potential traveling buddy was a screaming queen. Neil and I figured we outnumbered him and we would somehow figure it out along the way. We agreed to travel with Stanley.

I wish you could have some idea of what it was like in '64. For Christ's sake, blacks were still getting lynched at that time and it took a fucken act of Congress and the

President to force civil rights down the white throats of people north and south. Flagrant, foppish homosexuals might as well have been Martians at the time.

Neil, Stanley and myself drove right through the heart of America and being with Stanley made Neil and I incredibly self-conscious. To make matters even more challenging, Stanley was no shrinking violet. He was out there big time. I remember stopping for lunch at a diner somewhere in Kansas and Stanley went through his regular routine of wanting to know whether the tuna was prepared with oil or butter and if it was fresh or not. When we walked around our cabin at the Grand Canyon, he drew many eyeballs to our threesome. Gays were just beginning to come out around then in major coastal cities, but they were still totally in the silos of the heartland.

I know it took us less than a week, but we were nevertheless faced with a handful of nights where we looked at two beds for the THREE of us. Neil and I developed the 2-2-1-2 formula for choosing who would get the bed to himself and miracle of miracles; Stanley always got the single bed. I wish I could remember the hours of dialogue in the Ford station wagon, but they are long gone by now.

Before I get to the most memorable part of the trip, I would be remiss if I didn't tell you how incredible this country is. I am hoping there will be still plenty left to see by the time you are able to adventure out on your own. At the very least, our national park system will hopefully still be in place and you will have a chance to see the raw and rugged natural beauty of this land. It is funny that so many people want to devote their resources to changing this place, as opposed to preserving it. The cost of progress has a price tag that nature can no longer afford. Shit, there I go again, especially when I have the Hollywood Hills encounter to share.

Stanley's reason for wanting to go to Los Angeles was to visit with his friends. When we arrived in LA, Stanley asked Neil and I if we wanted to go to a party in the Hollywood Hills, a fairly exclusive section of town. We had been dealing with his homosexuality for the entire trip and it was not a contentious relationship at all. It was also never boring around him. We went to this beautiful house at the prescribed time and when we opened the door, the house was filled with men and that was naively shocking to us, although we should have known where we were going.

At that point in my life, I was fairly practiced at drinking too much, having the room spin and promptly puking my guts. I would then lie down and pray to all the Gods that the miserable feeling would go away. A night's sleep would leave me feeling weakened and wounded, but slowly recovering. True to form, I drank too much and tried following the rest of the predictable routine. The only problem was I was in a houseful of gay men and the host was paying great attention to me. He offered his bedroom to me and I was pretty far gone and just wanted to lie down in a dark room.

After several hours of sleep, I awoke to find the host, whose name escapes me, leaning over me and kissing me. Well, I did the only manly thing I could think to do and that was to start crying, while forcing myself to sit up. I didn't do the macho thing of punching him in the face or anything of the sort. I was terribly shocked and confused, not to mention naïve. We can be so certain as to how we will react in a specific situation, but it usually doesn't go that way.

This episode turned out to be one of the most important experiences of my life. I actually had an opportunity to choose between heterosexuality and homosexuality and opted for devoting my life to figuring out women, leaving no time for men.

Now, I am going to do something that will totally fuck you over in a mind warp. I am now in a time machine and trying to figure out a way to communicate in a manner that is completely out of whack. Let me tell you a story:

Somewhere prior to this latest tale, I know I made a big deal of not revisiting anything I had written up to the time I sit down and write again. At the time, it made complete sense because I didn't plan to return to something and re-edit for whatever reason. Now, down the line from where you are right now, I wrote that I would break with the idea of not revisiting any of this material. This occurred sometime in the future because I am now backwards in the narrative revisiting a statement that troubled me from the time I wrote it down about nine months ago. In other words, I have written a long piece over a fair amount of time and told you at some point I would sparingly reread everything I had written before I felt my work was done. *I suppose this should be in italics because it would be a warning that you are in a time warp.*

I had two choices and one was to simply re-edit what bothered me or to keep true to my plan and let everything stand on its own at the time it was written. The totally honest thing to do in this make believe world of mine is to tell you what is on my mind, regardless of what rules it breaks. What you have just read about the road trip until this interruption was written quite a while ago in an adventure that has kept unfolding, which you will continue to read about in the pages to come. If you are not confused, I am totally fucked up. The short version is I didn't like what I had written about the "choice" thing regarding homosexuality because it is not true.

I hope you understand this intrusion on my part, but what I had written has never sat well with me and I think it is important to provide some clarity. Thought about it a lot while riding with the Sons of Kauai today. The rest of this story will unfold over time and having already written it, I strongly recommend you hang in because it is worth the price of admission. Keep in mind, I am revisiting this page from a time in the future.

The line that never sat comfortably with me relates to my writing that I felt I had made a choice between homosexuality and heterosexuality up in the Hollywood Hills so many years ago. I am fracturing the time tunnel by going backwards to make a point and I apologize, but it has been bugging me for many months.

Men, more so than women, make a big deal out of their sexuality. In many cases, it belies an insecurity guys have about their manhood, their performance and/or their self-worth. I think we are all provided with some seesaw of tendencies and some go one way and some go another. When I responded the way I did it is because I really tried to think of the offer to go gay and move to Hawaii and I simply wasn't interested. From that point forward, I realized it was a fine line and if you have a strong sense of which side you are on, you take it. Most men like to think the masculine and feminine thing is like the Maginot Line and God forbid if you get too close to one side or the other.

Almost Back

Wanted to let you know we are about to get back into the narrative as it was written months ago. This is my second time through pages one to one hundred and first time through the one hundred plus pages that follow. When you read about my plan in terms of re-editing this story, you will have a déjà vu moment. Hopefully, I will not interrupt time moving forward, but if something really bothers me, I won't be able to let it pass. However, I think we are okay and we will go from this entry back into the unfolding story for you. I will quietly reread what has been written so far and the only guaranteed interruption is a visit to see you about ten months from the time everything else has been written. God, I hope this makes senses because I am completely confused. We now return to the narrative as it was written months before this last word you are now reading.............

After that incident, we spent a number of days socializing and he never crossed the line again. Before I left, he offered me a job in a bar he was opening in Honolulu (don't know if that ever happened), but I would have to switch jerseys and change teams. I remember being very appreciative and turning him down.

Aside from providing a terrific story to occasionally recount, this experience had tremendous impact on my evolution as a male. The problem with the vast majority of assholes who call themselves men is that they have a complete inability to recognize the balance of masculine and feminine in each gender. It is kind of the luck of the draw;

some are drawn to their opposite and others are drawn to their own. Most guys live in mortal fear of possibly having any homosexual thoughts and it often creates repressed hostility. Women seem to be a bit more together when it comes to their sexuality. They are far more complicated and subtler, which is why I like them so much.

Buddha and Things

"All that we are is the result of what we have thought. The mind is everything. What we think we become." The Buddha

Just got in from my Sunday motorcycle ride with the Sons of Kauai and it is always a great time to kick back and either do nothing at all or, in this case, write a little more. When I opened my emails this morning, I got my usual message regarding my Card of the Day, along with a quote from the Big Man. The Card of the Day is based on the 52 cards and four suits. I briefly dated a woman who does the cards and I pick it up each day just for shits and grins. I am a three of clubs, which is the card of the writer. What a shock! In my world, you either believe in everything or you believe in nothing. I am not sure how one can discount something like the cards, but believe in Jesus. I certainly don't want to be the person with that kind of authority.

Anyway, the card message always has a quote from someone attached to it. This one from the Buddha caught my eye and I figured it was time to lay a quote on you, something I will likely do in the future, too.

Most likely, I have already talked around this quote in some prior messages to you. Again, so much of this stuff is probably going to rocket over your head because it is terribly unrealistic to think you will get much of this in your first go around. Please, not saying this because I am some fucken genius or wise man cave dweller; saying it in recognition of the disparity in years between writer and reader. At your age, I likely would have thought most all of this is the raving of some old guy wanting to somehow influence my life, when I am merely sharing where I am at the moment.

Let's get back to the Buddha for just a second. You can read all about him if you are so inclined; therefore, there is no need to hit you with the Cliff Notes. It is the idea behind this particular quote that is so appealing to me. This is something for you to think about because you are nothing more than your thoughts. It is your choice as to how you want to occupy your mind. The younger you are, the more likelihood there is of your thoughts being influenced from the outside. You will get to know yourself better and better with the passage of time and your opinions and ideas will continue to change. Just remember, wherever you are is who you are, but don't get terribly vested in holding on because it is an exercise in futility anyway.

Listen, it is around 6P and I want to get some Chinese takeout for the evening. In between one of the above sentences, I ended up in an hour-long conversation with an old friend, Alex and left no sign it had occurred. Oh boy, is he ever worth a stand-alone sit down. In this specific instance, describing a person fills in lots of gaps in my past for you and it is thoroughly entertaining at the same time. I don't want to be any later because the sun is shrinking and the colors are graying, time for takeout.

Alex

As promised, a story about Alex and how we crossed paths a number of years ago. When I left the world of 9-5 and headed west, my life began to be populated by some interesting characters because you tend to find them dwelling out there on the limbs of life's tree. Certainly, our old friend Mario gets points in that regard. Hopefully, these kinds of people add color to your own life and make the art of living more of an adventure than a chore.

Back around 1997, I somehow got involved with Belize. I swear it escapes me exactly how or why, but it has something to do with some guys in Houston, who wanted to get involved in the timber business in Belize. I traveled there a couple of times and dealt with NGO's and some government forestry people. On one of the trips, I bought a bunch of locally bottled natural remedies and some jams and spices and set up a booth for a summer at the legendary flea market in Santa Fe. I even met with a hotel manager in Santa Fe, who claimed she had investors who would purchase a hotel property in Belize. So, on one of my trips I was exploring the possibility of purchasing resorts and ended up dealing with a guy who had our same last name. He was laundering his drug money through the resort operation and not necessarily the best person to do business with.

There I go again, getting off target. During one of the trips to Belize, I was sharing a motor boat ride to one of the cayes (look it up) off the coast with a scientist for the Wildlife Conservation Society, which owns the Bronx Zoo and does conservation research all over the world. He told me the WCS was interested in setting up a network of environmentally sensitive resorts, called eco-lodges, on some of the land they owned in Central America. He gave me the name of his boss back in the Bronx.

I know I haven't told you yet that I am expert in the arena of six degrees of separation, whose genesis you might even be able to track down if you checked. The idea behind this theory is that we are only removed from anyone else by six degrees, meaning within six different efforts, you will likely score a connection. When you leave the straight work a day world, you better be good at connecting with people or you are screwed. I know I am as good as anyone at this practice.

When I got back from that trip, I quickly tracked down John at the WCS and even our initial conversation went extremely well. I developed an excellent rapport with him as part of my effort to get involved in their proposed strategy of setting up ecolodges throughout Central America. It is important for you to know that I knew absolutely nothing about the hospitality industry, let alone the relatively new tourism phenomenon of creating close to nature experiences for well-heeled travelers. I did such a good job that John wanted me to meet with the board of directors, presided over by a legend in the conservation world. If I recall, there was even a date given to me for this high level meeting that afforded me around two months to create the show.

Now, I was completely screwed because I was in so far over my head that drowning was even a possibility. Here comes one of those six degree things: I had been dealing with a guy at a company that was one of the first in renewable energy resources, which had some connection to Belize that now honestly escapes me and who gives a shit anyway? After sharing my predicament with him, he suggested only one name and it was Alex.

I called him and we proceeded to spend several hours on the phone, talking about everything imaginable. He was living in San Francisco and had an extensive background in nature tourism consulting, in addition to an incredibly interesting history. Alex is Iranian by birth and was born into a very powerful family during the regime of the Shah of Iran. He comes from a tribal culture and a Persian one at that. He was forced to leave his homeland as a teenager because he was drawing unwanted attention to his family as a result of his leftist views. He ended up in Los Angeles with some relatives and began his adventures as an Iranian American. He spent a great deal of his time in international finance and had a high flying life as a young man, at least according to the stories he recounted to me. His life was a terrific global adventure and I hope he sits his ass down to record it.

Don't want to get bogged down in the details of his life because, after all, this is about me. However, Alex is one of those larger than life characters who can fill a room when he enters and grab the spotlight, something he clearly enjoyed.

He was absolutely blown away that I managed to secure such a high level meeting without having any credentials at all. This was a major coup by his standards. On the phone, we decided to work together and we prepared a presentation long distance and agreed to meet in New York City the day before the presentation in the Bronx. Alex thought it would be advantageous to bring in a third guy with an extensive background in adventure travel. John (different one) started one of the very first travel companies that put together rafting trips in remote locations around the world and other similar offerings. He was a pretty eccentric dude and very incidental to the tale of Alex.

The three of us met at a cheap hotel in Gramercy Park in Manhattan. Remember, I was in New Mexico at the time and I also had to fly in for the gathering. Alex is around 5'10" and kind of a broad shouldered, bearish size guy, who very much enjoyed his own presence, something mentioned earlier. We got along extremely well in person, a carry over from long phone calls we had in an effort to get our act together for this meeting.

Next morning, we were on the subway on our way up to the Bronx Zoo. During the ride, Alex asked me what we would do if they turned us down and I clearly told him that would not happen. I had already learned from prior experiences in maverick terrain that you have to proceed with complete confidence in the outcome. We got there and ended up racing across the full length of this gigantic zoo because we had gotten off at the wrong stop. We arrived at their offices, soaking wet from perspiration and out of breath. They were waiting for us in the conference room. Alex and John did most of the talking because I had produced the show and they needed to be on stage for the discussions. We got the contract right at the meeting. We didn't even have a company name, primarily because we weren't a company at the time. We hadn't gotten that far and just focused our initial effort on getting the consulting deal. Actually, the legendary conservation guy, who sat at the head of the table, actually asked, " Who are these guys?" This is a story Alex loves to tell, embellishing it each time it is told.

This odyssey started sometime in '98 and continued somewhere into 2000. I traveled all over Central America, primarily with Alex. We were really out there in the middle of nowhere, usually staying in pretty shitty hotels and mostly sharing a room. Let me tell you, you really get to know someone under those circumstances and vice versa. We visited Costa Rica, Honduras, Guatemala and back to Belize for me. Alex was very much at home wherever we traveled, which was a great assist for me because these were brand new adventures for yours truly. On one trip, we helicoptered into a former "killing field" in Guatemala, and apparently there were armed men in the hills above us, thinking we were CIA operatives. It was an interesting way to earn a living and nothing I ever would have imagined for myself.

The business was actually doing very well in its short history, with several other clients, in addition to the WCS. Over time, we started feuding over small issues, which was symptomatic of a clash of egos and Alex totes a larger one than I do. For me, Alex was a very colorful friend and a good one, but partnerships were not his bag. I always had a ball talking to him and the conversations were very animated and far ranging. We ended up getting a business divorce, but we always stayed in touch through the years.

Several years after the demise of our consulting business, Alex purchased a bankrupt Costa Rican airline and created a very successful internal airline. I followed his progress and we talked with a fair amount of regularity during that time. Out of the blue, he asked me if I wanted to write a conservation-focused blog for the airline. Part of Alex's Persian nature is being a dreamer and poet and influencing the lives of those around him, whether they are interested in it or not. He felt I was not living up to my potential on Kauai and that I needed to get out there more and to do that through writing. I thought he was nuts. I didn't speak Spanish, I lived on Kauai and I didn't know anyone in the conservation world of Costa Rica. He encouraged me to visit, which I did. I met some good people and decided to take the gig. On that trip, I met a guy by the name of Alvaro Ugalde (look him up) who would be the equivalent of John Muir (you guessed it, look him up) in our country.

I took Alex up on his offer and started putting together a plan for the blog. In one of my classic six degrees maneuvers, I managed to get right in the middle of a major controversy, involving the breeding habitat for Leatherback turtles and government efforts that were threatening their future. In all modesty, I must say I did an incredible job of communicating the story in English to scientists and conservationists in Costa Rica and around the world. Personally, I am very proud of my contribution and amazed I was able to pull off the blog challenge.

In Alex's typical, theatrical fashion, he hired both his sons to work at the airline at fairly high executive positions. Alex cast a very large shadow and his boys wrestled with him, trying to get out from under. My writing thing got caught up in some internal family struggles and ended after about a year and a half. We continued talking after that and he followed my ups and downs with Bill, trying to get the business off the ground here. At a low point, he asked me if I would think about writing for him again. He had since fired both his boys and there was no longer any administrative friction.

This precipitated another visit to Costa Rica to meet with staff at the airline and several other key travel people in the country. It was clear that the only way this would work is if I moved there. Let me tell you, I gave it very serious thought and figured it might be my last great adventure. I would go to Costa Rica and make a living as a writer, which certainly appealed to my very large romantic side. The world of places like Costa Rica have a certain rawness that you will never find in the so-called developed countries. In the end, Big Harry came through here with an investment and I am now in the horse and cattle feed business. True to form, Alex and I stay in touch and had one of our far ranging conversations last night when I was in the midst of writing to you, hence this detour.

I think we are only as interesting as the experiences we have and the people we meet along the way. I know for certain I have had my share of both, but they seemed natural to me, an integral part of my deeply personal journey.

Technology

Before I get going on technology, I have to tell you what an incredible experience this process continues to be for me. I know it has already been mentioned more than once so far, but this weirdly worded and disheveled representation is my excuse for an autobiography. Unfortunately for so many of us, we seem to think only famous people get to write their life stories. Bullshit is what I say to that. At the very least, I feel it is so important on a monumentally deep level for you to connect with my story. It is like having a crystal ball, looking backward to a time totally unfamiliar to you, with stories told to you by someone you will probably never get to know all that well in this lifetime. In a way, I want to make my story your story, not to be copied, but to be incorporated in your consciousness and providing a voice annoyingly in the background of your own journey. Maybe I get to be sign posts along the way that help to keep you from driving off the road late at night.

When I was a kid, families still gathered in their living rooms to listen to nationally broadcast radio programs, soap operas, mysteries, comedies and all sorts of other entertainment. During that time, television was making its presence felt across the country. The images were black and white and the picture and sound quality completely sucked. There were shows like the Lucky Strike Hit Parade and Uncle Miltie. Phones were these contraptions that sat in one place and you would pick up the receiver, maybe on a twelve-inch chord and you used a rotary dial to make the call. In many places throughout the country at that time, you would call the operator in your town, who you likely knew from the grocery store and she would make the call for you, often sharing gossip as to what was going on around town. Music was played on 78's on a victrola and the audio was usually pretty lousy. The ability to actually tape record anything at all was unbelievably liberating and expanded the ability for people to copy and share sounds. Somewhere along the way, stereophonic sound was introduced on recorded music, finding a home on the burgeoning number of FM radio stations.

The above was the technological landscape for a while. Telephones were improved with push button dialing and eventually, the miracle of miracles, the chordless phone.

Television discovered color transmission and the audio quality of recorded music increased dramatically, a blessing for music lovers of all genres. We ran through a couple of pre-computer, tape iterations, like 8 track and cassette. I am not exactly sure when the CD was introduced and whether it preceded the computer revolution. In the spirit of all this being recollections, I am not interested in researching any data because it doesn't matter if I am wrong, as none of this has anything to do with issues of accuracy.

Somewhere around the same time, computers, fax machines and mobile phones began quietly creeping into our lives. I think it was all around the mid-eighties. I distinctly remember absolutely freaking out over the fax machine. How the fuck could you send a photograph through the telephone?

I left New York City on June 1, 1987 and it was the very beginning of this communications revolution. I know I got my first computer soon after arriving in Santa Fe. When I first moved there, I was living in a very small adobe house that was burmed in the back and the walls had tires stuffed with sand for insulation. There was a very small out building and it became my office and the home for my computer. The places I have lived and how I lived within each is for another time, so let's just stick to the march of the machines for now.

Sometime during the mid-nineties, the world was forever changed with the introduction of the Internet and its instant access to information. It is pure science fiction thinking what has happened in a mere sixteen years or so since that time. The hardware and software technology has grown exponentially. Now, everyone is attached to a techno-umbilical chord of some form or other. It started with the ability to email each other instantly and accessing all sorts of information and resources just as quickly. These machines have become more and more sophisticated in their ability to collate data.

At this point in my life, I can't say that I give much of a shit about the latest and greatest technological development. There is a price to be paid for everything. The price for being given life is death. The price for the incredibly liberating world of technology is the stultifying anonymity that comes with it. In many ways, the cyber connection has replaced the human connection and that saddens me. Very often, our obsession with progress has been at the expense of our humanity. Now, people have an easy option to avoid any meaningful contact with others because they can whip out the latest gadget, operating the latest software and do anything imaginable.

I can't even guess how all of this will mutate in between now and the time you're read this. For all I know, you will have a computer chip implanted in your armpit and it will do virtually everything for you beyond taking a shit. Clearly, we continue to miniaturize the products and coordinate the assembly of information. There will likely be some master device, housing all your information and enabling you to do virtually anything. You will have some satellite gear that taps into the central source. I wonder what things will get lost in the process. Before anything else, we are human beings with basic needs and while technology is revolutionary, we are evolutionary and the machinery can easily get ahead of us.

Not Negative

Don't get the wrong idea about technology and me because I think it is unbelievable what has happened in such a short period of time. The ability for technology to absorb information has had the effect of speeding up time. These machines are able to instantly shuffle the data deck of cards and come up with incredible hands that trump anything we can think of, especially in the time in which they can accomplish this feat. The problem with any of this stuff is not equipment, it is us. Nuclear fission was a phenomenal discovery and its power seemed like it was from outer space. Of course, the first thing we thought about was how we could own this power and use it to our completely selfish advantage, hence the atom bomb.

The development and rapid fire spread of the Internet is nothing short of a miracle. It has been remaking the world. It has brought with its invention an incredible freedom, leveling the playing field and allowing small to become big within minutes. The social implications have been staggering, especially in the recent political uprisings around the world. Something called the Arab Spring began even less than a year ago and it has toppled repressive governments. Of course, the joke is likely to be that these barbaric dictatorships are going to be replaced by very conservative religious groups, who will likely quell the timeless search for the jewels of personal freedom, which precipitated these very uprisings in the first place.

Certainly, technology has revolutionized communication between people. Socially, the glowing screen, coming in a wide variety of sizes, has replaced the old school face-to-face connection. I can sit in a darkened movie theatre and all around me heads are tilted downward and hypnotized by the small screen and whatever gifts its bestowing on them that cannot wait. Facebook is like dropping your pants and sharing your butt with the world. Twitter is a dyslexic, contracted communication between people, who are apparently totally consumed with what some person has to say about mothing.

It is hard to say at this point, at least for me, if all this paraphernalia has been worth it. We certainly don't appear to be treating each other any better. It is difficult to be terribly optimistic about what lies ahead for you. The signs for the future are pretty crappy and I don't think they will improve.

Time to get back to what I am supposedly doing, which is sharing my life with you as best I can. By the way, each time there is a header, it means I have flipped open the book one more time and begun making entries. There could be a break of hours, a day or longer and it isn't always necessary to report in for duty. The night of the week could be important or not, just like the activities preceding an entry and I could go on about this or drop it and leave it to you to follow. So, we will continue to make this up as we go along. I will never finish this story while I am alive because as long as there is life, there is more to share.

I guess it kind of sucks that I am sixty-six right now and who knows how old you will be when you are reading even this sentence for the first time. Whenever you do, know that I am also writing it to you in that moment when you first read it. I can only communicate with you from wherever I happen to be in my life, which happens to be double sixes. At the same time, I am not talking down to you or presupposing what you will understand or not. In some ways, it is like writing to an invisible reader, but as I am sure I have already told you. as long as it makes sense to me at the moment, it's all OK. You kind of get to experience my life as I do, while I also do my best to pull moments and people from my past.

There is just so much I can write to you about what has already happened in my life. I am gradually pulling the past into these moments of sharing. I have had so many different vocations, I have lived in so many different homes and I have had a number of very memorable relationships.

OK, starting to feel I little too much like work, which means it is time to stop. A little tired from a hard day of physical work, clearing land and carrying logs, as we get the site ready for the business. Not feeling compelled to share anything, a sure sign to give it a rest. Later.

Anything at all

Back at you, my boy. It's another Sunday and an exhilarating motorcycle ride up into Kokee, out here on the west side of the island. It gets up to around 3,500 feet above sea level and the road is a great series of twists and turns. When you take it right, you feel like a matador, dancing with a two-wheel steel bull. I am usually in good spirits after a ride like that and coming back to any empty place leaves me with some energy to be transported outside myself, so here I am.

As you well know by now, I am simply making this up as I go along and will likely repeat that little mantra periodically. The more I think about it, the more I think most of this is going to end up being fairly contemporary. Remember, when we go back 50+ years, it is me at this moment trying to describe something that passed through me many moons ago.

In my best Zen, there really isn't such a thing as reality and this is a perfect example. If I wrote to you when I was not even twelve years old and doing my first slow dance ever with Carol, in the basement of her house, the recollection couldn't possibly match the experience at the time. Whatever was going through my mind as a young, almost pubescent boy couldn't possibly speak in the same voice that I speak in now. While I am likely not much smarter in matters of the heart, my romance canvas is now covered with a palette load of subtle hues and light and shadow.

It is good for me to pause every now and then in this exercise, which I have done before and will do again, because I am busting my balls to carry a high level of integrity in all of this. It is important to check back in with the mother lode, the spirit behind this unusual effort. Even if my luck changes and there is a woman in my life, she will simply become a part of this so far secret narrative between me and myself, at least for now. Frankly, I would rather have less free time and have to tell her I need a little quiet time in order to catch up with this story, or whatever we end up calling it. Hey, you work with what you got.

No matter what age you are when you read this for the first time, you will be old enough to understand an awful lot. If this is truly your first time, I want you to do me a favor, try and keep track of every thought that rockets through your consciousness and see if it takes more than a few seconds to forfeit the challenge. We can count our breaths, but the pace of thought can likely be monitored electronically, but not consciously. This is a little of the challenge I face with this effort. If I could telepathically transmit my thoughts as they occurred, boy, would we have a very long and probably tedious story?

We have some coming attractions in the next several entries. My mother, Ida's birthday is later this week on December 9th and it is inconceivable for me not to devote a good piece of myself to her story. Your birthday, as you know, is on December 13th and I will likely want to write something deeply personal to you. Ten days later is the date when I met a woman here by the name of Laura and that is quite a story, whose time has nearly come to tell; a magnificent and excruciatingly painful six or so years here on Kauai.

The time for getting married for life ended when your grandmother and I split up, so the next best thing is to have a life punctuated with a number of very special relationships. I am blessed to have had a handful of such connections during my life. Somewhere in between these recollections we will hit the fifty-page milestone, which will likely be cause for some mention on my part. We will wait for that sign and see what comes up for me.

I got some classic Blues in the background, along with easy overhead lighting in the private temple I live in, but there are no magic words to transport you into this precise moment. In some ways, I think art was invented in an effort to bridge the uncrossable chasm between all humans. Love is like a magic carpet ride between two people and you can get close, but there is always some speck on the lens, no matter how hard you try.

At the same time, you need to understand the huge difference between being alone and being lonely. No matter what charades we play on our psyche, we are alone and no one else can feel exactly what we feel. However, that reality is a far cry from feeling lonely, which can at least be mitigated by a phone call, a held hand or a soulful look from another. Understanding the essence of aloneness makes you more receptive to genuinely reach out to another and soften the loneliness.

Ella

Just heard a wonderful cut of Ella Fitzgerald singing, “Someone To Watch Over Me”, an exquisite sound that you will most likely think is ancient and boring. The genuine thing has a timeless quality all its own and lives on, just like Mozart and the Gershwin brothers. Hearing Ella was the only inspiration I needed to bang my keys and continue my very own, “Songs in the Key of Life”, a tremendous album by one of my era’s musical incarnations, Stevie Wonder. Believe it or not, I even have a Stevie Wonder story. I was a young guy still in college, and a couple of us went to a place called Steve Paul’s The Scene in midtown Manhattan. Little Stevie Wonder was probably around fifteen years old and he was opening for a musical clown by the name of Tiny Tim.

There are definitely precious few benefits gained from the crushing march of time, but one of them is hopefully the accumulation of experiences that give your life the feeling of being a wonderful landscape painting and having the broadened vision to take it all in.

Kind of cool to be sitting here at my instrument, composing more of these life songs, drinking a glass of wine and listening to some quality jazz. I suppose the only thing missing is a cigarette hanging from the corner of my mouth. I actually began smoking around the age of fifteen until my mid-twenties. A long, unfiltered tobacco stick in a red pack and called Pall Mall was my brand of choice. It felt like a cup of strong black coffee, also something I loved and actually still do, although I fake it with decaf most of the time now. I was cruising up to buying three packs a day, which is a butt load of smoking.

Miraculously, your grandmother became pregnant with uncle Dan. Back then, it was not a given that pregnancy initiated the end to smoking, drinking or doing most anything to bring a suffering, pregnant Mom an ounce of relief from the ordeal of an exploding midriff and elephantine boobs. However, her doctor told her it would be a good idea to stop smoking because there was already plenty of research pointing to the damage of smoking. As much as I loved my Pall Mall, I told your grandmother I would immediately quit smoking to support her. Well, she lasted a week and mine lasted the rest of my life. It is one of my greatest accomplishments. Once I actually made it through that first week, I knew I had my boot heel on the neck of that awful addiction.

I suspect kids will always be stupid because that is part of being a kid. Cigarette smoking is one of the dumbest things you could possibly do. I suspect you will have already secretly tried some alcohol and I am not sure pot will ever go out of fashion and experimentation is likely inevitable, unless you are swallowed whole by morality.

Trust me, I am not one to ever take the high ground. Preaching virtue was never intended to be my vocation. Be joyful and in the moment as much as you are capable of at any point in your life. Being in the moment is nothing more than investing your complete presence with each breath you take, a terribly tall order and a state of mind you will never actually attain, but it is always about the effort, Shane. We always get points for trying, regardless of outcome. To me, people who claim to be enlightened or say they are living in the moment have already screwed the pooch.

Had to get up a few minutes ago to start heating my Gourmet Meals for Single Dummies selection for the evening, which is a vegetarian curry bowl. Had a couple of thoughts while hovering around the kitchen sink and its environs. One is I am getting to do something I have always thought about doing and that is trying to capture brief moments of my thoughts and freezing them in type. Without you there was no incentive because there was no audience. When I thought about writing to you, it allowed me to dodge the bullet of any perceived egocentricity. Trust me, there is nothing exceptional about any of this. It is simply your grandfather wanting to provide you with a very modest present for you to check out every now and then.

I must write more to you about music, which has been my constant companion throughout my life. In keeping with our Ella motif, this very unusual exercise we are both engaged in is like an improvisational jazz piano, with a deep bass and sweet percussion in the background.

OK, I am going to be moving on for now. Time for my gourmet dinner, another glass of wine and whatever other diversions I come up with. Just so you know, I have definitely swallowed this talking fish and we are simply going to keep at it and see where it goes.

Cheers, my prince. Talk with you soon.

Rocky

I am in the mood for a story and not one that is too long. So, we will share the tale of Rocky. In 1983, I was working as a time salesman at the USA Cable Network, which may or may not be around, along with the entire concept of cable broadcasting, This is predicated on whenever it is you are given permission to risk your very soul by reading this tome from Tutu Kane, the Hawaiian name for grandfather. As a former New York Jew, now sort of practicing Zen Buddhism, it is a reach for me to go by that moniker, so we settled on Grandpa Larry.

It seems there was an opportunity for our cable network to carry a late night music and dance show, emanating from a club in Philadelphia. Myself and another guy hopped a train to Philly, getting there the night of the recording of the proposed show. We were somewhere downtown. I was already a terribly compulsive runner by that time and had every intention of running the next morning.

You also need to know there were a series of incredibly predictable, but very button pushing movies, going under the overall umbrella title of “Rocky”, which I suspect will still be seen in years to come because of its iconic nature, for better or worse. The lead character, Rocky Balboa, supposedly came out of a very tough, working class part of that city. In the very heart of Philly is a stately looking museum of art with an impressive series of broad stairs taking you to the top, a grand plaza and main entrance. I believe in the second incarnation of the pugilistic franchise, Rocky, already having become the long shot winner of the heavy weight belt, has a huge statue of himself planted right in the middle of that plaza.

Now, with that background, we can get back to my own story of Rocky. Being a committed runner and knowing the story of the Rocky films and those incredible museum steps, my morning run right through downtown Philly was definitely going to wind up at those stairs. Well, I made it to those stairs, running through the city in just my shorts and a sweatband, while everyone around was respectfully attired and on their way to work.

As you run up this series of long stairs, the view plane gradually changes as your line of sight moves up these stone steps just a little ahead of your feet. The moment my eyes could shoot across the mezzanine, I instantly saw this huge concrete pedestal, where the large statue of Rocky was placed for the filming. His statue was gone and all that remained was this pedestal and the exposed rebar that originally held Rocky. Right in the middle of this mess of concrete and rebar was a 10" high marble sculpture of a standing oriental priest of some sort. My instantaneous reaction was that this small, marble spiritual messenger was placed on that pedestal solely for my benefit. Without hesitation, I ran to the pedestal and took Rocky in my grasp and ran back to my hotel room.

Rocky has been with me ever since and always occupies the place of honor in whatever home I have lived in. He is the last to leave and the first to enter. I always put him in a place where he can keep an eye on me.

This statue came into my life at a very interesting time. I don't think I mentioned that I spent my thirties in therapy. We will undoubtedly get into that some time down the road, but for now let's deal with where I was at that point. Spirituality was beginning to creep into my life and the therapist I was with at that time reinforced this growing awareness. It was probably around the time I began fiddling with meditation and those summers in Honesdale, Pa, with a nearby spiritual center that I visited. I was definitely moving to the Eastern disciplines like Buddhism, but it was still early in my own journey.

I consider Rocky my only possession and he will already be yours by the time you read this or I will give him to you if I am still around. One way or another, it would be good for me to know that Rocky has gotten a new job. I don't pay much attention to him, but every now and then, I clean him off and say a few words to the old guy. He even holds his staff in a way that resonates with my sense of having been a shepherd in some other lifetime. When I assume my imaginary pose, holding a long walking stick and looking out over a large expanse of land, it is familiar to me on a cellular level. I was likely a shepherd and a poet, off by himself and dreaming of a world where compassion was the rule.

John Lennon and the Buddha

I want you to know that if you were sitting here with me right now, I would want to talk about the same thing you will be reading at this moment. This process of ours is a spontaneous one and no forethought is permitted beyond a subject. One way to keep this as fresh as possible is to allow it to be organic.

It is December 8th today and on this day the Buddha supposedly attained enlightenment around 2500 years ago and John Lennon was murdered just over 30 years ago. For some reason, this coincidence caught my attention.

At the time of John Lennon's murder, I was certainly more into him and the Beatles than I was into the Buddha. I was in my mid-thirties when Lennon was cut down just in front of the Dakota, an elegant compound across from Central Park on the west side of Manhattan. I have already made an effort or two to explain music's importance in my life. From the 1950's onward, music became the domain of young people. Back then, its power was very fresh and unstoppable. Rock 'n Roll enveloped the universe and became the language that drew thousands together just to see a concert. Seeing the Beatles perform at Shea Stadium was an unbelievable experience for me. At that point, I wasn't a screaming teenager; I was around nineteen, basically the same age as those four guys.

The evening of his death was an unusual one for me. For the one and only time in my life, I met a woman at a bar and went back to her place and ended up in bed. News of his death was on the tube later that night and it was a devastating moment for me. There I was, in the bed of a total stranger and suddenly feeling so incredibly sad and alone about his murder. Many of us cling to our youth far longer than we ought to and the door shut hard behind me with his loss. Just as there would never be even the possibility of a Beatle reunion after that, there was also no magical mystery tour taking me back to my youth. People were touched the world over and the level of sadness was incredible. He was an outspoken artist and didn't seem to take any shit from the establishment. Many people wonder what kind of music he would have been making had he been allowed to live.

The Beatles were a true phenomenon, an occurrence that could only have happened if the stars were aligned in a very precise orchestration. A special conspiracy of events needed to be perfectly in place for four young men from Liverpool, England to take over the world. Anything at all could have derailed this musical and sociological juggernaut. If John and Paul didn't meet on the bus and have a conversation or if they kept their original drummer, Pete Best, who knows?

What a perfect segue to the Big Man. There are a handful of basic tenets in Zen and one of them is this cold phrase, dependent co-arising. Buddha believed that absolutely everything was interconnected and impacted by everything else. The standard explanation goes something like, when a butterfly flaps its wings in Ghana; you can feel the breeze on your neck in Brooklyn. Now, what does this have to do with John Lennon and the Beatles, you might ask? Well, imagine the infinite number of permutations and combinations that ended up spelling their name and catapulting them into the stratosphere of artists who changed the world.

Both the Buddha and the Beatles have had an impact on their time, but we will have to wait and see if people are still listening to Let It Be in 2,500 years. The Big One has had serious staying power. This guy dedicated his life to seeking the Absolute Truth of our lives and I think he did a fine job of sorting out the major tunes we all dance to throughout our own sojourn here.

You will undoubtedly have moments in your life, which you may have already had, when you question the meaning of life and ask yourself why you are here. Siddhartha devoted his own life to essential questions like those. Much of what he came up with is pretty tough to follow because it requires that we become the Buddha and most people don't think they could ever be like him. He would likely take issue with the naysayers because he never wanted to be deified and believed we were all Buddha's and this is heaven. God lives within each of us and yet most all of us cannot fathom this truth.

In his view, everything is constantly changing and there is nothing to hold on to. We do our damndest to believe in permanence, especially when it comes to our view of ourselves. We really don't exist the way most people would like to think. I believe that at the heart of our suffering is our inability to come to terms with our mortality, preferring the mirage of being this unwavering presence in the world. One minute from now, you will not be the same person you were before. So, who are you? You exist in this very moment and the medicine for this ailment called truth is to be as present as you can be as often as you can. This may be of interest to you or not and that is not my providence. I am only sharing and definitely not preaching.

Big news!! I have just surpassed fifty pages of writing by my count and that is a milestone. I tried something like this quite some time ago. I was living in a brownstone in Brooklyn that your Dad and uncle Danny loved to spend time at on the weekends. They ran with a gang of some local kids and stayed out until after dark, playing in the streets and going up to a big high school playground nearby.

Anyway, back to the writing part of the story. I just had this feeling I ought to write, having no idea what my voice was. I bought a typewriter and when I was ready to start, I put it one the bed and rolled the paper into place. I stared at it, walked away, stared at it and after a time, sat down on the bed and placed my fingers in the appropriate pose. This went on for a while until I finally broke down in tears and sobbed for quite some time. Whatever I was thinking was clearly much too painful for me to share even with the typewriter. Opening yourself up can be a scary business and I was simply not ready back then.

Now, fifty pages into this incarnation, it feels very joyful to me. Thank you, Shane.

Homage to Ida

It is hard to let December 9th go by and not talk about Ida, my mother, your great grandmother. Today is her birthday and it is as good a time as any to write about her, although there is no way words will do her justice.

It is ironic that her passing nearly nine years ago is the event that elevated her to a very rare place within me and it is automatically what I think about when she surfaces from the vault of my memory. There is no question it will be the subject of a story on next May 22nd, the day she departed.

My brother, Marty, just called me back and we spoke about our mother for a while. Actually, his birthday is coming up in a couple of days and I will likely write about him, although I am not sure how you write one entry about someone who is directly blood connected and someone you have known your entire freakin' life.

My mother was born in 1910 and grew up in a ghetto-like neighborhood in Brooklyn, where many Jews migrated from Russia and other European countries. She was a beautiful young woman, based on the few photographs I have seen. She went to work in an office after high school and gravitated toward bookkeeping. Unlike most women of that time, she married in her early thirties, considered late by the very conservative immigrants of her parent's generation. She married my father, Daniel, who was about ten years her senior.

My memories of the first nine years of life, when my father was alive, are not very sharp. I will hold off on my neighborhood stories for another time because this time belongs to Ida. Their generation was a transitional one, struggling to shed their parent's European roots and embracing the freedom of America. This applied more to my mother than my father because he was Russian born and even further behind in the adjustment. When my father was alive, she was the good wife. She stayed home and raised the children and took care of the house. Her world was pretty insular by today's standards, a time when women were really considered to be second-class citizens, certainly not bright enough to be in a man's world.

While I don't remember the exact date, our lives changed dramatically in April 1954, when my father, her husband abruptly died of a heart attack. Our house was paid off with the insurance, but there was not a dime in the bank and this lady had to raise two young boys, nine and twelve. In those days, the single mom syndrome was a rarity. It was devastating for all of us and she got her shit together and got a job at a nearby Jewish Center as their bookkeeper. It paid all of around $125 per week and she somehow managed to raise Marty and me.

I always liked my mother as a kid and was concerned about her as well because if she croaked I was screwed. My brother and I began working when we were very young and one of the reasons was to try and lessen the load on her. In addition, I know I wanted my own money and not allowance. She managed her two roles as provider and parent pretty well, considering there were no precedents to follow back then.

Listening to a guy by the name of Marvin Gaye, singing " How Sweet It Is". If you don't move when you hear it, you ain't alive. When I got up to fill my wine glass that song came on and I thought I would let you know. I am so fortunate to have grown up with music from the Fifties and every decade thereafter. I simply can't imagine music so special ever again and I wonder what the hell you will be listening to as a kid. Today, music is so corporatized; the original stuff is forced to seek out all sorts of alternative pathways to its audience. Maybe there will be new genres, but for the life of me, I can't imagine what it could be.

Back to Ida. You know, it is such a long story to tell because it spans the first fifty-five years of my life. The vast majority of the events have slowly lost focus and faded from memory, besides this is not a diary held down by details. She did the best she could with meals, but they were always very basic and that was okay with my brother and me. She helped with homework and she was always interested in our education. We had quite a bit of freedom as kids because she was not home much of the time. Somehow, my brother and I were never really assholes about it all. While we were certainly no angels, we took no comfort in screwing her over with too much bullshit.

Even though I lived at home through my four years at Queens College, I started slowly moving on during that time and was dying to move out as soon as I could. When I got back from active duty in the Army Reserves (Now, there's a story!), I finally moved out and went to the East Village. The connection certainly changes when you leave the house and start building a completely independent life.

I wasn't single all that long when I married your grandmother, which was likely a bit sooner than it needed to be and that really changed the relationship with my mother. On some level, she began to feel a bit like some obligatory duty, but the least I could do in return for her sacrifices on my behalf was to stay close. She did most of the calling, especially when I was younger. As she began to get older, I did make more of a point of calling. Calls were pretty short and essentially updates of where I was. In the later years, there were fill ins on her health and doctor's appointments.

She was quite a remarkable lady and fiercely independent, which is something I began to understand over the years. As I already mentioned, I don't think intimacy was her bag and she basically spent the vast majority of her life without a primary relationship because my father was about it for her in that realm. She had a handful of girlfriends over the years and they would get together for dinner and other occasions, but she was alone much of the time. I know she was an avid reader. She was a life long Democrat, but not really all that liberal. My adventures were exasperating for her to deal with, but she always ended up being supportive, even if she had no idea why I was doing half the things I did.

It is a miracle how she managed with money because she never made very much. After I finally moved out, she sold the house I grew up in and made some cash, but not all that much. On a number of occasions during my life, I found myself in a jam for some money and she came through, in spite of professing not to understand my choices. It wasn't often, but it was always crucial or I never would have gone through the trepidation leading up to a call. She was there for me when I needed her and I am deeply indebted to my mother.

I would like to think that as I got older, I came to appreciate her much more. We would have some honest conversations about personal issues, often about her getting older and how it was challenging for her. I began to understand how important the quality of life was to her. We all tend to be preoccupied with longevity, while ignoring how we live our lives. Do yourself a big favor and look for quality in your own life.

Ida was far from perfect, but the last time I checked we are all missing pieces here and there. Growing up, it is important to break from your parents and very often there is discord, especially from the children who are not quite ready to take complete responsibility for their lives. It is convenient to blame your parents. I think freedom only comes when we can see and embrace our imperfections and not look for blame. When you are finally able to forgive yourself, you forgive everyone else.

While this paragraph simply follows the last, there is more to it than that. After the last one, I shut down the story and got up to prepare yet another one of my special dinners. I felt compelled to come back to the story to simply say I am not nearly a good enough writer to do justice to a story about Ida. Like your Mom, she gave me life and did the best she could to nurture me and make sure I left the nest in one piece.

Whether she actually comes up again in this ongoing tale remains to be seen. I am pretty sure I will want to share the story of her passing, which I already mentioned. Let me just say that from my present vantage point of sixty-six years, I have immense love, gratitude and compassion for Ida. This entire story literally wouldn't be possible without her so I am indebted to her for my life and for whatever comes, some of which I get to share with you.

Three years old

It's been a couple of days and I am happy to report on my addiction to this process. I just have too much to share and this is a stupendous outlet. If you have gotten this far into the bottomless pit of my temporary consciousness, you have clearly had your ticket punched and you are totally along for the full ride. Welcome on board, my boy.

I really wanted to write you yesterday because it was your third birthday. I didn't get to talk with you and frankly it would have been extremely brief as you were only three and one shouldn't have very high expectations of conversational abilities at that age. In addition, had we spoken, you absolutely would not be remembering it as you read this story anyway.

As you already know, you didn't go to Disney World when it was initially planned because you were not feeling well. This will undoubtedly be lost in the blur of childhood memories, but you did go this past weekend before your birthday. I got some photographs of the trip, but didn't want to write to you until I had a chance to speak with your Mom or Dad for some fill in on the adventure.

Most of the time, I can catch Andy driving home from work at Novo Nordisk, an international pharmaceutical company, to your house in Hoboken. I really wanted to talk with him about Disney World, so that it might be my narrative to underscore the wonderful pictures of your trip. We had a great talk today about the trip and some other things. I really like your Father very much and think we have a special kind of connection and I hope you are fortunate enough in your life time to be old enough to stand eye to eye with your Father. I think I might like to write about a transcendent time in our relationship, but this is about your trip and your birthday.

The photographs are incredible from that time in your life. You had such a look of enchantment when you were with the Disney characters. According to Dad, you were absolutely fearless and totally enthralled by a make believe life that became a reality to you for that brief time. Believing in magic or the unknown is a terrific character trait in my humble opinion. Young people like you were in those pictures have this raw ability to reshuffle the deck of reality on a whim for themselves. Speaking for myself, I lost that ability for quite a while, but I was eventually drawn back to a time when the boundary between real and not real didn't seem to matter all that much. What matters to me now is how something feels, with my heart as the yardstick.

For me, it is an absolutely incredible gift to know you exist. So far, I think you are a good kid with some unbelievable potential that may or may not be realized in your life. How could I possibly know anything beyond speculation? Magic is the answer and I think if you stay connected to your own magic, you are going to be just fine. There is a part of me that likes to think this collection of tales is going to be a safety net of some kind for you, which is partially my intention in doing all of this. Believe me, falls are inevitable in this life and if this little edition softens the blow or helps you find your own way; we will have created a successful partnership.

I sent you a replica of a whale for your birthday because I thought it would fit perfectly with my post card back to you a while ago with a breeching whale on it. Apparently, the card was a big hit in your class. I would be very nervous if you were still carrying around the whale with you because your mental health would be at risk. It is likely lost in the ghost menagerie of stuff you acquired during your early years.

Anyway, it is a pleasure to know you and to be a part of your life, even at this distance. You're in luck because I will be visiting in January and it should be interesting now that we have begun this Magical Mystery Tour together. I know I will be writing about it to you while it is happening, which really ought to be a trip and a half. Andy and Andrea treat me like a freakin' king and it is very touching to be cared for with such affection. Anyway, that is down the road a bit and there will be more in between.

Let's See What Happens

Have nothing better to do at the moment, so I am here to see what comes out. Sometime there are specific stories or opinions I want to share and this is one of those times where there is nothing between the paper and me.

There is still a part of me that wants you to be able to understand all this and then there is another side simply telling stories and it doesn't really give a shit, because that is not the point here. As long as I can look at anything I have chosen to save on these pages and feel a sense of ownership, it's all good with me. It is funny; we never look at ourselves as a gift to others and always feel the necessity to ignore that truth by giving as many presents as we possibly can. It is like our own selves have no intrinsic value, which is very sad indeed. Giving of the true self is priceless and as you get older, you will hopefully get gradually closer to an understanding of who you are and a path that serves your highest ethical sensibilities. Believe me, this is not a line of idealistic bullshit. There is no substitute for time and experience, commodities you will accumulate along the way. I have a reasonably good, mint condition collection of both.

Need to take a Van Morrison moment because he is part of the background. This guy has been a music icon for over thirty years already and he is one of the many musical treasures I have been privileged to call my own.

My favorite thing is talking about life in this moment and trying to get to the heart of that fleeting episode. After so many years in the trenches, I like being able to simply be Larry. I really don't think I had the ability to do this until I popped my sixties. It is a very liberating time for me and it is special to share this with anyone who happens my way. The younger we are, the more we tend to look outside ourselves for affirmation, a potent hangover from mommy and daddy days.

This exercise, or whatever name I continually try and come up with for this dossier, is a privilege afforded to me by me. It also has been serving as a wonderful salve for the periodic pangs of loneliness. Pretty sure we talked about the truth of being alone and feelings of loneliness, which is what I am referring to now. Being on your own or in a relationship is an interesting balance of trade offs.

Don't know if I told you already, but I love women and find them endlessly alluring and fascinating. There are a handful of ladies I look forward to talking about and I will. They are the ones who gave me the greatest highs imaginable and the lowest lows, the nature of the beast. Now, here I am at this point in my life and I got to tell you it is really liberating to be completely free of any responsibilities that are an inherent part of a relationship. Frankly, I don't know if she is out there at this point. Clearly, I am a nut case and it would require another similarly altered lady in order to reinvest at this time in my life.

We talked about you and Mickey just before and how you had this magical look on your face, your body ready to explode with excitement. While I know it is pretty fucked up to believe in magic at my age, I do. It will take a magical moment to ensnare me and force me out of my cocoon. Of course, we know this is still possible because the Portland escapade was not even two months ago, if you can believe that.

I wish I could ask you what you want to hear about, but under this unique circumstance, I have no idea of agenda. I need to think about the next story because it is not there right now. We definitely need to go with some history because this is not intended to be a lame manual on how to live life, although there is a bit of the preacher in me, as you must know by now. Speaking of that, the idea behind all of this is for you to have some comfort regarding what your grandfather on Kauai was all about. More than anything else, it is the voice I want you to hear and not the details. Believe me, this has nothing to do with whether you agree or disagree, understand or misunderstand; it is merely your ticket into my soul.

Taking a quick look at the recent entries, it is clearly time for a longer story. My observations are short and my stories are long. I need to make sure you get your money's worth! I will think of something for the next time, not to worry.

I just want to add something to the above short opus and not consider this a brand new addition, merely a brief continuation. When I finished writing, I thought how incredibly imperfect this process is. It is impossible to capture a fleeting moment of thought, considering the rapidity with which they strike. It means I know this whole thing is fraught with inadequacies and flaws, but it is absolutely worth the effort for me to write and for you to read.

While I was briefly away before, I have come up with our next entry and it ought to be a good one. I am going over to Oahu this weekend to visit with a friend, Ken H. You are gonna like this one. I will likely set it up before the trip so we can focus on the prime cuts for the weekend.

Turn the Page

Sitting at the airport, waiting for my flight from Kauai to Oahu. Not much time now, but figured I'd get started anyway. Before telling you about Ken and this trip, we need to go back to 1964 and the presidential election between LBJ and Goldwater.

I gave up a career in medicine in my sophomore year at Queens College because it was a pretty bad idea in the first place, requiring more intellectual focus than I could possibly muster. A Jewish kid from Queens was expected to become a lawyer, doctor or dentist, the last one being a mystery choice to me. I was fortunate to be bright enough to get by without really killing myself and after retiring from medicine, my academic objective became getting out with as little hassle as possible and as quickly as possible. I slickly shifted over to political science because one of the professors, responsible for more than a third of the credits needed for the major, was extremely easy. Her tests somehow managed to circulate before each exam.

I filled out my mind time with courses in psychology and radio and television. I have always had an interest in what goes on inside each of us and probably would have been a terrific therapist. I will tell you my therapy stories down the road. The radio and television choice was two fold, the courses were easy and I have always been drawn to entertainment on one level or another. I have extremely comedic genes and have always been able to use my humor for every conceivable circumstance imaginable. There is no telling where life might have taken me had this quality been nurtured when I was young. As I have already mentioned, we were expected to pursue academically oriented careers and there wasn't much tolerance for artistic expression, especially if that is what you were drawn to as a youngster. If you did, it was something you did, as long as it didn't interfere with your true purpose, bringing pride and joy to all your relatives, dead or alive.

Go back with me in time to the fall of 1964. I was in a radio and television production course and the professor asked if any of us were interested in working election coverage at one of the original television networks, NBC. Not one to turn down some spending money, I shot my arm in the air and got myself signed up. It turned out to be a gopher job, but I got to spend time in studio H where the coverage was taking place. The broadcasters at the time were Chet Huntley and David Brinkley, long time journalists from the days of print. I saw these young guys walking around in uniforms and they were called pages, another name for an usher. After the election job, I began bugging the network about becoming a page. It took about six months to finally get the job, which turned out to be one of the best jobs I have ever had and it sure wasn't for the money, a paltry sixty six bucks a week for a full time position.

The majority of the pages were a good deal older than me, many of them in their late twenties and early thirties. They came from all over the country in the hope of becoming actors, writers, photographers, dancers and anything associated with show business. A considerable number of well-known artists and people within the industry were pages at the beginning of their careers.

You need to remember I was not quite twenty and still living at home because I was going to Queens College. By that time, I had considerable freedom, while Ida really had no choice and she was pretty good about it all. Still, meeting all those people was a fabulous experience for me and we would hang out together often.

I would leave class every afternoon and take the F train to 30 Rockefeller Plaza, the home of NBC. Back then, an incredibly talented comedian by the name of Johnny Carson hosted the Tonight Show, which may or may not still be around for you. As a result, I got to see every major star and musician from roughly 1965 to 1968. The names won't mean much to you, but it was a veritable who's who in the entertainment world. One of the more exciting evenings was when the Rat Pack showed up. This group, which you can read about, consisted of Frank Sinatra, Dean Martin, Sammy Davis Jr. and Peter Lawford. There are endless stories from that time. I felt very comfortable around all of these people and most every one of the big names understood that pages were budding actors, etc. and treated us more like insiders than fans.

This was one of the great times in my life and I did it for around two and a half years, right through graduation until I had to go away for active duty in the Army Reserve. Keep in mind this was during the height of the Vietnam War and it was either going to Canada or a safe stint in the Reserves.

By the way, right now I am sitting by myself in the baggage claim area at the airport on Oahu. I am killing a little time until I head out to China town to meet up with Ken. This is a good time to take a break because there is far more to the story than time permits right now.

Miracle of Miracles

I am now back in the Oahu airport, waiting to go home after a short 36 hour stay with my friend, Ken H. Eating some crappy Chinese food and waiting for my flight. To make sense of this weekend is no different than trying to make sense of my entire life.

I guess it is a fruitless exercise to make sense of any part of my life, so why begin now? I flew over to Oahu to see Ken because he was here in his capacity as president of the most important actor's union in the country. We befriended each other when we were both in our early twenties and pages at NBC. As so often happens with relationships, we drifted apart for several decades and I think I reached out to him to reconnect. We enjoyed each other's company that many years ago and it stayed alive within each of us through the years. He became somewhat famous as the star of a number of television series and Broadway shows. I suppose there was a part of me that felt very comfortable around people like Ken, because I could have easily been like them and chosen an unpredictable path, but I didn't. I saw him several times when I was in the broadcast advertising business and he was a TV and Broadway star. For whatever reason, we connected a number of years ago and the comfort and familiarity were instantly rekindled. For me, the many phone subsequent conversations were a wonderful affirmation of a time long ago when I could have easily gone the way of the performer. Our conversations over the past number of years have been absolutely joyful for me and he is always effusive in terms of complimenting me regarding my gift for humor.

We had a great weekend together and I think it warrants a bit more focus than I can muster right now, considering the travel and Mai Tai consumption of the day. I need to get my shit together for the flight home, plus I have to tell you about Patrice, an artist I met just before leaving to see Ken. I really don't mean for this to seem like a soap opera, but it is what it is. Going to shut it down, but I promise I will finish out the story because it is a beauty for sure.

Back Home

I am back home and have had a day of work between the Oahu weekend and right now. Actually got to see Patrice a couple of hours ago, so let's catch up with Ken H. and then hit it with my cocktail companion this afternoon.

Met up with Ken at a Chinese restaurant in downtown Oahu. Members of the Hawaii chapter of the actor's union accompanied him. It is worth the price of admission to be around people in the entertainment world. Animated conversation is a prerequisite. I was asked by one of the people, "What have you been in?" In acting parlance it means what shows have I been in. I explained I was just a regular person and a friend of Ken's.

Ken and I hit one of the hotel bars on our way up to the room. After throwing down a couple, we went up to our room and ended up speaking about all sorts of things for a couple hours. Ken has great memory and over the course of his career, he has worked with and met many of the major names in show business over a forty-year ride. I let the humor run wild and became a full time joker, mixed with some serious conversations about the state of things.

The next day was spent around the hotel pool and the bar, a favorite destination for my friend, who can on occasion drink like a self-destructing Irishman or maybe it's a Scotsman, which one escapes me at the moment. As an occasional over indulger myself, I need to tread lightly on others. It is his life and I enjoy our incredibly entertaining phone conversations and these rare visits. I don't look very good in judge robes anyway and try and avoid sentencing anyone because of their imperfect nature, an affliction we all suffer from.

Invariably, somebody always ends up recognizing him and that precipitates these inane conversations with people who somehow think that actors are living very different lives from their own. This, of course, is a terrible disservice we do to ourselves, thinking that life at its core is very different for the rich and famous. Believe me, they are just as screwed up as you and I, but too much adoration will definitely fuck with your mind. I noticed Ken wouldn't do that many things for himself and would instinctively ask people to do things for him or to ask for something special at a restaurant. Imagine, he is not all that famous, so I can only speculate how outrageous some of these people become. By the way, one of the reasons why these folks expect to be waited on is because there are endless numbers of people who will do exactly that for them.

Anyway, it was a treat seeing my buddy, Ken. Please, don't get the wrong idea about him. We have a great connection and it is a pure joy to speak to him and to hang out on those rare occasions when we get together. He is a real actor to the core and possessed of a fine intellect. When you let the genie out of the bottle, which is what so many artists do, it can be hard to shove it back in and shit happens. Ken, if you read this, I love you, man and our conversations have meant the world to me. I am absolutely at my funniest when I speak with you.

Patrice

Now, there is Patrice, a woman I met at a special agriculture and crafts market I helped to put on because of my connection with the farm bureau here. Assuming you have led an urban existence, you probably have no idea about farm bureaus, something I will likely cover later. She had a booth at the event and is a plein air artist, meaning she paints the outdoors while in the outdoors. I would conveniently pass her booth throughout the day and we would talk.

First Kiss

You will likely read all of this as a seamless narrative, but that is definitely not the case. I just took a break of about a week because I didn't like how I was writing. Whenever this feels like an obligation, it is time to shut it down and wait for the urge to return.

I asked Patrice out and we met several days after that at a Mexican restaurant. I have absolutely no idea what your level of experience with women will be when you read any of this. Regardless of my age, every time is the first time for me. It doesn't get easy and I don't think it is supposed to. I find myself very self-conscious and I carry on an internal dialogue with myself, while I maintain a completely false sense of security on the outside. In Patrice's case, she is a beautiful woman with fabulous blue eyes. So, while I am talking with her, I am talking to myself and trying not to stare too much. It is a very precious place to be and it never loses its freshness, no matter how many times it happens.

On the second get together, she came over to my place. She brought her two black Labs in the bed of her truck and she was wearing a great two-piece bathing suit, having just come from the ocean. I did whatever I could to make her feel as comfortable as possible because I wanted her to relax. You should know I rarely if ever have anyone come to my place, due to a strong sense of privacy. My home is the only totally safe place from the world outside. There is a feeling of serenity in my space and it is very disarming for the few who visit.

I also respect the privacy of those around me and don't want to dig deep into the details of her life. Unfortunately for her, she is going through the trauma of a busted marriage that lasted far too long. It impacted her relationship with her son and that is something crushing for a mother. I like her very much and that is what is relevant for this story.

The conversation was very warm and filled with much laughter. When she went out of her way to lean into me, it was pure electricity. Throughout my life, I have been a fairly lonely guy and that moment of connection with a woman is priceless. There is something magical about it and I hope you have that rare privilege in your own life at least once and once again.

Some point toward the end of the evening, we embraced and had a luscious, first kiss. Don't get nervous, at no time will I go places that are none of your business. For me, there is an element of trust between myself and a woman of intimacy that should never be violated, distance and the passage of time are not sufficient justification. Plus, I am your grandfather and you do not need too much information.

When two bodies are tightly pressed together, for a split second, it feels like the hearts are actually touching each other. You look deeply into her eyes and as they gently close, your open mouths somehow create a perfect seal. You stop breathing and the world comes to a stunning halt. It is an absolutely perfect moment.

Along with everything else that is going on with me, Patrice will likely weave in and out of the monologue. I have been single since my early thirties and relationships have been a blessing throughout my life. I had my first girl friend when I was around twelve. I had her as in had a girlfriend, without the biblical implication. Give me a break, I was just a kid. Whenever I have found myself in between partners, there is a feeling that it may never happen again. Frankly, I am not sure if I was ever meant to be truly with another. The younger you are, the less you tend to think about the challenges and you too quickly buy the myth of happily ever after. Unless you can honor and support the differences between yourself and your mate, there is trouble ahead.

At this point in my life, I think I could pull it off, but it would take a very special lady to put up with me. If the love is powerful, the connection strong and the trust is without question, it has the makings of a good one.

Absolutely nothing I share with you is intended to be advice for you to follow and I know it is something repeated throughout this monologue. I am simply sharing my life and my opinions about most anything. If something in here smells of profundity, please disregard. Just as I have cut my own path through the universe, you will do the same. It's all in the heart, which is what makes writing about things like the first kiss so pleasurable.

The idea of being an independent, feeling, thinking human being, walking in a forest of strange occurrences, is incredibly overwhelming at times. Being truly open to the full force of life is a lot to handle; actually it can be downright terrifying. What am I doing here? Do I have any purpose? What truly matters? The singularly important questions have no answers and never will. While I think it is crucial to ask these questions, it is even more important to understand they are not intended to be answered. I believe a life is about seeking and understanding that all we can possibly do is live our lives with these unanswerable questions as signposts to keep us on our own path.

Don't want to lose sight of our entry heading. The first kiss with Patrice was everything it is supposed to be. In that moment of absolute silence, she spoke to me in an unmistakably clear voice and I heard it. Man, I hope you already know what it is like, but if you don't, you will. Your entire body bursts into cool flames, an exhilarating fire of passion. It is sensations like this that have resulted in great poetry, magnificent works of art, all failed attempts at trying to capture a moment that is far too elusive.

I told Patrice I was writing this story for you. Sometimes, I tell close friends I am writing a book, but it is for an audience of one. She even offered to provide a cover, which I thought was very sweet, but way ahead of this personal effort of mine.

I looked at the very first sentence and realized we have been at this for about two months now. There is so much more from my past yet to share and everyday provides me with fresh experiences. As I have probably stated before, this is about getting to know who I am and not so much a chronology of my experiences.

Bing Crosby is singing "White Christmas" in the background because it is the season. I consider Patrice my very own present and the metaphorical unwrapping is priceless, my boy.

Feelings

I have been feeling a bit more emotional than usual and laying low seemed like a good idea. It then dawned on me that the whole idea of feelings and being aware of them has been a touchstone in my life for many years.

My boy, while you probably haven't realized it just yet, the heart rules everything in our lives. We feel way ahead of thought, whether we are conscious of it or not. The more in touch you are with this, the less likelihood that you will fall victim to your emotions, plus they will win out, one-way or another anyway.

I am a veteran of around ten years of therapy, primarily during my thirties. In my opinion, most modalities are off the mark, especially the ones that deal with trying to change who you are. Those schemes have you adding behavior as an overlay to deal with your issues. After years of Zen practice, I would say the direction needs to be exactly opposite to that idea.

On a personal level, our life's work is to keep stripping away the layers that have accumulated in our minds. In Buddhism, there is a term called True Self or Buddha Nature and a host of other words and phrases that attempt to define the indefinable. This kind of understanding is visceral, non-intellectual and experiential and something you ultimately feel and that is all. It is a counter intuitive process and runs directly in the face of convention.

I know I have already launched into Buddha for President diatribe and there is no need to repeat it here. This time of the year has always been emotional for me and don't ask me why. Believe me, this has fuck all to do with Santa Claus, rather it is about endings and beginnings, which seems unavoidable as you approach the end of one year and the start of another. It seems to be a time when you look back at the year soon to end and ponder the year to come. Like it or not, it is also a recognition of the passage of time and that doesn't make most people terribly happy, even though it is rarely dealt with on a personal level.

The younger you are, the more externals impact you and there is no training for true self-discovery, other than the passage of time and lessons learned along the way.

Parents want what is best for their children, but more often than not, it is about what will make them feel good about all the time and effort they have put into growing their child into an independent being. Right now, it is way too early to know how your parents will nurture your individuality, so we will have to wait and see what happens.

Judgment by self or another is a totally unproductive exercise and very limiting on true personal growth. No one has the right to live your life for you and our objective really ought to be inhabiting our selves as much as we are capable at any time in our lives. The more you connect with your feelings, the closer you get to being who you truly are. Peer pressure is a total crock of shit and is generally elicited by others feeling threatened by someone's uniqueness and their commitment to travel their own way, with the heart as the engine.

Another word that comes to mind is intimacy. First and foremost, you need to be intimate with yourself before you can do a decent job of being there for another. I was certainly one of those people who got married before I could see myself, warts and all. Everything emanates from ourselves and unless we are on track, we will ultimately be derailed along the way.

Of course, all of this is brought on at this time because I have barely begun seeing Patrice. Amongst other things, being in a relationship shines a bright light into our private

mirror, forcing us to see things about ourselves that aren't always that attractive. Being intimate with another is both glorious and terrifying. In order to do it right, you have to shit can all the pretense and get naked, otherwise you are simply building something on a foundation of illusion and delusion.

So, here is Grandpa, once again embracing the challenges of intimacy as best I can. I guess if you do it right, it never gets easy because every single situation is completely different, requiring the very same level of sensitivity in a one of a kind circumstance. You get your ticket punched, strap yourself in and get ready for the emotional roller coaster ride of your life; otherwise you are not really present.

Our baggage increases with age. When we are young, the load is much lighter and as we get older and lose strength, the weight of the baggage tends to increase. For my part, I have tried hard to keep it lean and have had limited success in that regard. The objective is to find out what truly matters and discard all the rest because it just slows you down, stooping your emotional posture until you fall over.

One of the many cool things about being given another chance at connection is that you have an opportunity to chip away at all of your predictable fuck ups and see if there is another way that honors who you are and holds the other person very dear at the same time.

I certainly don't want to give the wrong idea that feelings are simply based on the presence of another in your life because that couldn't be farther from the truth. All of our memories are based on feelings and not thoughts. Feelings have a timeless quality about them and they can haunt you like a ghost or let you fly like an angel.

When you can accept your own feelings absent of judgment, you are in great shape. Your heart demands honesty or else your emotions go underground and you become their victim. You know, if someone was writing me this bullshit at your age, I don't know how I'd react. This is the closest I can get to unscrewing my head and putting it on a much younger being. I hope you are a very emotional, caring human being, a bit wiser than your years, possessed of an inquisitive mind and a heart free of judgment.

As a kid, I always felt I was a little different than my friends. It had nothing to do with being smarter because many of them were far brighter than myself. In all modesty, I was a charismatic character, who was always comfortable being out front. In hindsight, it had something to do with reacting to people in an open way. All through college, I was a fairly popular guy and it was something I took for granted because it just fit me in a natural way.

Strap Yourself In

Earlier today, I had a really different thought about this writing to you. While you wouldn't necessarily know it, tomorrow night is New Years Eve, leading into 2012. I find my place at this precise moment in time with some things I want to say and there are two people I want to write to. I can write both in the present and the future if I write to you and Patrice. Mind you, up until the moment she reads this, she will have had no part in it whatsoever.

Know that Patrice will be reading this shortly and it will be much to her surprise, believe me. The only trick is to understand that when I say "you", I will be talking to Patrice right now and to you whenever you crack into this time castle.

"This has been one of the most extraordinary years of my life. However, I hope I am able to say this for every year-end as it comes rolling towards me. What I find most exciting is that I am still able to find life's magic, regardless of the years and their bruises.

I want both of you to embrace all that life has to offer and to always proceed with open hearts. Patrice, fifteen or more years from now, this young man with my blood in his veins will be reading this wish for you as well as himself What this means for you is that my wish is timeless and comes from a place in this universe far greater than myself.

Shane, I am proud to say that after all these years, I still find women a complete mystery, unfathomable and well beyond my capability. My boy, I don't know if you will marry your high school sweetheart and live happily ever after or have a series of relationships or whether you will convert to Catholicism and become a celibate priest.

For better or worse, I can only write from my experience. I married your grandmother when I was 24 and was fortunate to have had a couple of girl friends and relationships before that. Remember, nothing I write is intended to force you to conjure up an image of your grandpa stark naked with a woman. At another time, I will talk about the women in my life, but not right now. I am not saying this for Patrice's benefit because she will be reading all this, rather it is miles away from why I feel the urge to write this way to both of you.

I wanted to tell you both how incredibly blessed I feel to be alive and at this place and in this time. I have had an incredibly colorful past and wouldn't be here without all of it. This gift of life is beyond any description imaginable.

A while ago, I hit upon the use of the word " interlude" It is an episode of a determinant. length and applied to an endless number of situations. Patrice and I are having an interlude. People's paths cross for more reasons than there are drops in the ocean. The romantic ones can be memorable beyond any description. Romantic relationships are meant to burn and the fire starts when both conspire with the heavens to bring this interlude to life.

Patrice, I haven't told much to Shane, but I did go off a bit on our first kiss because it was so beautiful to me. He also knows this a relationship that began just a couple of weeks ago. It is extremely fresh for both of us and currently lives in a very sublime place going by the name of uncertainty. Funny thing, interludes have indefinite life spans and it is no stretch to shift it right over to life in general.

Years end and years begin and lucky ones like us get to straddle the two. I have always found it a profound time to take stock of what the hell I have been doing and what the future holds in store. Shane, this has been a wonderful year of transition for you, primarily because you started school. Unknowingly, you have already stepped onto the path of your eventual independence, when you reach outside your mother and father and begin shaping your own life.

This has also been an unbelievable transition year for Patrice. She has had to let go of a way of life that has been her own for nearly twenty-five years. Women are not like you and me, my boy. The maternal energy is a force to be reckoned with. Mothers love their children in a whole more primal level than we could ever imagine. For many, the idea of home and nest ranks up their nearly as high. When a woman finds that shattered before her eyes, it is a painful thing. Shane, when you read this, you say a prayer for Patrice and hope she found all that the Universe has to offer.

I was thinking about my incredible good fortune at the end of this year. I guess the highlight would have to be the work coming together. It was a wonderful affirmation for me and in my own quiet way, I celebrated my tenacity and faith. Around seven years ago, I committed to the work with Bill and I was not going to stop until I completely ran out of money. Let me tell you, I came closer than anyone in their right mind could deal with. Spiritually, I continue to chip away at Mount Rushmore. Learning from my experiences continues to be the wellspring of my education. I live in one of the most beautiful places in the world and every single day, it's stunning face smiles on me and I am blessed.

I will spend New Years Eve alone in my place and likely pass the evening with a good video and one of my Gourmet Meals for Single Dummies. Not sure what I will serve myself, but the selection is awesome. Patrice, your pesto is unbelievable and I will make it into a meal that I will actually cook! Patrice makes a killer pesto and shares it with friends during the holiday. I picked up my ration yesterday and have been periodically denting the container with my right forefinger.

Shane, I hope you have a strong life force; one that permits you to experience all that life has to offer. I confess that one of the reasons for this exercise without end is to provide you with a gas tank for the journey ahead. It will take you wherever the winds decide, but you will always be at the helm and as long as you steer a course with your heart, a safe port will always be near by.

You know, I was going to write tomorrow, but I think I will be too emotional and I will make it my own time instead. Patrice, my dear, I hope the New Year brings peace and unity back into your life. You are a marvel of a woman and without question, one of the most unique women I have ever allowed into my life. Shane, you have just slammed past three and you are dancing to old rock 'n roll songs, microphone in hand and hips on the move. By the way, there is video to back up this assertion.

Want I want to tell you both is that my heart is full with thoughts of visiting you, Shane, in a couple of weeks and continuing to explore the meaning of life in my interlude with you, Patrice.

Shane, this is advice for you. You treat women like fucken queens, do you hear me? I don't care if it is the first girl you meet or the last woman you ever encounter. They are very special people and they deserve to be treated with tremendous respect. My relationships with women have had a much more profound effect on me than my friendship with guys. It's a special thing, a voo doo of the heart.

I hope neither of you mind my putting you together in this short episode. You know, I don't know if this interlude with Patrice will end in days or whether I will even be around when you read this, Shane. Doing this makes it seem timeless to me. These thoughts occupy a strange place in time and its recipients are separated by barriers that are beyond my abilities. If something lives through this multi-dimensional time warp, let it be my true heart. The idea that I can touch you, Shane, and Patrice at this single moment, knowing one will embrace it immediately and another in decades to come is too much for this mortal mind.

I will try very hard not to write either of you tomorrow and I will likely get mildly bombed and bask in the gratitude for this privilege I have been afforded."

Backwards and Forwards

I have done some of what I promised regarding New Year's Day, but the writing part didn't hold up all that well.

Well, I have just come back from a terrific ride up to Kokee and. the sky was clear, providing a spectacular view of Kalalau Valley. It is hard to imagine a sight any more breathtaking than this one and I hope you get a chance to see it some day. Yes, it is Sunday afternoon, New Years Day. What a wonderful day to begin a New Year with.

I have been emotional all day, tearing up unexpectedly and having that cotton in the throat feeling. The overwhelming gratitude is sometimes more than my system can take and my insides leak out through my eyes. This process of writing to you has had a tremendous effect on me. Most of us go through our lives fairly numb and this discipline has thinned my already thin skin even more. I am so appreciative of you for having given me this window into myself. Now, I often think to myself, what will I tell Shane?

I don't think you will mind my last entry to both you and Patrice. For the record, it is back to you and I now. Other than that piece, no one has seen any of this because it is far too personal and for no other eyes than yours.

When a woman enters my life, it is like dropping a boulder in a very still pond. The ripples are everywhere and my private dance with myself changes instantly. Trust me, half the time these budding relationships go absolutely nowhere, but they unleash my heart and it will sometimes have me run amok. The older I get, the more likelihood of complications when it comes to women. Patrice's situation is right up there in the realm of challenges and we shall see what happens.

As you know, this was never intended to be some straight ahead autobiography, giving you the facts of my past, which will teach you nothing about Grandpa Larry. The Master Plan still remains providing you with my history, which will continually be interrupted by whatever the hell happens to be going on in the moment. It is challenging for me, because the past feels a little boring and I much prefer to deal with freshness of my day. However, I am not interested in ego masturbation and this is all about you and being done for you. So, we will flip between the past and the present, plus some light doses of prognostication and pontification, with very, very little likelihood of fornication.

I have been thinking that this would be a good time to start sharing the mind-boggling array of jobs I have had throughout my life. Of course, it will be interrupted regularly by something that may have just happened or is about to happen or may never happen. Now that you're in this boat, you are pretty much screwed and have to let it take you wherever the current decides. It is like being up the creek without a paddle, in a manner of speaking.

I guess I was twelve when I got my first job. Both my brother and I were aware that money was very tight for our mother, after the extremely untimely death of our father. Mind you, she never once complained to us about the circumstance, she simply did what she had to do to take care of us. Ida was an incredible woman and it took me many, many years to understand how extraordinary she was. We figured if she was working so hard for us that it was right for us to help and I don't recall ever feeling victimized by my situation.

There was a delicatessen within walking distance of my elementary school and we got time off for lunch back then. Kids would flock to this awful establishment and I became a lunchtime waiter for around a year. I would rush there before everyone else and serve hot dogs and French Fries to my classmates. The reward for this effort was fifty cents a day and it was a goddamn fortune to me. Two dollars and fifty cents a week was very rich and most importantly, there was no need for allowance from my mother.

Not sure exactly how my next job came around, but it was a great experience. At age thirteen, in the seventh grade, I worked part time at Turnpike Men's Apparel, a small men's clothing store on Union Turnpike. The owners were Al and Milt and they were unbelievably generous to me. I would stock the clothing and clean up, keeping everything where it belonged. At the same time, I had no problem acting as a salesman, which was amazing for a young kid. They let me pretend I was a grown up and made me feel as if I could handle whatever I was doing. I was privy to all of the internal workings of their small business and it was phenomenal. For many years after I left the job, I would stop by and hang out with them. It was disconcerting to see them slowly age, a sensation I now understand from the other side of that mirror. I can't remember what I got paid, but it was very liberating for me and I also dressed reasonably well for a kid my age. This was the beginning of my education into the bizarre make up of human nature and I can't say that it left me feeling terribly positive either. When you wait on people, you find out more than you would like to know. At the same time, it was incredibly gratifying to have a totally positive transaction with a customer. It is no less true today, you take it wherever you can get it and be thankful for the gift.

I left the world of men's haberdashery for a summer job at The Shelborne, a beach club at Lido Beach on Long Island. The sub-culture of the beach club may still be around now, but I have no idea if it will survive by the time you get to this. Back in the late fifties and sixties, many people had busted through into the middle class as successful small business entrepreneurs. The beach club was a place where you would take your family each summer and pretend you were living large. The less affluent would have "lockers", cubbyholes for changing clothes and setting out a beach chair or two. Those who could afford it had cabanas, single rooms with a bathroom and electricity. All had the option of the ocean or the swimming pool, where they could sit with their own kind and feel good about themselves. Lest you think there is any sarcasm or elitism in my note, it is not intended. Many of these guys worked their asses off and over came all sorts of prejudices to achieve their version of the American Dream. These clubs were built primarily for Jews, who were completely excluded from the well established, WASP establishments.

In my first year, I found myself working the grill, doling out franks, burgers and fries. At the end of each day, my face and arms were coated in a mist of cooking oil. My brother and some older guys worked there and I would ride there with them. In my second year, I became a locker boy, not nearly as prestigious as cabana boy, but a step up from the grill nevertheless. I would sweep the walkways, retrieve food and drink and act as a young slave for the families that inhabited these cubicles for the summer. Both summers were wonderful experiences for me and what kid wouldn't want to be at the beach during the summer?

In the summer ending my senior year at high school, I got a job as a waiter at an old folks home in Rockaway Beach. No way I can remember the name after all these years. A high school friend and I worked there Monday to Friday, sleeping in small, very depressing quarters in the basement of the hotel. Half the people were sitting on inner tubes, drinking hot milk and staring off into the distance, looking for the arrival of death, lurking somewhere on their horizon. It was pretty fucken depressing, but it was a job and another comedic, character building experience for me. Someone with a better memory than mine would be able to recall all of the gory details, but I simply cannot. One elderly guest offered my friend money to take him to the beach and push him out into the ocean to die. I do remember that story and it definitely didn't make me feel good about growing old. Back then; life somehow came to an end at a certain time, whether you wanted it to or not. Personally, I would take a bullet before I found myself surrounded by a table full of human prunes with no light in their eyes.

Whale Ho!

This is likely the first in an endless series of interruptions recounting my Jackson Pollock influenced employment history.

I am too tired to check about any prior kayak mentions somewhere behind this particular marine tale. At the very least, I probably mentioned that I got a kayak when I first arrived on Kauai and that I take it out during whale season.

Today was the maiden voyage of the HMS Feinstein for the 2012 whale season. I loaded her in my truck last night so I wouldn't have to deal with it in the morning. There was no work today, Monday, January 2nd, hence a perfect way to begin my kayak season for the year. Did my usual meditation, computer, yoga and running, before heading out to the high seas.

I take the kayak out from the beach at Kukuiula Small Boat Harbor and have been going out of this same spot for nearly eight years now. Kayaking alone in the open sea, one would be smart to exercise some caution and familiarity with the water is one of those precautions. I head straight out, keeping two landmarks behind me, which keeps me on course regardless of winds, waves or current.

I have gone out many times and spent hours by myself with not even the sound or sight of a single whale. Speaking of sound, their blowholes generate a gargantuan sound, like wind rattling through an open window with a slight bass, throaty sound. On a still day, this sound carries great distances and there is no mistake about its direction.

Usually, I know it is going to be a good day if I can hear them or see them, even at a distance when I am on my way out. Today was picture perfect for my whale hunting adventure. The ocean was pretty calm and the breeze was very soft, allowing sound to travel great distances. I got my sign less than an hour into my journey, hearing the blowhole sound and seeing several of these gentle behemoths off in the distance.

Today provided one of those world-class whale moments for me. After seeing a number of them close to the horizon and slightly closer, I ended up no more than fifty feet from at least three of them and it is a sensation that is simply indescribable. When they are on the surface, they move effortlessly curling their backs up and then sliding down into the sea, which must help propel them through the water. Sometimes, you get to see their monstrous tail fin when they complete the full body curl and head straight down. They dive in this gently curved shape and it is simply breathtaking to witness. Seeing the stare of their eye is another spine tingler. With tears flowing from my eyes, I offered a deep gassho (Zen bow), bringing my palms and fingers together and thanking a far greater power than myself for the privilege of this experience.

Over the years, I have gotten incredibly close to these creatures and each time feels like the first, leaving me stunned and incredibly grateful. If we play our cards right, there will be more of these adventures and it will be impossible to keep them out of this story. The natural world provides us with experiences that freeze us right where we are, stopping time and flooding the senses with seemingly otherworldly impressions. Make sure you get yourself out of the goddamn cities and spend some time with God's work because there is nothing like it.

One fleeting moment with surfacing whales is worth millions in spiritual currency. Thank you for letting me share this moment with you.

Back to Work

I am pretty sure I went back to Turnpike Men's Apparel in my freshman year at college. Frankly, I don't remember, but there was never a time when I was without a job and it makes sense to me from this distance. I continued to visit Milt and Al for a number of years after college. I know I got along with them extremely well years before and there were always smiles when I showed up at their store. They treated me like a grown up after a while and that was a first.

The following year, my sophomore year, was the job with Greyhound at the 1964-65 World's Fair in Flushing. This has already been described in some detail, mostly in the context of Stanley and the cross-country saga. It started in the spring of 1964 and was definitely a very exciting experience for me. Major US corporations had massive exhibits, as did countries from all over the world. Companies spent millions of dollars on their presentations. Driving those high priced golf carts with couches in the front was tremendous fun. We would get hired out for the day or evening by very wealthy people who simply wanted to have a "limousine" at their disposal. These fiberglass-constructed machines would occasionally burst into flames because they were fairly shitty vehicles. No one was ever hurt, but they'd break down frequently. It was a terrific gig for a young guy to have and I had a ball doing it.

After the cross-country odyssey, it was back to college time and in my junior year; I scored an election night coverage job with NBC, which precipitated my becoming a page in the spring semester. I can't say enough about the page experience for me. The cast of characters was classic and blew open my homeboy horizon's. These people were living on their own, mostly with roommates and they were experiencing life in NYC for the first time. Keep in mind the time I am referring to is the dinosaur Sixities.

I managed to keep the page thing going right through my graduation from college and beyond. It was very unusual for someone to be a page for so long, but they made an exception because I was still in school. There were ranks in the staff and I rose to the rank of White Key, which is essentially the equivalent of being a mythical white buffalo. Very few people were awarded this rank and it was actually quite funny to me. I always had a gift for getting along with very diverse people and it was partially my humor and brain that made it possible.

Every afternoon, I would take the F train into Rockefeller Plaza and enter this magical world of show business. As my seniority increased, the Tonight Show became my regular gig and that was a very special experience. I was very comfortable in that environment and a slight twist of fate could have had me leading a completely different life than the one I have led. Entertaining people is a gift I have and it is always in my back pocket, ready to be pulled out whenever the spirit moves me.

Now, time for a pot story that is also one of my favorites and it is linked to the paging experience. The Sixties sub-culture had already taken hold on college campuses all over the country. Remember, we are talking about the mid-sixties, when anti-Vietnam War demonstrations were spreading and flower power was blooming. The New York City college system was a bit slower to catch the winds of change, partially because most everyone was still living at home, which dramatically curtailed personal freedom. We were still drinking beer in the fraternity house during my senior year and no one was smoking pot.

I graduated in June 1966 and was still................

I can't continue right now. I know I told you I ride my motorcycle with a fabulous group of local guys and we call ourselves Sons of Kauai. The fellow who rides in the front, Jack, is a special Hawaiian. He has been singing and playing the ukulele his whole life. Hawaiian culture had royalty in its society. Hundreds of years ago, even before the US stole the country, Jack would have been a prince. He is a wonderful guy, who embodies the aloha spirit and we have developed a strong bond over time. I know this because when we greet each other on Sunday morning, we embrace and he makes sure to touch his head to mine, a native custom.

As guys get older, many of them have prostate issues and Jack was diagnosed with some problems. For some reason, I had a bad feeling about it and the prospect of cancer was pretty much a certainty. Just got off the phone with his wife, who told me that his surgery lasted much longer than expected and that his bladder was also involved. I began crying and I still am. Goddamnit. I can't imagine riding my bike on a

Sunday and not looking ahead to see Jack leading the pack. I know he had a bad feeling about it all and he wrote his wishes to his wife before he headed to Oahu for surgery.

Shane, life is so fucken short and I want to you to fill your days with love and life. Live your dreams and be grateful for everyday you are allowed to be here. It generally works ass backwards. When you get older and the time begins to really diminish, you finally start to value your life. Try and do it when you are young and have the time to truly explore all life has to offer.

I can't continue a story about the first time I got high when this news has hit me like a sledgehammer to the heart. I'll be back in a while, but I need to find out about Jack tomorrow. I can't separate myself from the moment and when it absorbs me like this, there is nowhere else to go.

The Next Day

It is now the next day and I have not gotten an update from my friend, Jack's wife. She could call at any time and it could send me in a tailspin again. This is a very unusual place and there is a spirit here that you won't find anywhere else in Amerika, purposely misspelled because it feels so terribly foreign to me right now. Kauai is a place of incredible beauty and power. There are some original people who embody its essence and Jack is one of them. He is a strikingly handsome man, with a wonderfully engaging smile. When we are out riding, he is the first one to talk with tourists and he embodies all that is aloha. Right now, I don't have a good feeling about his health. He came back from Oahu last weekend, so he could ride with us and I sensed he felt it might be his last ride. I decided to ride with him wherever he wanted to go last Sunday because it was the least I could do. I can't even begin to tell you how much I have learned and how enriching my experience has been, riding with the Sons of Kauai. I am an adopted son of this island and these men and women are my brothers and sisters. I feel so incredibly privileged to be allowed into their lives and to be treated with so much affection.

For now, let us travel back in time to the mid-sixties. The music was exploding all around us and is still to this day, some of the best music you will ever hear and it continued into the seventies. Young people were feeling completely free from their parents and all the constraints of appropriate behavior, whatever the hell that is. Hair was growing long and clothes were outrageous. It was a time of unprecedented transition, with no road map beyond your next footstep. There was an intoxicating mist blowing through every doorway and window where high school and college age kids lived. It was in the streets, in your food and definitely in your attitude.

Somehow, I managed to stay detached from the revolution until I graduated college in 1966. There were war protests on campuses all over the country by then, but it didn't hit Queens College until right around my graduation. Columbia University was sure making headlines, but the borough of Queens didn't catch on fire right away.

During half of my junior year and all of my senior year, I was working as a page. I think people were still fairly discreet about pot around then. The staff was quite a collection of characters and some were more intriguing than others. Kenyon was without question one of the strangest of the lot. He had to be somewhere in his thirties and he was British. Like many of the others, he had a very theatrical quality to his demeanor. He wore these incredibly old, double-breasted suits to work and there was a mysterious quality about him. However, he was incredibly friendly, absent any of the silly British snobbery.

Myself and a friend from college, Dan, had become increasingly interested in getting high, to see what the fuss was about. Well, one night, Kenyon invited us over to his eastside Manhattan apartment to give it a go. I went with Dan and another page by the name of Fred, who turned out to be a fairly religious Catholic, which we only found out about after we inhaled.

Kenyon lived in at least a four-story walk up somewhere in the east sixties. We went into his bedroom, which had fabric covering the walls, meeting at a point in the ceiling, to give the feeling of being in a tent somewhere in the desert, where Lawrence of Arabia might stop by for some tea. Right away, we were in an exotic setting for our first time experience. We shared some joints, along with minimal instruction from Kenyon, while we waited for whatever was to come. So, there we are, sitting in the tent and within minutes it became abundantly clear that we were stoned. Dan and I were red eyed and laughing, while Fred began to freak out about this experience being in direct contrast to his Catholic upbringing.

Our gracious host suggested we go out to a nearby bar called Friday's, which was the original link in a chain of TGIF's all over the country, which may still exist by the time you get to this. The upper east side of Manhattan was one of the first scenes in the country where young people came together and began indulging in the new freedoms. We virgin stoners entered this high-energy, brightly lit bar and simply laughed our asses off the entire night.

I think like anything else, your first experience with something is a lasting one. The more satisfying it is, whatever it is, the more likelihood you will do it again and again. While it is hard for me to believe, that was over forty-five years ago!

We can let the smoke clear for now and continue the endless employment saga. In the year of our Lord, 1966, the Vietnam War was in full bloom and upon graduating college; I was clearly at the top of the list. The people at NBC kept me employed well beyond the limit for pages and I ended up being "promoted" to handling uniforms and hanging out in the locker room. By that time, my legend was secure and I needed time to find an Army Reserve unit that would allow me to avoid going to that awful war and likely being killed.

My friend, Dan and I ended up finding a unit in Staten Island that was part of something called the Army Security Agency. The reason why this outfit had openings was because the actual training time could run as long as ten months, as opposed to the standard four months in National Guard units. We immediately signed up and during the summer of '66, I became a soldier, in a manner of speaking. While waiting to be sent away, I remained at NBC. Everything was essentially on hold until my active duty stint.

This is a good time for a break in the story. I will recount my Army tale next, assuming there are no contemporary interruptions and as you know by now, there is every reason to believe something will pop up and send my off in an unpredictable direction.

6AM

Writing to you now at around 6AM, at least an hour before the winter sun rises over Kauai. I have always been a pretty lousy sleeper, even as a kid. I don't think I have ever gotten anywhere near eight hours sleep once in my life. Getting up before dawn is a strange and wonderful time, at least for me. There are no distractions from the outside and the cocoon of the darkness creates a very secure emotional environment. I am actually surprised it has taken all these pages to finally write to you at this hour. I compose my favorite love notes during this time, although I am a little out of shape in that regard. When I look out into the darkness, there is nothing to see and it seems to serve as a mirror to my internal world. It is easy to engage myself in the thoughts and feelings that are closest to the surface. Reflection seems to be effortless around now.

I am hoping to contact Andy once there is a little daylight here, so I can get a chance to talk with you and see each other on the screen. You are now sleeping in a bed, a milestone for children. I talked with your Dad yesterday and he told me when he looks in your room now and sees you tucked in under the covers, with your head resting on a pillow, he gets the sensation that you are growing up and it is an amazing feeling for him. He also told me your vocabulary is expanding dramatically, another sign of your maturing. You will be going to your first karate class pretty soon and he is very excited.

This whole living business is such a miracle and something we don't take enough time to appreciate. Just a few years ago, you were a tiny little creature, barely moving and tightly wrapped in a blanket. The changes occur so rapidly, it is amazing to witness. Rolling over is a major development and the evolution into a young boy happens within a matter of several years. Even at this distance, I marvel at the progression, always wondering who you will become, knowing that your True Nature is already firmly in place. The challenge for your Mom and Dad is to recognize this and foster your uniqueness. For you, my boy, the lifelong journey will be getting in touch with the truth of who you are and understanding that it is a priceless process without end.

War and Peace

My ten months of active duty and the subsequent six years of reserve meetings were awful. The first night in Fort Dix told me everything I needed to know and I was not a happy soldier.

However, before I go ragging about my military experience, I must tell you an experience that happened years later in Santa Fe, NM. In the summer of '89, I promoted a concert series called Music in the Pines, which I have already mentioned, but deserves its own entry sometime down the road. For some reason, I wanted to hire Vietnam vets to handle parking and security for this series, which was located on the side of the mountain on the way to the ski basin. I got to spend time with these guys during that summe. I began to understand the incredible toll war takes on our soldiers. These guys never recovered and their emotional wounds would bleed all too easy. Every fucken person who fights our idiotic wars are victims, some physically maimed and others emotionally wounded for life.

While it likely sounds terribly trite, violence absolutely breeds violence and solves nothing at all. The perverted idea of supremacy shreds the much more compassionate idea of equality. Every goddamn war has greed and unbounded ego at its core. Human history offers the finest testimony to the complete futility of violence as a solution to any circumstance. The Korean War, the Vietnam War, the wars in Iraq and Afghanistan and God knows the wars that will occur by the time you read this, are a sham. They perpetuate the idea of dominance as the only strategy available to powerful countries and others seeking that same power. It is a flawed idea that has never worked and will never work. As long as there are masters and slaves, wars will be fought and I think the prognosis sucks. This is what we do and what we have always done. The ability to think and feel pretty much separates us from all other sentient beings and while it has served us admirably on so many levels, the one eighty of that has been dark and ugly, the perfect definition of a mixed blessing.

In order to promote democracy around the world, we have invaded countries, killed their people and destroyed their land. I don't know about you, but this is not how you win the hearts and minds of a people. God knows, we are definitely not the poster child country of a democracy and have absolutely no right to show others the way to freedom. We had an opportunity with 9/11, when the world embraced our country, but it was squandered by the blood lust of blame and we created our culprit in Saddam Hussein, who had been our best friend only years before.

I am sure my complete disgust with violence as a solution to any situation will likely be another recurring theme throughout.

Basic training was absolutely surreal, to say the least. I was around twenty-one and most of the kids were in their late teens and from small towns all over the US. Reservists were commingled with regular Army recruits and it was a real culture shock, considering my background compared to theirs. You are constantly being yelled at by some moron about nothing of any consequence. I think it lasted about eight weeks and I was ecstatic when it ended.

Following basic training, I was sent to Fort Devons in Massachusetts. Being part of the Army Security Agency involved getting a top secret clearance, if you can believe that, along with going into rooms that had combination locks on the doors. I learned Morse code for the purpose of identifying "enemy" transmitters. There were a lot of Jewish guys in this unit, all avoiding the draft. One person in particular was very well versed in every single religious holiday and all of us always got off so we could observe them. The best ones fell around a weekend, which allowed us to go back to NYC. A small group of us took an apartment in Boston on Commonwealth Blvd, but I am sorry to say there are no stories to regale you with because it is gone somewhere in my decaying grey matter and they weren't all that thrilling anyway. All of us were single, which meant hitting the Boston bars and things like that. I definitely don't recall getting laid while in uniform.

During that time, I had a brand new, red VW beetle that I wrecked one night on the Grand Central Parkway. I fell asleep and rolled the car, but came out of it without a scratch. The two cops who arrived on the scene were betting I was dead. I realized then that there is a plan for each of us and our lives will end when they are supposed to and there is nothing you can do to prolong it or even shorten it. On that night, the realization came to me that there was plenty of life left and it was simply not my time. The VW was totaled, but the message was clear.

Anyway, the military thing lasted for around six years following my active duty and it was a pain in the ass. I either went to one weekend a month meetings or weekly evening meetings, depending on the unit I happened to be in at the time. Most of the units were very liberal regarding hair; keeping in mind this was the late sixties after all. I had fairly long hair at the time and I would wear a very ugly short wig to my meetings. Several of us would shave the back of our necks, so when the wig was on nothing showed below the line.

My military experience is not one of the highlights of my life and pretty much nothing comes to mind in terms of stories worth sharing. With all the things that have happened to me, this whole thing is very low on my list. My uniforms always looked awful on me because there was not an ounce of vanity on my part to look like a serious soldier.

Back then, when you went away on active duty, your company had to either hold your job or offer you a similar one in its place. Fortunately, my job in the Guest Relations Dept. was no longer available and I ended up working in something called Network Station Clearance. I was responsible for making sure that TV stations affiliated with NBC were carrying as many of the network's programs as possible. These locally owned stations did not have to automatically carry everything the network programmed, so I would spend time on the phone talking to TV stations around the country. I guess the best part was having an office and a secretary. I started wearing suits and carried an attaché case to work. Finally, I was a grown up, praise God.

It really felt like an incredible milestone for a twenty two year old. During my tenure as a page, I had made many friends at the network and there were some hard partiers in that group. Several of the older guys lived in a seven room 'cave" on the corner of Avenue A and Fourth street in lower Manhattan, called the Ageloff Towers. It was an aging, former luxury building from decades before that still had a doorman. I finally moved out of the house and into this circus of a place after my active duty. We would have parties and people would end up in the living room for weeks at a time. Right across First Avenue, the Hells Angels had a brownstone. It was definitely on the edge of civilization and I loved every minute of it. Finally, I could do whatever I wanted. I drank a lot and smoked a lot, both cigarettes and pot. I was a young bachelor, working at a TV network and answerable to no one personally.

This was an interesting crossroads in my life and I likely ended up going the wrong way, but what the hell did I know back then? I was clearly exhibiting bohemian tendencies and I was torn between the suit and the bomber jacket and Honda motorcycle I had acquired soon after taking up residents in the cave. The bomber jacket was a black, cracked leather item with a big white woolly collar. The bike was a small 250cc black motorcycle and I drove it all over Manhattan and took it out on highway traffic. This was my first bike and I survived upright the entire time I had it. It was years before I had another one, but we need to get back to the crossroads issue.

The thing that really captured my attention on that night when I worked the Johnson-Goldwater election in '64 was the excitement of the creative energy of television. Subsequently, I ended up becoming a page and it was the theatricality of that environment, which really got me. Unfortunately, I had no training or familiarity with show business because of a fairly conventional upbringing and one that did not foster creativity. Trust me, not throwing blame or regret around, rather just an observation after all these years on the road less traveled and my reticence to step out all the way back then.

Being on your own is very challenging, especially when you are young. Convention would have had me finding a Jewish, career woman and getting married, living on the East Side in a decorated apartment and eventually moving to an unaffordable home on Long Island, all of which I had the privilege of doing. The road less traveled would have had me setting out on a journey of self-discovery, tapping into whatever creative urge grabbed my attention at the time. Alas, there was just not enough traction there to direct me to that other road.

I was struck with something I need to share. In a way, writing from this vantage point is kind of like cheating, because it is an injustice to the young man back then. It makes me feel a little uncomfortable, as if I have become some wizened guru with all the answers, which is miles from the truth. I think as you get older, you simply get more used to not having the answers. The fuck ups become more familiar patterns and they can be a bitch to change. Acceptance is a lot less challenging and time consuming.

Something

It has been a couple of days since my attempt at recounting a time in my life when I had a choice to make, although I was not terribly aware of it back then. When I was in my early twenties, I could only operate with the emotional and intellectual tools I had at my disposal, just like you at whatever point you are in your life when you read this. While I am separated by many decades from that time, it is all me. I don't like dissecting my life from long ago with tools that have taken years and years to evolve.

Back then, I was living on my own for the first time in my life. I was confused between the predictable life that I was taught to believe in, versus a way of being that I was too young and inexperienced to handle. I was enjoying my freedom and complete lack of accountability to anyone, for the first time in my life. As I have already mentioned, I had befriended a colorful group of guys, many of them well into their thirties.

The choices for me were both personal and professional. In terms of work. I was definitely enamored with the idea of wearing a suit and pretending to be a grown up. I never would have shed that dream because an alternative life style was totally foreign to me. Socially, I was very single and not terribly cool, in spite of the so-called free wheeling times. The scene always made me self-conscious and awfully shy. I didn't know what to do or say, which has pretty much not changed a hell of a lot in all this time.

For now, we will save the woman thing until after we have slogged through the endless number of gigs I have had and manufactured for myself. My personal vocabulary is definitely better suited for those sordid tales, but I want to get all this other stuff down first.

We left me handling station clearance and making sure that the affiliated TV stations all carried Bonanza on Sunday at 9PM, etc. A daytime soap opera was doing very badly because many stations were not carrying it, which diminished its audience and its value to advertisers. An executive from an advertising agency called Young and Rubicam came to see me to talk about this problem for his clients and subsequently offered me a job at the agency, which I took.

Back then and likely true today, media of all kinds is one of the important businesses in New York City. Keep in mind, when I started, there were just three national television program sources and they owned the advertising world. The only way large corporations could reach mass numbers in the US was by advertising on NBC, CBS and ABC. On some minor level, I was part of this elite club. I confess to thinking it was cool back then and I worked my ass off. It was also expected that you change jobs with some frequency in order to move up the ladder within advertising agencies.

I stayed at Young and Rubicam for a couple of years. I think I started working on General Foods, scheduling their dog food and cereal commercials in daytime television. The level of self-importance that some of these agency and network people had was pretty goddamn lame. I basically did what I was told and tried to do quality work. Much of my time was spent making sure I didn't schedule competitive brands together, pretty mundane shit. Regardless, I still got to be part of the club.

I have a confession to make, I find writing about this part of my history extremely boring and difficult to infuse with any excitement. When I was going through it all as a young man, I was totally into it. Being a successful advertising executive was a very attractive trajectory at the time. I married your grandmother in 1969, while still working at NBC and life seemed to be good, although the seeds of my eventual departure had already been planted.

When you are young, you are always waiting for the next birthday, the next chronological milestone in your flight to independence and so-called adulthood. While I may have gotten there numerically, I really don't think I was all that well equipped to make the choices I was making. Doubt rarely enters your mind when you are young and life is filled with promise. There was somewhat of a make believe quality about it all for me. Choices never felt indelible and their long-term consequences didn't seem to be much of a factor, at least in my world. When we are young, we often make such important decisions, ones we are not really capable of making.

And now a word from

I will get back to the work resume, which is feeling monumentally tedious and not all that important. In around twenty some odd years, I worked at four advertising agencies, two cable networks and one television program distributor. I am most alive in my writing when I am passionate and it is challenging to feel passionate about that time in my life. Now, if you asked me back then, my response would likely be quite different, but missing much of the dimension time has provided me now.

Let us get back to the present for a moment, which is where I happen to be spending my time. I have written to you a little about Patrice and shared communication with both of you. I will do it again, but quite differently than the first time. Early this morning, I sent her the following email:

> *"Good Morning*
>
> *I will pass on Thursday. I have this behavior pattern that has been painfully consistent in recent years. I see a woman I consider to be beautiful and I am struck by lightening. Deafness and blindness occur almost instantly. Her story and situation can clearly make her unavailable to me, but in my best Cyrano. I believe love will conquer all. I can go through painful break ups and still return again. I can be told that friendship is the idea and still believe that it is something other than that.*
>
> *If you told me your emotional life is in such painful turmoil, but you were really*

beginning to care about me and could we just move forward delicately, we could talk about it. I know that my writing is effusive and that is likely an understatement. On the other side, I need to get something back and it has to be more than simply finding a convenient slot in your schedule. This Thursday, you are on this side of the island and have a busy schedule, but you want to see some musicians you know at a restaurant. It is not about wanting to spend time with me, even though that is likely true. There are things I need to be told and subtlety doesn't work for me because I am too damn thick headed and completely unaccustomed to hearing a woman tell me sweet things.

My heart is in the right place, but my brain seems to migrate to my posterior.

I believe life is beautiful and that relationships can be beautiful.

Every single word I have written to you has come from my heart and I would take back nothing I have written, said or done. Your emotional plate is spilling over onto the table and it is not your fault. My heart goes out to you because you are a woman who deserves much more from your relationships. I am a guy who wants to be devoted to a woman and I have that within me. Whether I am ever blessed with that situation in my life remains to be seen, but I am worthy of it.

I know I get way ahead of myself much too quickly and it doesn't serve me well. Part of it has to do with the knowledge that this life of ours goes by in a blink and I just want to get to the marrow of it. I have been very unfair and not terribly sensitive to your personal struggles and I apologize. I simply want to be powerfully attracted to a woman and be matched in return and that is likely unreasonable because no two rhythms are ever the same. However, the direction can be the same and it could just take a little time for harmony to happen.

It feels that my attention is perceived as pressure and not embraced for what it is. At the restaurant, I came up behind you and kissed you on the neck. I am not sure why, but it was not a recognition of our friendship. We kissed very affectionately in the car after dinner. I don't know what you are thinking. I am out there pretty good and you are unavailable, because of all that is going on in your life right now. I am emotionally unencumbered and have a boatload of goodies in my heart, but I don't know if you have any room in yours at this moment.

Please, if I am a jerk, off the mark or insensitive, let me know. Tell me to go to hell. Tell me you are incredibly touched by me, but need time to heal a broken heart. Tell me our needs are different at this moment. Tell me absolutely nothing and let it drop. Call if you want to talk. I know if I tried to do this in a conversation, I would have screwed it up and I had a better chance trying to write this to you.

I just don't have it in me to meet for a lite dinner, tell you how beautiful you are, look at you with tremendous affection and then part company and get together again for another lite dinner. In between these meetings, the expressions of affection flow freely from me and while they don't fall on deaf ears, they fall on a wounded heart I cannot heal.

Love Always

Larry"

Shane, this is the bread and butter of life. Here I am at sixty-six, dealing with the same goddamn woman stuff you have likely dealt with already or will certainly deal with in the years to come. For what it's worth, I have no advice at all in matters of the heart. I am a novice and will go to my grave absolutely clueless about the other gender that actually rules the world, although most often in very subtle ways.

When you unselfishly make someone's happiness more important than your own, you have entered heaven on earth and it sure as shit ain't easy. Before you get there, you have to be able to think about why the fuck you are here and what your own life is about. Making someone happy is such a gift. Whether you like it or not, you will likely have your own wrestling match with the best path to follow in the world of relationships. Maybe, I am just giving you a head start, maybe not. To be clear, another's happiness cannot trump your own, unless being compassionate brings you a special happiness. It's the compassion thing.

I literally just spoke with Patrice and it was incredibly touching. I told her two things at the end of our emotional conversation. The first thing was that I would be there for her regardless of circumstance, no questions asked. The second thing was that if her heart was open to a loving, caring man, I am the guy. Trust me, not easy stuff to lay down, even in my grayness.

Here Comes Grandpa Larry

I know I'm not giving you much notice and probably should have mentioned it before, but I had planned a trip to see you guys shortly after I started writing to you a couple of months ago. There was really no point in getting into it until it was happening.

Right now, I am sitting on a plane bound from Phoenix to Newark. I spoke with Andy and he told me it was snowing. He was at Tae Kwon Do with you, which is now a favorite Saturday activity. The ride is incredibly bumpy and very jarring, with the plane jerking up and down and side-to-side, one of my most favorite experiences.

I haven't visited since last July and today is January 21st. I started my flight last night, so my eyes are itchy and my body has no idea what time it is. Uncle Danny has flown in from Israel and we will have a chance to be together. I am coming in typical Hawaiian style, wearing slippahs and dressed for a slight chill. However, the temp is somewhere around 25 with several inches of snow on the ground and I am guaranteed to freeze my ass off. At this point, I am simply hoping we don't get diverted to another airport because of the weather. I am only in for a few days and don't want my time screwed up. I have a real aversion to cold and will likely spend most of the time in your house, although I always go out and run several miles along the Hudson in the morning, regardless of temperature or wind-chill.

It is going to be fun writing to you during this trip. I will tell you about yourself at the ripe old age of three. I am feeling more emotional than usual and I am looking to spread the love while I am with the family.

I began this verbal voyage with you nearly three months ago and it was also on a plane. It is amazing how far this process has come in such a short time. Back then, the beginning of all this had a monumental feeling about it and now, while it is not matter of fact, there is certainly a level of comfort about the process.

Didn't mean to leave you in the lurch about Patrice. By now, you have probably gathered I have these tendencies when it comes to women. As a hopeless romantic, I often venture where the heart has no business going, but I have no desire to change. We will probably see each other on some basis or other and maybe I will be smart enough to take only what she is capable of giving and do the same from my side. The aggravation quotient needs to be kept to a minimum for me because that is not the idea behind relationships.

I had a ball talking with my friend Ken H. last night. He called as I was getting ready for the trip. Sipping a shot of tequila, we had a terrific conversation about women. Ken achieved acting success in his early twenties and he had more adventures with the ladies than any guy has a right to. On Broadway, the beautiful gypsies, who make their livelihood in chorus lines and non-starring stage roles, surrounded him. No matter what the circumstance, women are in charge and it has a great deal to do with sex. They have a different relationship with this powerful force. A man will screw any time at all, but a woman holds the keys and when she is ready, then it is OK for us. We have always been led around by the nose and while it might be a tough pill to swallow for some of us, it is a truth of biblical proportion.

Ken is around my age, but his overall health, including way more weight than he needs to carry, has a lot to do with getting a kidney transplant to replace his failed duo. His adventures are somewhere back in his past and he gets a kick out of the idea that I am still at it. He appreciates the fact that after all these years and all of the heartache and broken relationships, I am still absolutely and totally a fool for love. It is pure poetry for me and is clearly my muse when it comes to this writing business of mine. I can sit at the computer and bang out a tear jerking love letter to a woman without even pausing to think about content. All I do is copy the language of my heart and it is a language only I can hear. It has no sound or letters, it simply flows, in the same way that nature's beauty makes us shine when we bear witness to her achievements.

I have been working very hard these past few months on the feed business I told you about. We deal with heavy machinery, moving dirt, chopping trees, fabricating equipment, putting up buildings, etc. Right now, my hands look like I was in a street fight and lost. I have scabs and open cuts all over. Working in the woods, wearing muddy work boots and using drills, hammers and ratchets was never anything I have done before. Both your Dad and your Uncle have never done any of this kind of work and it was foreign to me until only a couple of years ago. I suspect they will freak out when they see my hands and even voice concern that I shouldn't be doing these things at my age. Something tells me, you know exactly what my reaction will be because you are privy to this confessional and they aren't. Of course, in the strangeness of this time warp of writing to you now, knowing you will read it in fifteen years or so, makes statements like the last one feel a little twisted.

So, you and I will have some fun during the next handful of pages. Other family members will be dropping by. My brother, your great uncle, Marty, will be visiting on Sunday with his wife, Vicky and Andy and Danny's cousin David, their son. Marty and Vicky have twin sons, David and Jonathon. They're good guys and I like spending some time with them. Actually, the last time I was in, it was partially to go to David's wedding to Kendra, which is the last time I saw you. Are you writing all this down because it feels like a scorecard is called for?

We all went to the wedding and stayed in a great house in Woodstock and we had a ball. It was a wonderful change of pace from the usual visit to your home in Hoboken. Personally, I have had my fill of urban living and much prefer being away from large numbers of people and the business of that life style. While I grew up a city boy, that break in my early forties with the journey to New Mexico opened up my internal world in ways that would not have been possible marching on pavement and sidestepping charging throngs of humans.

At some point, we will catch up with the employment history business, but I have revisited it in my head and don't feel inclined to get into much detail. I am so much more comfortable painting my picture with the bright colors of adventure, romance and impulse. Right now, feeling like it is time to put away the machine and I will fire it up when I get to your home. No need to worry, no one will get to see this tome until it is ready. Trust me, they have no idea what I am doing and will likely shit when they read it, but that is down the road some. OK, buddy, until later.

In Bed

Well, I am in bed and trying to get warm. It is pretty damn cold for me, with snow on the ground. Your Dad and Uncle Danny and you picked me up at the airport. I was still dressed for Kauai and leapt into the back seat of his car and there you were, sitting in your car seat and being very animated. It was great to see you again and I was surprised at how comfortable you were with me. It's like you knew that I was Andy's father and Danny's father because there is a strong blood tie between us. We had a ball riding back to your house.

Pretty soon after we all got back from the airport, you had your macaroni and cheese dinner, while we drank large glasses of single malt whiskey. You are going to sleep later now, which means you are likely a part of the adult's dinner more often than not. We had a great time this evening. After you went upstairs to sleep, your Dad, Uncle and myself stepped out to the backyard and split a joint. It is not nearly the first time we have done that, considering both of them have been around it for around twenty years. Trust me, I did not introduce either of them to smoking pot and never would have, but it was unnecessary.

Anyway, we spent the next couple of hours entertaining each other, although I will admit that your uncle is overly preoccupied with violence and machismo issues, which can get a little tiresome, especially at this point in his life. Hey, who am I to question anyone else's way of engaging the world, my son included? We talked some politics and I think your father is a little naive about the extremes our government would go to entrap Americans who are perceived as a threat. Thanks to the horrific tragedy of 9/11, our freedoms have been eroded at a catastrophic pace. Personally, I am not happy about the loss of freedom in the name of patriotism, which seems crazy to me. I am not selling my worldview to anyone, so we ended the evening with some laughs.

I will check back with you later tomorrow evening at the end of the day's activities…………

It's around 11PM now and everyone has left. I am sitting on the made up bed in the room on the second floor opposite Emmy's room. I am pretty tired and can't stay up too long writing to you.

The day started pretty early and I did my usual morning Zen sit and then I went downstairs and your Dad was there with hot coffee already brewed. You and your Mom came down shortly after that and it was great to see you in the morning. You are an incredibly cheerful, outgoing and affectionate little boy. In spite of my limited visits to this point in your life, you have definitely figured out something is up with me. While I am for the moment, Grandpa Larry, there is no way you have any idea that I am Andy's father, but I am somehow in a special place.

After your breakfast, Dad and I went out to run along the Hudson River. I nearly froze my ass off because it wasn't even twenty degrees. My brother, Marty and everyone else showed up around 3P. You had a good time with his son, David, and his wife, Kendra. We had a terrific dinner prepared by your Mother, who is a spectacular cook if I haven't already mentioned it, plus you likely know that by now. You were the life of the party and were completely at home with a houseful of people, who might look familiar, but were still not everyday visitors.

When you are not looking, I really like staring intently at you, trying to catch the subtle changes in your facial expressions. You were/are a very sweet spirit and it would be quite something if you can somehow manage to protect and nurture it, as you grow older and ever so slightly wiser.

OK, kid. It is past my bedtime and I will catch up with you tomorrow.

In the Kitchen

Sitting in the kitchen waiting for you to wake up from your nap. Your Dad and I went to your school today. The letter for the day was L, so Grandpa Larry from Hawaii showed up and spoke to 40 or so of your classmates, ranging in age from 3-5. I had a ball going through the alphabet and using Hawaiian words to explain the letters. V for volcano was clearly the most exciting word and there were endless questions about volcanoes. You were sitting next to me in a little rocking chair and you kept talking to me while I was attempting to explain the letters and words to your friends. I think you were very filled with yourself to have both your grandfather and father there at school.

Tonight, Andrea's mother and father are coming over for dinner. I have always liked Steve very much and have had great conversations in the past about all sorts of things. He and Brenda are very good people and they are very loving. We will eat great food and likely drink too much as well.

Well, I was right on both scores, we ate and drank too much, but all of us had a great time. I liked Brenda and Steve when I first met them. Frankly, it isn't possible for your jewel of a mother to have happened without some very serious nurturing and her parents provided a wonderful home to grow up in. From your standpoint, they are quality people to the max. They dote on you and it is very sweet for me to see.

Dinner was terrific and you were right in there and not being a dick about it. You were very sweet and focused on food and the music of Lady Gaga. As a kind of loner, it was enriching to be a part of such tenderness between people. There is a lot of love in your home, Shane and it makes all the difference in the world. Emmy arrived during dinner and you went wild. She came down and instantly fit in with the family and sat right by your side. Emmy has no mixed loyalties, she is your bodyguard and no harm can possibly come to you as long as she is nearby.

It is a great privilege for me to come in all the way from Kauai just a few times a year and to be welcomed with such love and affection by you, your Mother and Father. I had a world-class talk with Andy today and it consumed three rounds of drinks in the middle of the day to get to it and through it. We talked about some things that went on when he was a child. The substance will remain between the two of us, but the more you can help explain the emotional landscape for a child, regardless of when you tell them, the closer you get them to resolving their conflicted feelings. Of course, that is another reason for providing you with this secret road map into the mind of Grandpa Larry and those who cross his path in this narrative.

Today, me, you, Andy and Danny went to the Brooklyn Children's Museum. You ran around pretty good, from one exhibit to the next, reacting seamlessly to the three of us, clearly something you are getting used to. We came back and left you for a while with Emmy, while the three of us went out for a couple of beers. I have substantive conversations with Andy, but Danny keeps it simple and doesn't usually have much to say, which is fine with me. Everyone was pretty tired tonight and Danny left early, after promising to pick me up tomorrow morning at 4:45A to get me to the airport. This time with you was the most fun yet because you are developing your own spontaneity, which seemingly comes from nowhere. I just think it is your mind getting accustomed to its own ideas and not always operating in response to someone's question or statement.

Homeward Bound

On the way home and on the first leg of the trip, flying from Newark to Phoenix. Sitting in a plane, thousands of feet above the ground provides a great perspective on the visit that just ended.

You are a terrific kid, a joyful and engaging spirit. I like to watch your face, partially because it is so sweet and you also happen to be very good looking. I hope I get a chance to see you grow into a young man with all of the uncertainty that will come along with your evolution.

I really love your Dad very much. We had a very bumpy time when he turned twenty and looked at a much larger landscape than he was used to. It is the world after college and as it approaches, some young people are thrown back into their internal world, where they can do some important repair work or repress their shit and carry it on their back, very often for the rest of their life. In the case of Andy, he met his demons head on and the result so far has been the development of a special human being.

He is a protective Father, which makes all the sense in the world at this point in your early life. We will see how comfortable both he and your Mom are in allowing you more and more freedom to take more and more chances. I know he thinks I am writing some kind of innocuous children's book to you, with only occasional departures into naughtiness. We are definitely going to blow their minds with this collection.

It is always fun to talk with Andy and Danny about our time together, after I left their home, replaced by weekends and several weeks during the summer, which took over our history early on in their development. In many cases, their memories are clearer than mine. Aside from their reminiscing about our time in Brooklyn together, they actually remembered a woman I was seeing right around the time I left for New Mexico. Her name is Helen and she will now get included in the stories of the women I was fortunate enough to spend time with during my life.

I did the best I could back then with my boys. We spent around ten years together when I was the single parent, caring for my sons during our weekends and vacations. I know there were plenty of good memories because they recount them to me when we get together these days. I was miles away from perfection and I am no closer these days, but I took my role very seriously back then and I guess that is still the case.

As I have told you a number of times before, this exercise is still an experiment. There is no road map for me to follow and this is an improvisational theatre of my mind. I still wonder if there is enough inside to make this a tale worth telling. I haven't completely let go of the page counting consciousness and will likely feel some sense of accomplishment once I hit the century mark, which I am closing in on. Still, when I abbreviate some stories or episodes, I am always concerned about being too cryptic and losing precious pages. Of course, the other side of this is that I simply started writing because I wanted to share my life with you, whatever that ended up looking like.

Hopefully, there will always be unfinished stories from the past to tell, while I ride one tangent after another in the world of the moment.

These past five days of travel have allowed me to rest my body a little, which gets pretty beat up during my day life at home. There is plenty of heavy lifting and lots of other work that physically stresses my joints and muscles. My shoulders have been very sore because of the lifting and I am hoping they have had a little time to heal. I arrived with some fresh cuts on my fingers, which were a never-ending source of attention from you. We even put band-aids on the boo boos, partially so you wouldn't keep looking and asking questions about whether it hurt or how I got them. I get back to work for Thursday and Friday and I will try and finish out the week without adding to my war wounds.

Your Mother and Father have been so wonderful to me that I can't begin to tell you how appreciative I am. They go out of their way to keep me in your world by reminding you about Grandpa Larry in Hawaii. Their attention has helped to bridge the gap created by our infrequent get togethers. This last visit may have actually cemented me in your consciousness and I will try and keep it fresh by using Skype and allowing us to see each other.

On the second leg of the trip home and I have a little bit of juice left in the computer battery. I have pretty much given you a summary of the events of our time together, but I am hard pressed to share the feelings with you as they are strong ones and not easy to call up at will.

I have known your Dad and Danny from the moment they took their first breath. I held each of them in the crook of my arm, fed them and changed their diapers. After I separated from your grandmother, seeing them was the highlight of my life. I always tried to make our time together exciting. We spent summers on Long Island and in a farmhouse in Honesdale, PA. where they still remember shoveling cow pies in the barn.

They traveled to see me in New Mexico a number of times and we had a ball. Maybe I will remember to ask them how old they were on the first trip. They were city boys and I was living a pretty rural life, which was a real change for them and I know they enjoyed it. The highlight had to be our camping trips. We would go for several nights and we would always be in a spectacular setting. We would throw Frisbees, footballs and softballs, all provided courtesy of yours truly. Sitting around a campfire at night is one of the best parts of any camping trip. You spend time gathering the wood before dark and then you get it going before it is totally black.

The whole divorce thing for me was particularly painful, because as a kid, I decided that if I ever had children, I would never leave them. As you know, my father died just before my tenth birthday. Divorce and death are no different in the eyes of a child and I somehow managed to screw their lives up by leaving them. I never tried to make it up to them or become victim to the guilt. I just chose to love them as best I could, regardless of the circumstances and hoped it work out in the long run. I hid very little from them and they got to see me throughout our relationship as a pretty honest guy. Remember, I said honest, not perfect. The story behind my leaving is not really for you to know, but I have been pretty candid with your Dad.

Here we are, all these years later and my boys are men. Not only that, one of them has become a Father and I get to see him love his son the way I loved him. This circle of love is a blessing that I am humbled to experience each time I visit you guys. I try not to behave like the patriarch of the clan because I think it is unbecoming. However, I can take a very quiet pride in the wonderful son I have helped raise and I get to see him treat you with devotion and adoration and love. Shane, I am a lucky man.

Think I am going to call it quits for now. We will see what the next sit down brings up for us. Might be time to go off on a tangent, but who knows?

Didn't Plan On It

I finished the above entry last night, sometime after getting back from the visit to you. There was no plan to write you tonight and I actually figured a break was in order, partially because I was feeling a little rut bound. I don't want to lose my way in this opus, while continually re-finding my voice. The idea of what I wanted to do is clear to me, but at times the subject matter feels like it's getting away from the voice I am comfortable with.

The trip was everything I could have hoped for. You are an absolutely terrific little guy and it was such a joy to spend the time I did with you.

The truth is I mostly care about what I am thinking or doing right now and recounting history misses a passion I simply can't give it. We will get to the jobs, some of which were routinely boring and the later ones have some good stories tied to them.

It's around 7PM on Thursday, January 26, 2012, which will anchor us in time for your purposes. It was my first day back at work and it turned out to be a wet one. Most of what we need to do now is outside work, so it does slow us down, but we still have to keep at it. The rains on Kauai can be very intense and while they make the island the vibrant place it is, it is still a pain in the ass every now and then. Feeling a little tired because I do put my sixty six year old body through quite a bit these days. Nursing a very sore shoulder and there are healing cuts on both my hands. My left leg is also challenged because of a fairly catastrophic incident in my life, which will be recounted sometime in this coming February, around the anniversary of the event, which caused my delicate condition.

Sitting in front of the screen and the sun set over an hour ago. The rain persists this evening and it is often a very comforting feeling to hear its muted percussion all around. Drinking some wine, smoking just a touch and listening to some good acoustic music on the local, public radio station. These are some of the times when this process feels very creative and visceral to me. I am in my space and I am in the moment, focused only on this communication to you.

Back to being alone again and shining the light on the latest mirage, which would be Patrice. I think I want to have a relationship I deserve, one that has been earned while on my journey of self-discovery. If you were asked to paint your life at whatever time you get to read this, you likely wouldn't feel it was being done in some indelible medium because there is so much time ahead for you. In my case, it wouldn't be crazy to think about long term as not being as long term as it used to be and to take what I do today a little more seriously. It doesn't mean you stop having fun, it means you have a different kind. When I use the word "seriously", I am saying that I understand the consequences of my choices.

I have an extremely active internal dialogue and one that has been going since I was a young kid. There is a part of the process that involves the invisible vocabulary of this kind of communication and I am aware of writing this conversation since the beginning, although it has been in indelible mental ink. This is probably why there is a natural quality about this writing for me. I think I mentioned this somewhere upfront in my writing to you; this is meant to be nothing more than eavesdropping on my internal chats. In addition, if you don't encumber your mind with propriety, it's amazing the places it will take you.

Anyway, it looks like we are going to be flying solo for a while and that will become its own story to share. Frankly, I knew Patrice was not going to work out at all well. The immediate hit you get about most anything, including a relationship, is usually on the money. After all these years and a number of relationships, I still haven't gotten it right yet. Who knows?

Getting a Leg Up

I wrote just above that I would save the leg story until it got closer to its anniversary, which happens to be February 17, 2005. However, it is actually bothering me tonight a little ahead of schedule and I have only passing concern that it might be infected. It is hard to tell some times because it is an unusual circumstance and one I tend to minimize, in fear of becoming a nutcase about it. Obviously, there is a happy medium to be found. Sorry, let's get back to the story.

I was canoeing with five other people in Hanamaulu Bay, likely the dirtiest of the island's beaches. A big wave took us from behind and my shin was pushed hard into the bench in front of me. It was cut to the sheath around the bone. I was in the water for at least another 45 minutes trying to get into shore. When I got out, I drove myself to the Emergency Room of Wilcox Hospital and one of the paddlers followed behind.

When I saw the ER Doc, he cleaned the wound and sewed it up, which was traumatic all by itself. I asked him about antibiotics to preclude infection because of the dirty water and he did not agree because I was not infected at that time, an incredibly stupid call by any stretch of the imagination, considering it occurred less than an hour before.

Thirty-six hours after that, it was clearly infected and not looking good. I went to my physician at the time and all he did was cut a stitch to let it drain and give me some sample antibiotics prescribed for upper respiratory infection. The next day, I was in serious trouble and went to the emergency room. A terrific young doctor named Gregg met me and he was key in saving both my leg and my life. I went into surgery right away to remove the infection.

I stayed in the hospital for two weeks and had two more surgeries to debride the wound. They were very concerned about saving my leg and my life was clearly in danger during part of my time in the hospital.

It is impossible to go further and not mention Laura. We had started seeing each other a couple of months before the accident and it was quite a time for her. She was a nurse and a damn good one, so she became my advocate at the hospital. I was very screwed up and without her divine oversight I can't imagine the possibilities. She saved my ass at the hospital and during the aftermath, which took months. She was a totally stand up broad, in the absolute best sense of the word.

After the surgeries, I came home for a month of healing, followed by a return to the hospital for plastic surgery. This is probably a good time to mention that I never looked at my leg from the time I had my first surgery until the bandages were removed after plastic surgery, which took up about seven weeks. I experienced unimaginable pain during my time at home. If my leg was down for more than twenty seconds, it would hurt unbearably. I was on crutches. I gave myself meds through a shunt, a series of exposed portals that led into one of the veins in my chest.

Every other day while at home, a nurse would come to change the dressing on my leg, which was hooked up to a small suction machine that covered the wound. She would change the dressing and each time be forced to rip off fresh growing skin around the wound. My response to this excruciating pain varied from singing, to crying to gritting my teeth.

I was alone in my place the majority of the time and getting around on crutches was quite an ordeal, considering I couldn't keep my leg down for more than a handful of seconds. My wonderful neighbors would often bring me food at night, but I had to fend for myself during the day and it was really tough. During this period, Laura would come over in the evening and my heart would just fly at the thought of her coming into my space. By caring for me and about me, she helped my healing. We will talk much more about her when we get there.

Following the skin graft, I stayed in the hospital for another week and was not allowed to move, beyond shifting myself onto a repository for my byproducts. I think my Zen practice helped me immeasurably during the period, but being close to death and actually feeling it was the game changer. It is impossible to describe, but on some pre-conscious level I was damn sure death was around me.

I came out of the grafting experience and had to wait until it was possible to move around without too much pain and then started rehabbing my leg. I went to rehab with a total commitment of getting my leg back. I worked my ass off every day without exception. At home, my therapy consisted of three, hour-long sessions, repeating the mobility and strengthening exercises provided by rehab. It was absolutely awful and without a dogged determination, I would have been physically compromised for the rest of my life and I knew it.

Subsequent to the actual experience, the doctors informed me of the severity of the injury. My last session with the plastic surgeon had him advising me what I would have to deal with regarding my leg. Having no feeling is the least of the problem. There is very little skin over my shin because so much flesh was removed and as a result it is subject to injury and bleeding at the drop of a hat.

Truthfully, I have no idea how I got through the whole thing. I think it was my Qi, my life force that lifted me out of this awful trap because there is no other plausible reason. Aside from having to be conscious of the leg, the entire experience definitely changed me. When death has been at your door, it is hard to take anything else all that seriously. However, it has made me a much more passionate man because I got really close to the invisible side of life. I was in very bad shape and it is a minor miracle that I have my leg and that I am running, doing yoga and working in the field today.

The subtext to this story is that I had no medical coverage and I wanted to sue for malpractice. There was no question in my mind that the two first doctors I interacted with were negligent in their standard of care. Nine lawyers later, it was clear that I would have a terrific case if I were dead or permanently impaired. My devotion to my healing was an impediment to a malpractice suit and I gave up the fight. The original bill was around $50k and interest and penalties likely have ballooned it to nearly $100k. The statute of limitations sets in after seven years, which is this particular anniversary. Frankly, I think they would have gone after me if they didn't find there were serious procedural fuck ups on their part.

Well, there you have it, the saga of my left leg. As awful as the entire experience was, I feel blessed to have gone through it and survived on the other end. Far more than my leg was changed on February 17th.

Your Guess Is As Good As Mine

In the solo mode, Saturday is relatively predictable day. I take my time after my sit and don't hurry the yoga or the follow up run. I might diddle around a little after that. In whale season, which is right now, I will get my act together and take the kayak out in search of these magnificent creatures. It is nothing short of a privilege to be allowed in their presence. Surf was too rough today and after my beer I didn't feel like working against the trades and the unpredictable waves that happen in high wind, so I made my way back.

Got home and cleaned my gear, a part of the ocean kayaking ritual. Up next, cleaning the bike for tomorrow's ride. I've got it down to around a half hour by now and nobody can see what I missed. Then, I buzz cut my hair with a number 6 blade, a change from my long time use of number 5. I let my hair grow a little longer than usual on my visit to you and the full head of silver hair makes me look just an ounce more attractive and what else matters?

Ran out to get a bottle of wine and some sushi as an appetizer for my dinner, which is, of course, one of the Gourmet Meals for Single Dummies. This one is a pasta and shrimp dish and I am sure it will get me going when I have it, sometime after nightfall. Got some sweet acoustic music in the background and all is good right now.

Music has come up yet again. I hope there is lots of music to listen to that gets your body moving and transports your mind to some other place. I have likely loved music for sixty years because I connected with it early on and I have had the good fortune to live through many incarnations of the sounds people are listening to. When the doors of

Rock 'n Roll blew open and grabbed the attention of young people, the roots of this music in Blues, Country, Jazz and Gospel also got the attention they deserved. My musical listening life has been very, very rich and increasingly eclectic. I certainly don't think I am the poster child for the mantra of Sex, Drugs and Rock 'n Roll, however I would never deny the significance they have all played and still play in my life. I say thank God for that.

Probably OK to balance my musical riffing with a bit more on my NYC employment record.

When last we caught up with Mr. Feinstein's employment history, he was working at an ad agency by the name of Young and Rubicam. He worked in the TV Programming Dept. and the use of the word "programming" predates the computer thing. It refers to a time when advertiser's actually placed programming on the television networks. My job was to put major advertiser's dollars on network television and that basically didn't change at the four agencies I worked for as I made my way up the ladder. Agency number two was Ogilvy and Mather. Worked for a really wonderful guy there by the name of Art. There were plenty of egomaniacal assholes in that industry and he was on the other end of the spectrum. The next stop was Doyle, Dane, Bernbach. The guy I worked for was a bit of a wild Irish man and it made work much more exciting. My responsibilities were considerably more substantial than at the first two agencies.

Doyle, Dane, Bernbach was the agency I was fired from and the only job that ever left me before I left it. I had actually worked for the person responsible for the firing at the previous agency and thought I had a good relationship with him. Corporations eat people and shit them out whenever and wherever they feel like. The bottom line is like a line in the sand for them and they will do anything to preserve it. The personnel floor was like a morgue and everyone was in dark clothing. I had to endure this idiotic ritual within an hour of getting the news. It was a totally horrific experience, going home to a heavily mortgaged house, two young children and a relatively shitty marriage. This is when I had my run with the Mafia and the hot 8 tracks I told you about earlier.

After around six months, I was finally hired by Dancer, Fitzgerald, Sample and stayed there for a record breaking six years. I even got profit sharing with this gig. There were some really good people there. Six years is a long time to be in an office environment with a fairly consistent population. I worked as hard as anyone else to make client deadlines, etc. During my tenure, it became obvious that I was not going to be given the responsibilities I could handle because I was slowly becoming an iconoclastic figure within that business. There were people not nearly as smart as me getting fat jobs and I realized it was time to move away from that side of the industry.

The other side is sales and it is always a very forgiving place as long as you surpass your numbers and it doesn't give much of a shit about anything else. When you don't make your sales forecast numbers for a certain period of time, they are as equally unforgiving. I moved over into media sales for one of the early successful cable networks, called the USA Network.

The transition to selling was a little jarring, but I didn't have great difficulty. Pressure comes with any sales job and I was able to avoid freaking out from it all. It was not an easy sell back then because the whole idea of network cable television was still pretty knew. It was the very beginning of the fragmentation of electronic media and God only knows where it will be when you read this. Selling is a serious business and it only cares about results. In the early days of cable, it was pretty damn hard to sell advertisers on the medium.

After a couple of years at USA Cable Network, I moved over to something called The Financial News Network, a precursor to many of the business channels that proliferate cable today. The initial offer sounded great, but the reality was a little more challenging. I didn't stay long before moving to The Weather Channel, yes, The Weather Channel. Somehow, someone managed to make a national cable network that dealt with weather, 24 hours a day, 7 days a week, 52 weeks a year until you choke on the weather. It ultimately became a relatively successful, nationally distributed network and is still around all these years later.

Right around then, my internal fuse had been lit and it was only a matter of time until I walked from it all. My final job in the City was with All American Television. It was run by a bona fide character in the broadcasting business, George. I was the VP of Advertising Sales and actually had a fairly significant amount of pressure on me because it was my responsibility to deliver the advertising dollars to support their efforts. Several people worked under me and I was very chill with all of them. I was definitely not into busting chops; rather I worked much more personally. I actually dated the sister of one of the sales people I hired. Candace, the woman I dated, deserves her own planet in the small galaxy of women I have known, in the biblical sense and otherwise. Anyway, the office was very relaxed and often on Friday afternoon, I would go into George's office and get high with him and another friend or two.

Ultimately, my time ran out on the life I was living. I let my hair grow and pierced my ear and made plans to move to Santa Fe, which is a very long story and a stand alone in terms of tales to tell. Actually, that might be a good story to tell, but I have to make sure that I haven't talked too much about the move earlier. I am close to starting at the beginning of this tale and reading forward in order to clean it up and take stock of what has already been shared. I would look like an asshole if I kept repeating the same story and I would prefer not to be cast in that light. I have been at this for quite a while now and without keeping notes, I am not completely clear on what is out and what is gestating in the wings.

Back

It was a very big deal picking up the show and moving to Santa Fe. When I was at All American Television, my last job in NYC, I bought my little adobe womb out on the Cerrillos Flats, just outside of Santa Fe. My plan at the time was to visit my place in New Mexico periodically, but I simply couldn't live the life I was living and just had to go full bore on the journey.

I can't talk about Santa Fe without bringing Norma into all of this, even though I was going to deal with the ladies at some time in the future, I feel like talking about her now.

I know I mentioned I spent my early thirties to early forties in therapy with two different guys. I met Norma in a group therapy environment and I was thunderstruck. She came into the room wearing a white lacey outfit with sandals that leather laced up her calf in a very dangerous look. She was a statuesque beauty by any standard you would want to employ. She was an actress with a fairly decent career as a young woman in England and was here trying to make a go of it. She was in an awful marriage to a guy who was living on the west coast and their interaction was minimal and never pleasant.

In the therapy environment, I got to know Norma very well and she heard a lot about my past during these scheduled sitdowns. One of the rules of this therapist was that people in group were not allowed to get together in a relationship. Well, I was feeling that after seven years or so of fairly intense therapy, it was time to move away just a little. I couldn't think of a better way of getting drummed out of group therapy than getting together with Norma. There was a strong connection between us during the several years of group therapy and I didn't have to twist her arm.

In all my life I have never, ever been with such a magnificent embodiment of beauty than Norma. She was close to my height and had the grace of a swan. Sometimes, I would catch her sleeping, with the covers below her knees and her entire hip and more was exposed to the light, like some perfect marble rendering. It would just blow my mind. In many ways, I got to live any guy's fantasy about being with a truly gorgeous woman and spending plenty of time with her.

My relationship with Norma lasted over a period of ten years, with two lives. In the beginning, we had a talk about getting together for a drink, which we did. We went back to her place and I had a spectacular time and was hooked on her. This was in the early eighties. It didn't take long for me to share my boys with her and she was amazing and blew their minds. She was wonderful with them and we spent quite a bit of time together as a couple and the boys were right in there. We had some great adventures and your Dad and Uncle will never forget Norma.

She was married during this whole time, which added an element of danger I could have done without. I don't know why they stayed together and after a time, she wanted out and it took quite a while for him to go along. It is impossible to figure out why so many people get together and stay together.

Anyway, one night, she told me she got an acting gig with the New Mexico Repertory Theater. It required her being away for around two months, which was far too long for me to be apart from her. I met her out there one weekend and not only did we have a fabulous time together, I really felt a strong desire to live out in this part of the country because of its incredible beauty and open space.

We split up for the first time and I don't remember why or exactly when. However, it did leave me wondering if I was drawn to Santa Fe because of its connection to Norma or because I was drawn to the place. Less than a year after we split, I visited there again and within three days, I bought my place in New Mexico. There was never a doubt in my mind that this part of the country was just what the doctor ordered.

I reconnected with her sometime after moving west. She had moved to Los Angeles and was closing in on her divorce. We got together again and saw each other in LA and at my adobe paradise in the Cerrillos Flats.

I was getting increasingly into simplifying my life, partially because of my Zen practice, which bloomed out there. I was getting into a fairly basic way of living and Norma was accustomed to a level of comfort that I could neither afford nor want for myself. The second incarnation was not as long as the first, but it was not short on drama. This time around, I helped her through her actual divorce and even traveled to LA one weekend to help her move into her own space as a free woman.

I think we would have had an awful time of it if we actually got together at that point. I was having vagabond tendencies and didn't see how either one of us would alter our lives for the other at that time. It was a very unpleasant split up that I actually initiated because I didn't want to get together on the basis that we would spend the rest of our lives coupled, because that would have been the direction we would have gone in under those circumstances. She was very angry with me and I just remember sitting on the floor of my little adobe home, balling my eyes out after we hung up the phone. In addition to the awful pain and finality, I was certain our lives were on very different trajectories, but I really did love her.

I learned a lot about beauty and the kind of traps it poses on these recipients of great genes and outstanding looks. They are just like us and nobody allows them that courtesy, rather being more comfortable with the idea that they have it knocked. Norma had her share of demons about her appearance. I repeatedly told her, with all sincerity, that she was most magnificent when she awoke in the morning and I got to see her face.

There are really only several other women in my life that are in that very small pantheon of being life-changing experiences for me. God Bless You, Norma. I know where you are and you will live at least as long as I have you in my heart.

I Wonder

It is another evening and I am still very affected by my sharing Norma with you. The last time I spoke with her, she had remarried a very nice guy, but she had bone cancer and it didn't sound very good, in spite of her marvelous way of dealing with it. There are some stories that never end and Norma is one of those stories for me. After all this time, I hold on only to the sweet memories because that is the true, sane payoff for dealing with the inevitable, inescapable problems and issues that arise between two intimate people. If my memories are any measure, I am so far in the plus column, you couldn't squeeze anything other than love out of me for her right now.

Who knows why some relationships survive and others do not. Norma has been with me since the evening I first laid eyes on her many, many years ago and she is still with me after all this time. My boy, it is this idea that keeps me out there, looking for a lady to be with for the foreseeable future, which would be glorious. To a certain degree, that has also been behind some of my choices over the decades. I have also been somewhat unfair to these ladies by not separating my desire for a strong relationship with the realities of whatever our circumstances were at the time. I am either all in or all out and have been that way for a very long time. It has sometimes gotten me into relationships too quickly and at other times has pushed the other person away.

I am thinking at this point that I am going to vibe a woman liking me and wanting to be with me and not being shy about it. Long before I was ever born, it was always the guy who had to take the initiative and I believe many women are still under its spell, but there are many ladies who have gotten out from under that bullshit and they have shed the myth of their impotence.

It must be just a little strange to read this, considering it is being written by your

Grandpa Larry. You know, writing to you in the present about my work, the women in my life and all sorts of other stuff means that nothing really changes as you get older. I know that most everything I am sharing with you is going to resonate deep within you at some point in your own life. I am keeping it pretty close to the ground on this written journey. Over the thousands of years, our basic humanity has not changed one fucken iota. What I am writing to you has a primal quality about it and that voids the age difference and probably gives it a bit of a timeless quality as well, if I do say so myself.

You know, I have been wondering what kind of world you will be in. I think I probably mentioned somewhere before that predicting your world is outside my purview. However, I can tell you how I feel about where we are right now as a country and as a planet. At this point in time, I am definitely not the bearer of good tidings.

I know there are still plenty of tales to tell about my very spotty professional past because I believe we left me leaving my last job in NYC and heading to Santa Fe. There are a number of women I must tell you about as well. Living in the paradise of the Southwest for years and now in heavenly Kauai also leaves much to be shared between us.

So, I think I am going to head toward the one hundred page mark by getting off on where I believe we are at now and what I think the world will look like in less than twenty years. Between now and laying down that particular prognostication effort, I will think about this mini-treatise of ours and the milestone of actually writing nearly one hundred pages, the most I have ever written hands down. I think applause would be appropriate at this juncture.

OK, I have to go now. My clothes are coming out of the dryer and I want to get to them before they wrinkle. This thing that I want to get into deserves a clean start, no laundry pun intended. I like the idea of focusing my attention this way and it will be interesting to share with you our present cluster fuck and its repercussions in the years to come.

My Prerogative

One of the many cools things about writing this is I can change my mind about anything at all in the process because it is mine and mine only. I am not sure I need to get into some kind of focused diatribe on how completely fucked up the world is and likely beyond our ability to repair.

However, if I did, I would probably start with the Buddha, primarily because I am totally in line with what he is alleged to have said over 2.500 years ago. I am no student of Buddhism and would never imply that was the case, but my endless attraction to Zen is that we are all the Buddha and our very simple task is to embody that Truth. According to the Big Man, tremendous inequities in a society are at the core of their greatest challenge. Today, we have an unbelievably huge gap between rich and poor in America and all over the world. Personally, I am not one who believes this behavior will ever change and to one degree or another, the past several thousand years have borne out that predilection within all dominant cultures. On a macro level, what we have done, we will continue to do.

The economic inequities fuel the anger between the societal bookends. The level of discourse in America right now is about as strident as it could possibly be. On the plateaus of power, no one ever tells the truth. Down on the ground, no one seems to understand their reality is being manipulated, regardless of how they lean. The sides are awfully righteous and blind to the realities on that very ground. While one will never find it, the quest for the truth is what matters most. What are the best qualities of our species and how do we bring them to the fore? We never stop to think about what makes us human and how we can live up to the enormous responsibility every other sentient and non-sentient being has placed on our shoulders, from a blade of grass to a pebble in a stream to a redwood to a whale.

If past is prologue, you are walking into an absolute shit storm. I can't imagine the price of oil and what sacrifices were made as the reality of a diminishing supply began to sink in to the global psyche. I do not pretend to know what unknown energy source will mushroom just like oil and create a seamless move across this unavoidable gap. Today, there is nothing in the pipeline, so to speak, with any remote shot at replacing the cheap energy generation of good ole petroleum. Energy is a big one and I personally don't see anyway at all to avoid a painful rip in the fabric of society as a result of the hardships brought on by increasingly expensive oil. Trust me, the environment will pay an awful price for the extrusion of oil and gas from below its skin. The rich will absorb it and everyone else will suffer.

The direction of our political system is absolutely fuck awful. Money has completely polluted the process beyond any recognizable semblance of a democracy. Politicians pander and stand for nothing beyond whatever is expedient for their re-election. The forces of corruption and abuse of power kick any president in the genitals before he or she gets to sleep one night in the White House. Once again, I am not even remotely optimistic that this will change by the time you read this. God only knows what the cost of being President will have mushroomed to and what added compromises come with the tab.

There is no room for compassion in the current political rhetoric. Today, you have to be able to help yourself regardless of what circumstances life may have dealt you at the moment. Nobody needs help anymore in this uncompassionate world. Independence can breed irresponsibility regarding the plight of those around us and compassion withers on the vine.

Governments are failing financially, socially and politically all around right now. When I was growing up, I figured countries would kind of stay the way they are, albeit with mythical relationships thrown in from the indigenous of those lands. Most of Europe, with the exception of England, decided to have their own currency, the Euro. I am not sure that one size fits all, especially in such an old part of the world, where blood history runs very deep. So far, I am not hearing any terribly encouraging news on that front. There seem to be implosions occurring across the world with financial markets, human rights abuses, environmental degradation and a host of other nauseating goodies.

The countries we have already invaded and others we will likely visit in the future, are each one worse off than before we got there to offer redemption. Our policies are about control and not about freedom. There are thousands of nameless martyrs, who have stood up to the bullets in Tunisia, Egypt. Libya and all over the African continent, which I think is what they deserve to be called in the broadest sense. My guess is that whatever vacuum gets created by freedom fighters, it will be replaced by just another cabal of the powerful, whether by bullet or bible.

Pretty sure I ran off on technology before this moment. I wouldn't even hazard a guess what that world will be like in techno terms. At some point, ethics is inevitably going to cross swords with technology. The incredible power and possibility of technology will run into the basic global human right of privacy. I also think this is a train wreck in the works. The powerful thrive on information and the more they know, the more powerful they become. I am not giving a line of shit here, for what it is worth.

I just don't know how things are going to shake out in your time. I think about my life here and all I have gotten to experience and make part of who I am. Hell, I got to ride on the rock 'n roll train when it was just leaving the station. There we men of promise, like John F. Kennedy, his brother, Bobby and Dr. King, cut down by an evil that lurks within many of us. The Sixties were an indescribable time for many and even the witnesses were affected by it. The story today is about technology and the endless number of ways to communicate and share, in addition to having our stories collected by third parties and suffering the loss of that precious privacy, a basic tenet of America, supposedly.

My ride has been incredible and I just don't know what yours will be like. In my youth, society exploded and made young people influential citizens in the course of events. In many ways, the Sixties gave this gift of youthful self-worth a life all its own. It was wonderful to be around, regardless of whether the flower was your power or not. Those folks actually thought they could change the world back then.

Frankly, I am not sure it is possible to top my time here, in terms of what I have witnessed and been a part of. For you, the past is a tall order to follow and I simply can't venture a guess what your universe will look like. I may be lucky enough to be around, but the luck thing makes me a little nervous at the same time. All of this is being written to be read by you, whether I am fortunate enough to be breathing or not.

Word From My Leg

I know I have told you the story of the leg accident and briefly mentioned in passing a couple of weeks ago that my leg was bothering me. Well, it kept bothering me and the cut was not healing properly. A couple of days ago, I picked up a nasty odor coming from this small wound. Having no feeling in the leg as a result of the earlier accident doesn't help to figure out if there is surface pain and whether something is actually wrong. The truth is, when any wound begins to smell like a wet dog, I should have realized I was definitely fucked up and needed to see a doctor ASAP.

The above occurred after a normal morning of sitting, yoga and running. I was beginning to think something was not right. Without thinking about all this, I called my friend, Michael, whom I have written to you about earlier on. The moment I told him about the leg stink, he told me to hang up the phone and get to a doctor immediately.

Fortunately, my doctor was in on a Saturday morning, the day of this occurrence. I know him pretty well and I am familiar with his disposition, which is very relaxed with me, but not this time. He looked at my shin and said the bone sheath was exposed and there was infection, which could actually be serious. I could tell he was a little concerned about the infection, especially considering my history with that same leg. Keep in mind, I am writing this before knowing any outcome, just addressing the experiences today.

I am not taking this lightly. Regardless of how many times I write about my experience with my leg, there is no way to describe the true nature of that accident because it was off the charts of our normal vocabulary. The facts might lose a little focus, but those feelings are always crouched nearby and they will spring at a moment's notice. They came up very hard today, especially at the doctor's office. When he wrapped my lower leg in gauze with an ace bandage outside, I was right back in that time in my life when I teetered between here and gone.

Fortunately, I have you to talk to and it is a tremendous relief for me. No one could possibly understand what that challenging time was about for me. The journey was its own little epic and I have tried to distance myself from it. However, the fact is, my leg was seriously compromised seven years ago and I can't ever forget that.

The doctor's advice was to treat the leg with special care until we meet in about three days, at which time he will check on my leg and have lab results regarding the nature of the infection. I am stuffing my face with antibiotics and we will see what happens. It could be fairly serious or not too big a deal. I don't know, but when I do, I will report back.

It is hard to focus on anything else right now. I was dumb enough to ask if I could run and the Doc looked at me like I was delusional. I have to baby the leg and I will do just that. You will not have to worry long, because it could pop up in the next few paragraphs, On the other hand, I get to sweat these next few days, hoping my body will rise to the occasion and take care of business.

No News

Writing the night before my second appointment with my doctor, who has already made an appointment with a surgeon right after we got together. I know my doctor is being hyper-cautious and I much prefer more attention than less, especially when it comes to my leg.

The idea of seeing a surgeon about my leg conjures up the worst possible memories I can imagine. At the risk of being repetitious, I was actually close to death in the aftermath of my canoeing debacle. It is hard to top being in the same room as the Grim Reaper for shits and grins. I honestly and truly do not want to go back there. The thought of any additional surgery on this poor leg of mine does not make me happy.

Then, I think about being starkly alone in this world and having absolute no one I can share this with who could conceivably understand what this does to me. Being completely unattached certainly has its virtues, but not during a time like this. This idea of communicating we have created for ourselves affords me the opportunity to talk to myself and grounds me for that little bit of extra strength. I have to take whatever comes my way and I am feeling up for the challenge, yet again.

I could say whatever I want, but the bottom line for me is going to be what I find out about my leg tomorrow. I can make you a deal right now and that is I am going to be here a while, because I have barely gotten started in our little conversation. Tomorrow is likely to be eventful for me and I will share with you whatever happens. I wish you could pray for me, but it would be a little late in coming.

Before I sign off, I will throw in another musical target. Find Mel Torme and listen to him. He is very different from what you will likely be listening to at this time in your life, but his ability to stylize everything he sang is amazing. He had a unique sound and a butt load of folks were into that kind of music. I have embraced all music for a long time, at least from the time of my crossing from NYC to Santa Fe. Once there, I realized I loved all music and if I liked it, the genre was inconsequential.

I love writing with music in the background, provided it feels synchronous with wherever I am at. This thing of ours feels much more like composing a life when there is music to provide a soundtrack for the words. Sitting home alone in the evening, a couple of wines and bongfuls to show for it, I am right here, right now.

Let's kick some leg ass tomorrow. Stay tuned.

Pins and Needles

I know you have been unable to eat or sleep, worrying about the outcome of my leg drama. It's all good. I have dodged a bullet. Went to see a surgeon today and she told me she thought it would be much worse. I figured that was an excellent beginning for the prognosis. The only hassle is that my shinbone is exposed and infection lurks in the background, along with hoping that new skin will grow over the wound in order to avoid a skin graft. Having had a big fat skin graft on this leg seven years ago, I can tell you it completely sucks and I would avoid it at all costs.

I have been ordered to forego whale season on the kayak because ocean water is awful for a deep wound like mine. I can't run until she says it's OK. I will have to bug her about the running, but all of it is a very small price to pay, considering the severity of the alternatives. Being a stubborn mule makes learning to adjust very challenging, but I have finally gotten the message about my leg and I am through fucking with it. My left leg is now the star of the show, getting top billing and avoiding a repeat of my lack of consideration for all that it has been through on my behalf.

The leg business rifled its way to the head of the line here and we can now happily put it aside. I am probably too happy to write much more about it because some things are so deeply personal that it is impossible to convey to another. In addition, I would rather revel in the news and not even attempt to focus on exactly how I am going to explain it all to you.

Based on the count so far, this would appear to be the start of the 100th page, which is another cause for celebration, at least by me. I know I said when we hit this milestone; I would go back to the beginning and edit and/or elaborate on whatever has been written to this point. By the way, 100 pages is a shit load of pages for one person to write, especially if you are not in the business of doing such things. I may pick up the thread relating to work and my travel from NYC to Santa Fe, which kind of stopped dead in its tracks a while ago.

For the moment, I am going to go off and be by myself and with myself. Not sure what is next, although I am not much in the mood for going backwards and reading what I have written. There is a part of me that wants this to simply be an accident of the word, without any preconceived idea of its merit beyond what you derive from all this. Anyway, I love you Shane and we will talk soon.

Travelin' On

One last word on the leg incident, you enjoy your life and try to really appreciate the privilege of being alive. You don't have to go insane about it, you just keep searching for limits in your sense of being and you bust your balls to overcome them. I appreciate life a great deal and getting whacked with the leg thing makes me that much more grateful.

I think we will try and do a road trip for now, one that keeps me moving through time and place. I will do what I can to keep that as the underpinning for a while. You just need to remember the NYC adventures and my leaving for Santa Fe with a mortgaged home there and no income upon my arrival.

I just took a quick peek at my excuse for a resume and I have at least fourteen viable job entries for the fifteen years I was around Santa Fe. Frankly, I don't have the energy right now to start at square one and move around the game board of my life. Something tells me I need daylight for sorting all that shit out. I knew I was busy living in New Mexico, but never quantified the number of bona fide gigs I actually had during my time there. I am pretty sure I can slip back into that period of my life with a lot more freshness than I can with my twenties and thirties in NYC. I know there was somebody home all during that time in my life and it continues to this day. However, I can tell you from this vantage point that my somebody kept changing as years accumulated much more quickly than I like. I really began to embody who I am continually becoming when I got to my little hacienda in the Cerrillos Flats. I felt too young, even at the end of my time in NYC. I began to grow up out there in the incredibly expansive landscape of the Four Corners.

I bought my little 5-acre hacienda and was there for only a week back in February 1987 and now at the beginning of June, I was now driving up a dirt road onto another dead end, dirt road where my little adobe womb was located. For my first six years out there, this was my home and it was very special. I put up a hoop and every now and then, regardless of temperature, I would shoot and dribble, but not very well. I thought it was cool to have the hoop out there in the middle of nowhere. I had a small room outside the house and that became my office, which was kind of cool, because it separated some of the daytime lunacy from a more tranquil living space.

It is amazing the world I built for myself in the high desert. I felt completely at home, away from the onslaught of urban life. I calculated that I had over a year to live there before I needed to be concerned about money, but it is really not a very long time. I knew just a handful of people, partially from my initial visit and names that were given to me before I left NYC. However, there was a wonderful flow to my life in New Mexico and I treasure all of it. I don't think I compromised very much when it came to earning a living. I had an incredible series of adventures and as I have already said, it will require a road map and flashlight to navigate those high desert adventures.

I like this particular approach for me and I will stick with it unless something invades our space. It took a handful of days to get my first job. It involved marketing a John Huston film festival, taking place in Santa Fe. God willing, this is where we will pick it up again.

Sangre de Cristo's

I have written about the trip across Amerika, which is purposely misspelled to reflect my own distance from it right now, as I did in some earlier recollections. It was a fabulous odyssey and for some reason, I was fearless, even without any plan at all. I had bought my home around four months before I gave up most everything I owned and headed west. My time in Santa Fe began in early June 1987.

I had met several people on my initial trip to Santa Fe and followed up on a contact from Candace, you remember her? We had a very brief go of it when I was preparing to leave NYC and connected several times in Santa Fe. She has mailed me a birthday card for at least 25 years in a row.

It took around three days for me to fall into a gig. I bumped into one of my prior connects at some outdoor celebration and he told me about a John Huston Film Festival and that there might be some work. Well, I worked around four months helping to market this event. Aside from providing income, it was my entrée into the town and it worked beautifully for me. I took to my new home with an open embrace and the return was incredible.

The income stopped when the festival was over, but it was still unexpected to get something so soon. It was followed up rather quickly by a conversation with an old page friend, Dennis. He was in a fairly high position at a publishing house, McGraw Hill. He and I managed to wangle a way for me to get paid for exploring the start up of a statewide magazine, called Careers. They wanted to see if they could have a college graduate oriented magazine that focused on employment and empowerment. I traveled all over the State, looking for potential supporters/advertisers and I got a good education on how things happened in the State. For reasons having nothing to do with this small project, Dennis was fired about six months into the exercise. Like the film festival, I got to meet a tremendous cross section of local people and then it was over.

I am wracking my brain to remember how I met Gerry, but I can't bring it in. He was and still is a writer and storyteller. We became friends and I would get together with him pretty regularly. I liked him a great deal and considered him a buddy during the length of our connection. It seems he and another fellow owned a publishing company called Lotus Press. There were books on Ayurvedic medicine (look it up), Native American stories and audiotapes by Gerry and a number of others. I worked with them for a time and handled their marketing. I traveled to book shows, with a booth of our material, soliciting business from attendees. It does qualify as having been in the publishing business for sure.

This takes us up to early 1989 and my next adventure. I helped promote a Rudolf Nureyev (another one to look up) concert with a guy by the name of John, whose claim to fame was being one of the key people on stage during Woodstock, which I hope you don't have to look up, even after all the years since it transpired. John was one of the people I met at the film festival and he was actually running it for much of its short life. We ended up pitching a guy an idea to do a summer concert series, halfway up the 15 miles to the Santa Fe ski basin and located on the side of mountain, with a restaurant below. It might have been the restaurant manager's idea, but it doesn't change the experience.

John turned out to be fairly difficult and the money people were not happy with him. I was asked if I would take over the promotion of The Music in the Pines concert series and I stepped right into it. Believe me, I definitely earned my creds in that arena with this summer long extravaganza. I was responsible for the whole deal. I booked the talent and crafted a very diverse, very high quality music series. Another guy I met at the Festival, Dick, had become a friend and we hung out together and did so for many years after that.

I made him my production person because he was in the theatrical business and knew about staging and sound, etc. Dealing with the artists and/or their tour person was always a trip. You'd better pay the artist, often in cash, before they go on or they will not go anywhere.

One of my highlights was booking Bonnie Raitt (Yup! Look her up. Terrific). It was by far our biggest selling show and pretty much pushed the facilities to the max. Considering we were on the side of a mountain, requiring a picnic style seating and bus transport from a lower parking area, it was pretty damn outstanding turnout. I bumped into her band the next night at a place called the Pink Adobe. She came in and invited me to their table. I sat with her and had a side conversation about my life and its adventures and she was very attentive. After a couple of margaritas, they were moving on to another club and she wanted me to come and yours truly said no. During that time, I was seeing Norma in her California incarnation and felt it would be cheating on her to go off with an incredibly charismatic lady. In hindsight, I was a schmuck for not going along for the ride, but what can you do?

I was fairly public during that time, partially due to my being on stage in front of anywhere from 700 to 3500 people for about thirteen Sundays in the summer of '89. Not sure if I mentioned it earlier, but I became a volunteer fireman out where I lived in the Cerrillos Flats. I had all the gear and became a part of their roots community. They remind me a little of the Sons of Kauai that I ride with now. Those volunteer firemen dealt with some very heavy shit, while the bikers are only about cruising, but they were both incredibly welcoming and I quickly became a local guy. I bought an old pick up truck, got a hybrid wolf and even wore cowboy boots on occasion.

One of the firefighters, Ed, had a friend who owned a British record label, Run River Records (Don't look it up). However, I am beginning to fade and this little adventure deserves to be told fresh. I will pick it up from here, unless I don't.

On the Turntable

Run River Records is one of the better work stories in my repertoire and roughly covers 1990-93. When you are plunged into an existing group, like a local volunteer fire department, you gravitate toward some and always stay good with everyone else, which is definitely my way. Ed and I talked quite a bit and became friends, who got together socially. He lived in an incredible spot along Hwy 14, south of Cerrillos and north of Madrid. In the realm of small world, my friend, Michael, who had a part in my starting this whole thing, ended up building a great new house on that land for a woman, who bought the place from Ed, but we are here to talk about records.

Ed said he had a long time acquaintance, who had strong roots in Santa Fe and was now living in England. Apparently, he had inherited some change and started a record label, primarily due to his sincere love of music and its appeal to his Hemingway tendencies. Fred was a hard drinking man, who spoke about his adventures and mixed in literature at the same time. He was definitely an interesting character.

I am not sure if I started working for the label before Fred and I actually met. I was very committed to making a go of this venture, primarily because I love music and have enjoyed contributing in any way I could. I totally enjoy hearing music for the first time, regardless of genre, as long as I think it is good. As far as I am concerned, my taste is impeccable, but that does not always translate to commercial success.

My primary responsibility was to secure a US distribution deal for a totally unknown British record label, featuring Celtic, Folk and Country Western, if you can believe that. There were some terrific Celtic artists and their records were incredible, however Celtic music is definitely a niche and BIG business is not interested in niches. One name that come comes to mind is Steve Tilston. Great guitar player and overall musician, who is in keeping with the forever history of the troubadour in the UK. He still is an incredibly gifted artist long after our initial meeting. On top of that, we had several young bands, guys who played and wrote really good Country Western sounding music. I had never heard it before and really believed it could be groundbreaking if it ever got the chance, which it never did.

The entire time I worked on the label, I was still living in my little adobe house in the middle of nowhere. The one room building on my land was where I worked the label. By this time, I realized my life was simply going to be a testament to my way of being here and now. I would get up each morning and do my run, plus I began sitting before I left this home and then I would simply walk outside, up a short path and into my office. During the winter, I would crank the electric floorboard heat and make it nice and cozy. I was calling people in the music business all over the country and sending out samples and looking for a deal.

At some point during this history, probably closer to the front side, Fred paid for me to fly over to the UK and I stayed at his home, plus hotels in various parts of the country. I was definitely not a well-seasoned world traveler at the time and it was incredible for me. Basically, I went there to see the artists perform live in local bars all over the country and to spend some time with them. Let me tell you, running in the UK totally fucked me up. By that time, running and I were inseparable, so the shoes got packed for the trip. Fred lived in a beautiful part of the country, which I can't seem to pull out of my memory bank. However, running there was a real treat. The countryside gave off a feeling of having been here for a very long time. There were a handful of not so close calls because I couldn't figure out where the hell to look first because of the driving on the other side of the road thing. The trip was great and I came home to get back to work on the label.

I ended up getting a deal for the label and it took every bit of smarts I had at the time. It was with a major record label. You need to keep in mind, we are talking pre-techno time when you produced CD's and there was not much of a network to expose less commercially viable music, unlike today with the web, etc. Once again, the future of music, not to mention technology, is something I place in the realm of science fiction, a genre I never liked anyway. If you should have the ability to hear the entire breadth of music, get started and just keep going, with no end in sight.

Fred started to run out of money at some point during this process. He had just enough money to get into trouble and not enough to buy success. We all gave it a good try and there was no animosity. Fred was not the happiest guy in the world and he drank himself to death a number of years ago. Figuring out where you are in this world is a tricky business and many of us are lost, which is a great tragedy.

I did take another quick look at my excuse for a resume to check on dates and it became instantly clear that each job thing was a story unto itself and not something to weave into some continuous flow. Coming up next is my dabbling in Belize. Right around that time, I started seeing Gail, who is definitely someone I want to tell you about.

Planet Patrol and Beyond

I spent the next couple of years after the record label doing my own thing and it mostly involved Belize. Truthfully, I am racking my brain trying to recall how I got involved with Belize in the first place, especially while living in New Mexico, a total brain fart.

I traveled there a number of times and found myself in the business of importing herbal remedies, spices and some other items, which I sold at the flea market just north of Santa Fe. I established an exchange program between the kids at Pojoaque Elementary School in NM and a village in Belize called Maya Centre. They wrote letters to each other and I taped recorded messages that I shared with each school I went to the village several times and slept in a tent next to a friend's house. There were any number of dead end roads driven down by yours truly in an attempt to make some kind of living that would allow me to live between Santa Fe and Belize. I definitely admit to being a sucker for romantic adventure.

Actually, the impetus for my initial involvement is vaguely returning in some dying flash of remembrance. South of town, where I first lived in my adobe incubator, there was a fair amount of acreage that belonged to a group that lived somewhat communally and went by the name of Synergia Ranch. They had ties to Belize and I simply slipped into that connection and followed up on some leads. I remember spending several nights on a three masted, Chinese junk replica, the Heraclitus, sitting in the middle of a magnificent location, next to one of the many spectacular cayes that dot the coastline around Belize. This junk had a connection to the ranch. It was a surreal visit, to say the least. The crew were very young and I definitely felt a lot older.

Right around that time, I began pushing the envelope regarding practical issues like money in the bank or money of any kind for that matter. When you make a choice to go out on a limb and follow it regardless of how tenuous it may be, it is hard to come back, or at least it was for me. I enjoy dreaming about how I want my life to be and decisions get made on that basis. It was an unspoken deal I made with myself when I left the so-called normalcy of life in NYC.

My personal zenith in that way of life hit its southwestern crescendo when I almost produced a film. By that time, I had been living with Gail for a while and had sold my place, moving in with her and then moving around together for a number of years. As I have mentioned, she will get her own headline and full on story. Anyway, one of our neighbors in a place we were renting back then was a Native American teacher at a college called the Institute of American Indian Arts.

Glen and I became good acquaintances over a short time and he shared that he was a screenwriter and comfortable around directing. He had written a so-so screenplay about a kick ass story. It seems that around the turn of the 20th century, a half-breed Indian was robbing banks and trains and killing at least a dozen people along the way. Supposedly, he hid a treasure in gold in some location or other in Washington State. He allegedly gave money to a number of local Indians, so they could buy the paper from the local bank and own their own land, making him a Robin Hood like person. The deal is it is actually a true story and this guy was totally for real, which is what made it particularly interesting to me.

I got together with Glen with the idea that I would produce the film and he would direct it. Somehow, we scored the consummate Hollywood agent to find a home for our project. Hilly was a short, Jewish guy, who actually had a collection of Napoleon memorabilia in his home. I think most Hollywood agents are short, Jewish guys with

Napoleonic tendencies. Hilly got us a meeting with Roger Corman, the forever king of B movies. Glen and I flew to LA and met with our agent and then drove incredibly fast to Roger's office. It seems that Hilly and Steve McQueen had a driving connection. You definitely want to check out Steve McQueen, one of the truly iconic actors who filled every bit the big screen.

After racing at ungodly speeds, we arrived at Corman's office. Glen and I spoke with Roger and he said he liked the script and we had a deal for a $750K film. While that is very little money by conventional movie standards, it was enough for us to produce a low budget movie. We all stood up and shook hands. Hilly was absolutely flabbergasted we made a deal with Roger, based on our total inexperience.

The week or so after that time in LA was indescribable for me. I got back to NM and I could tell Gail I was producing a movie and not to worry so much about money. It was a very emotional time for me because I felt that I somehow had vindicated my father's own failings at the success game. Very silly trying to cross our lives. I am sure he did the best he could and he worked his ass of to be a success and provide for his family. He went out on his own with that in mind and he got kicked in the nuts, like some many of us limb walkers.

We were starting to cast the movie and thinking in terms of logistics, etc. All of sudden, Glen gets a call from Roger asking if we could do another film for him before our own. This meant we would now be producing two movies, which was mind blowing for us. I was essentially broke and now I was producing two movies for Roger Corman. This additional film was supposedly based on the life of Geronimo. When the script arrived, I nearly puked. This shitty script was written by a couple of guys in LA, who never even met an Indian in their entire lives. It was demeaning and heavily used the drunken Indian stereotype, amongst other insults.

I had been living in that part of the country for around seven years. Based on my experience there and now here, I know I have the ability or agility to be allowed to touch the soul of a place. The screwing of Native Americans was something I couldn't figure a way out of. The US made treaties and broke them with reckless abandon, based on whatever was most expedient. There are many, many tribes throughout North America and every one of them lost the war and have basically been prisoners of war since they were banished to reservations.

I will get to the stunning conclusion of My Life with Roger in a moment. I love trying to look for any daylight, even in a dark tunnel. After many years around Native Americans, I figured their cause for equality would never happen. Their power is in their language and culture and that is the only way to win a modicum of longevity in a long ago lost war. Of course, being a Jewish schnook from Flushing, Queens provides me with the imprimatur necessary to justify my expertise in the field, kidding here. I know it is the right way for the thousands of people and hundreds of tribes that struggle regarding their place in the world beyond their cloistered reservations. Their power is in their culture.

I suppose the above sets the stage for my reaction to the Geronimo script. Producing two films for Roger Corman was the absolute shits and I would have had no problem with the tasks ahead. Personally, I did not want to do this first film because of how Indians were portrayed in a number of scenes. Glen, who is a full blood Native American, wanted to take the job because it would enable him to get his own film made and it would make him the first Native American to actually direct a film, so it had some deep significance for him. I convinced Glen to tell Roger we would take on this project, but to ask for just a few changes. The next time they spoke, Roger abruptly hung up on Glen when Glen asked about making some changes in the Geronimo script. At that very moment, my movie mogul career went swiftly down the opportunity crapper.

You probably think we are done with this saga, but you are wrong. Glen convinced me that we should go to his reservation in Washington State and make the movie on a shoestring, using whomever we could get to play the key roles. For several years prior to this, there were a number of extremely low budget films that exploded at the box office, including El Mariachi, which struck a chord with Glen. Of course, trying to purposefully recreate an accident is impossible.

At the reservation, I lived in a room in a double wide that belonged to Glen's sister and husband. For a couple of days, it seemed like there were decent possibilities, but it quickly began to unwind. Glen got drunk on several evenings and he was a nasty guy, which didn't sit well with me. I have no problem with drunk, but I do have one with nasty. I decided the gig was up and I would have to get back to Santa Fe and look for a job, God help me! I was actually broke and Gail deserved better and so did I. I had to wire a friend to send me money, so I could afford the drive back.

Once I got hot home, I began that arduous task of looking for work. I was pretty well known locally by now and had connected with a huge number of people in town. As much as I disliked media sales based on my years in NYC, I knew my credentials would be impressive in a small market like Santa Fe. The next entry will likely have the heading, KBAC-Radio Free Santa Fe.

Radio Free Santa Fe, But First

" Time is the coin of your life. It is the only coin you have, and only you can determine how it will be spent. Be careful lest you let other people spend it for you." '

The above is a quote from Carl Sandburg, one of our truly great poets. I literally just read it at around 7PM on February 15, 2012 and I am at the word piano, composing yet another entry about ten minutes after reading it. Will probably break for dinner and then get on with the Radio Free Santa Fe portion of this epic quest for truth and justice. First, I must have a gourmet entrée of eggplant Parmesan and delicious pasta. Life is good, Shane.

OK, let's back to Carl for just a second, playing off his reference to time being the only real currency for each of us to own outright. You have to have your shit together to understand this inescapable, undeniable truth. I don't know if this is something you will be able to really digest at whatever age you happen to be when you are granted permission to read all of this incredibly dangerous propaganda.

How you spend your life is a matter of choice, realizing at the same time that is a bit too clean to totally be on target. There are people born into unimaginable poverty and for the life of me I can't imagine what it would be like. When I talk about how you spend your time as being a matter of your choice, I am obviously dealing with where you happen to find yourself at this moment. You are likely pretty comfortable and not sleeping in the rain on a muddy hillside, unless it is a genuine remake of Woodstock.

Our sole possession is our life and it is therefore completely up to each one of us to do the best we can with the time we have been given. Personally, my mantra would be to follow your heart. If you listen to your mind, nine times out of ten, your heart is going to kick you in the ass.

I am starving. Talk to you soon..........................

Dinner was great, but I don't have time to talk about it, or else I won't tell my radio story.

I am not quite sure how I found out about a Sales Director job being open at a start up radio station in town. The guy doing the hiring was already on their payroll and is someone I had met in my many meanderings through all sorts of different circles. He did hire me for the sales gig and a person responsible for the musical sound of the station was also hired. I don't remember quite how it happened, but when the owners from back east came to visit, they fired the guy who hired me and said that the music guy, Ira and I would run the station. Ira was senior to me, but we got along extremely well, partially because I loved music and really liked his taste.

Ira and I were basically charged with putting a radio station on the air in Santa Fe. It was my job to project its image into the business community so they would advertise with the station. We hired a couple of additional sales people, who reported to me. This was my life for about three years. While it was the dreaded "job", most of the time it was great because we had absentee owners and as long we were increasing our advertising revenue, they kind of left Ira and myself alone.

KBAC-Radio Free Santa Fe quickly became THE radio station in Santa Fe. Ira and I pretty much created its personality in the community. We supported things like AID's Walks and did remote broadcasts from all sorts of events around the area. We played a format called Adult Alternative. I am sure there is an ancient definition of what that means musically. It played to an age of at least twenty-five and more likely thirty-five plus. In some ways, it was a tip of the hat to FM radio of the Sixties and Seventies when there was real freedom in programming the music. This was before radio got completely corporatized, like virtually every good idea that finds its way to the market place. Greed gobbles up all the good ideas.

In the beginning, it was great fun to be involved in the creative process and birthing the station within the community. There is no magic to sales and mirrors don't work. In sales, the only gauge of success is sales, no exceptions. Of all the things I did with the station, sales was the part I liked least, which is kind of tricky, being the Sales Director. I really enjoyed writing and producing the client's commercials. Being around the music was always a boost for me and we promoted plenty of concerts in Santa Fe, often at the Paolo Soleri, a fantastic amphitheater under the spectacular skies of northern New Mexico.

The radio station really started doing well and we were running in the black after about a year or so. We had a terrific run before it started to suck. The original owners began to get interested in selling this newly successful radio station to a bigger fish. The closer it got, the more demanding the job became and I am not sure if I was fired or I quit, but I was ready to go regardless.

At the time of my departure, which I knew was coming months ahead of time, I began to get involved in the nature tourism consulting business and was feeling increasingly confident that it would actually work, but that is next on the menu and I can only tell one story at a time, otherwise it could easily become a mechanical process. No thanks.

Naturegate, etc

My first foray into Belize stayed with me for a number of years, even while at the radio station. Subsequently, I met with a hotel manager in Santa Fe, who claimed she had access to funding for a resort or two in Belize. I took some vacation time from the station and went to Belize to check out one particular guy who owned two resorts. Believe it or not, his last name was the same as ours. It was well known that he dealt in transporting drugs on a fairly high level and was not someone you trifled with. It was a very interesting series of meetings, plus he put me up at a place called Blackbird Caye Resort. While sitting and traveling on a skiff to get me out there, I met a scientist from the Wildlife Conservation Society. He is the one who told me that his organization was interested in establishing a network of eco-resorts in Central America, where they had quite a bit of land.

Fortunately, I realized I have already done a whole bit on my old friend, Alex, so I don't have to go through the story of Naturegate. It was that trip which triggered my sojourn in the nature tourism consulting business, which had about a two year run for me, ending sometime in 2000. I thought it was a very adventurous way to earn a living, going to plenty of remote areas in third world countries, although I don't like that term because it somehow implies we are a first world country, which we sure ain't.

The rules are always made by the strongest, but it doesn't mean they are right. Pardon yet another tangential comment, which has nothing to do with how cool I thought this consulting business was for me to be experiencing.

I was with Gail during much of my time in Santa Fe, starting toward the end of Run River Records and going through the Naturegate saga, a total of around eight years or so. Still not the time for telling the whole Gail story, beyond saying she was a gifted yoga instructor. Together, we promoted a couple of workshops, one of which was in Baja, Mexico and another actually at the Synergia Ranch. I acted as the producer of the events and dealt with the logistics, finances, etc. We made some money and I thought it was great that she put herself out there in that manner because she was more than good enough.

My comfort level with living on the edge was rarely unsettling, at least for me. When I got together with Gail, it was sometime in 1993 and I ended up selling my little adobe house after we decided to live together in a space that would allow for a yoga studio. I made a couple of bucks on the sale. I negotiated a fair deal with your grand mother to pay off the balance of my child support, which wasn't all that much after the years of providing it. I bought a red Toyota truck, which I am still driving nearly 19 years later. I drove it to LA from Santa Fe and put it on a barge for Kauai. It nows has over 190,000 miles and has a complexion that reflects a very active life, which includes camping deep in the woods of some remote Southwestern splendor and now residing in the Kauai climate. I lived off the remainder of the domicile sale proceeds and used it to keep my motor running during the down times for a couple of years.

More Still

I got a couple of bucks from the divorce with Alex over Naturegate. I relinquished any interest in the company, which was fine because it was impossible to work with him; at least it was for me. He hit on a bankrupt airline, which he turned around only several years after we split. Who knows? I could now be living in Costa Rica, overseeing marketing for a successful internal airline.

When you live in the world of professional speculation, you always have to have something, somewhere on a back burner. Plan B is the way to gracefully exit a catastrophe. Just now, I called my friend, Pete, to recall how we met because I had yet another brain fart. Of course, this happens to be germane to the subject at hand, which is what did Grandpa Larry do next?

For one summer, I had a booth at the Santa Fe Flea Market in Tesuque, which you already know about. One day, this longhaired, Southwestern styled guy by the name of Pete came over to my Belize booth, which was a miracle unto itself, considering the stampeding mobs that completely avoided my space. He had a theatrical quality about him, plus a little bit of peacock showiness, God bless him. It turns out, he was thinking about shooting a video on the healer I had purchased Rainforest Remedies from, which I was now selling at the market. Her name escapes me, but we spent some time together in an effort to get her medicinals to a larger audience.

We became friends and Pete was a stone called trip. There is something terribly infectious about show business and I can easily see how you can get really drawn into it. He was very much into Native American culture and the Blues, if you can believe that combination. I really wasn't making any money with him in the beginning, because he didn't have any money of his own.

In the process of trying to sell Blues programming, we stumbled on the idea of securing concert style Gospel Music videos and editing them for broadcast. We would insert several commercials, encouraging viewers to order a copy by calling an 800#. Keep in mind, this was before the ability to order and pay for products and services over the internet. I can't even begin to imagine what is technologically available to you as a consumer.

Pete and I rode the Gospel train for nearly three years. Again, I know this piece was already mentioned, but it belongs here, too. I carried on with him from '99 until I left for

Kauai in '03 and beyond. The Gospel business started some time in 2000 and testified until it faded away after I had been here on Kauai for six months or so. I didn't ever think we could ride this horse forever, but it provided me with some comfort regarding my move from Santa Fe to Kauai. The fact that it turned to shit shortly after that doesn't take away from its contribution to my relocation.

I was involved with Pete's company, Sagebrush Productions, for the balance of my time in Santa Fe, regardless of whatever else I took on to pay the freight. Ultimately, it provided my parachute for the unrehearsed jump into Kauai.

One of the interesting things I did during my Sagebrush tenure was a fairly detailed marketing plan for a company involved with a technology for desalination, something I knew absolutely nothing about. Somehow, this gig came through Pete and I was paid to put together a global perspective on desalination and the role this company's technology could play in that effort. I suppose this particular news helps to better understand the ridiculous depth and breadth of my entire professional career, always getting involved with something brand new to me and figuring how to quickly make myself at home in that new environment. The names change, but the rules are always the same in my line of work. The most important rule is that you make up the rules as you go along.

I am not sure who introduced me to John, but, unlike Pete, who I talk to regularly today, I can't ever call him because he killed himself quite a few years ago, however that is the end of the story and not the beginning. Aside from being legitimately bi-polar, he was an avid inventor and an extremely bright guy. He was looking for someone to handle the marketing of his Breastbottle Nurser, a silicone breast shaped, soft bottle. I am dead serious here.

He lived in Virginia, but spent time in Santa Fe, so I sometimes dealt with him long distance and other times, face to face. He did set me up in a very small, one room building office space, which was very sweet. He paid for the new "computer" for me to use in the office. My job was to get press coverage for this unique baby bottle and to develop sales/distribution outlets for the product. I think I did a pretty good job, working within the parameters of the situation. Bless John, he was not a terribly stable person and I think he had times of unbearable suffering and the reasons were the least of it, it was the depth of the drop that mattered.

I committed over two years to this effort and it was another one of those outrageous adventures into a world I could never have imagined and have always learned from. The venture ran out of money and John had to really pull back. I had a great run with this one and even went to a huge baby accessory convention in Vegas, which was otherworldly.

We are starting to close in on my time in Santa Fe, at least from this one sided perspective of work adventures out in the high desert. Gail and I had split up around the demise of the Breastbottle Nurser and the birth of The Gospel Collection, which I had been working on with Pete even during my time with the baby bottle. It was OK with John, as long as I was doing my best to promote his bottle. Unless I am mistaken, I had one phone for the bottle biz and one phone for Sagebrush in this cool, little one-room space in a great part of town.

Around the time the breast bottle collapsed, I chose to move out from Gail and I immediately went to the Pink House, which I will tell you about, I promise. Following a fairly long house sit at the Pink House, I moved my life and workspace out to a wonderfully, funky adobe house I started renting just north of Pojoaque, pretty much in the middle of nowhere. I was living in this architectural accident, with rooms arbitrarily added over the generations. I had maximum privacy. I would spend my time on the phone and computer, lining up Gospel material for the Gospel Collection.

I was sort of bequeathed this place by Dick and Mogi, who are somewhat new to this expose. I most likely brought up Dick when I wrote about the Music in the Pines concert series. They had been living in this place for probably twenty years and they had bought land right down the road and built a house on it. After moving out there into their old house, I would often walk to their place in the evening, under the dazzling southwestern skies. I would indulge in the herb with Dick and we always had a grand old time. Those were my last two years in that part of the world and I was living in some spectacular country out there.

My last official gig in Santa Fe was an incredible experience for me and really infected me with the idea that I might have a knack for writing, God help me.

There was and likely still is a very large Sikh community just north of Santa Fe in a town called Espanola. They are an Indian originated religion and there were many Anglos who decided to change their lives to join this community. They had created a number of very successful businesses to help underwrite their efforts.

Once again, I don't recall how it happened, but somebody from their Golden Temple business got in touch with me regarding marketing work with a brand called Yogi Tea. I met with them and shared my idea of having short travel related adventures printed on the different varieties of tea bags. They went for it and as a result, I wrote these incredibly romantic, fairly tale like stories and kept them short enough to print on a box of tea bags. When I had a tea story to write, I would put the package on the kitchen table and I would circle it for a few days and then, out of nowhere, I would concoct a very short story for that tea. I liked getting paid for writing, which was a first for me. I had been writing for years in a variety of business positions, but never presented with the opportunity of a blank space that had to be filled with my imagination. I wrote these little stories about exotic locations all over the world and just made the shit up. They were pretty cool tea stories. I just went to dig up the portfolio I put together with all the stories on the actual tea package. Remember, these are completely fake. Here is one that sort of involves Uncle Danny:

> *"In college, I thought about being an archaeologist and got as far as a course in Egyptian civilization. Always had a fascination with the pyramids, artwork and the historical intrigue of that early empire. Career and life took me in other directions, but I finally got to take a vacation there last year. The highlight of the trip was getting up before dawn and taking a fifteen minute cab ride from Cairo to Gaza, the home of the sphinx and a grouping of three pyramids. Got there just in time to see the sunrise on the eastern facing sphinx. Nothing can prepare you for this experience. There they stand in the middle of the endless desert seemingly out of nowhere, with Cairo a mirage in the distance. I remember placing my hands on the cool limestone of the Pyramid of Cheops, imagining myself in the court of a great pharaoh. Before heading back to my hotel, I stopped at one of the little shops that sell an endless array of perfumes and spices for tourists. I bought small handfuls of licorice, cinnamon and orange peel, which I still have to this day. At home, in the quiet of the early dawn, I sit with my cup of Egyptian Licorice Tea and its familiar scents from that little shop and I am royalty in the land of the great pyramids."*

It was great fun to let me imagination run wild and come up with adventures that involved names of teas like Spicy Mountain Peach Tea and Tropical Hibiscus Tea. With the Egyptian tale, I called your Uncle Danny to ask him some questions about the pyramids and it certainly helped to give it an authentic feeling. I also wrote copy for their line of Peace Cereals.

Golden Temple takes us ever closer to my departure for Kauai, but I am in no particular hurry to leave. The fifteen plus years in that part of the country is impossible to recount. I wish I could go back in time to re-experience so many of the awe inspiring natural settings I was privileged to see, sometimes camping out and get swallowed up by the experience. I was able to begin relaxing in New Mexico and I am continuing that exercise even as I write these words.

When it comes to that high desert time in my life, it is a gumbo of my off the wall work life, important ladies and the boys, all going on amidst a kind of natural splendor that you have to see to believe. I don't know if any of these natural treasures will still be available to you and if there is ultimately an effort to protect nature and not prostitute it. I can't say I am feeling it now. Let me tell you, some of the country I got to see shouldn't be fucked with by anyone. We are dead unless we keep reminders of the pristine nature of this world, until we twisted and choked the life out of most of it to meet our selfish needs.

Got to share something with you that has nothing to do with any of the above, but what do I care? Got together with Ken and Susan last night. I am not sure if I have told you about them yet, but I don't want to do that right now anyway. Susan is a real journalist, who has earned her living that way for decades and is now retired. Well, they know I am writing this and I talk with them as a writer, not because I want to share content, which I don't. When I told Susan I had written about twenty pages in two weeks, she made a reference to that being a slow rate of production. You know, this could have taken me a week to write or an endless number of years. The interesting thing is when you read it, you have no idea of the time it took to get this all down, but that doesn't really matter in the long run either, now does it?

This feels like a terrific natural break for us. I might stay in Santa Fe for a while to share the personal side of it all. As always, I am predictably capable of getting a bug up my ass and going off on a tare once again.

No Bugs Up My Ass

My fifteen plus years in northern New Mexico were everything I could have hoped for. I left New York feeling cold and alone. Certainly, over the course of my decades in the City, I had made many friends and it was my home and pretty much all I knew, with occasional trips away. I actually think my two summers at the farm house in Honesdale, PA with my boys, which came toward the end of my Big Apple tenure, really opened me up to the possibility of living in a place that felt open, with the exquisite beauty of nature always lurking around the corner of every glance.

I really think it was during those summers with Danny and Andy that I began to open up to the need to be closer to nature. Our two summers in the Hamptons were not what you would call rural experiences, but it was great to feel far away from the City. The house on the dairy farm in Honesdale was what really got to me. I would get up very early in the morning and walk out into the fields and do my meditation, which I kind of fooled with in my thirties. I would run on the back country roads and follow it with a decent 10 speed bike ride on those same roads and more.

It was big country out there in northern New Mexico. The network of State and

National Forests offered this magnificent web where nature was held prisoner by the seasons and that was all, no human interruptions. I had endless camping experiences, sometimes by myself and my dogs, or mostly with Gail, who was an avid camper.

Oh, what the hell, I might as well talk about Gail, primarily because she is totally integrated into my life in Santa Fe. After about six years out there, I was completely at home and new all sorts of people. I am not one to have a circle of friends; rather it is like these concentric circles of unrelated people, which is a way to get to know a large numbers of folks.

A friend of mine, Richard, is a writer and we ended up connecting over something having to do with Belize because he was a travel writer with a history there and I had my own connection, as you now know. By the way, I like Richard very much and we have stayed in touch through the years, plus he was out here to visit a number of months ago and we connected just like old times. Fuck, did I already talk about him? You know, it hard to keep track of my life sometimes.

Richard had an incredibly eccentric friend, Jim, who I also befriended. Jim was an insanely talented person, who did not have very marketable skills, but he did have a trust fund to live on, God bless him. He was famous for throwing fabulous parties at his place in town. His house had space ship elements about it. He had a great sound system and a screen, primarily for his slides taken on his world travels. He was a gifted shooter and the visuals were great. I think I went a couple of times before and mostly ended up spending time by myself, feeling a little uncomfortable, primarily because I suck at artifice. It is interesting to be both incredibly shy and incredibly open, depending on the circumstance.

I think Gail approached me at one of these gatherings, as opposed to my doing the work. We had certainly noticed each other at this particular party and once the first words were spoken between us, we kind of locked together at that moment. We slept together that evening, which I know was absolutely something she did not make a habit of doing. Trust me, I mention this only to provide subtext for our relationship and for no other reason. I don't think most grown ups actually do it on their first time together and it is more unusual for a woman. They are usually smarter than we are, while we get hard and go crazy. Honestly, I mention this with absolutely no bravado attached, rather as a sign of two people who just aren't thinking about consequence at a given moment.

Gail was and is a gifted yoga instructor. She was drawn toward Eastern cultures and had visited India several times before. She was predisposed to things of a spiritual nature. Considering the life I had led in the City and my desire to move away from it, Gail was like made to order. In case through some fluke Gail reads this, I want her to know she is a terrific woman and more than anything else she opened me up to the worlds of yoga, spirituality and nature. I am deeply indebted to her and she is one who looms large in the constellation of my relationships.

We hit it off pretty well and spent time between our two places, hers in town and mine out there in the Cerrillos Flats. As I mentioned, I eventually sold my house and my three dogs went with it and then I moved in with Gail in town. We made several moves over the next years. At the end of my Run River days, I returned to working at home and that wasn't the greatest environment to have spill over into my life with Gail. I was well out on the limb by then, but I had never once defaulted on whatever it was I was supposed to drop in the kitty. I guess, in some ways, my choices in recent decades have been for and about me and what are the odds of finding someone who is exactly as neurotic as myself?

Gail was into the details and sloppy didn't work for her. Now, this was a perfect mindset at least for camping because absolutely nothing was left out and this was terrific, considering we would be traveling to the middle of nowhere in some humongous swath of wide open land. I think my life style was a bit unsettling for her. There was a malfunction on the physicality side of things. It's funny, you would think a yoga instructor would be very physical in his or her own lives, but Gail was not terribly demonstrative in the world of affection, but no way in the world I am going to unload on her. I suppose it would be fair to say we both wrestled with intimacy, while not necessarily on the same team. I know she had a rough go of things as a kid, plus growing up Catholic simply adds to the baggage. Before it grew cold, we had sensational times together. The boys spent plenty of time with her. They visited on several extended summer trips and we went camping on some of them, something they had never done before and I know Andy hasn't done it since. Danny does lots of camping in Israel, which is great. He rides his bike to remote beaches everywhere within its small boarders. There is very little that compares to waking up in the morning in the middle of the Rockies, surrounded by huge trees and spectacular views of borderless lands.

I am not sure if it is a fair thing to say in terms of a relationship, but the greatest gift I got from Gail was yoga. Don't get me wrong, for most of my time with her, I was very much in love and would have done anything. I actually asked her to marry me and she turned me down. It was a very sad moment for me to realize that the person I had idealized as a spiritual being wanted security and a diamond ring. We stayed together after that, but it was never the same. I asked your grandmother and Gail and that has been all as of this moment and probably forever after. I didn't own my way of being in the manner I do now. It was many years ago with lifetimes in between.

We were together somewhere between seven and eight years, which is a very long time to be with someone. There were memorable moments together for sure, but it was not satisfying for either of us in the end. If I recall, I did us both a favor and said I was going to leave. I did. It doesn't feel that I have done justice to my relationship with Gail and may want to revisit it because she will always be important to me.

There was one other lady in Santa Fe and Beverly is her name. However, I can't keep the continuity going between these two women, each one requiring a place of her own. I think the story with Beverly is one of the more interesting girl stories I have to share with you.

Keeping It Real

This writing thing get a little tricky when I get into other people, especially ones that are years into my history. I was specifically thinking about it in relation to Gail, but it would fit the handful of other women whom I carry with me to this day, not to mention all of those experiences viewed through today's emotional prism. This process has made me feel very forgiving and unwilling to dig into the dirt of my relationships. Being single and not a widower clearly defines the nature of all my connections right up to this moment; they all ended. Stuff went wrong in every relationship I have had or I would still be with one of them or mourning her passing.

There were certainly relationships before I met your grandmother. As a kid, I had crushes, but they were before the sex connection took over my brain. When you begin to settle in a little with your hormones, you can absolutely have a real girlfriend, someone you talk to the future about and you can have sex with her more often than you will ever be able to have again. Enjoy the multiplicity while you can.

For a part of my junior and senior in at Jamaica High School, I was heavenly blessed to have met Joanne. She was from Florida and staying with relatives in Jamaica Estates, the uptown neighborhood in our larger community. She was gorgeous and had a figure that only a sixteen year old can have and boy was I lucky. Not being terribly evolved as a teenager, our conversations were not terribly deep, but we were definitely boyfriend and girlfriend and I still have my high school prom photo and Joanne was my date. We spent the night on a beach, pleasuring ourselves under the blanket. I seem to recall she had to move back to Florida and I don't think it carried over into the beginning of my college time.

There are several other women I want to tell you about and I will get there.

I want to say a little more about Gail and about the idea of not looking for garbage.

Gail blew me away because she appeared to be a woman who was very comfortable with many things that were new to me. I learned a great deal from Gail and I am grateful for all she gave to me. This is my story and it is about what I have dealt with and how I now deal with my experiences, filtered through where I am at this very moment. At this moment, I have nothing but gratitude for everything and everyone that fills my memories from way back then all the way to right now.

When Gail and I split, it was clearly up to me to move out, primarily because she owned the house we were in and I was just putting in my 50% of overhead. I did not have a stick of furniture, which made a quick move pretty challenging, but it was necessary under the circumstances.

Wouldn't you know, it, I immediately heard about some woman in an upscale development called Eldorado, who needed a person to house sit for her and take care of her poodle, Angel. This is the previously mentioned Pink House. The move was pretty seamless. Yes, I had a slew of emotions about leaving Gail, but it was clearly time for both of us. The house was nearly all pink and there were more crystals than I had ever seen before in one place. I think she was a bit over the top with the spirit stuff, but who am I?

This now sets the stage for Beverly. Spending nearly eight years living with someone is a very long time and when you break from that, it is shocking to all your systems. I think I was in relatively good shape because the split had been a long time coming and it was definitely for the best. I do remember saying to Gail that I wanted to try very hard to be friends after the break, something I never cared to do before. Over time, I think we have sort of pulled it off. You know me, I let it all hang out when I write, but she is not quite that way and that is fine with me, as long as I don't temper anything I write. I send her photographs of you periodically because we went to visit your Mom and Dad, before you were born. We had a ball and it was precious to watch Gail try and take in the overwhelming energy of the City. She was a Colorado girl and didn't have an urban pedigree.

Now, I am living in the pink house with Angel, an unbelievably irritating miniature, white poodle. It was actually a lovely house and it was a real blessing to be able to move out from Gail and make such a soft landing.

It was during this period I met Beverly. Damn, I just remembered when we met. There was a terrific artist living relatively close to Gail and myself. He occasionally had parties and I saw and spoke with Beverly at one of them. He may have actually given me the number to follow up on. Beverly is a gifted artist and a lovely woman. Her hair was silver and I found her striking. We went out a bunch of months after I split with Gail, but I am sure I was still affected by it. Beverly would come out to the pink house, especially on weekends. We had some wonderful time together and were pretty close. On top of that, she was a bona fide psychic of some sort or other. Trust me, she could pick up on invisible shit and she was on the money. She had a place in town and I would come over for the evening and leave in the morning.

When I started getting to the end of the line with the pink house, I connected with my friends, Dick and Mogi, who turned me on to their funky casita north of town, which I reminisced about already. Beverly was unbelievably supportive and helpful during the whole move. She recommended the appropriate colors for the different rooms, based on the energy they ought to have. As an aside, even in this small adobe house, I actually was able to have a room strictly for meditation, which was extremely cool. I really enjoyed this new place in the middle of nowhere and got to thinking that I needed to be by myself for a while. This totally fucked up the thing with Beverly and it is as close as I can get to regret about a relationship. I am pretty sure this one was totally on me and I might have fucked up, but it is one of the many things that will remain an unknown until the end of my time.

Beverly and I still communicate and sometimes talk on the phone. By her own words, we had and still have a wonderful connection, but the demise was painful and pretty cold on my part. I often wonder what it would be like to have her here on Kauai. She recently reminded me that when I hurt my leg, she called nearly every day and I was so out of my mind, I didn't even remember.

Alone and Time To Go Back

I think I will split this little episode between the state of being unattached and the chaos of this endless story, so far, a one directional diatribe of mine, meaning it is now time to change direction and go back to the beginning. There is a great deal more to share from my distant past and I have barely touched my Kauai life.

You know, each time I open this document up; it starts at the very first page and I have absolutely avoided rereading it because I didn't want anything behind me to influence the moment directly in front of me. My sense is that going back to the beginning will likely result in some kind of additional wordage, which will be a change in the process. I may or may not let you know that something written is a result of this revisit or not. Just as a reminder, there are no rules here because it is my game to play.

I have been alone for a fairly long time recently, with only a small number of false starts thrown in. There is no question that I am a huge fan of intimacy and being close with a woman is one of the few things that makes life worth living, at least for this aging fool.

Other than your grandmother, I have only lived with one other woman and that was Gail. By the way, living with a woman means there is only one bedroom for both of you and everything after that is incidental, sort of. So, at age sixty-six, I have lived with a woman for only a maximum of fifteen years, which means the rest of the time I had my own space and was totally unattached to anyone for several years at a clip some of the time.

Right now, I am in my ohana, which is all of one room, but it is walled in such a way to provide a more spacious and private feeling. I am wearing an old flannel shirt that I often sleep in. I have on an ugly pair of blue poly –something shorts. There is some solid jazz playing on the radio at a fairly high volume. My total focus is on writing this to you right now. There are no distractions. However, please don't think I would ever refer to a woman as a distraction.

Living the way I am right now is the height of selfishness, but I definitely don't consider that as something with a negative connotation. Being selfish does not mean to me that you are doing your thing at the expense of another, the standard inference. There is a thin line between selfless and selfish and I don't have a steady enough hand to draw that particular line.

It only takes a brief conversation or merely a glance to get me back on the love train and denying everything I thought about the joy of being on my own. While that is at least half true, doing whatever I want whenever I want is sometimes more attractive than having to always be connected with another. Unfortunately, I don't really think there is a perfect compromise between the two. Each way requires that you do without at least some of the goodies from the other way. It is a tough call and one that is often resolved by time and/or circumstance.

Well, that's it for now. I am going back in the time machine to page one and I have no idea what awaits us. There will certainly be typos and some minor tweaking, but I'll bet it will be an opportunity to expand and expound. At the very least, I will let you know when we have cleared that task and at that point, we will start fresh and keep moving forward.

Fresh Start

True to my word, the 120 page autopsy has been completed and while this is a direct segue from the preceding paragraph, there are two weeks or so between then and now.

It was definitely interesting going back to page one and actually read what I had written. I think, for the most part, it made some sense and didn't totally suck. There was definitely the aroma of preaching about it and please take what has been written to this point and what is to come with a grain of salt in that regard. There were also a bit too many references about what your state of mind will be when you are allowed to read all of this. Clearly, your state of mind and level of experiences is all yours and there is nothing for me to do about it. Maybe a little too much Zen and likely more to come, but I will try and keep a lid on it.

120 pages may or may not seem like a lot of writing, but it sure feels that way to me. Over the course of around four months, it is difficult to remember all of my meanderings. I realized there was a bunch of stuff left out in certain places and I took cryptic notes to include some pieces into the puzzle of my past.

It was pretty challenging to read my writing and I couldn't do too many pages at a time because it was easy to lose focus. I didn't disturb anything with updated contributions, as that would have felt like tampering with the basic structure, which is to take it as it comes and not mess with it. Where appropriate, some blanks were filled in for purposes of clarity. Honestly, I thought it would be funnier than it turned out, but my best humor is adlibbed and not in anyway deliberate and there is a deliberate nature to this, which we'll just have to put up with.

There is no particular hurry to get into the Kauai volume, which is at least relatively fresh in my clogged memory pipes. I feel like continuing to shovel the pre-Kauai relics and will cross the ocean when the mainland life is relatively well covered. At the same time, I will not hesitate to tell you what is going on at its precise moment of occurrence out here.

In the spirit of contemporary communication, I did just come up from the garage, where I polished up the Tangerine Dream, hopefully for a ride with the Sons of Kauai. We have had torrential rains here for around two weeks and everyone has about had it. The sun is supposed to shine tomorrow and I wouldn't miss a ride with the bruddahs, especially after a run of lousy weather.

My leg is fine and nearly 100% healed. I have been running on it for a couple of weeks now and the Doc said in around three weeks, I can go back to kayaking in the ocean, which might allow me to catch the end of whale season here. It's all good.

A couple of nights ago, I had a great conversation with your Dad. I am pretty sure he had several scotches under his belt because he was much more expansive than usual and it was a real treat for me. Mind you, he is usually pretty forthcoming and our communication is good. It is a pure joy to talk with my blood son about anything on my mind and encouraging him to do the same. He definitely talked about you and he is madly in love with you and the feeling is indescribable for me when I hear him speak about you in the way he does. Your Mom is in the midst of putting together a massive gig, involving service stations that sell natural gas, recharge electric cars and provide conventional fuel. We had a good time talking about it, especially the part that related to the distinct possibility of incredible wealth coming your way. Your Mom is hot shit and has the ability to laser focus on issues and the innate intelligence to carry an idea forward to fruition. You could end up being an incredibly wealthy kid, which means you will be able to fly here and surf during school and summer breaks. He also lectured me about being more careful with my leg, which was very sweet of him. It was a role reversal of a kid telling his parent to be careful. As far as I am concerned, if Dad is still taking chances at my age, then there is life in me and that is reason for celebration and not caution. Trust me, I am over hurting my leg because I don't take appropriate precautions and that is pretty much the story, but it was great to get lectured to by Andy.

One of the things I was looking for during the backwards read was any mention about a milestone in your father's life and one that changed him dramatically. When he was entering his senior year at Rutgers, the motor stopped running. On a good day, this is a pretty overwhelming time for a young person. You are about to get out of college with a degree and for the first time, there is no plan and no parents to take you by the hand. My split with your grandmother and all that ensued around it were probably festering long enough to burst forward at this desperate time for your Dad. He was rightfully very angry with me for leaving the house and then leaving him and Danny for New Mexico when he wasn't even thirteen. Whatever the history and dynamics with your grandmother, that is not a path I will take you on. I tried as best I could to let him wail on me without getting defensive or trying to dissipate or redirect his anger. My hope was that he would stomp our history to death and become open to a new connection, one that would be far deeper than it ever could have ever been without this coming apart. A marvelous young man emerged from this private nightmare and it allowed us to get closer than I could ever have hoped for.

Right around the time I went backwards into this story, I started communicating with Beverly. You remember her, don't you? I started this recent go around by sending an email about my writing this thing and having very complimentary words about her already written into it. Emails followed back and forth and then a phone call. I asked her to come out here for a visit. We have had a connection that has survived around twelve years and there is a strong attraction. She totally has my number and that is a wonderful challenge for me. Her being psychic gets her into places where the doors appear closed. We shall see what happens.

OK, kid. I think we will call it quits for right now. I'm feeling like going back to NYC and covering more of my forty plus years there.

Not In A New York State Of Mind

Billy Joel wrote and recorded a song called New York State of Mind. He did a lot of really solid work and he was just some Jewish kid from Long Island. You should listen to him and so many of the artists who grew from the roots of the musical explosion in the Sixties.

Anyway, not in the mood to retrace my steps in the City right now. I should likely start that story at the beginning, in the house and neighborhood I grew up in. As I have already stated ad nauseam, the history is not nearly as much fun as what is going on right now and isn't that the way it should always be?

I spoke with my dear friend, Eiju, over this past weekend. Pretty sure I have mentioned him already, but this is one of those instances where I really don't mind the repetition. The reason why I don't mind is simply because Eiju is a pretty exceptional guy. He knows I am writing this extraordinary epoch to you and we have talked about it a number of times already, based very much in a Zen way of looking at things.

Bear with me if I am repeating some stuff. When I first got to Kauai, I began doing a Zen practice at a temple here, which is a story to be shared when we finally land on Kauai. Eiju visited this temple when I was going there and we had a really good connection. Eiju is a wonderful soul, who embodies so much of what the Buddha was and how I think he viewed the world around him.

When we talked before this last time, I asked him if he would write something to you for this book. Of all the people I know, he is the only person I would think to ask because his way of viewing himself and the world around him resonates perfectly within me. Keep in mind, this guy is a Zen priest and that is who he is in the world. Some of the people who choose this path are fabulous human beings and there are others who are driven by selfish, ego driven interests. Eiju is solid.

He has been trying to track down his own grandfather. Eiju lives in Mendoza, Argentina, but like virtually every one in Latin America, his roots are Spanish. He told me he would love to know about his own grandfather, but he has nothing to hold on to because nothing was left for him. Whatever he writes will be worth the price of admission. While he is absolutely no saint, he is not a sinful man, no matter how you try and twist his story. I am always deeply flattered that we talk as complete equals, looking at the world eye to eye and heart to heart.

I will try real hard to start the next entry with 69-30 179th St, Flushing, NY 11365.

69-30 179th St, Flushing, NY 11365

That is the address of the house I grew up in and spent twenty-one years, more or less. It was a great neighborhood for a kid. These were all homes built right around the end of the Second World War and they had front and back lawns and separate garages. Families moved to this area to realize their dream of owning a home. These places were all white, but had mixed religions. Blacks were living in ghetto like places all around the City. Most parents hung with their own, but the children on the block all played together and friendships were based on age.

The younger you are, the smaller your world is. For me, it started with the people who lived on 179th St. I had a couple of good friends and my older brother did as well. The paranoia that grips nearly everyone today didn't exist back then. We were not exposed to the abundance of fear that has now become normal, definitely since 9/11, but it was going on before that. We would play on our own and walked or rode bicycles to other locations, including the playground and the movie theatre. Now, you are told to never talk to a stranger and to never let someone touch you inappropriately. While I understand the necessity based on what has happened to all sorts of kids, it also breeds fear and distrust.

Until I was nine, the household was relatively normal, although my father was on the road quite a bit, while most of the other Dads were around. You know, it is hard for me to describe that time in my life. Actually, it is challenging to recount most of my history, primarily because of the distance and all that gets lost in the passage of time. I wish I could tell you how it felt to me at the time it was all unfolding. Until my father died, I was probably into a comfortable flow. I was extremely popular and always had a good sense of humor and enough intelligence to navigate most obstacles.

In April 1954, my world was rocked forever when my father suddenly died. He had a heart attack and was gone in less than 24 hours. My brother, Marty, was sleeping with our cousins in Brooklyn and I was alone in the bedroom we normally shared. At some point during the night, the hospital called and told my mother he had died, which precipitated a flurry of activity. The well-intentioned strategy at the time of sparing children any upset regarding the death of a parent or other loved one was to separate them from any of it. My brother came home quickly and for some reason or other, I greeted him at the door to tell him, "Dad has gone to the pearly gates".

The immediate time of his passing was very difficult for me. We were shuttled off to a former neighbor, now made good and living in a ranch house on Long Island. In the interest of protecting us, they actually ended up making it much more difficult to come to terms with, but that is how it was. I know we were forbidden from going to the memorial service and I don't think we were allowed to the burial. For better or worse, I liked my father, which may be due to his liking me. My relatives told me much later that he had a good sense of humor, which is likely where mine took hold. I loved making him laugh. He and my brother, Marty, did not get along so well and I got to see aspects of my father that were far less than complimentary. He was a disciplinarian and took it out on my brother sometimes.

As a family, we were flat broke after his death. My father's insurance paid off the mortgage on the house, which saved our asses. However, my mother had to go out pretty quickly and get a job. She began working as a bookkeeper at the Hillcrest Jewish Center. We had a black maid, Mary, who was a wonderful woman and incredibly good to my brother and me. There were no African Americans living in the neighborhood or going to my first schools, so Mary was my only exposure to black people back then. I think I might have liked growing up in less homogeneous environs.

I remember my first day back in class after my father died. All the kids were looking at each other and whispering the news about my father. Divorce wasn't nearly as popular then and I was also pretty young to lose a parent to death. Life quickly became normal for all of us and we did a damn good job of keeping our act together.

Marty was three years ahead of me in school and we followed each other through college. We were both incredibly popular and it was not easy for me growing up as his younger brother, but I managed to do a good job. I was always in the smart classes, but not nearly smart enough to be at the top. Some of my classmates were scary smart and competing was a non-starter. However, the majority of them were socially awkward and I always had the gift of engagement. I got along OK with the tough Irish and Italian kids at school and was equally comfortable around all the terribly smart Jewish students. I even skipped the eighth grade, which made me a year younger than others in high school, but I was good with that. I joined my brother's fraternity and became president in my high school senior year. It is really a bitch to go back fifty years and come up kind of empty in terms of my true feelings and thoughts at the time. We are stuck with having to look back at the past, but farther and farther removed with the passage of time and it's tough to pull up.

Things were pretty simple in the Fifties and early Sixties. America was flexing its muscles globally and we first began selling the Dream to the world back then. It was a time of legitimate growth in the country, as opposed to the paper growth scam that has infected our economy in recent years. It was a time of great promise and kids going to school and getting a good education would likely do just fine for themselves.

As a kid, my social circle began to expand as I progressed through the grades. By the time I hit the sixth grade, I was the "leader" of a gang of fairly bright Jewish boys. We used bicycles as our mode of transportation. My first girl friend happened during that time. Her name was Carol and she was a sweet, young kid. At that age, you might as well be walking in an art museum blindfolded because you have no idea what treasures await, but the innocent anticipation can be unbearable. We would do slow dances in her basement, listening to 45's, one at a time. We broke up for some inane reason or other and my gang and I were accused of terrorizing her and causing her to stutter. I was actually threatened with not getting into the program allowing me to skip the eighth grade. I don't remember how it got resolved, but it worked out okay in the end. I am sure there was some stupid bullying involved, but I never meant any harm to Carol back then.

Before I get to junior high school, I wanted to share the state of being alone with you. Every now and then, it dawns on me that so much of my time has been spent completely alone. It is just me and my thoughts and feelings, sitting and walking around in this ever-changing mind and body of mine. There is much about this state that can be incredibly profound. The most important thing for us is how we think and feel about what happens to us and what goes on around us. Without the distraction of others, this being alone thing gives you an opportunity to really root into your True Self, not to be confused with the illusory self. So far, whenever I have written to you it has been within my solitude. The Washington State trip and the visit to you have been the only times I wasn't sitting at my desk, all by myself, writing to you. At home, there is always music in the background and at the very least, a beer or glass of wine within easy reach of the keyboard.

Over the course of my life, it is impossible to calculate all the time I have been by myself. I think of camping in northern New Mexico, all alone, with my dogs for company. In my heyday, I had three dogs and they were never on a leash and I never picked up their shit. We were out in the open country and they would just go and come back for meals and for sleep. The only exception was the dog love of my life, a hybrid wolf by the name of Sikhis, which is a misspelling of the Navajo word for friend. I was really getting into being out in the southwest when I first got there. In some sense, I felt like a metaphorical cowboy in NYC, kind of not belonging and standing out. Real characters grow up in the challenging outdoors and the independent spirited East Coast dwellers and immigrants are the ones who came out West to make a life. It was great to be just another character out there and not to be looked upon as different. Even then, I was on a trajectory of self-exploration and the desire to feel the world I inhabited. To deeply feel the life in your inhalation and the lifeless pause in between, followed by your letting go with an exhalation, seems to be the path chosen for me. I have never believed we are completely in charge of anything. We live our lives the way we are supposed to live them and nothing can be done to change the outcome. On that basis, any path you choose has to be the right one, so you might as well follow your heart. It beats the shit out of detailed plans.

My constant companion throughout all my life has always been music. I know musical ditties abound in this narrative, but there is no way I could ever overdo how incredible its affect has been. Try and explore all sorts of music. I have already alluded to my early roots and how my appreciation has broadened. A major breakthrough occurred in my transition from NYC to Sante Fe. Something happened on my drive cross-country and I may just tell you this story and we can always get left back to junior high school and finish up that one later.

We already talked about my having to say goodbye to your Dad and your Uncle, who I loved more dearly than I can say. Trust me, you can't imagine the devastation that nearly ate me alive when I had to say goodbye to those two beautiful boys as the last thing I did before driving west. After the tears cleared my eyes, I found myself on the New Jersey Turnpike, driving my blue Dodge Colt with a moon roof. Rocky was in the front seat, along with a ghetto blaster and a case of cassettes put together by a friend in return for my giving her all my NYC furniture. I wore a NY Yankees baseball cap all the time on this ride and believe me, I was not into hats before this. I think it was a gift from your Dad at some point. I had it for years and years and lost it in Belize off the side of an outboard powered skiff.

Getting back to the story of the musical road trip, I listened to these cassettes through headphones, secured over my baseball cap. I loved listening to Graceland by Paul Simon. Legend by Bob Marley was a huge favorite on the ride. There was a great Bruce Hornsby and the Range cassette. There were others and the music gave me a wonderful cocoon to travel in.

I can't remember the exact stops on the trip. For some reason, I remember an overnight in Tulsa, OK and liking it. I got up early each morning on the five day ride and I would run and then follow it up with a spin on the ten speed bike I had strapped to the back of the Colt.

In some way, the world began to open for me on my drive and it has continued to this day. I needed to be transplanted to another place and the trip across definitely sowed the seeds. It is impossible to describe the feelings at that time. I basically decided to step off the face of the earth and land in a place completely different from anything I had ever known. Music carried me on the ride and it often carries me to this day and beyond. Maybe you should start with some of the early Blues singers like Bessie Smith and Billie Holiday, who were groundbreakers. The Blues have been here forever and in many ways so has Blue Grass, one from the slaves of the South and other from the poorer than poor in Apalachia.

The big band era gave birth to Frank Sinatra and you must listen to him or you will forever know nothing about music. Rock n' Roll started with black groups and mutated to Elvis in the early fifties. I hope you dig back into the archives and get to enjoy some incredible contemporary music and I would define contemporary as something right for its time and an expression of it.

We will get back to junior high after this word from our sponsors..................

George J. Ryan

The above was the name of my junior high school and I have no idea who George J. Ryan was and why a school had his name. Truthfully, I am not in the mood to talk about that time in my life when I was in my early teens right now.

Let's stay with today, which is Saturday, March 17, 2012. It has been rainy and windy for several weeks and at least it has broken for a while. I polished up the Tangerine Dream last weekend, but the weather completely sucked and it was not even remotely inviting for a two-wheel whirl around the island. I wanted to get out on the bike this morning because if the weather holds, I will be riding with the boys tomorrow. Not only was today a good day for a ride, it also gave me a chance to get on the big boy and make sure I am comfortable, which I was. I wore my jeans, running shoes with no socks, T shirt covered by a camouflage, military style, heavy shirt, finished off with my black leather vest and red knit cap. Of course, the shades are forever ubiquitous. I am pretty sure if people didn't know better, I could pass for a real biker, as long as I went by quickly in the opposite direction. You feel different riding a bike and it is fun to dress the part for my rolling role.

After my morning ritual of meditation, yoga and a run, had a little breakfast, smoked a bowl and headed out on the Dream. First stop was a local farmers market that I usually visit on Saturday, partially owing to my having been a prime time player in making it happen. Probably mentioned that I somehow got on the board of the local farm bureau and this is one of the areas that caught my interest. Establishing a market place is a natural way to grow producers and consumers, especially in the world of agriculture. Cruised over there for a little lunch. I usually get a taco from some good folks. I say hello to many of the farmers and vendors because I know them and they know I have been involved with the market since its inception.

We want to avoid too many Kauai details right now because that will carry us too quickly to the finish line at a time to be determined. Don't know if I told you already, but I am going to end this particular effort on Halloween next year, a year from the time I began. This gives me plenty of time to take care of history and to get us up to the present, which keeps on changing every day. There are people who journal their entire lives, but this was never my intention. I always wanted this to be a book.

I left the market and went to see a terrific film, The Artist. It won the Academy Award and many other cinematic awards this year. It is a silent film about the silent film era and its awkward transition to sound, which happened some time around the early nineteen thirties. Decent movies don't stay here very long because we are such a small market, so you have to quickly get out of the house if you want to see it in the theatre. I have spent much time on music, but I enjoy many art forms and believe each one has its own special integrity.

The cinema is one of the last holdouts for the fading concept of live audience. Film, theatre, dance and music are meant to have asses in seats because an audience brings these efforts to life. Technology has been pushing hard for an audience of one. Everything comes to you and you extend no effort to go out and actually be with a larger experience, one that goes far beyond you and whatever device happens to be the latest and greatest palm puppet.

The older I get, the more I appreciate the accomplishments of imagination over intellect. Believe me, in my wildest thoughts; I never imagined my life here on Kauai. I am sixty-six years old and living all by myself on an island that is as far away from Amerika as you can get. This last Friday, we were unloading equipment for the feed business. One of the pieces weighed five tons all by itself! We hoist this stuff out of containers, and pull them fairly high in the air and move them to their next location. I am around forty foot containers, dangling in the air and pushing these three-ton boxes to control direction. My work boots are caked with mud, my hands are dirty and getting calloused, my jeans are covered with dried dirt and footprints of encounters with stuff. The humor of all this is never lost on me, not even for a second. I think it is hysterical for me to be here, doing what I am doing at this time in my life.

Had a great conversation with a friend at the Saturday market today. She is the wife and office manager of an incredibly nice lawyer, which I know is a serious conflict, but it is true, even nice people become lawyers. They are going to NYC in a couple of months and they swapped out their home with folks in The Village and others on the Eastside. She said they stay on Hawaii time when they are in the City, so they get up at around 11A and go to sleep around 3A. They go out to late night clubs to listen to music and most of the audience is likely in their twenties. On one occasion, one of the people on mike called them out for being up past their bedtime. When she told me that short story, I said to her that we definitely age on the outside, but that has nothing to do with what is going on under the skin. For me, I embrace life more now than I ever did and it is because I really appreciate the gift and I don't give a fuck what I look like on the outside. Although, I confess to snipping hairs that have no business growing where they do on my face right now. A comedian by the name of Billy Crystal had a wonderful routine about aging and realizing that hair decides to now grow in your nose, ears and your eyebrows, often a fiercely independent corkscrew of a strand.

I have been talking with Beverly, although not too often. We talked today for a while. Having been lovers so many years ago carries a level of familiarity and intimacy that hasn't diminished over time. Texas and Kauai are much too far apart for anything other than fantasy, at least for me because I don't have any desire to leave this place.

We may have a Mary story in the works, but it is much too soon to give it any attention here. It is one connection away from being noteworthy. However, at this time, discretion would seem to be the direction of choice.

Losing it right now, so let's say goodnight.

Good Luck With The Storm

We are going to try something we haven't done before. Remember, I sent a note to you and Patrice at the same time, in a manner of speaking. Sitting here on a Sunday afternoon after a good ride with the boys and looking for mental mischief. When I got back, there was an email from Beverly, whom we have spoken about as well. Feelings are interesting things; they can survive years and distance and still weave their magic. It has been fun connecting with her recently. Oh, listen, I don't want you to think I am somehow fixated on women, although I am. Much of my life and learning is defined by and anchored to my relationships with women.

As you know, the muse is usually nipping at my butt on Sunday afternoon, following the ride with the Sons of Kauai. I read Beverly's short note and felt like writing a little bit in return. When I was finished, I immediately thought of sharing it with you. I liked what I wrote to her and thought it would also be cool to see how I communicate with someone else other than you.

My work has been and continues to be peeling away all the layers until there is only a question mark. The better you know what you are about, the better the odds of having a rich life. However, there is no magical answer and it is a fruitless exercise anyway.

First is her short note, followed by yours truly:

"L

Actually, the forecast calls for "severe weather" tomorrow which here in Texas can be pretty darn severe. Let's hope this does not involve tornadoes. However, by next weekend, there will be sunshine and I will be walking on it! So I am battening down the hatches and going forth with optimism.

I was given a book last week as a very belated Christmas gift and am now reading it. It is called "My Grandfather's Blessings." Know it? I think you might enjoy it.

Thinking of you this evening and talking to you in my head. Hope you had a lovely day.

B

Good luck with the storm.

As you may remember, I am not a very good reader and now that I am writing this little tome to the kid I am even more reluctant to read anything, beyond the loads of business and news stuff I read each day. I have no idea where this modest ability to express myself has come from, but it is definitely not rooted in my extensive library of favorites genres.

So, you are now talking to me in your head. Is that like hearing voices? Don't make me nervous regarding your grasp of reality, whatever it looks like at this minute. I think it is very sweet and wouldn't have minded hearing what you had to say, when you were saying it. In my case, I have had some of my best conversations with someone when they were not around to divert the perfect pitch that can happen between your ears.

Today was the first decent Sunday in at least three weeks, mandating a motorcycle ride with the boys. My bike was polished and ready to go. I outfitted myself from the neck up with my wrap around shades and a red knit cap pulled down over my ears. Had my new business logo t-shirt under a surplus camouflage shirt, topped off with my old black leather vest with the logo of the group on the back. Jeans and sockless running shoes covered the rest of me. It is like being Batman. I morph into a callous and menacing figure on a tangerine colored motorcycle, which completely screws up that mean image. I am also the only guy with a large hooped earring and definitely the only who was even remotely interested in seeing the film, The Artist.

It is a great weekly ritual. We ride around the island and many of the guys I ride with have been here for generations and know virtually everyone of the locals and are often distant relatives. There is lots of waving and many shakas, the Hawaiian hand gesture used by those who can. We ride en masse to funerals and visit very sick relatives of the riders. Many of the guys are terrific with visitors, who invariably find our parked group of shiny bikes very interesting; partially because when we stop there is always laughter and hand shaking and an overall good vibe.

We rode to Hanalei this morning. Our island has gotten hit very hard with heavy rain and on occasion, heavy gusts. Parts of the island got 50 inches in ten days. I hadn't been up north since before the rains hit, so it was something to see parts of the road taken out, etc. We got up to Hanalei at around 11A and I ordered my breakfast wrap of egg, bacon, cheese, lettuce and salsa. Of course, I am the only one who ever orders this. The rest get something greasy, salty and/or jammed with carbs. Washed it down with a large can of Foster's Ale, a reasonably palatable Australian brew. Drinking before Noon is allowed if it is Sunday and you are riding your motorcycle with The Sons.

Rode back around the island to our final resting place on the south shore, called Poipu. Got home around 3P and threw my dirty jeans in the laundry. Sipping an afternoon wine and sitting here in a pair of shorts with open windows and doors, inviting the trade winds in to the space. Got some rock 'n roll on the radio. I'll tell you, I never, ever would have figured I would be living this kind of life at this time in my life. Any number higher than 65 is the equivalent of getting your ticket punched for the last part of the ride and if you are fortunate enough to choose the ride, you owe it to yourself to make it a good one, at least in my world. My younger boy was chastising me for taking chances around large equipment and extremely heavy gear, often swinging in the air. I told him it was a terrific reversal of flow because it is usually the father telling his son to be careful. On some level, I think it is great for him to experience Dad still out there and taking chances.

I will probably write a little more to the kid, which is definitely a habitual thing at this point.

Take extremely good care of yourself.
Larry"

Don't be offended, but sometime I refer to you as the kid, which is maximum endearing. Good, I didn't think you would be after getting this far.

I promise we will go back to the seventh grade in Queens sometime soon. The pre-pubescent time in my life was not all that exciting, although I had no idea at all back then. The best we can do is to know the world we live in at any time in our lives. The 14 year old and the 66 year old are not quite the same person. When you see a young tree growing in nature, you can't have any idea how many branches it will grow or whether the trunk will split into two large growths. Back that far, I can recount events, but not embody them very well, which is not as much fun to write about as something being fresh and current.

Life may get more interesting. Meeting Mary for margaritas on Wednesday and your guess is as good as mine. She is a very good-looking woman and an artist, which means there is a possibility she will be sufficiently crazed to think I make sense, a very scary thought.

Seventh Grade and Beyond

I remember each year school started with a good amount of trepidation on my part. Going to a different school after seven years in the same place was definitely a freak out for me. Elementary school was a bit of a womb and I traveled through the grades with the same basic group of very smart Jewish kids. Now, I was going to George J. Ryan in the SP or Special Progress class, which means we skipped the eight grade and went form 7SP to 9SP and then on to high school.

Junior High was a larger school and pooled from a wider net, including plenty of students who were not necessarily as educationally fortunate as my original schoolmates. This was in the late fifties; when boys had pompadours, garrison belts, engineer boots and a pack of cigarettes rolled up in their T-shirt sleeves. Needless to say, the brighter kids did not dress like this and I really felt as if I was straddling both worlds. I was very lucky and somehow ended up OK with the tough guys and still kept my smart friends. If I remember correctly, I think I ran for some school wide office in the ninth grade and ended up winning. There is actually a photograph of myself and the other school officers with the top official in the borough of Queens. My private joke was wearing a label on the inside of my sport jack that said something like, "This is made out of 100% horse shit".

I had my second girl friend and her name was Margie, a really pretty, freckle faced, red head. Pretty sure we held hands and kissed, but I don't recall necking or the touching of private bodily parts. It is a terribly vague memory at this point and details are hard to come by.

I know I was very popular and kind of took it for granted because it was not something I actively sought nor did it make me self-conscious. It was just how it was for me. Somewhere in here I got Bar Mitzvahed and I was thrilled to have the whole Jewish thing over with. Hebrew school was mandatory from some early age until achieving my ethnic manhood at age 13. Even then, these events often became orgies of conspicuous consumption because I think so many Jews were so insecure back then and they wanted to make an obvious statement regarding their success. Since that time, they have grown to be absolutely ridiculous. Wondering what your pageant will be like and of course it will be years behind you when you read this. I hope it wasn't too garish and I don't think your parents would go for ice sculpted swans and shit like that. They have great taste, which is primarily your mother's doing, along with your dad's happy acquiescence.

The ninth grade was a prelude to Jamaica High School, lurking in the shadows of summer's end that year. This was somewhere around the late fifties, Playboy Magazine, V neck sweaters, chinos, Edsels, hip Jazz, R&B, Soul and early fall out from the explosion of Rock Around the Clock. It was a time of innocence and optimism, along with a healthy dose of denial, as African Americans were still being lynched in the South and living in a subtle apartheid in the North. Women were second-class citizens and they rarely broke out of that defiling stereotype. Of course, we have to keep in mind I was all of fourteen or so at the time and I was as clueless as any other young person that age. I had survived the death of my father and was thriving in this world of my creation, which is what mattered then.

Sometime during all of this, I went to sleep away camp for a handful of summers. Ida managed to find the money to get my brother and me out of the City for a bunch of weeks during the summer. Being away from home and on your own is both unsettling and liberating. Getting home sick was a common affliction for many of my bunkmates. I was never homesick, but I was always concerned about how my mother was doing. I know this because for some reason or other, Ida saved the postcards and letters, which became mine along the way and I think it was following her passing. While that concern seemed completely normal to me, it was clearly a result of our unusual family situation. Anyway, these camps were a blast and it was like a fantasy existence somewhere out in the mountains.

Just got up and walked around and when I came back I couldn't figure out why the hell

I was writing all of this about a time in my life that I remember in shades and shadows of feeling and thought. It is still me talking about then, because I didn't get here without going through the infinite experiences that contribute to a life lived. I wish I could share my life as a fourteen year old, but that is simply beyond my capability. What I am certain of is that every single occurrence in my life has contributed to my being right here, right now and I don't have one damn complaint.

We will still go back to New York until there isn't anything more worth sharing and there is a ways to go before we get there. Keeping in mind that my City stay lasted around forty-two years, there are lots of things to be shared, but I am equally interested in writing about my contemporary journey, pieces of which having already been carelessly leaked to you. However long this first volume becomes, I am figuring around a third is going to be about my imprisonment on a paradise called Kauai.

While we are on the subject of this volume, not sure if I told you about deciding to run this version out for exactly a year and close it out this next Halloween. By that time, I likely will have milked as much of my history as I care about squeezing from the teats of time. It gives me plenty of time, but it puts closure on the task at hand and we will see where I go from there, as I am apparently addicted to the process.

In the spirit of full disclosure, I have to confess to sometimes stopping at the end of a paragraph and coming back to it a day or two later without telling you, probably because you wouldn't give a shit anyway. This time around, I stopped with my Bar Mitzvah and picked it up with the ninth grade.

In between the last entry and this one, I got together with Mary and it was a curve ball for me. I knew she had fairly early stages of Parkinson's disease, but it was not something I gave much thought until we actual sat together over margaritas. What caught my eye initially when I saw her perform was a beautiful face, an exquisite figure and elegant carriage. The concept of her illness became an immediate reality to me and for some reason or other; it made me feel very protective. On a good day, we are all terribly fragile beings, but rarely open to it. Having an illness like hers makes that fragility inescapable.

We had a couple of margaritas and talked about all sorts of things, much of it very personal. We talked about her illness and it was very touching to me. This whole story of mine is still very new to you and there are all these women. Believe me, I am no Lothario, but you happen to have caught me at a time in my life where I am in between and I guess this is what seems to happen along the way.

I enjoy the company of women, but I certainly haven't figured out how to make it work in a way that best serves her and me, whoever she is. The other side of that is maybe having a series of long term relationships because that is how it is supposed to be for me. We are going to get together after this weekend on Monday and I will let you know how it goes. She is really lovely. We shall see.

T is for Tie Dye

Just got a photograph of you wearing a tie-dye T-shirt because the letter "T" must have been the letter for the week at school. You are definitely a cutie. Have I told you, it is very weird being a grandfather, the son of my own son? We share genetics and mystical connections, but I am not the person you see everyday and clearly not your father. If we are lucky, we will get to have our very own relationship, one that is set on a bit more equal footing than at the present time.

I know I need to finish off junior high school because that is part of the contract with myself, which is to share my history, shining a light into yesteryear, a time long ago and far away. The biggest thing about ninth grade was the knowledge that Jamaica High School was looming in the background. It was huge in comparison to my school and it was ethnically mixed with plenty of black kids from the Jamaica area. We took some kind of tests before high school and my aptitudes got shoved in with the smart ones, namely math and science. It would have been really cool had I tested for a more creative pathway, but I was supposed to be a smart Jewish boy, who would become a doctor or lawyer. This sounds like something probably mentioned before, but frankly I don't want to bother fact checking.

I am looking forward to getting through high school and then college. At that point, I will tell you about the places I lived in the City and the one or two important relationships I had along the way, which would exclude your grandmother because we simply can't talk about it, out of respect for both of you. Everything else about my life is an open book, but not that chapter.

Beautiful Day

It is a spectacular Sunday on Kauai today. Had a great ride with the bruddahs. Each year, the original motorcycle gang in the State, the Ali'is, have a run and many of the island bikes turn out at a local beach park. These guys and the women with them are the quintessential image of bikers, but Hawaii works its magic on all factions and these folks are incredibly gracious and generous, regardless of how ominous they might appear to outsiders. To me, if you take a day like this for granted, you are simply an asshole. This is a blessing, no matter how you slice it. We owned the roads today, with a group of at least a hundred bikes that stretched ¼ mile on the highway. People waved and honked their horns along the way and cars stopped to let us pass through intersections. This is very hard to properly describe, unless you ride a bike.

I don't know how much I want to talk about high school. Obviously, while living through it, it was quite a time for me. I got by with decent enough grades and was beginning to approach the zenith of my popularity. In my senior year, I became the president of a fraternity. Every Friday night, we would go to Roger's on Union Turnpike and hang out, occasionally going inside for a soda or burger. Took the bus to and from school until my senior year when I bought a used Renault Dauphine, a little shoebox of a vehicle you must check out. It was the consummate piece of shit, but it was my consummate piece of shit and I loved it. It actually had a crank that I used on more than occasion to start the heart of the Dauphine when I couldn't get a pulse.

When you are young, you are always looking ahead to the next milestone. When you are much older, you are in no hurry at all to hit any markers and the smart grey ones find ways to be extremely fulfilled right where they are. When a milestone starts getting confused with a tombstone, it is time to slow it down.

Aside from being preoccupied with exuding coolness, college loomed large from the very beginning of high school. It was assumed that all of the young people from my sub-culture would be at least going to college and probably going on after that. My grades were decent, but not fantastic. My SAT score was similarly calibrated. We had absolutely no money, which meant the only possibility was being accepted to a college that was part of the City college school system. Until my notice came in, I was shitting in my hat because I had no idea what I would do if Queens College rejected me. My incredible anxiety is one of the things I remember from that time. While I will modestly fess up to being pretty damn bright, academic pursuits were not it for me. My creative side lay dormant and has only begun to truly awaken in the last handful of years. For some of us, it takes many years for the internal voice to be audible and intelligible, which would make me a very late bloomer.

Certainly, life begins getting awkward in high school, partially because of raging hormones, which tend to fog the mind. It seems parents have great difficulty dealing with a time they went through themselves, but somehow refuse to give their kids the benefit of the doubt regarding their deviousness. Already went through my liaison with Joanne, which was simply dying and going to heaven time for a high school man boy. It was difficult for my mother to discipline me or by brother once we hit our teens.

However, we rarely screwed up because of the special dynamic each of us had with her. It feels like to me there should be this long entry on high school and that transitional time in my life, but I can't seem to work up the juice and that is for several reasons. One, you will definitely have gotten through 12th grade before you get anywhere near this, making it history for both of us. Second, four plus decades later it just doesn't resonate with the same impact it did all the way back then. So, screw it and let's move on.

Just had a mini-revelation regarding my selfish script and that is I will begin my Kauai adventure on or after May 22nd, which is around two months from now. The reason for this is very simple; as that was the day Ida had a debilitating stroke and it was the day I flew into Los Angeles, with a one-way ticket to my new home on Kauai. This occurred nine years ago and it is impossible to begin to talk about this part of my life without paying homage to her one more time and we will.

I began college, intent on becoming a doctor and was going to take the requisite credits to apply to medical school. Already wrote about how that worked out so well. When my medical career ended, my only goal was to simply graduate from college with the necessary number of credits and I didn't much care about what I would be doing. The page job in my junior year directed me to the career I had in broadcast advertising, although I had no idea whatsoever what the next twenty plus years would be like before it began.

I remember being considered the heir apparent for the presidency of my college fraternity. Something about the popularity thing started feeling terribly transparent to me and I began to feel increasingly uncomfortable with the faux responsibility. I aligned with the lunatic fringe in my fraternity and sufficiently offended the membership to preclude my being considered for the post.

Covered most of college already, so I am not sure what remains to be said. I do remember being anxious as hell to be on my own and out of my mother's house. Right through college, everything was totally programmed and it seemed others were always in charge, but the approaching end of college was an incredible time for me. I was busting to get out of the constraints of being my mother's son, rather than being Larry.

I am not sure when it hit along the way, but I can vividly remember the sensation of finally being on my own and no longer accountable to anyone. If your life is spent pleasing others, it ends up being at the expense of your own growth, at least that was the unconscious force at play for me at the time. When I was introduced to the misfit pages at NBC, the die was kind of cast.

I am racking my brain to recall if I ever got laid in college and for the life of me I don't remember. Of course, that means even if I did, it was obviously not terribly memorable.

Next, I think we will run through places I lived during my adult stay in the City, spiced with a couple of ladies along the way.

Pardon the interruption from yet another ending, but I had to come back to this story after looking at a photograph of you, proudly wearing your gi and your newly presented white belt. The look on your face is busting with happiness. That's all. Couldn't let the moment pass and not share it with you. Now, definitely done until next time.

On My Own

When I graduated from Queens College in June 1966, I did stay at home because my stint in the Army Reserves was due to come up in a matter of months. By that time, I had exceeded all of the tenure requirements in pagedom and had no choice, but to take a position as the quartermaster in charge of uniforms for the pages. I had an office of sorts, which was adjacent to the locker room, where all the guys hung out and played ping-pong.

After the active duty business, I moved into the Agelhoff Towers, which has already been described. After hooking up with your grandmother, we moved into a small, renovated one bedroom brownstone on West 77th St. I liked that part of the City because it had an element of the funk about it, which was a comfort to me. We didn't stay there all that long and moved to a luxury high rise on East 82nd. We inherited a Buick from Ingrid's mother and had to wrestle with alternate side of the street parking, which was a bitch, sometimes wasting over an hour to look for a spot on the correct side of the street.

I am not quite sure when we began dealing with an interior decorator, who was a friend of your grand mother's family. I don't know if I thought it was hip to be looking at swatches of fabric for a couch or any of the other accoutrements that were a part of an upwardly mobile life style. Not sure I took any of it too seriously, as the hole got deeper and deeper for me. On the one hand, it was cool to be starting to live a more affluent life style than I was accustomed to. On the other hand, there was something about the pretense that made me uncomfortable.

When your grandmother announced she was pregnant with your uncle Danny, a complete surprise to me, we converted the dining room to a baby's room. A word on the baby thing, if you don't mind. Should you find yourself in a committed relationship where there is a likelihood of offspring, make sure you are a part of the decision and not a passive recipient of a life-changing situation.

The family was off to Glen Cove, Long Island after that, a terrain already covered somewhere along the way. Brooklyn was the next stop for grandpa. I found an emergency place to move into that was located in an area close to Park Slope and that takes us pretty quickly to Pat.

While I was squirreled away in the basement of the home in Glen Cove during the divorce proceedings, I met up with a lovely woman by the name of Pat. Not sure why it is important to mention after all these years, but I never cheated on your grandmother, not once. For some reason, I just didn't think it was right to do that, plus I totally suck at lying. Once the formal separation business began, I felt free to do whatever I wanted because the marriage was irrevocably over. Pat worked in the broadcast advertising business like me and we got together.

Pat lived with a roommate in Brooklyn Heights, a sweet neighborhood right along the East River. I would frequently stay over there and after a while, I introduced the boys to her. I don't have a single bad word to say about her. We had a wonderful time together and on one long weekend, all of us took a trip to Boston and there are photographs to prove it. That reminds me, I have two overstuffed photo albums that are yours. Great pictures of your Dad and Uncle when they were very young. If I hadn't just escaped from an emotional jail, I might have stayed with Pat back then, but my freedom was something I needed to have for a while. We were together for nearly two years and she was with me through the whole incredibly unpleasant divorce. After Pat, I eventually got together with pin up beauty, Norma, but that was a little down the road.

After my emergency residents not far from Pat, already mentioned above and one that allowed allowed me to simply move in with my belongings, I found a ground floor apartment in Park Slope on 7th Street. It had a small yard in the back and it was a great space for the boys. I enjoyed the neighborhood because it was just beginning to go upwardly mobile back then and had a colorful mix of long time, ethnic homeowners and the more upscale white folks who were moving in and renovating these old buildings.

My place was something called a railroad flat, meaning there is a long hallway and rooms one after the other. When the boys were over, the door was always open and they would stream through from front to back with their friends and do it periodically during those weekends when they stayed with me.

Hector was a neighbor who lived right across the street from me. He was Puerto Rican and his wife, Maggie, was Australian. We became pretty good friends and would hang out together. It completely slipped my mind regarding this rehash of my past that Hector got me involved in the ownership of a bar in Easton, PA, but this might require a fresh attack on my next visit with you. It is a good story, trust me.

Flickers, But First..........

The bar saga is a good one, but I need to squeeze in a current event. I told you briefly about Mary and how excited I was to meet a woman where the possibility of connection was genuine. As a result of recent escapades and my ongoing stupidity, I was determined this time to follow her lead and not rearrange the basics with my twisted view of how I wanted things to be. The communication on the phone and through email was absolutely terrific. The second date was as good as it gets. We were holding hands and I massaged her back while we sat and watched the sunset. The dinner was very romantic and the conversation was incredibly sweet. Several times during the course of our meal, I leaned over and kissed her on the cheek. Just before parting company, Mary reached over and gently cupped her hand behind my neck and drew my toward her for several delicious lip locks. So far, so good, right?

Two nights after that second date, we spoke on the phone and the first couple of exchanges fit perfectly in to the flow of things. Then, out of the blue, she uttered words I have heard before in my previous romantic adventures. It goes something like this, "I don't know how to say this, but......." The moment it began, I immediately thought to myself, you have got to be kidding me? Sure enough, it was followed by an admission that she had been seeing someone for a while and wanted to give it a chance to happen. For reasons that only she could possibly understand, our brief relationship was skipping along on a path of lies. The good news is this had not been going on for a long time at all, so the fall was not very far, but it still hurt a great deal. There is also the possibility that the other guy scenario was a fabrication engineered to end our budding relationship, although the rationale behind that logic escapes me. I can hardly imagine how Parkinson's impacts all of your choices. I wish her grace and resilience.

I must sound like some kind of unbalanced lunatic, bouncing from one failed connection to another, but I swear that is not the truth. At least in this particular instance, I was the victim of deception and there wasn't even a hint of anyone else in our talks. It is a very disheartening experience and at this moment, I am feeling the need to retire from this quixotic quest for a solid companion. Shane, for the life of me I just can't figure out why so many of us behave the way we do toward each other. I am a disarmingly honest guy with no desire to wall any part of myself off from another. Trust me, not feeling sorry for myself, just tired of investing in the mirage of genuine connection. Whoever she is, she may have to find me because I am feeling played out on my side.

If you have been seeing a woman for one day or one year and she says, "I don't know how to say this, but....", it is time to retreat and regroup for another day.

Now, on to the almost forgotten tale of Flickers. Somehow, I managed to stay at one of the advertising agencies, Dancer, Fitzgerald, Sample, for enough years to qualify for profit sharing and had around thirty grand in the bank as a result of my ability to swallow a routine longer than I imagined possible. My Park Slope neighbor, Hector, had a friend who lived near a beshitten town called Easton, PA. Its sole claim to fame was being the birthplace of Larry Holmes, the Easton Assassin and heavyweight-boxing champion of the world. While he never got the recognition he thought he deserved, he was a very big star in Easton. At one time, that part of PA was a major coal-producing region, but its time had passed and the downtown was a depressing succession of vacant storefronts.

Hector introduced me to Richard, who had an idea to open a bar and restaurant in downtown Easton. Its motif was the silent movie era, hence the name Flickers. I stupidly decided to invest my nest egg in this scheme and suddenly became the absentee owner of a bar, every moronic guys idea of something really manly to do. I would drive down on weekends and help in the construction of this horribly unique experiment. One of the many brilliant ideas was to coat the bathroom walls with pictures of silent movie stars, a very compelling touch for a blue-collar community. Hector and I rented a house and stayed there on weekends. The boys would come with me on our weekends together and Norma came on a number of occasions as well. I know they had a good time, but it was a terribly expensive form of entertainment based on its outcome. They would hang around when it opened and it must have been an experience for them.

The color of this malignant tumor was purple, which led to rumors of it being a gay bar, which couldn't have been further from the truth. We had bands on weekends and served a Sunday brunch, with copies of the NY Times available with your Bloody Mary. This was a world-class fuck up, which opened over July 4th and promptly closed on Labor Day. For a number of months, I would pack up my stuff every Friday after work and head down to Easton. It turned out to be yet another education in what not to do, which is one way of taking a painful detour through the land of experience. My nest egg disappeared, only to be saved by a very talented accountant, whom I have stayed with all these years, partially due to his genius around this escapade. The return of that green allowed me to plunk it down on my Cerrillos Flats estate, even leaving money for survival, etc.

While I have likely mentioned this before, there is no better education in life than costly mistakes, whether financial or emotional. The guy's dream of owning a bar should likely stay as a dream because the reality is a bitch.

Back to NYC

During the Flickers debacle, I was still living in Park Slope. Some time after the demise of the venture, Hector and his wife moved to Australia and I heard from him once or twice after that. My landlords sold the brownstone and I had to get out of Dodge. I ended up in a two-bedroom unit on the second story of a house in Astoria, Queens. This neighborhood was famous for being a Greek enclave, one of the City's many ethnic centers. I guess I lived there for nearly my last two years in NYC and it was a good home for the boys and myself when they visited.

Sometime toward the end of my Astoria sojourn, Norma left for California to sort of live with her estranged husband and I actually don't remember how we ended this first part of our relationship. My time at All American Television was fairly stressful, but that is the nature of sales. I think I did a fairly decent job, but we were not necessarily selling top of the line programming for advertisers. One of the highlights was selling a premier broadcast of a remake of Godzilla, which should give you some idea of the challenges faced.

After Norma left, I was on my own yet again. I somehow managed to meet another English lady, Helen and we were together for probably around a year or so. She lived in the West Village and worked at a Jamaican style restaurant right down the street from her place. She was a bit of a hippie lady and it was fun for a while to be a part of the life style. I do remember driving down to her place late in the evening and waiting for her to get off work. It was like being the totally cool guy, who went to a restaurant near closing time to wait for his lady to get off work. We would then walk back to her place and spend the evening. She was a sweet lady and I think she liked me quite a bit, but it started to play out for me after a while. I know the boys got to spend time with her, partially because your Dad recalled it during my recent visit to see you all.

I was beginning to give serious thought to leaving the City during my Astoria time. Uncle Danny was already in his teens and your father was fast approaching that time as well. When my lease expired in Astoria, I really didn't want to tie myself down to another place. Through my work at All American Television, I met and became friendly with a Canadian TV producer, who kept an apartment on the east side of Manhattan. It was actually one block away from the high rise I lived in with your grandmother years before. I put what furniture I had in storage and moved into his place. He didn't charge me any rent and I stayed there for well over six months.

During that time, I had a brief run in with Candace, the sister of one of the women who worked for my in sales. Saw her briefly and we would end up getting together again in Santa Fe. She is a wonderful character and everything you would expect from a professional lady, immersed in the culture of Dallas, TX.

Not sure what else to tell you about my forty-two years in New York. You know, you start out wanting to be older than you are, always thinking it will be better and it never is. However, there is no way to tell someone that inescapable truth because you get their on your own or you don't. Life is simply what it is, regardless of your age. We are like human recipes, filled with an infinite variety of flavors and spices, each one taking its own special time to blend into our lives. We are an endless work in progress and the biggest miscalculation we make is to think we have arrived at some special place, no longer subject to the inevitable changes that wait each time a split second comes and goes. It would probably be cheating to know this too soon because time is the teacher and the lessons are never ending.

There are so many experiences and memories and I wouldn't cash any of them in for a free ride. My childhood on 179th street was a good one by most any standard, in spite of the loss of my father at age nine. During the 1950's, innocence and trust were the norm. Kids went around unsupervised and never thought about the danger of talking to strangers, etc. It was a time of great promise. America had ascended to the throne of the dominant society in the world and we became the yardstick by which all countries measured their success and failure. We were pumping plenty of oil out of the ground and we were the manufacturing kingpin in the world. You would get a job with a large corporation and stay there until your retirement. There were actually homes with white picket fences as the suburbs exploded. The American Dream hypnotized the country and created great envy outside our borders. We gradually took on the role of the world's savior and developed expedience as the measure of our relationship to other nations. All those years ago, we sowed the seeds for the global dilemma that is creeping across the planet. Excess became the standard measure of success in our society.

Most parents of that era had either lived through the Great Depression or migrated here to escape oppressive regimes in Europe. That time was like a miracle to so many of them, who came out of a place where their lives were at risk from famine or tyranny or both. Trust me, I am not laying blame, just describing a time in my life and making a lame attempt at explaining it to you all these years later. I was just a kid and had all of the normal concerns for someone my age. I hoped I would be tall. I was afraid of having a small penis. I was keeping an eye out for hair to grow in the manly places. I wanted to be liked and fortunately I was. I was a crappy athlete and hoped it wouldn't affect my popularity. I wanted to have good grades and not cause any shit for my mother. I smoked cigarettes behind my garage with friends and got caught with a pack in my pocket. I shop lifted a candy bar from a store when I was pretty small.

My teens straddled the late Fifties and the early Sixties, a time of transition, although most were unconscious while it was percolating under the radar. I entered high school as the Fifties were closing out and graduated in 1962. JFK became president and Camelot, a make believe story, became our bubble of optimism, which exploded with his murder in my first year in college. During all this time, blacks were regularly lynched throughout the south and women were second-class citizens. The raw, underbelly of the country was bleeding, but it was miles away from middle class Queens. At the time, I had no idea how fortunate I was because my world was pretty small and I was consumed with very typical teenage, earth shattering issues. One of the things that bothered me a great deal when I was growing up was the way adults dismissed our problems because we were young. I remember all too well my heart being broken by a girl and it hurt like hell at the time. My fears felt pretty damn real to me when I was growing up. Your world is all you know and as it gradually expands with age, so does your awareness, or that is at least the hope for us all.

I'll get back to my teens in a minute or two, but I need to take a sharp turn. I know I mentioned I have been communicating with Beverly, a lover from my past. This morning, I wrote her a note about my trying to function in this world as if each day is my last and how that would impact on most everything I said and did. Shane, the truth is, regardless of age, any day could be your last one here because it is completely outside our control. The things we put off to another day for whatever reason becomes a habit all too easily for us. We don't quite say what we mean and we edit our actions, thinking there will always be another time. Beverly just sent me a response and she recounted the loss of most of her family at this point in her life. She described this time in her life as a rather peaceful one, working, coming home, caring for her dogs, watching the season's change and writing in her journal. Her last sentence went like this, *"If it were the last day and I knew it and we were together, I probably wouldn't say anything. I'd just hold your hand."* It stopped me dead in my tracks and I cried uncontrollably. That is one of the most touching moments I have yet to experience. My eyes are still burning and I am sniffling a nose that just finished crying.

Now, I return to high school with a slightly different attitude. Forget the platitudes and global references. I was all of fifteen when I entered the tenth grade at Jamaica High School. Having skipped the eighth grade, I was a year younger than many of my classmates, except all of the super smart ones who were in the same program I was. You will undoubtedly be able to testify that hormones are all the rage in your early teens. Somehow, you intuitively figure out what that's all about and life takes on a whole new meaning. Voices change and stiff little hairs start popping from your cheeks and neck. Spindly hairs get more company on your pits at the same time.

I definitely balanced social and academic pressure. It seemed so bizarre that at age sixteen or seventeen, you are forced to make career decisions for the rest of your life. For me, my sense of certainty has diminished over time and after all this time, I would confess to being clueless about most everything. The rush to adulthood is almost like a game in retrospect, but back then it was pretty damn overwhelming.

I think I took the Q17A bus to high school for my first two years and bought a very used Renault Dauphine during the summer leading into my senior year. Having my own car was close to the coolest thing in my whole seventeen years of life. Cutting classes was a ritual everyone felt the need to experience. Having the ability to break the rules is part of the exercise of freedom from control that is an inherent characteristic of teen time.

We pretty much covered college already and I definitely don't want to get the feeling I am padding the pages of this saga in order for it to qualify as a full-fledged book. We've done my jobs, my homes and my relationships in NYC. I am feeling like I should concentrate on my glass of wine and let this rest for a while. I really don't want to start my Kauai stories until we get to May 22nd, which is about six weeks from now. We will see what I come up with between now and then. Frankly, the note from Beverly has really thrown me and I probably need to be alone with that for now. Got Chicken Long Rice waiting for me and I think I will heat it and have myself a fine dinner. Love you, Shane.

Where Did The Fear Come From?

Still wrestling with encapsulating my first forty-two years and will likely come back to it shortly. What I am trying to figure out now is what happened to the world from the time of my childhood until now. Fear, anger and polarized philosophies have infected the culture and I am attempting to sort out where its roots came from.

As usual, I have absolutely no idea what your world will be like and any guesswork on my part would not be terribly positive, based on all the contemporary signs. Fear in all sizes and shapes has grabbed America by the throat and it is not likely going to let go. We are all much more easily manipulated when fear infects our lives. The McCarthy era, which predated my adulthood, used fear of Communism as a way for the government to crush dissent and it worked for its time. When it ended, a benign time ensued and that was my childhood. I was pretty young for the Korean War, which was the beginning of the most idiotic foreign policy imaginable. Any threat to American interests anywhere at all, was deemed to be justification for carnage in its name. The list of wars keeps growing and there have only been casualties and no victories whatsoever.

I think the ongoing threat of Communism allowed those in power to create this external distraction regarding the red menace. When the Berlin Wall finally fell in 1989, what would replace this "excuse" for the transgressions of the military industrial complex, an idea made famous by a long ago president, Dwight Eisenhower.

This has kind of gotten my momentary attention because I can't think of anything to rival what has happened here, especially since the fall of the Twin Towers. Prior to that, the Moral Majority had a good run in the 1980's, very effectively inserting Christianity into the political dialogue. The political influence of corporations began to grow in the 90's, as their tax rate coincidentally began to drop. Media is right there in the mix and as their numbers increased through cable and the internet, they had to find new ways to reach their audience and another word comes to mind and that is manipulation. A wonderful confluence of power began to gradually coalesce and the ability keep its consumers and/or constituents on edge proved to be a very effective strategy for them to achieve their goals of increased power and wealth

I swear I am not some crazy, paranoid lunatic, banished to a small island in the Pacific. There is nothing terribly unusual about all of this because you will easily find a well-worn path by every goddamn empire that precedes our Amerika. In my very informal Zen practice, there is something called the Four Vows. One of them offers that greed, hatred and ignorance rise endlessly and I believe it is a sad affliction of our species. It seems we have predictably turned on ourselves in the past years, ever since records were kept, even on cave walls.

By the way, Buddha's birthday is allegedly tomorrow, April 8th, which will likely warrant a mention of some kind, assuming I am back at this.

Once again, I know a bunch of this rant-like posturing has come up already, at least once before and will likely reappear before the end of this exercise. Our personal freedom, which was pretty much taken for granted, has been disappearing at an alarming rate. A law was recently passed that allows our military to arrest US citizens who are deemed by them to be a threat to our security. There is no trial and no rights for these people; they can simply be imprisoned, effectively disappearing from view. The Supreme Court resisted challenges to this heinous State overreach. This very same group of black robed barons ruled that corporations are people and as such, have the right to spend unlimited money in the support of political candidates. Pedophile priests and athletic coaches are being uncovered at alarming rates. The political rhetoric is beyond belief, with all sorts of freedoms being threatened and there is a sinister taint to it all. Honestly, I am not sure how much longer all this can go on without some kind of tear in the fabric of society.

So, what the fuck does any of this have to do with me growing up in the City? Now, that is a very good question. I guess I don't have the discipline to talk about my life fifty or so years ago without bouncing forward to this moment. If anything I have written throughout this piece sounds even remotely pompous or pious, please completely disregard because I am fairly certain I have tendencies in those areas, but I mean no harm.

I really do think the world has changed dramatically since the time I was a kid in the fifties. Probably, technology is the ultimate mind fuck in today's excuse for reality. All of this stuff is so incredible and so empowering, but spiritually debilitating. It is easy to delude ourselves into thinking we have transcended the primordial ooze we came from, but our ooze slimes out every now and then. The Fat Man would likely say we haven't traveled very far from our birth and we need to understand who we are and not who we would like to be. Anyway, I will probably do a Buddha rap tomorrow.

We have a presidential election in the works for this coming November. Obviously, I have no idea how it will turn out, but I will let you know how it is going before I sign off. Barack Obama, our first half-black President to hold this anointed office, is likely going to be running against a hyper-white, Mormon, Mitt Romney. This guy has been part of a group that has ruptured companies for profit and made millions. He is a surrogate for big business and those in favor of deregulating government and allowing the legitimately disadvantaged to whither and die. Barack came in as a guy who was going to really make a difference and there was a certain expectation that also came along with his being a semi-African American. This son of a bitch has grabbed hold of all the executive powers stolen by his predecessor, GW Bush and taken even more power into the White House. Either this dude had no scruples to begin with or the elite interests of this country kidnapped and hypnotized him.

All of this kind of shit may have been going on when I was a kid, but I really don't think so. I don't think there is some miraculous connection between my aging sight and some equally miraculous increase in my insight. No, the world has changed quite dramatically over time and no way it is my imagination.

Shrink This

Time for a break from the state of things and getting back to this story of mine. Been thinking about uncovered highlights from my time in NYC and ten years of therapy is probably due at least a bit of attention.

The marriage to your grandmother soured in a pretty unpleasant way and I was really getting concerned with my ability to cope. I was especially tortured about my two sons and what this would mean to them. I was in my early thirties and until that time, my feeling was that therapy was for others, but not something for me. My tune began to change as the pressure began to feel unbearable. A friend of mine recommended his therapist and left with no choice, I made an appointment.

Ben was a big bear of a man with a magnetic presence, used to full advantage in the therapy dynamic. I was always a fairly introspective person, but had yet to develop a vocabulary to navigate the emotional twists and turns. All of our contemporary dilemmas have traceable roots to our past and more often than not involved some parental dynamic or other. I know there are numerous therapy modalities, but our history provides all of the clues to our present circumstance.

Once a week, nearly every week, I took the subway to Forest Hills for my fifty minutes with Ben and that lasted about seven years. It is definitely an adjustment to be in a relationship where there are no secrets, or at least there really shouldn't be any for it to be an effective one. Being able to tell someone everything and to do it in an atmosphere without judgment is almost too good to be true and it actually is because you pay this person for that rare privilege. It is a wonderfully painful, self experience and if you are in good hands it can be invaluable. Most of the time, when you are in therapy, you never bother thinking that he or she is also human. Certainly, in the beginning we give them all of our power. It is kind of like going on emotional dialysis and they become the human instrument to provide us with a shred of clarity in our muddy lives.

Ben certainly provided me with the support I needed going through the whole separation and divorce, but it had a much farther reach than that. There would be times where I could barely wait for our appointment and others when I just didn't want to go at all. I don't think many of us have any idea how much control our feelings have over all our decisions and choices. The more in touch you are with the invisible feelings, the better you understand your life. Mind you, it doesn't make you any smarter, very often it simply helps you understand why you repeatedly fuck up in a very predictable pattern. Revelations were not in short supply during much of my time with him. At its best, the therapist becomes the perfect parent you never had. At its worst, the therapist enjoys the control just a little too much.

I have a huge debt to Ben for all he did for me. Sometimes, those fifty minutes would carry me through the days and hours until we got together next.

In Ben's case, I don't think he liked to finally become useless in his client's lives and he may have held on too long. During this terribly complicated process, the shrink helps you to see yourself and then give you back your power, making him or herself unnecessary in your life and sending you on your way. About a year into our therapy, he suggested I attend one of his groups and I did, which is where I met Norma. Group was a phenomenon, like a make believe family with a referee.

After nearly seven years with Ben, it was feeling to me like it was time to move on and on some level I was looking for permission from him. Believe me, I didn't want to leave because of some feeling of having reached a perfect state of being. I just didn't want to do what we were doing any longer. The most incredibly pleasant excuse I could ever possiblly imagine was getting together with Norma, immediately putting an end to my membership in group because this was considered a major transgression. Believe me, she was way more than an excuse. I did everything I could during our group time together to keep the stallion in the barn, so to speak. We continued our private sessions for a number of months, but I guess we mutually decided it was time to move on.

While it was clearly time to end with Ben, I didn't feel my work was done and after a while I found another therapist. I am very bummed I cannot remember his name, but I do remember our time together, which was completely different from my experience with Ben. Ben was this big guy whose presence overwhelmed you and he was a head therapist. There was a physicality and spirituality left untapped and this new guy was all about it. Maybe not remembering his name goes back to my comment about having the process be about the client and he could have done his job so well that he disappeared.

His office was on the upper west side of Manhattan and sometimes I would just walk back to work. We did physical therapy like me banging on a couch pillow with a tennis racquet or struggling with him in some strange postures. I cried a lot with him and very often it took nothing more than his finger on my septum, feeling like he would crack my chest wide open. I would take poses and often it was the shepherd, holding his walking stick and it definitely felt biblical to me. I had already been seeing him when I "discovered" Rocky in Philly and we talked about it extensively. He was a good guy and a very effective therapist, quite different from Ben, but no less important in my life.

A number of months after I stopped seeing him, I started on my real journey, which began with the heart wrenching choice to leave New York and head to Santa Fe. I know that our work together, which had a lot to do with the spiritual quest, was an important factor in me giving myself permission to start on the path, one I am still stumbling on today.

Big Al

"*Try to become not a man of success, but try rather to become a man of value.*" - Albert Einstein

It has been nearly a week since I have had the time to sit down and let my brain tap dance through my fingers on to the magic keyboard. Been particularly busy with work related projects, but as you know, I am forbidden to deal with any of my Kauai life until May 22nd.

A little tease is in order, lest I appear secretive, heaven forbid. Presently, I am in the horse and cattle feed business, which I am pretty sure, has been mentioned, at least briefly. As it turns out, I am pretty tight with the Mayor of our island, a big bear of a man with a good heart and an OK mind, but in his defense, he is a politician, after all. He allocated some money for a study on the feasibility of establishing a Kauai beef industry, meaning the beef gets consumed by the island, as opposed to shipping nearly all of it to the mainland, the present state of things.

I was able to get a very smart guy awarded the grant and he lives in Walla Walla, WA, yes, Walla Walla. Joel is incredibly knowledgeable and slightly zealous, but that is a spill over from his church upbringing. Anyway, he was in this week, so there were meetings and such while he was here. In addition, I am a fairly important person in the agricultural community and a board member of the local farm bureau. I know this is hard to believe and it is for me too.

I spent the past two days helping to put together a Garden Fair, bringing in orchids, plants, trees, equipment, etc, not to mention a food court and an adjacent farmers' market. Pretty burnt out, figuratively and literally, having been in the super ray Hawaiian sun all day and dealing with hundreds of people.

It is very interesting to be well known in a fairly large circle and it is easy to see how adulation on a grand scale can really fuck you up. It is dangerously self-inflating and it is no problem for me because it is extremely temporary, thank God.

Here I am, alone in my space, with the Beatles on the radio, singing" Have to Admit It's Getting Better", finishing a bottle of Stella Artois and knowing I have some gourmet lasagna waiting for me in a quivering Tupperware container. A picture perfect day and presently looking due west at the setting of the intoxicating Hawaiian sun, back lighting puffy clouds that are undecided about whether they should start the day or end it. It isn't quite like Robinson Crusoe, but it sure as shit is a long way from sitting on the stoop as a little kid living on 179th Street in Queens. I never would have guessed it, even up to ten years ago. Back on the stoop it would have been some fairly tale that I likely would not have understood anyway. No complaints, my boy.

I also had a special treat at the Garden Fair. It is an event I have been out front on for at least five years and I know most all of the vendors and I absolutely love pretending to be the Maitre D'. I am always upbeat and entertaining the troops. That is one of incredible gifts of having a first class sense of humor, you generally know how to get at least a smile out of anyone. I happened upon Herman, an aging surfer, who coincidentally dispenses marijuana to the local crowd. I very innocently sat down with him on a curb, which was out of the intense sunlight, under the shadow of a big tree. We talked about what he was up to and then he said, "Hey, I want to give you something." When somebody says that and discreetly extends a closed palm, it is only one thing. So, in the interest of full disclosure, I confess to being under the influence of an illegal substance, whose status may finally have changed by the time you smoke this.

Now, this is very important. I am not endorsing any part of my life as a recommended direction. I don't care what that applies to because it is my universal intention with this undertaking that all I am doing is sharing my experience and none of it is recommended for home use. In my case, at least in terms of writing, I often like what this indulgence does to my sensibilities. I am essentially having a good time and if I am able to convey the feeling through my words, that really ought to be OK. Plus, you have to cut me some slack because I am going to be 67 at the end of May, a ridiculous occurence. I am not as young as I used to be, but I am not looking for some sympathy here either. I have earned my life stripes and I will do whatever pleases me, especially if it doesn't do harm to anyone else.

In my case, it is definitely a fight between stubborn pride and a sense of grace. I like how I am and still completely enjoy what I am able to do at this point in my life. At the same time, I am well aware that my stamina and strength have fallen off. Running for 35 years, nearly ever freakin' day of my life, I am extremely well tuned to the slow down over time and I would be a schmuck to perceive otherwise. I would be lying if I didn't admit to it being depressing at times. My idol is Fred Astaire, a most extraordinary dancer whose performances aged beautifully and he exuded a phenomenal grace through the years. I guess it is probably more intense at my age than yours, statistically having far less time than you do.

I know you are asking yourself about now, "What the fuck does this have to do with Big Al and that quote back there? It is 7:30P and I am starving for some no-brainer gourmet lasagna, and the hunger is now interfering with my communication skills. Will catch up with you in around a half hour or so.........

I am back, but dinner is not ready just yet. In about 15 minutes, there is a decent Client Eastwood movie I could see again, called Mystic River. Today was pretty tiring, but the thought of getting back to the story is my priority.

I guess that quotation from Al caught my eye and I just instinctively grabbed it and slapped it onto our tale of a life still lived, at least at this very moment. As a human on this Earth, success and value are not necessarily joined at the hip. In my case, I have been absentmindedly following Mr. Einstein's instructions. It is honestly something to take to heart any time in your life and your reaction to it will mutate as time changes you. In my not very humble opinion, success has become the battle cry of these contemporary times and self-worth has mutated into a currency language, rather than a language of the heart and conscience. I am sure this qualifies as one of the running riffs throughout this thing we are creating and all of this is your fault anyway.

I think we are good for now. We finished up the shrink thing a bunch of paragraphs ago and I am not sure where to travel next. Maybe, I will retouch upon my transition to Santa Fe and how it magically filled my life. Take good care of yourself, my beautiful grandson, Shane.

Where To From Here?

When I left the City for Santa Fe on June 1, 1987, I can't say that I had a plan. I owned the house I already described, having impulsively purchased it about three months before my formal departure. I remember contacting some of the TV stations in Albuquerque about advertising sales. My NYC credentials were considered big time by these people, but that is as far as I got because I just didn't want to do that shit any more. I knew it really well and I did not like it all. I am not a Willy Loman like person and never did fit the mold, which made me uncomfortable a great deal of the time in the buying and selling environment.

Thanks to a creative accountant, who I still use to this day, I recouped nearly all my profit sharing money, which I had subsequently flushed down a toilet in Easton, PA. God Bless you, Lee. As a result, I didn't feel even remotely panicked about my situation. I might have had three contacts before hitting the road, but back around then, I began giving over to whatever fate had in store for me. I have had some terribly painful experiences since then, but the influence of fear has gradually diminished for me. I know I am not going to live forever, but I feel blessed and I believe it has something to do with the path I have chosen, which never seemed like a choice, just a direction. I care more and more about my time here and it is percolating through all sorts of choices and decisions lying ahead.

It is impossible to describe the emotions when I ended the final leg of my drive to my new adobe home out in the middle of nowhere. I drove up the driveway into my place and parked my car, having to walk around and down to the little burmed adobe womb. If I recall, after a quick unpack, I walked down the dirt road a piece to the couple who had built my home and were now living fairly close by. I believe I brought a bottle of wine to celebrate my arrival into the new world.

During the course of my forty plus years, I had been around a little and had at least developed a sense of place for myself. This magical space was everything I could have asked for. Didn't know if I mentioned in an earlier Santa Fe tale, but I did ride that ten-speed on some of my cross-country stops and it did come with me to the Cerrillos Flats. Usually on weekends, I would do my run and then take a good long ride on the bicycle. It was before my meditation and yoga inoculation and I did run a little farther back then. It was so amazing to be in this dazzling slice of nature and it will always hold a dear place in my heart.

For me, leaving New York had a lot to do with who I wanted to be and what kind of life I wanted for myself. I felt remarkably normal in the completely foreign physical and cultural New Mexico terrain. It was the Fred Astaire Syndrome for me and I was completely at home. Someone coined the phrase, Let Your Freak Flag Fly and I think it is good to salute this flag, but it is the graceful thing once again that determines the depth and quality of that expression. Doing what I can for the cause in a way that suits me. Every now and then, I think what I would do if I was an angel? How would I treat people? I try to behave that way, but it is a bitch to pull off and I am intent on falling short each time because it eases the pressure.

Funny Thing

I was just sitting here and thinking I really had nothing compelling to write, but since last Halloween this has become an integral part of my life and not too much time can pass without my getting the urge. In many ways, this is like having a relationship; at least it is for me.

However, no matter how much I write, I will never be able to capture the moment a split second before I write, the too quick to understand language of that precise, pre-conscious blip. This kind of idea is one of many the things I like about Zen. There are pure moments of connection when Small Mind crosses the path of Big Mind. Zen is not meant to be understood in any conventional way because at its best it plumbs the depths of our darkest fears by shining the light of the Buddha within each of us.

I think I might be in for a fairly long run of solitude. Sitting here, writing to you many of my evenings, I am able to keep myself company in a very strange way and I am not inclined to disrupt it for now. As you know, this can change on a dime and it all it takes is a woman to catch my eye.

After Laura, who is part of my post May 22nd story, there was a dry spell and then some quick interludes I have already recounted. Each time, my life and its rhythm change to allow for another. I remember now how easy and unencumbered life is when I am alone and the change is always weighed by gain and loss.

Keeping it short right now. Been fighting a cold and coupled with work in the field, I am pretty tired.

Four Twenty

Today is April 20th or 4/20, which has been a ritual observance related to smoking pot. I think it may have started in San Francisco back in the day, but I am not sure and it isn't worth finding out exactly why because that is not the purpose of this entry.

I got back from working in the dirt and climbing two by four skeletal structures, while waiting for metal and motors, etc. Pretty cool that a guy just around sixty seven is walking around on two by's that are fifteen or so feet off the ground. Funny, this kind of activity doesn't feel strange or particularly strenuous, but I always keep my wits about me because I do not have the reflexes or agility of a cat, not that I ever did. Had some meetings in the morning before getting into my super geriatric cape and tights later in the day, so I could climb two bys in a single bound.

Even though I am fighting with a bit of an irritating chest cold, my mood is more celebratory than usual and now we get to four twenty. Trust me, it is not a religious holiday for me and this date has passed by many, many years without it feeling even remotely like a holiday, although I was never writing this kind of thing before either. Please, don't get the idea I am some kind of mindless, drug-addled old man who is perpetually wasted. Frankly, I am one of the most sober motherfuckers you will ever have the pleasure of knowing, definitely through this story and hopefully in our relationship to come. which will depend upon my luck.

Thanks to Herman, who I happened upon at the Garden Fair nearly a week ago, I was able to celebrate this special day. As soon as I put the pipe down, I got into some jeans, a long sleeve shirt and my slippahs, which is what we, Hawaiian's call flip-flops. Actually, I wear my slippahs everywhere I go, except when I go to work in the field. Here, it is cool to wear them virtually anywhere you go. Slipped on my shades and went down to the garage. I grabbed my Sons of Kauai leather vest and mounted the Tangerine Dream because I wanted to take a quick ride to the ocean and check it out. So, there I am, hunched into my ride and cruising down to the Pacific Ocean, with a wind at perfect temperature blowing in my face as I ride into it. By the way, if I haven't mentioned it before, Hawaii still doesn't have a helmet law and I take full advantage of that freedom. Rode a quick pattern and then came back to a little vino and just a touch more of Herman's Heavenly Helper.

A wonderful musician died today and his name is Levon Helm. He is best known as the drummer and singer with the Band. Yes, there is a band that was actually called the Band and they made some absolutely off the charts music. You must check them out if you haven't already. Although they are historically tied to Bob Dylan, they made some fine, fine music. You must see the concert film, The Last Waltz.

Today, I also celebrate musicians of my era, who changed the world and are now beginning to leave it behind. I don't know if there will ever be a time again when the Gods of Music decide to bless us with such an unbelievable abundance of sounds in just a period of decades. I think my music is going to be perceived as the new genre of classical music, like Mozart has been for generations. Some of the music of the Sixties and Seventies is truly artful, really good stuff. I hope you appreciate this music because it is such an integral part of my life and even your Dad's. He really enjoys a lot of the music from my time, the classics.

Right now, the local public radio station (don't know if these gems will still be around) on Kauai is playing his music and it is a real treat for me. Night is falling over the island and it is mostly black with just a hint of blue. Interesting place for me to be after all these years. Being alone feels less and less empty for me, maybe because I have so much to fill it with now.

Shane, if you really pay meticulous attention to being alive, it is amazing how much happens all at once and you can't possibly keep track of it all. Life is as full as you it want to be, no matter where you are or what you are doing. You better enjoy the ride because there are no refunds or do overs. When you live a full life, you have nothing to lose and everything to gain.

Cigar Store Hawaiian

It is the next day from yesterday, just so we are in synch. I had been thinking about getting back into the ocean with the HMS Feinstein, my steady, peddlin' kayak pal, acquired a few months after landing here. Did my usual morning, semi-compulsive routine of sitting, yoga and the run, but I stretch it just a little on Saturday because it is totally at my speed, having no obligations or tugs on my clock. I said clock, so don't even go there.

I rustled up some energy and took the kayak out to my favorite launch site, already mentioned. The trades were blowing pretty hard and the current was feeling a little strong, so I stayed fairly close to my favorite put in. The newly acquired outriggers are a Godsend. I would have stayed out longer, but it was too much to fight the wind and current. I had my beer and was working too hard, resulting in a retreat to my friendly beach drop. My legs are usually tired and my balance is a little off kilter when I come back in and I always hope it goes without incident, which is what happens most of the time.

On my way in to the protected beach site, I noticed a familiar jeep and went on over after I had dragged the kayak out of the water and put it in the back of my truck. I sat down with this guy and two other men. One was originally from Virginia, but had been living here for over twenty years and very much okay with locals. The other was a pretty hard-core Hawaiian native. Whenever I have been placed in situations where I am the maximum outsider, I am quiet, attentive and animated in my reactions.

It was one of those conversations that you are allowed to eavesdrop on, but you remain respectful and pretty much keep your mouth shut. The guy I know, who walked me over to this little group, left after a while and the words from the native Hawaiian that followed his departure were a little chilling. Believe me, I am the last voice for Native people because I command absolutely no authority and have no credentials and couldn't ever dream of having any. I am not now, nor have I ever been Margaret Mead. I believe that places like Kauai and Santa Fe have a lot of energy around them. This potent energy can either be your companion or your adversary.

I hope I am okay with the spirit world of Kauai, which I know is part of all local people's lives here. I don't think they would have any problem with what I have written so far. It is nuts to think you are anything other than a guest on this planet and it is good to behave that way as much as possible. Treading lightly leaves as small a footprint as possible and I think that is worth thinking about.

It is the next day, but not worth a little heading because it isn't that a big a deal. My Hawaii story really began early on the morning of May 1, 2003, when I hit the rode from New Mexico to Los Angeles, where I would leave my trusty, now rusty '93 Red Toyota Truck at the appropriate pier down at the harbor for its trip to Kauai.

As for me, I spent that night at an inexpensive hotel in downtown LA, where I made arrangements to get to LAX for my one-way trip to Kauai. I am still not going to get into the story just yet because I am about a week and a half away, but it is much sooner than the May 22nd date, which has to do with the passing of Ida and totally commingled with the beginning of my life here. At some point in all of this, I started thinking to myself that I wanted to finish up the history and be more present, on contemporary, familiar terrain.

Good Mood

Been waiting for a couple of days because the writing mojo was not visiting me and I have never written out of any sense of obligation, only when I feel like it. I was also feeling stuck, tired of side stepping my whole Kauai story writing any longer. When the May 1st thing hit me, it was very liberating because I was beginning to lose some steam overall.

We are only week away from the formal launch of my voyage to and discovery of Kauai. I know I have told you plenty already, whether about my two wheel adventures, work stories, kayaking and a host of other mentions. It will be fun to give it some context, which set the stage for everything that has come my way out here.

In a pretty good mood this evening. Indulging in my merlot and lazing myself into another idyllic evening on Kauai. You know, it is not all that easy being my age and still having some faded stains of youth embedded under the gray. Actually, not sure it is really youth, more likely it is a growing appreciation for this life we are gifted. In my case, it breeds a continued amazement without a hint of resignation.

All in all, I think I am a pretty shitty writer, especially when it comes to descriptive writing. I can't do justice to a sunset, a rainbow, a pine forest, the forever ocean or a beautiful woman. My descriptive abilities absolutely suck. However, it's the life thing for which I know I have an unusual vocabulary. My whole life I have cared about the things I am writing you, but I just never had the ability to lasso it onto a page. Well, aren't we the lucky bastards? I have spent my entire life learning what I know now and I also know there is no end to that learning. Words on a page convey a certainty about them, but I continue to make all of this up as I go along. To me, it is the spontaneity that weighs in heavier than the substance of any of this. What I am writing to you is how I feel at the moment, capturing it as best I can in this sieve of a mind of mine.

Listening to some great Blues: Johnny Winter, Taj Mahal, Magic Slim, Lightnin' Hopkins, John Mayall. I hope they are still playing the Blues when you are old enough to begin to appreciate its emotional leverage. If you have any emotional scars, and we all do, the Blues is the salve. Fantastic.

Friday

You and I had a rare phone conversation today, right before the nightly ritual of insinuating sleep into your world. This is a delicate challenge for all parents. At some point, they really want you to go to sleep so they can have grown up time.

I was outside working when your Dad called and I immediately jumped up and walked away from the guys at work. First of all, I love talking with your Father and stop whatever I am doing when he calls and the same applies to Uncle Danny. It seems you were in a rare mood to talk with Grandpa Larry and it was a treat to speak with you earlier. While I couldn't understand a good deal of what you said, hearing you call me Grandpa Larry and telling me anything at all about yourself was more than enough to make my heart skip.

As you may or may not know, we don't see each other terribly often. If I had a magic wand, it would be very cool to have you guys living close by here on Kauai and you could walk over to my place whenever you felt like it and I would take you to the beach to surf, snorkel, kayak or fish. We'd be walking around with our slippahs and in shorts. As luck would have it, I am living in a spacious one-room place above a large garage and close to a bypass road and low-income housing. Believe me, not bitching at all, as I look out at the sun setting over some lush, green hills directly in my line of sight. I can look off to my left and see the Pacific Ocean. You happen to be living in a beautiful home in Hoboken, NJ, time zones and thousands of miles away. So, in yet another way, this exercise of mine is my way of shortening the distance between us. Whenever you read this, you will be living it with me, as it happens to me.

I may actually be at a place in my life where self-honesty is everything. I am just so happy to be doing this for you and for me. I've been doing the best I can for quite some time now and if all I have to show for it after my departure is this message in the machine, that's fine with me. Not sure if I wrote this in any of the endless preceding pages, but this is like writing a message in a bottle and dropping it into the sea of life until your are able to reach out for it and hold it close to you. Sometimes, I write as if I might be dead tomorrow and at other times, I write as if there are many more stories to tell and plenty of time to tell them.

You know, I would be saying all of these things directly to you in your face if I could, but I can't, so we are stuck with this highly inadequate recounting of one life and how it traveled through time and circumstance and ended up in front of you now. I can't imagine this undertaking for anyone other than you, primarily because I don't care a hell of a lot about what anyone else thinks of me, but I try as best I can to find truth and at least share it with myself. The added bonus for me is that I get to double my audience and it's you.

Chuck Berry, The Beach Boys, Stevie Ray Vaughn, Little Feat. While most people don't even know what a ukulele is, Hawaiian music is beautiful. Listen to the most famous of them to this point, Bruddah Iz. I know that is not a sentence, but I can't be bothered. I never thought of listening to Hawaiian music before and didn't really like it. When you live here and resonate with this place, the music all of a sudden becomes your own and it is mesmerizingly gorgeous. As always, wanted to mention those other music names to check out if you haven't already. Relax, close your eyes and put on some Bruddah Iz. In addition, if I haven't mentioned it, I don't give a flying fuck about grammar, especially for this purpose. Last time I checked, the mind speaks differently than many of us are accustomed to and there is really no reason to regiment it to some checklist of punctuation, syntax, etc. As long as you get, it's all good.

Concert for Bangladesh

Listening to the music from the Concert for Bangladesh, which took place at Madison Square Garden. I am certain it has already been mentioned in my rock 'n roll bragging pages and pages ago. I can't remember the last time I listened to all of it, but this afternoon will definitely be one time. You know, it was the first time this kind of devil's music was ever presented as a fundraising vehicle and leave it to George Harrison to be the spirit behind it. By now, you better know he was one of the Beatles and the most mystical of the group. His music with the band and on his own is incredibly soulful and gentle. We are in the midst of a serious musical flash back and it is a treat for me.

One of the fellows I work with told me about a site called Grooveshark, which will undoubtedly not even be a footnote fifteen years from now. As you have easily guessed, I truly love music. This site is free and allows me to pull up music from most all artists and all genres. Only discovered it a couple of days ago and it has been a revelation to me, but I am also very easy to please.

I still have a computer that gets emails, etc and if I am not in front of it, I am unaware of its activity and have to catch up whenever I get to it. My cell phone has no numbers stored in it. I can't use the fucken camera on the phone. I don't text either, or whatever they will call it when you start sending all sorts of messages to anyone anywhere by tapping on a keyboard or transmitting telepathically.

I prefer the Concert for Bangladesh. It was a totally human experience, with thousands of people on their feet for hours at the Garden and everyone there knew they were a part of something quite special. Music is a form of magic, capable of transporting people to all sorts of imaginary places in the mind and the heart. God only knows what you will be doing for shits and grins when you arrive at the place where your legs can pretty much hold you upright for extended periods and Mommy and Daddy are not quite as important in your forever-evolving world.

While we are reminiscing, probably time to share the story of Beverly and the idea of gentling fanning the glowing embers of a long time ago love. There have been emails and conversations about her coming here for a visit, something I am completely in favor of. I think the spirit of adventure ages for most of us as we climb the ladder of decades. The body clearly contracts over time and very often so do our expectations and dreams. The talk of getting together has triggered more fear than excitement for Beverly and it is important for me to respect that. She is a very honest woman, even if it is at her expense and she has shared being set in her ways and afraid to disrupt them. What are you gonna do?

I saw the Dalai Lama several nights ago on TV. He will definitely be gone before you get to this. He is without question peerless in all the decades of my life. Please, please find out about him and if you can, watch him on whatever screen you watch things on. He is likely one of the few people ever born who has virtually no ego to speak of. His power is in his honesty and humility. He is probably the great being of the last century, along with Gandhi. These imperfect beings understood the nature of this life of ours and were able to embody it and communicate it to others.

He was appearing on a TV talk show, hosted by a British asshole who has no business doing an Americanized show like the one he hosts. This host is very interested in the salacious details of all his guests' lives. Now, here is His Holiness, the Dalai Lama, sitting in a chair directly opposite the butt hole. So, anus face wants to know if His Holiness has any problems with his lifelong celibacy. Needless to say, he said no and he said his life is much more even as a result. While you will hopefully be hormone driven when you initially read this, I am less inclined in that area, regardless of what my bragging mind has to say about it. I am settling in to this idea of living the balance of my life in an even-tempered way.

Putting up with myself is enough of a pain in the ass and I now often wonder if I can have a companion pain in the ass, so to speak. The funny thing about any guy, who claims to wear the badge of a guy, is that a smile and a look are all it takes to send you to another planet, where all the old rules aren't worth shit. As a result, any of my pronouncements about my current state of being are qualified by the obvious and always game changer, a woman who makes you trip over your feet, leaving you speechless and breathless. Yes, I know this is a hyper romantic perspective, but why not shoot for the moon if you are going to bother shooting? It has been an emotional passport to the full range of feelings for me. I have been gloriously happy and painfully sad with the women in my life. Mellowing into a lifestyle where anything I do alone is perfect and it is not the worst way to spend a life at this point, but we will see what lies ahead.

The Voyage to Kauai

As promised, it is May 1st and time to begin my official crossing of the Pacific Ocean to Kauai. While there will undoubtedly be exceptions, the balance of this tome will be contemporary, or at least less ancient than much of what has preceded. As of today, all bets are off and we are going to spend the majority of our time in the here and now.

I left my last place in Santa Fe, a little adobe house just passed Pojoaque and before Espanola, on the evening of the 1st because I wanted to get to the pier in LA the next morning and it was around a twelve-hour drive. All of my possessions had been mailed weeks earlier, so I was traveling pretty light that night. It is hard to remember my feelings as I drove in the darkness, but it wasn't the same as that day years before when I left my two sons and headed out from NJ to NM. Back then, it really was a genuine leap of faith for me because I didn't have the spirit mileage I put on my soul meter while in NM. Fifteen plus years in the high desert country got me pretty comfortable living on the edge and trusting in the Universe to meet an open heart and embrace it.

Remember, I had been to both the Big Island and Kauai a couple of months before and made arrangements to move in with a guy, who suddenly found himself in need of a roommate. I had networked as best I could before that initial trip and kept it going when I got back to NM for the next several months. The skills I developed in NM of just charging ahead with every new venture served me well in the transition to Kauai.

I got to LA sometime in the morning, after the port was open to receive vehicles for shipping. I temporarily parted company with my '93 red Toyota truck, which looked a hell of a lot better then. I don't know why I connected with Candace's sister, who I had hired years before in NYC, but she was now living in LA with some guy. I killed the day with them and likely drank a fair amount because that was her way and I needed a little anesthetic anyway. She dropped me off at a pretty dumpy hotel in downtown LA late in the day.

I was in my hotel room, having made arrangements for a morning pick up to take me to LAX for my one-way trip to Kauai. Sometime in the evening, my brother, Marty called to tell me that Ida had a massive stroke and he was heading from Chapel Hill to NYC in the morning. Without any effort at all, I definitely went into shock and felt completely overwhelmed. I really had no idea what I was supposed to do. As a little nine-year-old boy, my biggest fear was that my mother would die and I would be an orphan, a fear that never left the child within.

Marty and I decided he would head to see her in the morning and I would go to Kauai, if only for a few days. I felt incredibly vulnerable and it was vital for me to touch base on Kauai and then head to NYC. On that evening, I felt like an emotional astronaut, floating in limbo space without a home. When we hung up, I tried to open the sealed window in my depressing, drab little hotel room and it was sealed shut. I needed air desperately and went down into the streets of a really seedy section of LA and got some food and walked in the rain before going back to my room. I really liked Ida and at age 92, this was the end of the line for her, something I knew for certain even from that distance.

The next morning, I flew to my new home and I was a certified basket case for the several days I spent there. My roommate met me at the airport and I was a bon fide zombie. I guess I was there for three days, during which time we got my space in order. It meant there would be a home waiting for me after I got back from being with Ida and having no idea what that was going to be like. Work wise, I was still very much involved with the gospel music business and had to keep that going no matter what was happening in my life. This period is essentially indescribable. It was definitely not familiar territory on any level and all I could do was stumble forward.

After the several days on Kauai I flew to NYC and met my brother at the airport. We went straight to see my mother at the hospital and the moment I saw her, there was no doubt whatsoever in my mind and heart that the task ahead was to help ease her into whatever lies ahead when this life comes to a close. She was hooked up to tubes through her nose and mouth. Her eyes were shut and she was completely unresponsive.

I may have to break now because this is terribly painful for me and it can't be done all at once........................

Whacked in the Head by a Two by Four

My plan was to seamlessly pick up were I left off yesterday and continue the incredibly personal narrative about my mother. However, as luck would have it, I got whacked in the head by a two by four this morning, which split my forehead open and allowed for my precious bodily fluids to exit a wound just above my left eyebrow. Working on a construction site is a relatively dangerous occupation and it is made even more so by my complete unfamiliarity, something we have already talked about.

I was standing safely out of the way, at least that is what I thought. However, this two by four had my name on it and it was hell bent on whacking me in the head, which it did. I was bleeding pretty badly and was driven to the ER. If you have never been to an emergency room, try and keep it that way if you can. The folks were great and the surgeon sewed a bunch of stitches in my head and I was on my way.

It is okay if you tell your Dad about this now, but I am not going to tell him , understanding we are talking about a now that is many years apart. He is a city boy just like I was and things like climbing ladders and hammering nails are extremely foreign to him and likely to you as well. There is a lot to be said about the physicality of this work and it can also be quite dangerous. When you are sitting behind a desk and make a mistake, you can either correct it or try very hard to bullshit your way out of it. When a two by smacks you in the head, there is no discussion, just blood.

Obviously, there is nor reason for you to worry about me because I am either an old man relatively in one piece or I am already gone. As always, when I say something like that, I am selfishly hoping I am still around to look you in the eye after you have read this or anything else in this endless letter for that matter.

By the way, listen to the Doobie Brothers, with or without Michael McDonald. They made some great music and it was some of the more sophisticated rock 'n roll for its time. Right now, it is churning through my computer speakers as I sort out the day for you and deal with the fucken pain in my head.

After the ER, I went back to work, but left for the afternoon and here I am. Feeling okay about getting back into the story before we were so rudely interrupted by that two by four.

The moment I saw my mother, I knew it was over for her. We met with the doctor and he indicated she had a massive stroke and if there were no signs of improvements within the first few days it was game over, or a life on machines to keep her alive for everyone's benefit, but her own. Ida had a document that clearly stated if she was no longer able to feed herself, it was over and life support should be removed. To say it was a stressful time is a serious understatement. Marty and I grew very close during the next few weeks because she was our mother and no one else's. He had the legal authority to make decisions, but he never would do anything without me.

We visited her in the hospital every day and spent hours with her. It was heart wrenching beyond your wildest imagination. They had to strap her arms to the bed because she would try and yank the feeding tube out. We went through this routine for about a week and a half and there was absolutely no change in her condition. My mother was a fiercely independent woman and until that time at age 92, she was always in charge of her life and she would never have considered becoming anyone's responsibility. By the way, whether it is genetic or not, I have exactly the same feeling about my own life. It is all about the quality of life and not its longevity.

It became painfully obvious during the course of our days at the hospital that there was no light at the end of the tunnel and it was time to consider her wishes and no one else's. I wanted to bring her back to her home and begin the hospice process. At your tender age, I suspect the term hospice is a new one. This is a service provided by angels in virtually every community and they deal with end of life issues for the patient and the family. Their role is to ease the patient into their passing and to support the family in the process. As I said, from the moment I saw Ida, I knew it was over and it was time to honor her wishes. By the way, she and I spoke about this stuff on many occasions and she was crystal clear with me about her wishes.

It took a while to convince Marty that it was time, but he came around and exhibited the same commitment I did. Your brother and uncle were not quite as empathic. Actually, Danny and I did not speak for a couple of years after because he felt I killed his grandmother. Let me tell you something, nobody and I don't give a flying fuck who they were, was going to get in between my mother and me. She was my mother and Marty's mother and this was our deal and absolutely no one was going to hold any sway in the decision. All of us have very unique relationships with our parents and no one is better suited to make those crucial decisions. In general, death scares the shit out of most everyone and the tendency is to project one's fears, etc. into a situation like this. We all want to live as long as possible and can't imagine it coming to an end. To me, life on the end of tubes and other machines, while lying absolutely motionless is no life at all. I am bothering to tell you this because I wouldn't want you think for one second that the decision to ease Ida through her passage was selfish or expedient or anything other than honoring her wishes. After all that time and sacrifice she made on my behalf, it was what she deserved from me.

We brought her home and began the hospice process, which meant no food or water, while providing pain medication to make her comfortable. In all my life, I have never witnessed such incredible courage and majesty. Her dignity was actually very hard to take because it was unimaginable to me. On several occasions, she was conscious enough for us to ask her if she wanted to continue or stop the process. She unequivocally assured us that it was all okay with her. Marty and I would alternate our times with her. We would hold her hand and talk to her. Every now and then, she would delicately bring her hand to her lips, which meant she wanted to have her lips moistened. Once or twice she did that and what she actually wanted was a kiss. A couple of times, while holding her hand, she patted mine to assure me that everything was okay and there simply aren't words. There simply aren't words.

My father was ripped from my life at a very early age and it left a horrible emptiness. Ida's passing was more enriching than I could ever have imagined. As horribly imperfect as my father's death was, my mother's was an indescribable affirmation and one that has left me incredibly blessed.

She was home a little over a week before she passed and it was a time of otherworldly magic and terrible sadness. Marty and I were devoted to the process and it was a blood thing that binds siblings together. She passed on May 22nd, a week before my birthday and you can expect it to come up again in a couple of weeks when we hit that date.

During this time, I had a mythical life awaiting me on Kauai. I was on the phone quite a bit with the gospel music business. Kauai seemed like a distant dream, although I was anxious to get into it. I cried pretty regularly during this whole time and my pain was palpable. You know, that's how it goes with life.

Shiner

Woke up this morning and my eye was swollen shut and turning a lovely shade of black. Went to work today, but took it easy. When I got home a little while ago, I took a peek in the mirror and my eyes looks pretty funky. It is swollen in strange places and gradually going through color transformations. Bill took a photograph and promised to send it to me. Believe me, if I showed it to your Dad, he would probably threaten to make himself my guardian because of my reckless behavior, especially for someone my age. As a three year old, you would probably find it very entertaining to see Grandpa Larry's black eye, but it will just have to be our little secret for now.

Now, let's get back to our story, before we were so rudely interrupted by a startling whack to the forehead. Ida's waltz with her maker began in earnest with her stroke and lasted nearly three weeks. I think I will put it aside for now and undoubtedly return on May 22nd, the day of her passing.

So, it is just about nine years before this writing when my life began here on Kauai. It has taken us about six months to get here in our story, which started in Portland with an empty page. I have no idea how we have managed to fill up so many pages to this point. I hope I have stayed true to my original intent, telling the story of a life, which happens to be my only possession. For now, my relationship to this story is the most important one I have. While I am trying to make sense, I am definitely not trying to make sense of my life. I have been somewhat looking forward to getting to this point in the monologue, free from the past and comfortably ensconced in the moment. Then again, who knows what will end up being on my mind when I have the motivation and time to share it with you?

The Myths of Capitalism and Immortality

A couple of days, ago, I scribbled the above heading on my calendar and decided it would be the next entry. Some of this is likely repetitious, but some of it is not as I continually change my mind about everything. There is a smattering of consistency, especially when it comes to the big stuff.

In writing about Zen, I am sure I mentioned impermanence and the inescapable truth that our lives here are limited. While some may find this depressing, that is their problem because the truth is as obvious as every heart beat we feel and every breath we take. This awful idea is too much for most all of us to accept. Our egos act as a wonderful shield from the inevitable. It is what we all share and in that regard, it ought to be the great equalizer, but it is exactly the opposite. In our active denial of this truth, we do terrible things to each other and to the planet. It is only a true understanding of our mortality that provides the pathway to real compassion, helping us find balance in the world around us. If one is able to live with the yardstick of mortality, measuring success takes on a whole new meaning.

If any of us ever stopped to think about the death of one of the hundreds reported in the news everyday, we would likely be very depressed. When a soldier dies, there are mothers, fathers, spouses, children, brothers and sisters and who knows how many others. An eighty-year-old woman dies of heart failure and she leaves behind incredible sadness and emptiness. The senseless suicide of a teenager, who simply couldn't take it anymore, rips out the heart out of anyone with a connection. I guess the most awful thing is reading about the deaths of thousands of children in Africa because of starvation. We don't give a thought to the little one's family, who are living in abject poverty and totally dehumanized.

I think the height of the denial of our mortality is to feel distance and disconnection from the death of a little African boy or girl. I am right in there with everyone else and guilty as charged. You would likely go mad trying to be a purist in this regard. You do what you can on any level you can and it makes a difference. Changing the world is like changing the wind, it is simply out of our control and there are larger forces at play.

The basic idea of capitalism is an homage to immortality. Economic growth and profit are all that matter in this system. How is it possible for growth to be unlimited? We have non-renewable resources like oil and a thirst for water that cannot be sustained and yet mindless growth blows away any hope of balance. A company that has a fifty million dollar profit in one year had better make even more money the next.

Our behavior is tragically predictable and every empire has imploded on itself due to avarice and a complete absence of humility that only comes with an acceptance of our inherent limitations. It continually takes place on a societal level, but I believe there have always been people who lived differently, looking for just a little bit more out of their lives. Selfishly, it would be fine if you had some tendencies in that regard. Should it be the case, you will likely live a more singular life with plenty of room for others as well.

There is certainly a part of all this that feels like the memoirs of a dying man, which definitely is true in the abstract, but at this time I honestly have to say that I am feeling really good. Believe me, this is not said with any blind unawareness regarding my dwindling tenure. This whole project is a blatant display of optimism and hope on an incredibly deep level between the both of us.

Honestly, I think I am actually bearing witness to a multi-dimensional bankruptcy, on both a material and immaterial plane. There are gargantuan forces at play and they devour all in their way. The trick is to shrink your world view to the circle you inhabit. You kind of pretend that everything is cool and simply live your life in the best way you can and that is all the validation you really need.

Gotta tell you, I have nothing to bitch about. Here I am, nearly sixty seven years old, with all my hair, in pretty damn good health, still extremely active and adventurous professionally and I am sitting in a sweet little place on Kauai, watching the tropical rays return to their source for the start of another evening here. I am sitting in a pair of shorts with a glass of wine to my left and telling my story to you. Fortunately for me, passion still lurks within my heart and pretty damn close to the surface, too We are both very lucky to share this experience, even though I have quite a head start on you.

There will be paths we likely have shared already and that stuff will be carried forward by you. This extraordinarily incomplete map of my mind, moment to moment, will perhaps get some new roads as you carry it all forward on your own road trip. We are having a remarkably honest conversation, even though you can't hear it or comment right now, but you will have your turn. There is no reason whatsoever for me to lie to myself about anything and I have tried as best I could throughout life to be straight. It's funny, as you get older, your eyesight deteriorates, but your internal insights become clearer, at least that is the hope. There are times when I find myself reacting differently than many around me because of my age and the different perspective it fosters.

Now that we are officially on Kauai, with no going back, I haven't quite settled on the rhythm for moving forward. There are definitely some stories I want to share, in addition to some that have already been recounted. Amongst other things, I hope I at least get started on moving into the yurt before our year is up. It is hard to imagine sitting in a yurt, on a large deck that huddles close to a little reservoir with terrific wild life around. While I think I can conjure it up in my mind, I know there is a road to travel between here and there. This is one of the many things we have to look forward to, assuming I get there before the last page.

Woodstock

I have always enjoyed Saturday morning, alone or with someone, the routine is the same. I get up at whatever time and it is usually pretty early, like 5:30A. The first thing I do is my Zen sit for 25 minutes. Generally in a good frame of mind on these days. After the sit, I go online and check emails and whatever news catches my eye. I tend to avoid the shitty news, which is pretty much all there is, but I find pieces to capture my attention.

While at the computer, I always get some music happening, whether on the radio or online. This morning, I plugged into the Woodstock album and it was great. The music was unbelievable and both the event itself and the soundtrack are now a throw back to a make believe time when hope was epidemic. It's the music that bookmarks this time in the country's history. I suspect you will view the spectacle and listen to the music at some point in your archeological efforts. I would encourage you to experience the sound of this event because there were some wicked tunes out there on Yasgar's farm in '69. Remember, when you view this you need to understand it reflected where millions and millions of young people were at the time. You have to listen to the entire audio that goes between the music as well.

If I have any around, I will also get high at a fairly early hour on Saturday and then have a very deep yoga practice. As luck would have it, my friend Michael sent some along with an incredible water color of the Buddha's eyes, which now hangs right over my bed. I want you to have this, along with Rocky, whenever that shit ends up taking place, which is unfortunate, but inevitable.

Being high and listening to Woodstock would seem to be a complimentary experience. I shut the music down in order to do my half hour run, which, as you know, has been a decades long ritual. Had a strong run, made just a little more interesting by pounding the pavement in a semi-altered state. The weekdays have always been an almost zero tolerance zone for me, so this Saturday thing is a little gift for the old man.

After all this, plus a sumptuous breakfast of yogurt and oatmeal, I hopped on the Tangerine Dream to check out the surf for a possible kayak adventure. The trades were blowing pretty hard and there is a south swell to boot, so it was a fairly active ocean. The weather was so beautiful and I decided to whip out the HMS Feinstein for an undulating excursion on the Pacific. I was out for a couple of hours and it proved to be a little too exciting. My recently purchased outriggers gave the kayak incredible stability, so it hardly mattered where ever I decide to go because I manage to bob around pretty safely, but some oceans are friendlier than others.

Being out on that kayak all by myself is about as single as you can get. While my legs maintain a steady rhythm on the pedals, my mind is free to go anywhere at all and it usually does. One of the things I thought about was making some kind of entry into this piss poor excuse for a journal. Today has been a good day so far and I thought I would share it with you.

As Best I Recall

It is the next day and Sunday to boot. Last night, I went on a computer date with a woman by the name of Mo, which is short for Maureen. Pictures are misleading both ways and people's self-evaluations are equally twisted. We talked a few times on the phone before getting together and it was okay, nothing more. I had a feeling she was going to be too old for me, which has nothing to do with real age; rather it is about mental age. She is 63 and I am weeks from 67, but she acted much older than me, preoccupied with the numbers and its challenges.

Personally, I don't get any particular boost from talking about how old I am and the challenges that come with the passage of time. At this very moment, there is a bright red, male cardinal on my lanai and that is what gets my attention, not the heightened hurdles on life's track. I am not one of those guys who feel the need to be with a woman decades younger, but I do want to hang with a lady who exudes joy and promise. There is also the vanity thing for which I have no apology. I have always worked pretty hard at staying in fairly decent shape and the older I get, the more my unchanged routine impacts on my condition. So, I am not some fat guy who wants to be with a Barbie Doll, I want to be with a woman who is in great shape and works at it. Plus, if I don't feel she is pretty and very attractive to me, I can't get passed that either.

I have always wanted to be with a woman who carried herself in a distinctive manner and have had the pleasure a number of times in the past, some of whom we have already talked about. At a time that feels appropriate to me, we will talk about Laura, my last significant relationship, in terms of longevity and intensity. She was part of my dream about Kauai, but dreams live behind your eyes in a make believe world. We will need some time to talk about her and this is not it.

It is Sunday, Mother's Day, one of many holidays created by Hallmark Greeting Cards. Regardless of the blatant artifice surrounding this commercially driven day, I hope you always, always, remember your wonderful Mother. By the way, if for any reason I thought she was a shit, I wouldn't hesitate to tell you. In the very beginning, I know I made a big deal out of being as honest as possible. I would withhold bad stuff before lying about it. In the case of Andrea, I absolutely think the world of her and have immeasurable affection for her. As part of this weird time warp between us, I just sent your Mother an email telling her I was up to a point in my story to you about Mother's Day. I shared with her what I just wrote to you because I thought it would be a wonderful gift to share with her.

This process that began last Halloween in Portland, OR continues to amaze me and I sure hope you don't think this is some effortless, thoughtless diatribe by a rambling grandfather, bleached senseless by the Kauai sun. I am right here, standing directly in front of you and looking right at you, no matter when you read this or how often. I am in every one of these words at the moment they are written and for as long they are read. The past, present and future are not three separate, parallel railroad tracks to Infinity Landing; rather they are terribly confused states of mind. I know you can't possibly read all this and instantly imagine yourself in my world, but I am trying to at least make you as comfortable as possible, even under these bizarre circumstances.

We could definitely talk a lot more about the work I am presently doing, partially due to it taking up most of my daylight time between Monday and Friday, every week. As you know, based on my leg infection and getting the two by four forehead whacking, a construction site is not necessarily home to me. Tomorrow, I begin splitting my time between doing my marketing thing and helping out at the construction site. I finally get to do the work that I know, which doesn't mean it is easy; it simply means it's a world I am familiar with. Basically, my job is to create this benevolent Frankenstein, who has some good products to sell. When I say Frankenstein, I mean creating the personality of the company, one that engenders good feelings and trust. In this darkly jaded world, I admit to liking that part of the process because there is a creativity about it, one that runs counter to the polluted waves of cynicism and greed that are flooding our country. The creative elements of this process are nearly offset by the rote nature of cold calls to unknowing clients. Fortunately or not, I have been there many times before in the quilt of my professional past and have just enough confidence to get out of bed in the morning and go at it one more time.

Every now and then, I pick up with a new paragraph, quietly piggybacking with the previous one. It would likely drive both of us mad if I was a constipated soldier on some totally literal and linear mission. I don't think I am taking much liberty at all in this and have been damn straightforward with you. However, every sit down doesn't automatically have to be opening a new box that needs to be freshly packaged and labeled.

All you need to know is that it is sometime after that paragraph about my work. You know, it is a bitch to feel the burden of profundity, or why else would I be doing all this? Sometimes, I do actually feel I have something profound to contribute and then I catch myself and bring it back in. Humility just fucks everything up, but in spite of that I am working at becoming more and more humble with time.

I just went downstairs into the garage and grabbed a couple of chocolate goodies that my landlady is keeping in the fridge down there. I came back up to my place and was immediately greeted by the aroma of some incense I was burning, which is definitely not the norm for me, but Michael sent some incense along with the Buddha painting and my medicine. The scent immediately lit up my senses and I thought about the smell of a woman and how I missed that at the moment. Now, the Rolling Stones are singing "Hey You, Get Off My Cloud" and here I am having only you to talk to. Whadda you know? It is working fine for me, so don't feel at all responsible.

I hope at your age you are able to intuit what an incredible privilege this life is. You don't have to climb Mt. Everest or eradicate Polio; you just have to live your life with an open heart and with total trust in what is to come.

While you're at it, find some time to listen to Joni Mitchell. She is a great singer songwriter and her lyrics and style are the sound of a woman, much like the incense had the scent of one. Music was and is such a magical part of my life and I simply can't help myself because there is fabulous music that has preceded you by years and I want you to know it.

Next time, we will start with a new beginning and not piggyback on the efforts of a prior day. Take er easy, Shane. Get your hands on the Big Lebowski, a hugely funny movie and that is one of the countless lines in the film, delivered by a mystical cowboy in a blue collar, urban bowling alley. The Dude is a really iconic character and worth the price of admission all by itself, but there is a ton of funny stuff in it.

A Mind Phone Call

It is a new day that shall go nameless because we have to have at least a modicum of mystery in the "I've got nothing to hide" approach to this effort. A bit earlier, I was thinking that the actual style of this whole thing is based on the premise that at anytime of my choosing, I can make a mythical phone call to you and simply have a conversation about whatever is on my mind at the time.

I talk without expecting any response from you and hope at some time, you will get to read the transcript and determine its value for yourself. While it is unlikely, should anyone else read this, it will in no way detract from the singular importance of ultimately having it in your hands.

It's a little late in the evening to get fired up with any longer than usual tales, the big ones.

I am also slightly vexed about how to bring us down to the ground because we are nearly two thirds of the way through the arbitrary time allotment of one year. While we still have a long way to go, I want our landing to be smooth as silk. Because we have already done a significant amount of spadework on my past, we have no choice, but to be more in the moment. I've already eaten through most of the meat, so we now have to get used to a leaner diet. Maybe we'll have more diatribes, mood pieces, how I spent my day stories, who knows?

It's been nearly an hour since I opened this page. Sometimes, actually most of the time, I am writing with complete focus on matching the moment and my thoughts and feelings at that precarious confluence. Please, not looking for sympathy, just want you to know this is being written in as ethical a manner as possible. This is mindful jabber as opposed to a more diarrhetic outpouring. In other words, I think about this shit before I write it and while I am writing it. As you already know, at the point after it is written, it is pretty much indelible for me. It would be like cheating the moment because you have the ability to revisit it. I am afraid it is not my style to mess around with the past, present or future. Like everyone else, whether they realize it or not, we are all holding on for dear life on a totally unique roller coaster ride with our name glowing right in the center of the structure. Our past often changes as we get deeper into the ride and our altered perceptions miraculously twist so-called irrefutable facts we have held close forever.

See you around, kid..

Putting It Off

I confess to putting off my conversations about Laura because it still hurts and that is the truth. She was chocolate for my emotional diabetes, a shot of tequila for my transplanted liver and a pack of cigarettes for my spotted lungs. Like any respectable junky, regardless of the monkey, there is something about going back for more that is indescribably consuming and blinds you to consequence at the same time. We had a six year relationship here and I have only been here nine, so the math alone puts it into some context. Along the way, we had incredibly painful break ups and for some reason, I was forever being held prisoner by a dream.

We met on December 23, 2004 at a party being held by someone with no bearing on the story. I reluctantly went by myself, which has never been my favorite thing; walking into a houseful of people I don't know. I kind of uncomfortably made my way around the gathering and I guess I was holding my own. The moment I saw Laura, she got my attention and I was keeping my eye on her, how she moved and talked and just looking at her. At some point, well into evening, I went over to her and have no idea at all how the conversation started. It would have been impossible for me not to tell her she was beautiful. We talked for a while and then walked each other out to our cars. I walked with her to her truck and she gave me her phone number.

I called the next day and we met late in the afternoon over on her side of the island. We drove to a beach and watched a mindblowingly-stunning sunset. This was not your average magnificent sunset, it was very unusual in its beauty and something we were both instantly aware of. I fell maximum hard for her and even remember writing your Dad that I was certain the woman of my dreams had actually come to life.

Laura had a tomboy quality about her, but it certainly didn't inhibit her sensuality. As it turns out, she was a completely dedicated surfer. Unless you have met a true surfer, you have no idea about the world they inhabit. Surfers live for the wave and there is no point in trying to get in between them and the curl. A good swell makes any surfer very happy and that worked just fine for me. When there is no surf, they can get a little cranky, but it passes. They tend to talk to each other about surf conditions and if you like someone, you will let them know about a good spot on any given day.

Wait, this is not about surfing, it's about me and Laura. I thought she was gorgeous and she had a pretty stupendous physique. My heart would race every time I saw her and that never changed, regardless of where we were at. It happened the first time and six years later, even on the last day.

When I met her, she was living in one of those Kauai neighborhoods that were rough around the edges. She lived across the street from an ice dealer (look it up) and there were awful domestic dramas, in addition to the drug traffic. I found her a better place and one that was close to where I lived. On the day of her move, which was a Sunday, I asked the Sons of Kauai at our gathering if they would ride with me to her house and help her move. At that point, she was being harassed by the ice neighbors and when around 25 bikes rumbled down the street, it was like a two wheel Secret Service to safely escort Laura out of that neighborhood. It was a textbook cool moment and I rode at the front of the group. It is kind of phenomenal for a newcomer to the island to get such incredible aloha from a group of bikers.

You know, you can have a girlfriend when you are fourteen or when you are thirty-four or forty-four. However, when you connect around sixty, give or take a couple, it is likely for it to linger for the rest of your life on some basis or other. I am over and separate from all of my past relationships, but Laura will likely be a memory taken to my grave, more so than any earlier ones, which dim over time.

I kind of did a stupid thing, although it was never my intention. Laura blew my doors off and she fit perfectly into some fantasy I had for myself about meeting a mermaid and living happily ever after. This served two pretty stupid outcomes: It blinded me from anything that threatened the perfection and placed an incredibly unfair burden on Laura.

Our relationship was still new enough to have plenty of untold stories when I had my leg accident, which we have talked about to death already. However, I would never get tired of saying that Laura saved my leg and my life during an absolutely horrible bunch of months, covering the accident and the rehab. She was a very experienced and very capable nurse for years and she spoke the language. While I was playing hide and seek with the devil, she saved my ass. No matter what I have said or have to say about her, owing her my life is a non-repayable debt.

My idea is to always work at getting closer to your partner, even if it is at your own expense. I think I was at a point in my molasses evolution to take a stab at it. I was simply nuts about Laura and shouldered the shortcomings because she was my mermaid after all. My God, we had so many wonderful times together and we told each other special things. Honestly, there were many occasions when I actually believed our coming together was cosmic and preordained. It would also rip apart slowly and painfully each time, with me swearing off any possible reconnection. I think most of the initiatives to get back together were mine.

I need to be careful and withhold any judgment because none is necessary. I believe Laura was holding on to something that she couldn't share and when you start keeping secrets early in your life, you freeze out others forever. I wanted to be closer and would shut down when it didn't happen. The cycle was predictable, but both of us would give it a go for a while. For her part, while she would rarely cop to it for fear of hurting my feelings, Laura would claim that sex was not as good as it could be. Now, I am telling you this not to embarrass either you or me or her, rather I am simply sharing what transpired. While I believed that's how she felt, I knew it was more complicated and I couldn't venture where I wasn't welcome because that is not a right you take, rather it must be given.

There is a balance you look for as you get older and begin to understand what your life is about, including its limitations. My feeling is that I was trying to operate on a level of intimacy that was simply too unsettling for her. I am no walk in the park myself and no matter how earnestly we tried, we would split up again and again. Needless to say, she would undoubtedly see it differently and that is how it goes in any relationship. No one is right, each has their own perspective and there is no point in arguing. I labored over including the sex reference because it is way more embarrassing for me, but we have a deal and I am not going to break it, especially this far into the exercise.

My leg was close to healed as my sixtieth birthday was closing in. My skin graft was some time in April and the big party was on the 29th of May in '05. Your Mother and Dad rented a great house right on the ocean for about a week. Your uncle showed up, too. I printed up invitations and called it a Celebration of Life. The turn out was magnificent. I invited the bikers, who showed up in full force, along with other friends and the doctor who operated on me three times and worked hard as hell to see me through it. It was a really large, incredibly eclectic group. After only a couple of months together, which included the whole leg scenario, she was at my side and wonderfully supportive.

By the way, that was the first time your parents came to visit and I sure hope they end up returning again and again, as long as they bring you with them. I know Andy, Andrea and Danny, who was good enough to come, had a wonderful time on my island. After just a few days, all your parents wanted to do was hang out in the back of the house by the swimming pool and directly up against the Pacific Ocean.

Over the years, I sent well over a thousand emails to Laura, the vast majority being odes to love. Some were angry and some instantly disposable. I never wrote them with the idea of saving them and I am hoping she finally erased them by now. I let it all out with her in my messages, similar to all of this, which is for you and me. My heart is in a safe place now. It will remain that way until I have the privilege of falling in love again. Love is definitely not about safety; it is about stone cold, naked intimacy.

It has been a couple of years and I still think about her quite a bit. Being smart certainly doesn't prevent you from repeatedly doing stupid things and I proudly wear my stupid crown for all to see. You can never outsmart your heart, but you can try and have a smart heart, which comes with the repeated fuck ups and lessons learned.

During the recounting of all this, the local radio station has been playing a tribute to Elvis, which is unusual. The King is the reason so many of us began to feel we owned our music and our own voice. In his own way, that guy was saddled with living other people's dreams for them and it was doomed. I was around nine when he first appeared on the Ed Sullivan Show, but I told you that story already. If you want to hear him at his best, check out his Gospel music. I guess Laura and Elvis have a lot in common for me. His sounds live on in my head and her memories live on in my heart.

Don't be shocked if we return to her between now and then................

Back So Soon

When you are wildly in love with a woman, there are these incredible moments, like exploding stars in the heavens. I have had my share, but time has not diminished my appetite. Have I mentioned that this story to you is my significant relationship at this time? I pretty much suck at multi-tasking and can only give my whole heart to one thing at a time. I would likely tell a special woman all of these stories along the way and that temporarily would satisfy my desire to share myself with at least one person. In her continuing absence, we have come up with this beautiful way of meeting my need. At this point in my life, I would like to affect those I meet. As ridiculous as it may sound, this is not an ego driven mania. I think by simply sharing who you are with others, you encourage them to do the same.

While I have been potty trained for eons, puppy love is my kind of love, at least at first glance. In my world, it takes a spark to light my fire and glowing embers don't even qualify. Single as I am, I don't know how well that strategy has served me, but as long as I have no serious complaints, it's all good.

I had an incredible ride with Laura and can't say I regret a single moment and some of them were not easy keepers. The childish excitement about seeing her was not something I even thought I had within me any longer. I was on the cusp of sixty when we met and over the course of our time together and apart, I began to appreciate the fabulous possibilities of shared lives, ones that support each other on their respective journeys.

This one knocked it out of me, Shane. It was a hard fall and even with my yoga, I got some serious internal damage that will not likely heal in this life and that is fine with me. I know more about the truth of all this than I am willing to admit now or ever. Whenever I include someone else in this, I am trying to write about him or her as if they might actually read it. I can be honest about my own feelings, but if I find evidence in any re-reading that I have talked shit about someone, it will go. This is about me and my stuff, with no intention of off loading any of it on anyone else.

I think this should be enough about Laura for now and if there is a reason to return, I will.

This particular burst has been written to the music of Tony Bennett and a series of duets with a terrific roster. There are endless songs about love and it turned out to be the perfect backdrop for this mind scene. I actually hope I am being obnoxious about music because I fell in love with it on my stoop in Flushing, many lifetimes ago and the affair continues to this day. I just switched to Pavarotti, an operatic tenor with a voice that brought people to tears and still does, myself included. You may think it sucks when you first hear it, but you will learn to love the sound of a soaring heart or a stricken one. My father, Daniel, had some kid of connection to opera and I never got the straight story. I think he was in Vienna in the early 1900's to study opera, but by the time I gave I shit, everyone was dead. Whenever he was home from a road trip, he would listen to live Sunday broadcasts from the Metropolitan Opera on radio station that only played classical music. He had a collection of classical music and opera, when the best we had was a 78rpm waxy record.

Having sort of finished with Laura and had a brief musical interlude, it would seem to be a fitting time to offer a different take on Sex, Drugs and Rock 'n Roll, a saying that was birthed during my eligibility for that club. The music part is easy because it continually pops up during the most unexpected moments in our chats. I would change the Sex reference to an intimate connection with another, not because I am disavowing sex, rather I am simply adding some dimension to the connection. The Drug thing is a little trickier. I think we need to be happy in our lives and feel that life, with all its imperfection, is still worth living. In the spirit of Doing No Harm, each of us makes our own choices and takes responsibility for them in this world. I hope you believe that I am not advocating any agenda in this realm. I have faith in who you will become between this moment and your reading this paragraph, or all of them for that matter

I had a Bucket List (yup, look it up) moment a couple of Sundays ago, when riding with the boys. With my 67th coming up in a matter of weeks, I figured if I make it to 70 in one piece, I will take a solo road trip. I would likely rent a good touring Harley, somewhere in the neighborhood of the Dakota's, Wyoming or. Montana. I will pack camping gear and make a well thought out trip for myself. I've been around the Black Hills, but that part of the country is really big and I have always wanted to see more of it. We will see how it goes; maybe I can suck your parents into bringing you to some point on the way. I think I can likely get some decent mileage out of the seven oh with them.

Well, it is time to leave you for the evening. I have been at this at least two and half hours and that is a long time to journey through my mind, at least it certainly is for me.

Nothing Much

Wasn't in the mood to let two evenings go by with out having some entry, so I am making an entry, two nights after the last one. You know, I have been quietly working on this for around seven months and we have amassed 175 pages, which is a pretty damn good accomplishment, if I do say so myself. I know I am only sharing a fraction of my world, which is whatever I manage to capture in these sit-downs. Nobody can ever get inside your head because there is only room for you in it. As for us, we are spending some time together and I am telling you stories that are as spontaneous as I can make them. It sort of means we are actually together and I think this will give you plenty to work with, even if I happened to have moved on by then, which is definitely not my plan right now.

OK, I have satisfied my need to maintain appropriate continuity and now I can clock out. Tomorrow is the date Ida died and it is a week before my birthday. I am certain I will want to talk a little about that experience and start building excitement around my special day.

One Week Before

We are officially seven days from my birthday, so I want you to make appropriate plans. Based on my current social status, it is likely the two of us will spend my birthday together. In the past, when I have been in this condition, I have always promised myself a good dinner for one, which I just may do this time around. We shall see.

As I have already mentioned, this is the day my mother passed away and it is now nine years. She left very quietly and had already been gone for a number of days before that. Everybody has their own projections around a death in their family, or any death that strikes them closely. Sometimes, it is hard to separate yourself from the departed. It was very challenging for your Dad and Mother and Uncle, especially your Uncle, who had this whole religious, Jewish thing about life and death decisions.

This reminds me about walking the walk and how that is a far cry from talking it, no matter how smart you think you are. I think life is intended to be experiential and not cerebral. In the case of honoring my mother's wishes, which she made abundantly clear to me on a number of occasions, there was never a doubt in my mind and consequences were of no consequence at all to me. I dropped a bunch of notches in their eyes and don't suspect it will be forgotten. This was only about me and my brother and we ended up in lock step. Doing what you believe to be the right thing can be pretty fucken lonely, let me tell you. I honored my mother's wishes and that was the least I could do, considering all of the sacrifices she made for us throughout our lives.

Maybe Ida's passing and the hard decision about easing her out of this life finally provided me that little extra dose of resolve. When you combine that with the dwindling reserves in my personal chronology account, it was finally time to make my own special brand of music. Finally, saying it is about the time remaining brings a very gentle sense of urgency, not to be confused with desperation.

The tricky trap is discounting humility in all this and its absence will forever set you astray, regardless of the degree of sincerity in the effort. You take your lumps walking in your own footsteps, but that is ultimately how you take full ownership of your life and you are debt free as a consequence. We are very preoccupied with affirmation from others and that is not how you do it. Serving the wishes of others, while foregoing our own is pretty empty at the end of the day. This shouldn't be confused with compassionate action, which comes from within ourselves and then shows itself in how we treat others. It's like the difference between a fastball and a curve ball, a different twist of the wrist with the same basic grip, but a different result.

I just had this flash that hasn't dawned me at any time throughout this thing we are doing. There is more than enough fodder for your imagination and I wonder what you think. Am I a self-indulgent asshole? Am I an extremely sincere and caring person? Am I an aging warrior, looking to leave his mark before he throws his spear into the ground and loosens his grip on the shield? Am I some schnook who really wants his beautiful, little grandson to know just a little bit about his Grandpa Larry as he makes his own way through the world? Well, I could probably cop to all of those at one time or another. Just between us, this is one of the absolutely coolest things I could possibly do for you and something you will carry with you from the day you first encounter it and until the day you pass it on to the next in line. On some indefinable level, it would be really something to know that this could live for many, many years beyond this evening and beyond your exposure to it.

Just so you know, there really isn't anything all that terrific on these pages, merely a life, coupled with a very slight ability to communicate about it, plus all the other crap that is far too important to leave out. Yes, it is a self-deprecating remark, but purposely so. It's that humility thing. There is a fair amount of time left in our year together and I will do my best to keep it interesting for you.

I sure hope you like music, or else a lot of this stuff isn't going to mean dick to you. I've told you a million times already, music exploded into my life as a kid and it still does it for me. You need to bury yourself in Motown and Stax Records if you are interested in some solid music. Much of the music during my life helped to knock down the color barriers between skin shades. Jimi Hendrix being black had nothing to do with his gift to make his guitar sing in its own unique voice. The headwaters of rock 'n roll threw all colors into the mix and that has been one of its greatest gifts.

52 Vincent

I was in a particularly shitty mood a day or two ago and realized I am only motivated to write when I have the available energy, which is absent during the darker moods. As you have undoubtedly experienced at this point in your life, there are highs and lows and a full emotional landscape in between.

When we are feeling good, we want it to last forever and when we feel horribly depressed, we want it over in a blink. Of course, the truth is we pass through a perpetual swinging door, with darkness and light changing hands right before our eyes. It is futile to tightly grip the highs or attempt to sweep away the lows.

The Zen idea of impermanence applies not only to our lives, but also to everything we experience within our lives. If you are determined to fly high then you have to be able to survive the inevitable crashes.

Periods of loneliness are nearly unbearable for me. The reality of my life eventually ending is often beyond my ability to gracefully embody. Sometimes, I think I spend too much time weighted down by the awareness of my mortality, while most everyone pushes it away if it gets anywhere near them. Certainly, racing through my sixties has me not wanting to look at the checkered flag, somewhere ahead and around a curve I can't quite see.

There are people who spend their lives learning a particular discipline or espousing certain political views or complaining about their plight or whatever else that conveniently gets in between themselves and their lives. From the time I drove away from Andy and Danny in the driveway of their NJ home over twenty-five years ago, I have steered clear of the innumerable distractions and tried to look directly into the mirror of life. I have had days and days completely alone, with only my mind to keep me company. Looking for the meaning of life and knowing all along it doesn't have any has been my own high wire act without a net.

Now, you would likely think I am somehow despondent as a result of not finding any satisfying answers, but you would be miles off course. I caught yet another nugget of brilliance from Big Al and grabbed it up for our trip. Seeing this happened to coincide with a slight run of depression, which I have been talking about. It didn't deliver me from my mood, but it laid down an essential truth that has kept me company for many years.

"There are two ways to live: you can live as if nothing is a miracle; you can live as if everything is a miracle." ~ Albert Einstein

We never stop to think about being alive and somehow take it for granted or think it is an irrevocable right we have. Each one of our lives is a magnificent accident, but the vast majority of us never give it a thought or we bury it in the rhetoric of one religion or another.

You will have to forgive this exercise in introspection, but my birthday is creeping up and it has always been a time to look backward and forward. The backward part is easy because it is passed, which is not quite the truth. Anytime at all, you can revisit your past and alter your perspective based on wherever you happen to be at that moment. I guess the best way to see into the future is to embrace exactly where you are and appreciate the miracle of life.

Moving on, I have mixed a lethal recipe for margaritas and will mule the package to a picnic the Sons of Kauai are having tomorrow, Memorial Day, which is the day before my birthday. We are riding up to Kokee and stopping at a terrific site with BBQ and bathrooms. We have gone there a number of times before and have had a ball. It was a beautiful day today and we did our usual Sunday run, going up to the north shore and hanging out at Pine Trees, a beach on Hanalei Bay.

All the same, I would much prefer to have a quiet dinner and sensual evening with the love of my life, a position that is currently vacant. Over the years, I have spent many birthdays by myself, something I have already shared and that is just how it goes. Something about it is at least a little depressing, but still feeling good and hitting the higher numbers is tremendous cause for celebration.

Got another piece of music you should listen to. Check out a British folk artist by the name of Richard Thompson. His lyrics are folk tales and slice of life morsels. '52 Vincent is a fabulous ballad of a young outlaw type, who falls in love with a red head, Red Molly, in black leather gear. She rides on his bike and they share a brief time together. The romance of the motorcycle is intoxicating and exhilarating, at least it is for me.

Ultimately, I think it is about maintaining a sense of romance, regardless of circumstance. I still think about women in a very romantic way, believing in the possibilities. As long as I can look at a woman and appreciate her subtle curves, her hair flowing in the breeze, the way her body moves and her wondrous gestures, I am good. It is the magic that is everything.

Happy Birthday to Me

I am home after taking myself out for a couple of margaritas at a local, somewhat upscale tortilla joint. I was tired after a day's work and sitting at home wearing a towel, but it was my birthday after all. Put on a clean pair of jeans and one of my better-looking Hawaiian shirts and went out.

I was sitting at the bar and admiring how people seemed to be so comfortable in such an artificial setting. I don't know how they manage to hide their self-consciousness so well, or if they are even aware of it at all. I have always been aware of my feelings and just a wee bit awkward in these social settings. I guess it is the artifice that rattles me.

So, I am sixty-seven years old today and this is the birthday that gets shared in this yearlong semi-epic of ours. I have had a lot of birthdays and I am grateful for each one. Birthdays are a time when it would be sweet to have a lovely, loving woman in my life and I have certainly had that pleasure over the years. At the same time, there have been birthdays spent alone, with very little recognition from anyone other than myself.

I am definitely getting up there kid and there is no denying it. I suppose I could find any number of reasons to be depressed, whether about my age or my circumstance. Well, not a chance my boy. It is a goddamn privilege to be allowed to be here and I sincerely hope that I continue to carry myself with that awareness.

Of course, there is that ridiculously romantic side that still fantasizes about going to a bar on my birthday and sitting quietly by myself. All of sudden and much to my surprise, a beautiful woman approaches me and says she has been mesmerized by my presence and wants to get to know me better. She is visiting from New Zealand and has been thinking about relocating to Kauai. She has an ease and confidence about her that is totally refreshing. Her name is Zoey. The rest of the story is intensely personal and only to be shared between her and I.

Slowing Down

Not sure how we will fill the time between now and our due date the end of October. At this point, my Monday to Friday life is pretty predictable. For the past six months, I spent my days at the construction site for Paniolo Feed. My skill level is pretty lousy, so my time is involves lugging heavy shit from one place to another. I drill, hammer and screw, following instructions from the guys who are much better qualified. Of course, it is understood I am on board to handle marketing and sales, but at this stage it is important to pitch in on building the equipment we need to process and produce the cubed feed we will be selling to the horse and cattle market in the State.

I get back to my place every afternoon some time after five and immediately jump into the shower because I am filthy and exhausted. Most of my professional life has been at a desk, on the phone or computer. I have had meetings of all kinds, but never climbed ladders and walked around a construction site. It is also a fairly dangerous environment and I have had an infected leg and stitched head to prove it. You really have to be alert.

Being in what appears to be a terminally single existence, I come home to an empty space and do whatever I feel like doing. I rarely hear the sound of my own voice, unless I get a surprise evening phone call.

Every Sunday is equally predictable. I get up early and go to my neighbor's house for a Zen sit and a bit of ritual. I rush back and jump into my motorcycle gear and then I am off to meet the bruddahs for our weekly ride. Other than that, my weekend time is unscheduled and not monumentally exciting. Every now and then, I go kayaking, but I hold off until the whales are in. If there is a decent movie, I will take myself to a Saturday matinee. Generally, I will pay a visit to a Saturday farmer's market at the local community college that I helped organize as a result of my being on the board of the farm bureau.

Habits make up such a large part of all our lives and there is much to be said for them. Habits help lift some of the decision making burden that follows us the rest of our lives. Habits allow you to do things without thinking about them. Of course, the downside is you can easily dig a series of ruts that get deeper and deeper, until your view is obscured by the walls of the habit obscuring the horizon.

I guess it is all too easy to lose sight of the fact that even the mundane is magnificent. The trick is to maintain a fresh outlook, even in the face of daily rituals that feel increasingly stale over time. Right now, my life seems just a little smaller than usual and I suspect it will change, because change is the only thing that is predictable for all of us.

I don't feel inclined to talk about Paniolo Feed, the business venture I have been involved with for quite some time now. I know we have talked about it before. I am getting a little tired of the daily construction ritual and can't wait to get the office set up, so I can get back on familiar territory for myself. The purpose of this entire exercise has nothing to do with complaining or expressing dissatisfaction with where I happen to find myself on a given day. It just so happens I am fairly tired by the end of a day and it definitely cuts into the energy I bring to our time together.

It looks like Grandpa Larry will be coming to see you in September. We will be winding down our story by then and it will be fun to highlight our time together. Apparently, you are a very cool kid and showing some wonderful traits and it will be a trip to reconnect with you after around nine months or so, when I visited last. However, we have a whole summer ahead of us and who knows what the future will bring to both of our lives until then. Your Dad will tell me about your adventures and I will tell you about mine.

Equilibrium

There will definitely be more to come about our looming get together because it will be our second one in this yearlong history

Now, we can get back to some more musing. I don't think I am at a monotonous place in my life; rather I like to see it as a place of equilibrium, at least for now. I am not sure it is that easy to live any less encumbered than I am at this point in my devolution. I live in a spacious second floor ohana with a view of the Pacific. The rent is exceptionally low and my landlady is a good friend. I don't pay for my phone, computer, electricity or water. A woman comes in once a month and makes the place spotless. I have 10 gourmet dinners prepared for me every two weeks. I live my life absolutely unaccountable to anyone else. As I mentioned, when this feed business finally came to life, I had already decided that moving to Costa Rica to write was an extremely viable option for me. When I actually went on the payroll, I was completely clear with myself that if this didn't go the way I wanted at any time in its evolution, I would walk and not look back.

Let me tell you, at a ripe old 67, there is not a single reason to take shit from anyone for a buck.

Now, I could sing the merits of coming home to an empty space and waking up in one and maybe for just a second or two I will do that. When I am home, there is no conversation to have, interaction to have or friction or sacrifice. I would definitely admit to being spoiled by allowing myself to do anything at all in my space, without concern of approval or loss of privacy.

Here's the bitch. I really like women and it is not likely the same way you would see them at this point in your life. Believe me, not taking away from your perceptions, but God only knows, I have been around a lot longer than you. Listen, I don't think there is anything more beautiful than the shape of a woman. The curves, the movement, the sensuality and sensitivity, make them irresistible to me and they also don't think anything like us. I definitely do miss the excitement of a terrific woman in my life, but the personal territory lost can be costly and it is hard to find that balance.

I think I might be able to hit that balance at this point in my life, but finding a woman at a similar place is pretty chancy and she also has to be hot and that combo is pretty tough to pull off. My window is a good deal shorter than yours, but I still make sure to keep it clean so I can see clearly, with very mixed success. I do live in an equilibrium of sorts, having hit that balance point with my life at present and that has nothing to do with it being perfect, a concept I long ago shit canned.

While writing all of the above, I have been listening to Mark Knopfler, another incredibly talented musician you should check out. He has a distinctive guitar sound, but I never grow tired of it.

Last Stand

This is the evening after Mark Knopfler. Writing a little later than usual because life got in the way. I have been writing and/or editing material from a fellow by the name of Joel, who got a grant from the County of Kauai to do a feasibility study on ranchers retaining more beef for local slaughter. Not sure if I have mentioned Joel before, but I will not edit this out if I have. As an aside, I would never have guessed when I was your age, the age of your first reading, that I would be involved with a study on retaining cattle on Kauai, HI, let alone helping to start up a horse and cattle feed business.

Joel is an interesting guy. He is at least the fourth generation farmer on land in Washington State. He is a real farmer and a damn smart one at that. Shit, if I already wrote this stuff pages ago, I am going to be hard pressed not to edit one entry or the other, but I promise it will not happen again until it happens again.

Anyway, we are working on the actual recommendation for this grant dealing with our local cattle industry and I realized that I was approaching this as a kind of Last Stand. I thought about that for a while and decided to share it. You know, when you start clocking mileage in your late sixties, you are most likely older than those around you. For my part, I very often forget that this extra time I have under my belt enables me to speak in a more forthright manner than many. What the fuck do I have to lose? I am feeling more principled than ever before. I am trying to do right by my life and there is a consciousness about it.

This Last Stand idea seems to be pretty pervasive in my life. Half the time, I am engaging people that are decades younger and I don't have the ability or control to alter my speech based on who I am talking to. I have this terribly unfair advantage of having been around the block too many times, but it is never a good idea to use it in a discussion.

I don't mean Last Stand to sound like Gunfight at OK Corral; rather it is a state of mind that comes with having made most every conceivable mistake one can make and somehow surviving intact. I wouldn't confuse this with wisdom, which is grossly overrated anyway. I will whip out my metaphorical guns and blast away until the coast is clear.

I have had to completely rewrite everything Joel sends and I talk to him with complete candor. We had to press this last week to get the report together. Joel and I are taking a very different tact in this recommendation. We are only asking for the money this project needs and allowing it to grow on its own merits. The usual way is to ask for as much money as possible and promise unattainable goals because it's all about the money.

Honesty and sincerity likely go along for the ride in this graying scenario. I think in many ways it is an enviable perch, but that same perch weakens with time and it will break. Between now and the time my perch breaks, I am going to try and be uncompromising and caring, an interesting combination. . It is an unexpected place to be and you will eventually get there, but now I would assume that is only a gauzy view in the dim distance, while you enjoy being young of body, mind and spirit.

Had a breakthrough in yurt logistics yesterday. It was decided that the yurt could go up in a soon to be vacated piece of land that is absolutely beautiful. It will sit in an open field of twenty acres and the views are stunning. It has a locked entry gate and is very non-descript looking, which will cut down on any surprise visits by nefarious characters. I don't know if it will be in place before our year is up, but we shall see. The news has gotten me re-jazzed about the yurt and creating a space that looks like me.

The yurt is kind of its own last stand. I want a space that will be comfortable for me for as long as I need it. On the basis that I can't think of a single, solitary reason to ever leave my home on Kauai, I could be in it for a while, at least that's my plan. I've got the bank to make a fairly decent set up and I will attempt to approach all of it with an attitude reflected in my new home. When we sell our first cube of Paniolo Feed Company product, I will get on the case. I pass the property virtually everyday and it is spectacular. Like everything else, there is a time and place for this.

Been A While

Not sure when I sat at the keys last, not that it was all that long ago. I am very conscious of this exercise of ours and twitches begin when the absence grows to a point that feels a little uncomfortable. After all, this is really my time and the least I can do is make the time for myself to sit here. It is not as if buckets of incredible things have occurred in the interim, but after all, this was never the motivation behind my stories in the first place. When you think of the billions and billions of lives out there, this is just one of them.

In my best Zen, "form that is no form" style, let's talk briefly about the Beatles, who have already been praised. This is just something for you to put into context. I am only a couple of years younger than the Beatles, if you can believe that. I put down that paragraph before this one and then went away to have some salad for dinner and now back at you.

Listened to a Beatles song while having my dinner and that is when it dawned on me that you might find the following a little weird. Remember, they exploded onto the scene around fifty years before this is being written to you now and add on the years until this writing has been deemed to be appropriate for you. I was on the upper end of teendom when they hit and it was an unbelievable experience. I got to live that whole era, including the music that came before, back to Doo Wop and Elvis. It was so new and untracked and it was a life changing tsunami for many who were in that right age range. You know if I am around and I think you are old enough, I won't be able resist slipping this entire ditty to you. If we have a chance to develop a true relationship, I will know when you are ready to become a Jedi knight.

At the same time, I was thinking about the Beatles thing, I had this technology flash having to do with liberation and imprisonment. In its short 15+ year evolution to this point, technology's impact has been world altering, permeating every habitable corner of this planet. It was and continues to be life altering for all of us because whether you partake or not, you are effected by it regardless. Ideas no longer have boundaries and they can pierce all the armor thrown against them. It offers the keys to freedom, but no preparation for the responsibilities or pitfalls that come with it.

The same things that enable the free exchange of ideas and information can easily be captured by the forces whose intent is to control freedom. As bad is it may have ever been before, this is the beginning of the World Series of Privacy Loss. Even now, it is not remotely paranoid to believe that the authorities can track everything about us because of this very technology we worship. This is one of a number of things I wonder about in the world you are slowly inheriting.

I am personally concerned about the whittling away of privacy, which is worth a great deal to me and I believe it is my inalienable right as a human being. As you know, I don't have a good feeling about our behavior patterns and there is nothing to suggest that the coalescing of wealth with governance will ever end. There were some folks who invaded America early on and did so because of their basic right of freedom. Many of the early Europeans came here to create a better world for themselves, getting out from under oppressive monarchs and churches. We shall see, won't we? I do know for a certainty that they completely fucked over the First People.

Now, let's talk about running shoes. Recently, I have been reading stories about the soundness of running in a nearly barefoot shoe. Running shoes have always had a heel that took the impact first. The recent talk has been about the natural way of running, which is on the front of the foot and not the back. As it turns out, your uncle Danny had recently purchased a pair and we discussed the merits of switching.

It's funny; both of my sons are life long committed runners. Believe me, I did the running when they were little, but I never pushed running on them, although I did take them running with me when they were old enough. So, I just got in my pair of a shoe called the NuBalance MR10, a whole different way of running and I will definitely try them in the morning. Told your Dad about them today and he was real interested to get a report from me. He is a pretty good runner and did some cross country in high school.

I am not sure you will give a shit, but I will likely share the following anyway. Having run in a certain style for over 35 years, it will be interesting to experience the difference.

I feel better now, how about you? Got in a couple of hours and it feels great. Be back soon.

My Feet

There is no protection from Feinstein Track and Field. I ran on the shoes yesterday and immediately sent an email to your Dad and Uncle, who owe their running addiction to yours truly. Here it is and the only thing to add is that the day after, I am having some right ankle discomfort, but I will not report that until a day or two has gone by.

"Tried out the Minimus MR10 this morning. Very different experience. I think slightly more strenuous, but today was the first day. You automatically run on the ball or flat of your foot and consciously avoid smacking your heel. It feels much more primal, seriously. I stayed aware for the entire run to avoid running the old way. You don't take long strides and you keep your feet under the core of your body. My years of yoga stretching may minimize post aches and pains, but we will see how I feel tomorrow. Downward dog is a good achilles and calf stretch. Ran with no socks to add to the simulated effect of running barefoot and it was fine. The interior is comfortable enough for that.

At this early stage, I would give the 10 a 10. Depending upon how I feel over the next few days, I may just run exclusively in the 10's.

Pops"

Just in case you think I am writing to you in some special style, you should know it is how I communicate. The note to your Dad and Uncle could just as easily be in this story and it would fit in very comfortably. That is the cool thing about trying to be genuine as much as possible.

I just sent a note to Laura, you remember her, don't you? I wanted to tell her something very sweet without having any attachment at all and I did it. You know, falling in love is never convenient and it is not supposed to be. I have been blessed in my life to have had a small handful of women and I don't know how I could possibly provide the words to describe the experiences. I guess if words could actually describe the flooded feelings during the countless moments of connection, there would be no need for efforts like this one.

I wrote some notes from several nights ago and wanted to make sure they are included. When I was writing then, I was listening to Diana Krall, a brilliant jazz pianist with an effortless vocal style. I have no idea what the state of music will be when you swallow this pill, but I have had throughout my life an unbelievable pastiche of musical styles, etc. So, you check out the broads who have been making music since we were able to record it. Ladies bring an incredible energy to all of their art and guys can't help being powerfully enslaved to it all.

Then I wrote a short note about incense. I lit a stick of incense on the morning of note taking and was absolutely overwhelmed by its mellowing affect. Listen, kid, when you have chance, light some incense when you find yourself alone and just enjoy it all. This last time when I lit it, it was so wonderful. My friend Michael had sent over some incense with his beautiful Eyes of the Buddha watercolor and several nickels of Mary Jane. The incense was really beautiful and I have been lighting it longer after the nickel was cashed in and burned.

I wrote a note to make sure I would include it and it goes like this. "*Music has been my companion for years and often my only companion*." When I am alone, a place I often find myself, music is always there to deflect the emptiness. While I have written to you before under some different circumstances, I am most comfortable with music in the background. If I was monumentally anal, I could remember the music from the key points in my life, but I never bothered to keep notes. From the awful confusion of my early teens right through to the even more pained images of life's end, music has always been and will always be the magic carpet, taking me to a place more beautiful than wherever I happen to be.

There you have it, my young man. I did get a call from your Dad on Father's Day and he actually put you on the phone. I know you will never forget that moment. You said something like Happy Father's Day and I Love You, both sentiments I know you felt from the bottom of your heart at age 3 1/2. Not to worry, I will not hold it against you.

I ordered a couple of Size 3 Sons of Kauai shirts, which I will bring with me in September. I had this idea that you needed to save these shirts and a bunch that will follow over the next years. Imagine, having this mind travelogue and some T-shirts to go along with them. How cool is that? I will tell your Mom and Dad to save the shirts. Believe me, if they knew what I was writing, they would absolutely shit. On the other hand, this is not some demented Mein Kampf; it is me telling you some stories. There are no ulterior motives, plus I can't imagine what kind of uniforms and logos would cause people to blindly follow my cause. Oh right, I don't have a cause.

I have my moments of truth when I do this thing. I do love the truth, even though it goes by too quickly to capture. While I have not written a single word for effect, I do hope this monologue touches you when you first read it and continues to touch you when you reread it. Believe me, I know while this may not be a worth a shit to anyone else, it is a treasure for you and those that come after you. I guess I do want this to be a bible; a bible of a life lived, no more, no less.

Right About Now

Right about now, I would like to be talking to a beautiful woman, preferably in person, but the phone would be fine. While this writing has been indescribable on too many levels, having a woman to talk to is incredibly fulfilling. It is dialogue, a living, breathing, responding human, and preferably one with a certain fondness for my company and visa versa. What I do with you all goes one way and it is like performing at my best to an empty room. It would be very special to be writing and getting a response in the moment. It is also always good to be called on your shit because we all got a fair dose. There is nobody to keep me in check and I apologize.

There have been long periods of solitude and one way or another, something happens and I move into another adventure. The talent pool is kind of shrinking for me these days and that might throw a monkey wrench in the timing. This could be a desert terrain of considerable size and I can't say I am brimming with confidence, but you never know what the Universe has in store for you.

A woman would sure change the writing style for you and me. I would likely share much of it with her because there is so much of me in all this. We've got a little over four months to cross the finish line and just maybe good fortune will smile on me yet again. I do love my uninhibited privacy a great deal and could never completely give that up. First things first, she has to magically appear before my eyes and then I will wrestle with my privacy issues.

If there were a woman with me these past months, I likely would have shared with her most of what is in here because it is where I have been on my own journey. I don't think there would be enough time to get into everything here, but she could always read the book and then I would be totally screwed. Only kidding, I have nothing to hide from an intimate partner. This honesty packs quite a punch and it is sometimes hard to hear, especially if you are harboring your own ghosts. All we can do is try to be honest, even at our own expense, but it is the best bargain you can make. I've had my share of experiences and I don't feel like I am done just yet.

Meanwhile, I have fallen in love with this tale we are telling and it's not because I think it is a masterpiece, it is just a haphazard patchwork of my life at any given time during this Halloween bookended year. By the way, we are about 2/3's of the way through this verbal workout. Can't say for sure I know where we are going between now and then.

Speaking of now and then, every now and then, I simply continue writing under one heading for as long as I feel like. Especially now, because the longer tales have come and gone and we are stuck with the drudgery of my everyday life. You will likely be the first one to know of any good news, although by the time you read it, boy will it be old! You know by now I am not one to terribly complicate his life and one result of that is often quiet and solitude, a lethal combination, ending up in not much happening.

It is a neat trick to be comfortable in who you are. I think it is a sensibility that can only develop with age. If you find that you have done the same fucken, stupid thing time and time again, there is a modest hope for salvation. I think it is worth the trip; at least it has been so far. Between us, I think I have developed a fairly keen insight into myself and I am continually amazed at how dumb I can be, even when a freight train is gunning down the track right at me. Being a fool can be very helpful and I strongly recommend your taking the time to be one, just get off the damn tracks. I sure hope you are funny because I am throwing flaming genes in that direction. It can be such an unsinkable life raft to keep you afloat amidst a flood of some pretty turbulent shit.

I didn't realize how appropriate the heading is for this little series of bursts. Right about now is when I have been sitting down and writing to you. The now is kind of a floater because it happens whenever I have the time and inclination to share. Beyond my September visitation, I would like to have a new headline item and a good story to go with it, which can carry us through to the finish line. We will have to see if anything warrants a miraculous treatment versus a mundane one.

Change of Pace

This is an unprecedented occurrence. I have needed a new laptop computer for quite some time. The one I have been using totally sucks. Recently, I got a new MacBook Pro, which will be a Model T Ford in your world, not that you will even know what a Model T is. I got a good friend who said he was a computer whiz to come over and transfer data from the old one to the new. As an aside, I have never met a computer captain who ever blamed himself for any screw up. It is always the computer's fault. Wouldn't you know it? He couldn't transfer the info from the Model T to the Ferrarri, even after three hours. Finally, I told him to take both of them away and bring me back the computer, ready to rock 'n roll.

What this means for us is I am sitting on my lanai and actually using a pen to write on some scratch paper I was able to dig up. When the magic box returns, I will transcribe this onto the page and you won't even know the difference. I don't know how much old school stuff you will have been taught in school. Very few people communicate with handwritten letters anymore. I was actually graded for penmanship early in my school life. I don't know if you will be using a keyboard. I suspect voice commands will have replaced the keyboard. It may operate telepathically. Hard to say from here just how advanced and pervasive technology will be. I can tell you so far it is really thriving.

Obviously, I am currently without computer, which means I am in a techno-void of catastrophic proportion. I am continually looking over at the Grand Canyon sized space the little computer has left on the desk where it rests and where I spend too much time. I am not nearly as connected as most young people today and yet I am at a loss as to what to do next. At the same time, I can feel a hint of liberation, having lost my umbilical chord to the entire world.

Normally, I would not be sitting out on my lanai and doing this, which also includes looking out at the ocean, with my pen raised in a very thoughtful pose. I would be inside, staring at my screen and periodically looking down at the keyboard, usually for numbers or punctuation, which I never got together in my junior high school typing class. Radio and telephones were well ensconced when I was a kid and television was still somewhat experimental in my early years. It is simply unbelievable to have come so far in such a short amount of time.

I probably already mentioned that technology has made time move more quickly. Technology thrives on speed and miniaturization. As you know, I think it is the most potent drug we have ever developed or discovered. I also believe that overdosing is as lethal to the human spirit as drugs are to our lives. We are tricked into always desiring what we don't have yet and the joy of the moment gets buried by the garbage generated from our distorted dissatisfaction with what is. The concept of being technologically connected works extremely well and I guess the only concern I have is with balancing this connection with our flesh and blood humanity, our ancient need to be touched and to touch others. Loss of privacy is the biggest danger in all this because it is virtually impossible to keep secrets from the machine and that is unfortunate and actually tragic.

The aforementioned is a perfect reaction to my being temporarily computerless. However, it really isn't all that bad writing the old fashioned way. It is more work than spanking the keyboard, but I wouldn't have written any differently because what is on my mind is what I write. My life experience is the same and my mind isn't working any differently using this medium. I did have to scrounge for the paper, but it was easy after that.

Get this, I am now actually writing on a paper towel because I couldn't find paper anywhere and there was obviously little to work with. This may be a bit too much for me and I am on the verge of shutting down. The good news is that while writing this handwritten note, my computer person called and we are good to go with the new machine. My total disconnection time will be just over 48 hours. In my world, I have not gone along with most of the innovation because I just don't feel like it, while in your world it might not even be possible to choose. I hope I am wrong, but my optimism is not very high. If I continue writing this way too much longer, I will need a quill pen and parchment paper. I need to make sure I always have a writing pad as a safety net because this has been like writing a message in a bottle, to be unearthed centuries later as some vitally important text.

The fact that you are now reading this brings us back to real time, in a manner of speaking. I am typing on my brand new computer, which I picked up last night at a dinner for the Kauai County Farm Bureau. The computer fixer is a relatively new acquaintance. Dan and his wife, Marta, have been here a couple of years and have a solid background in writing, photography, video and design. She is the lady who cooks my Gourmet Meals for Single Dummies and he is a good photographer and an interesting character.

The dinner was on a beautiful piece of land owned by a guy who made big bucks in the early years of the "dot.com" explosion, when technology was an intoxicating drug that attracted millions of dollars, which became billions of dollars on a good day and zero most of the rest of the time. We had a big white tent, out on a magnificent setting. I got there early to help set up because I am extremely important in the farm bureau, which will remain our little secret. The president elect is a wonderful local guy by the name of Jerry. We get on extremely well and we sort of both orchestrated a change in the future of this organization, which is a bitch to pull off in this culture.

Jerry enjoys his brew and he asked me if I wanted to go out to his truck to have a few. Far be it from me to offend anyone who is gracious enough to make such an offer. We cracked open a couple of Coors and we were leaning on the back of his pick up. We were facing an old VW camper. After about half a beer, a beautiful young woman opened the sliding side door of the van and proceeded to change her clothes in the back of vehicle. In the midst of this, her friend gets into the front seat and begins to put on her makeup, which if you have not seen yet, is an incredibly sensual experience to behold. He and I were mumbling incredulously at our good fortune. These girls were in their early twenties and just beautiful. Both of us agreed that the evening did not have to get any better because we already had the best time we were going to have at this event. Personally, on some level, it saddened me just a bit to know I was too old to do anything other than pay them a compliment, which I did, thanking them sincerely for the experience.

During the evening, I was studying this magnificent, tanned blonde in a loosely fitting black dress. Her posture was impeccable and I thought she was absolutely beautiful. Before I left to get my computer from Dan, I went over to her and told her I thought she was absolutely exquisite, even though I was more than old enough to be her father. To make matters even worse, she told me her name was Zoey. A beautiful, blonde young woman by the name of Zoey. Are you shitting me?

Picked up my computer from Dan and my meals from Marta because they were at the dinner. Got home in the evening and didn't want to even deal with the new computer until this morning. The first thing I checked was to see where our story was and to make sure it had safely made the trip to the new world. Pretty sure it's OK, even though the old one showed 186 pages and this one 166. It is most likely a formatting thing and not the loss of any of the story, but I will find out next time I speak with Dan. I need him to help properly set up the computer, something I have studiously avoided for many years and computers. I need to have my shit together for the feed business because I will be the only person handling sales and I need to have the back up, so I will bite the bullet and learn a little more than I know right now.

After an initial whack at the machine, I left the house for my Sunday ride with the bruddahs. I found myself completely out of sorts over the computer and it made me uncomfortable during the beginning of my ride. I had a good talk with myself and realized it is only the damn computer and not my life. I hope you have the ability to completely disconnect from the engulfing web of technology. I just don't want to think of you as having gotten devoured by the machine, regardless of whatever form it takes. That said, I think my new computer is a quantum leap from the one I had and I will try and make it my friend.

I don't know what to tell you, kid. Sometimes, I wish I could answer the questions you will be inevitably asking yourself, but on the other hand, I wouldn't want to spoil your fun. Personally, it is the questions that matter more than the answers. Actually, I think I have been traveling that mind road for a very long time. The questions kind of remain the same and it is the answers that change.

Like it or not, I am certainly aware of my age, more so than I can ever remember. The answers have more dimension to them, but when I was younger, I never would have accepted that idea. I guess at every point in our lives, we think we have it down, but I confess to being an outsider to that way of thinking. I never took myself so seriously to impose a totally ego-centric view of the world, being someone who had the answers. It took me a number of decades to determine that this life of ours is a journey, one whose ultimate destination is a certainty, but it is the effort in the journey there that counts. Losing my father so young definitely caused me to internalize all sorts of stuff I was too young to deal with. However, after that happened, I took a lot less for granted.

Growing up has been particularly challenging for me because I am not sure what that looks like. It certainly has a lot to do with filling out the expectations of others about how you are supposed to act. The less you are concerned about others, the more likelihood you will stay true to yourself. Somewhere along the way, being selfish got a bad rap and personally I think it is horse shit. Whatever we do or say comes through us to the outside, which has something to do with being responsible for your actions, regardless of outcome. We are the only ones who will create a fertile soil for our self-awareness to grow and the weeds come from without.

I am torn between the idea of our having inherent goodness versus a fractured energy that can easily turn dark. Gandhi is a superlative example of our higher self, eschewing violence for kindness. While he was a lightening rod back in his day, India is now a nuclear power and not necessarily what he had in mind. Hitler preyed on Germans who had lost a World War and were steeped in poverty and a crushed national pride. They nearly conquered the world, but ended up devastated as a result of his own maniacal excesses. Today, they are a world power and dominate the European economy.

The truth is, most everyone would go over to the dark side under the right conditions. I am certain there were Jews who were shot in cold blood by Nazis because they simply refused to capitulate, but they were exceptions to the rule. Most everyone waited on line and went into the showers to never come out again.

One of the many reasons why I am not overcome with optimism for the future is because we usually behave pretty badly. Immediate gratification seems to trump most anything, which is the mantra for every dominant society. On the other end, most victims will go quietly to meet their fate, but every now and then, a beacon of light shines to light the way. The younger we are, the more easily we can be swayed off course. Hopefully, as some of us get older, we have a better understanding of these things. In spite of that, most of our world leaders are older people and more often than not, they behave very badly.

On some level, the more selfish we are, the more likelihood we will have some grounded perspective regarding the tumult around us. It was Socrates, who said, “Know thy self.” Buddhists will maintain there is no such thing as an abiding self and that we are engaged with an ever changing world, moment to moment, breath to breath. As one who sits, I lean toward the Fat Man's view of things. I believe his way is to be as engaged as possible as often as possible and to do so without any expectation of outcome because it is a reward unto itself. From what I can gather, Buddha believed in our inherent goodness and that we are each already the Buddha and our charge is to embrace that ultimate truth. Before Jesus got institutionalized as a Vatican, he preached that God was within each of us. Those guys would claim we were born with the capacity to be God-like on earth. Frankly, I don't know.

Had A Day

Had a day to think about what I have recently written and it concerns me, lest I appear as someone who knows what the fuck he is talking about, because I don't. I wonder what possesses me to talk or write about humanity and make assessments about our innate nature. I guess if I am going to go over board, I would much prefer it be on the side of humility. I can't even provide anything remotely definitive regarding the conduct of my own life, let alone our entire species, which frankly is a bit of a reach. However, when we let the mind wander, we have to allow for most anything at all. As I have gotten older, I think I have become more uncertain about most everything and less and less concerned about it.

You know, right about now, I would like to be talking to a woman who had the ability to make me just a little nervous every now and then. I would slam the computer shut without hesitation. Pretty much all the time, I have had some decent gaps in between relationships. At some point during each of these deserts, parched of any hint of femininity, something has happened. It has occurred long after giving up hope of ever being with a woman that truly turned me on. While I am definitely not complaining about my history, it is the present that has all of my attention.

It would be great to make a woman laugh again, something I have been good at for many years. Conversations, hand holding, showers and some unspeakable things, are sorely missed by yours truly. As I have said before, this appears to be my relationship for the year and it really is a paltry price to pay for this unimaginable privilege of stuffing myself into a bottle and setting it afloat on the river of time. I am claustrophobic, but I try and not think about the bottle part of all this. I have been entertaining myself for decades and sometimes there has been an audience, just as you are my time traveling audience.

I am picking this up after a day or so and it is Friday evening, a time when I will go out of my way to enjoy myself. It is the end of a week and I get some quality time for myself. My spirits are good at the moment and generally they are when I write to you. I am certainly not writing this whole thing to purge myself of any baggage or asking you to pick up my baggage; you will have plenty of your own, by the way.

I was sitting out on my lanai and sipping some wine as the Hawaiian sun prepared to set and it is a beautiful time, believe me. A guy by the name of Tom Waits came on the radio and I thought that I would tell you about him, too. He is a great writer and story teller, usually focusing on society's underbelly and his music seems more jazz than blues. Then, it dawned on me that if I keep directing you to music, I am simply directing you to me. The diversity of music I am drawn to, hopefully reflects who I am, in addition to my modest effort to do the same with these stories.

Living the way I am right now, it is easy for me to imagine myself sitting in a paradise like setting, adrift in the Pacific Ocean, enjoying the caressing trades and knowing there is an ocean pretty close by and all around as well. The reason why that is easy is because I am doing that at this very moment. It ain't half bad.

I have an update on your evolution. Spoke with your Dad today and he told me you are talking up a storm and showing some mind power, but I will be the judge of that when I visit in September. My old friend Ken H. may end up joining us for a day in Hoboken. Being an actor, he will completely go over the top in describing my incredible talents, etc. Again, I told you before that he thinks I am one of the funniest people alive and that is very flattering, considering that his work has brought in contact with most everyone who has been funny in the past fifty years, or close to that. Your Mother and Father will be captivated by his charm and that would be fun to witness. I will let you know if he does show up.

I always envisioned myself living in a place and with a life style that allowed me to wear a pair of shorts and nothing else in my own home. I'll be damned, my uniform, especially when I am solo, is those pair of shorts. Most all the windows are open and the door is open as well and the entire ambiance is completely intoxicating, which works out well for me anyway. The best part of all that is I can pretty much pull it off throughout the year. I think the less we wear, the closer we are to ourselves. Mind you, I am not advocating for reckless nudity because that could easily be a very unpleasant experience, especially for those of us who keep at least some of our clothes on. If I believed I was totally private, without any possibility of interruption, I would not bother with clothes, at least I don't think so. Well, we will get to find out when I move into the yurt, which will sit on the back corner of 15+ acres, according to the last acreage count. For a city kid like you, that is a fair amount of land, especially on a small island like Kauai.

Pretty incredible journey, if I do say so myself. I am not sure at all what's ahead. Some of it has to do with how successful this feed business is, which will rely a great deal on my supposed talents. Hopefully, at some point not too far down the road, I will get the yurt up, which will be a mind blowing change and I am absolutely certain of that. There is always the possibility of a lady to round out my edges and that unleashes forces for which there is no antidote. In the interim, we'll just live a life and see what happens.

I put in a request for an updated picture of you. Told them I wanted to see a picture from head to foot, so I could get a sense of your carriage. I am looking forward to this visit most of all and I suspect that will continue from one to the next, as you gradually begin to occupy your elusive self.

Cracked open my new Cadillac Mac this morning and there was a terrific quotation from a magazine called Tricycle, a Zen Buddhist voice. Years ago, I subscribed to a service that allows me to read a Zen quote of some kind each morning, very often from contemporary authors, of which there are far too many. Personally, I think the original Buddha would be amazed at how his words have been dissected, interpreted, reinterpreted, not to mention all the side streets taken by so many followers on the Buddha Highway. No one owns this way of looking at the world because each person has to find their own way. I believe the core of this practice is communicated in a non-verbal manner, but I have approached this discipline in an undisciplined manner, taking great liberties with much of the teaching, but never doubting for a minute that I am a Zen practitioner. I kind of look at my Jewishness that way, sort of. I am a full blooded member of the Jewish tribe, which is anchored deeply in my genetic memory. Personally, I don't care for the religion very much and I never did. Just like in Zen, there are no good Jews or bad Jews, just Jews.

Whoops, I got off on one of my tangents, apologies. This morning's quote resonated very, very deeply within me and I wanted to share it with you:

"Dharma is not about credentials. It's not about how many practices you've done, or how peaceful you can make your mind. It's not about being in a community where you feel safe or enjoying the cachet of being a 'Buddhist.' It's not even about accumulating teachings, empowerments, or 'spiritual accomplishments.' It's about how naked you're willing to be with your own life, and how much you're willing to let go of your masks and your armor and live as a completely exposed, undefended, and open human person." Reginald Ray

I am sure the author is well published in Zen circles, but as I do not read any Zen related books or just about any books for that matter, I don't know the guy. While this clearly has a Zen slanted approach, its message is Universal, which is the case with virtually all of the Buddha's words. The simplest definition of Dharma is a reflection of all the teachings and practices of Siddartha, from 2500+ years ago. Stripped to its absolute core, it is that last sentence that got my attention this early AM and I am positive the Big Man would give an Amen.

As a young man, you will likely look at this with some reservation and that is to be expected. In spite of overbearing people like Donald Trump, hell bent on creating permanence for themselves by creating skyscrapers and everything else with their name plastered everywhere to be seen. A life lived in awkward pursuit of the last sentence in the above quote is why we are here, creating monuments of honesty in the moment, without concern for their longevity. Not wanting to flip backwards at this point, I am pretty sure I would have had an opinion on my years of therapy and would likely have expressed something very similar to this sentiment. Most conventional therapy reconstructs and I believe in deconstruction, "living completely exposed."

The endgame in this tail chasing exercise is that the closer you get to the stripped away self, the more you realize it is an illusion, our own sacred construct to keep us from going mad, at least that is the fear. The precise moment you think of your self, that self is here and then gone instantly. Honestly, not bullshitting you. Very quietly, I have devoted years of my own private mind time, at least looking for a way to explain all of this shit to myself. Zen is the closest I have gotten to a way of making sense of this world and my place in it, yet it still misses the boat because there is only room for one in this vessel we call our own life.

This also means there is nothing in any of these pages telling you what to do because your choices are your responsibility and no one else's. I know you will want to lionize my persona because you won't be able to help yourself. After all, I am pretty damn special. The horse shit scale just exploded all around me. If there is anything remotely special about me, it is not my life, it is simply my desire to share it with you and always laboring to connect with the words that corral the feelings.

I know I have been laying down some good shit in the past pages and part of the reason for that is not much of a material nature is going on at the moment. We are still in that zone of routines and minimal interaction. Monday to Friday, I am at the site and pretty exhausted at the end of the day. The highlight of my weekend is riding with the Sons, which I guess is OK, because at least I have a highlight. I love the guys I ride with and there is great warmth each Sunday morning we get together. It is great fun riding in a caravan, but lots of the conversation on our breaks is not my bottle of beer, so to speak.

It would be easy to label this period of my life as boring, but most of the time that is not where I let myself go, because it is a bogus address. I am a grateful guy and have shared that with you probably too many times previously, which is not the worst sentiment to reinforce.

You must be dying to know how I am adapting to my new Minimus running shoes. Running about two weeks on them and ankles, achilles and calves are fine. I have a dull pain on the left side of my spine, but whatever caused it, it is going away, which is easy to monitor in my daily yoga practice. Running on the balls of the feet is a serious adjustment and it necessitates breaking down years of operating in a very different way. I am still building up my strength and stamina because it is a quantum change in my whole approach to running. Maintaining the bounce definitely requires more strength and I am not there yet. On many occasions, I have run barefoot on grass and it felt very awkward because my body was disciplined to run on my heel in the conventional running shoe. Before I get tired and cranky, it feels very natural and invigorating to start out running with good form and a mystical sense of the first runners' feelings when they accidentally discovered a faster way of getting from A to B. Most likely, the "discovery" occurred when an early ancestor of ours ran his ass off to get out of the way of some blatantly obvious disaster or carnivore, one that would have abruptly and painfully ended his life.

Aside from running in the old way, I want to get some shit done in my life. Being is an OK objective, but Doing is the ass kicker. On the professional side of things, I want to get this island to be more self-sufficent, primarily on the agricultural side of the equation. The joke is I will likely be able to pull it off, which is an anti-Trump moment for me, because it doesn't matter who knows my part in it all. My public self is committed to that direction and I am reasonably well known in that role here. Pretty trippy as far as I am concerned. I don't know how it happened, but I became the place I call home. I love my Kauai with all my heart.

The yurt is an integral part of all this, but that is my private life and one which totally opens its doors to a woman or just stays with me. At the moment, the yurt is only about creating my space. Earlier in the day today, I spoke with Bobby, the smartest and most decent cattle rancher in all of Hawaii. Likely mentioned him in some context with Joel and all that business about local beef. He presently keeps his horses on about 15 acres, which we lease to him and I would occupy about 15 acres that adjoins his land. Cowboys are very cool and they are that way because they are pretty real. What you see is what you get, back to the theme of this verbal shpritzing in the first place. (Lenny Bruce schpritzed his audience with some very uncomfortable stuff. It was a pretty unique brand of comedy. Very rough and unedited. He broke all the rules and the rules broke him. Check him out.)

Bobby will plow the land and keep the grasses down because that is how you create good pasture land. Between the two of us, we would have nearly 25 acres of quality pasture land and that is a pretty big deal. I know any day now, I will come home and find people moving into the units directly in my face. No way, I will be happy with the total loss of privacy, but the yurt in the mist will make it palatable for a while, having no idea what it will be like to be living in a drive-in with 28 household screens and having that same number able to view my one screen. Am I out of here or what?

I want to say a word about repetition, which is likely rampant in this document. If this was a book intended for publication, it would get butchered by an editor for things like that. The mind doesn't necessarily work that way and over the course of a year, even Einstein would likely repeat a story or two. As I have maintained from the outset of this folly, I don't particularly care about anyone else reading this other than you. Frankly, I can't imagine anyone else giving a flying fuck about any of this, with the exception of your mother, father, uncle, grandmother and some of the other helpless innocents caught in this web of self-aggrandizing deceit by good ole Grandpa Larry. I suspect at the end of this particular Zen Highway, I will likely thank you for giving me this opportunity and not even be remotely concerned about anyone else reading this. I will most likely see about getting it out there. Writing something over the course of a year represents an incredible degree of focus and it is likely an accomplishment I might feel like sharing. The truth is, it is nearly effortless to publish an ebook, you put it out there and see what happens. During this time, you have been my only audience and it will continue that way until I figure out how to embrace the completed manuscript.

Stories about my adventures are relatively easy to tell and the only bitch is not remembering more of the funny stuff along the way. In some ways, it is the other details that are more personal because it has to do with how I feel and that is shaky ground to write from and it exposes most vestiges of privacy for me. Once again, the good news is I don't give shit because this only has to do with the two of us and anyone else is an uninvited guest, but they are welcome and I mean no harm.

Speaking of repetition, I cranked up Paul Simon's Graceland just a little while ago. Yes, it was one my musical passports from NYC to Santa Fe. Got me to thinking about how gigantic that move was for me. It was all heart, without much significant input from my brain, which I had begun to downgrade in importance anyway.

I was forty two, giving up everything familiar to me and traveling to a distant world, the world of mesas and flooding arroyo's and real Indians and very big sky. That trip, right around the time Graceland came out, is the beginning of a life long exhalation on my part. You learn not to waste your breath on the small stuff. You know my background pretty well by this point, but there is still no way you could have any idea what this gut wrenching and life embracing tango has been like for me. I jumped and didn't look down. This album is part of my personal sound track, playing in perfect harmony with all my thoughts and feelings at the time and instantly tapping into them anytime. The tribal effect of the South Africans, who "illegally" participated in this project back in the days of apartheid, is very special and embued with life.

A Break

Without backtracking on this path, I am pretty sure we talked about electronic dating, because I likely wrote about the woman I met through this techno- connector called Match.com. I hope I am not repeating this, but those sites are structured in the same manipulative manner as the casinos in Vegas. You will never find a clock anywhere in a casino and you have to go through the casino to check in, take a shit, whatever. These social services get you in and they are brilliant at keeping you around, one way or another. In my case, I signed up for an occasional one month spurt and then quit until they drop a hook when I have had my usually prohibited third glass of evening wine.

Anyway, the one month commitment is drawing to a close. Last night, for some reason, I checked the gallery of femininity also looking for their perfect man. Caught a lady we'll call Jessica. Nice looking lady and completely gray, which is cool. Just got here and splitting her time with Seattle, her home for many years. She wrote she thought she was pretty, which caught my eye as well. It is unusual for any woman to be so immodest and that alone interested me. Sent a semi-brilliant, provocative email and she called last night.

Remember, not long ago I inserted that Buddhist-like quotation about the ultimate goal of this life. At this late stage, I like showing it all. I would safely venture a guess that most people really don't get into that kind of stuff. If I had masks, they have been dramatically reduced and being truthful, especially in an intimate setting is what I seem to live for, at least at this point in my devolution (I'll bet I used that word before. It really sounds familiar).

You have to keep in mind that I am unfortunately 67 years old and that women even a decade or so under me, no double entendre there, have some serious expectations about a guy at this point in their lives. You now know better than anyone else, other than myself at this moment, what I am about. My check list has gotten much shorter and I think most women grow their list as they get older. If both are convinced there is bona fide electricity, they owe it to themselves, especially at this point in their lives, to embrace it with open arms. Now, that's my deal, but I believe their tendency is to complicate the chemistry. If you are able to make a seriously, genuine connection with another, the rest doesn't need to be all that difficult, but fear of true connection frequently undermines the outcome on both sides.

I am just looking forward to sitting down on a Kauai morning and having coffee with a woman, who sounded interesting enough during our one phone call, initiated by her. I will tell her the worst things I can possibly say about myself and see what happens. Nothing would be said apologetically, just honestly. Frankly, I will be shocked if she says anything other than I am an incredibly interesting person, but our incompatabilities simply won't work. The good news is that if she hangs around for the second act, you'll just never know where to from there.

Seriously though, being incredibly excited about moving into a fairly secluded yurt at this point in my life will not generally go over really well. The truth in there is that I am putting together a living space for myself that serves me on my journey. Being terminally immature is also a drawback. I just feel I have so much less to lose at this point and that is normally associated with much younger people. Any lady who can put up with me and love me for it, is a lady I have been looking for. While relationships have their challenges at every age, the older you get, the hope is you become increasingly honest with yourself. I guess I have cared about it more than many, especially at this time in my life. As luck would have it, I am no slouch when it comes to the word thing and at least I am perceived as sincere when those exchanges occur.

You put your money on a long shot, you put your entire self to win and you will never lose, regardless of outcome. I will meet Jessica and be certain that anything at all is possible. At the same time, I can't imagine fitting any possible type a woman would be looking for. For my part, I don't care if a woman is on my "path". I am not looking for a twin with tits, rather someone who enjoys her singular nature and has enough room to fully embrace who I am and venture forth. This is a tall order, my boy. However, my channeled Cyrano will never say never.

I'll let you know how it goes.

So far, so good

Today is July 4th and I met up with the bruddahs at our usual place. My plan was to leave there and head north for a morning get together with Jessica. Weather was kind of squirrely, but the north shore looked good and we all headed that way and I just peeled off for my time with Jessica.

She is grey haired, slender and just a few inches short than I am. She has been here all of nine months in total, with long visits back to Seattle for family and business in between. We had a wonderful conversation and there was chemistry happening. I am rather amazed that she pretty much took it all in and was still very open. Jessica has had a very busy life, with much business responsibility and a life focused around it, at least that is the impression I got. She has come to this intoxicating island to re-calibrate her life. What I have done with my life and continue doing, which is keeping it simple and avoiding excessive distractions, is something she seemed to be comfortable with. Whenever I thought I was throwing a curve, like moving into a yurt on 15 acres at this point in my life, she seemed good with it.

Can't spend too much time on this now and that is just as well. Soon, I will be hopping in my truck and going over to our biker party spot, which we call the pasture. Harold and Paula live on an incredible tract of land, set aside by the Wilcox family. Amongst other things, the main house and grounds are called Grove Farm Museum. Those guys live on a small road in a plantation style house and there is a beautiful piece of land at the end of their road. You can see the annual Fourth of July fireworks display from their place. The guys and wives and families show up for these kinds of things and it is usually a pot luck. Anyway, do need to head over pretty soon and I have to find a place open, so I can bring pupu's (look it up).

Regarding Jessica, I have been burned and bummed so many goddamn times that I simply need to let this unfold beyond our first three hours together. For my part, I am happy I met someone who I want to get to know better and feel absolutely certain of that, no small feat for yours truly. My privacy is well guarded and it is not something I am inclined to throw around carelessly. As of this very moment, there is a possibility and no more than that.

In order to always avoid the impression that this is some kind of diary, I am not going to tell you about the fireworks Fourth with the bruddahs........ OK, I know the pressure is unbearable and I am left with no choice, but to share it. It is always an incredible time at the pasture. I was actually telling people there what an unbelievable energy fills our gathering and something you would not see on the mainland. This group, regardless of participants at any given time, is a wonderful ohana and the aloha in the air needs to be experienced to be believed. Everyone hugs, shakes hands, men and woman hug and kiss each other on the cheek. The children will even do it with the adults. It is simply a part of the life of people who live here, but not very many of them understand how incredible it is, because it is what they know. I love this place and I love its people and I am now one of them.

A little more about Jessica, which precedes our getting together for the second time in a couple of days. I have never been with a successful businesswoman before, at least at the level she has been on. We had a phone conversation today and I talked about the feed business, amongst other things. I wanted to talk to her because she is a pro and her input is based on her experience and her success. While conventional success has never been my focus, I respect those who have achieved it, partially because some things have to get sacrificed along the way. In her case, having fun and simply embracing life were cast aside and I sense she wants to turn her attention toward things like that now. Generally, these things don't work out, but neither do most all relationships. It feels like it could be fun to venture into, but I do without any certainty at all.

As you know, I enjoy the fermented grape and a variety of cocktails, while she is a member of Alcoholics Anonymous, a potential source of serious conflict to be addressed very soon. Smoking grass is a whole other animal that I haven't shared with her yet, but it is coming and that will likely go over very poorly. Men and women very often give up too much of themselves in order to be with someone and the bitterness is everlasting. It is simply too late for me to give up most anything I do because what I do is who I am.

Four Conversations a Date and a Ride

Saturday is always a slow kind of day for me here, at least it has been for quite some time now. I just take my sweet ass time about doing anything at all. Without fail, I do the sit, yoga, followed by running on the balls of my feet, which I have spoken about at length already. My sit always takes the same amount of time because that is part of the practice. I sit for 25 minutes, no more no less. My yoga practice is slower than usual, allowing me to synch up my mind with the body. Eventually, I suit up and head outside for my usual run, feeling a little more relaxed than I do during the week. I do the same run every day because I have never traveled to do my run. I leave the door of my home or wherever I wake up and run and it has never mattered where I was living. No hurry with breakfast after that. I drink my bottle of water, while my body unloads the heat with a pretty good sweat. Yogurt, oatmeal with raisins and about 10 pills later, I am done with what needs to be done. By the way, the pills are primarily vitamins and minerals, all geared to keep the heart machine running smoothly.

First phone call was to my Zen priest friend, Eiju, who lives in Mendoza, Argentina. Like many people threaded through my life, we have talked about him somewhere before, but as you know, I am prohibited from going backwards to check. Talking to Eiju is like talking to the Buddha. His life is as a priest, carrying on the traditions of Zen and engaging people along the way. He has a modest following, but I am certain those people feel very blessed to have him in their lives. It is a thrill to talk with him because we speak a common language, in spite of the fact that he has his struggles with English. We see our lives and their place in the world in a very similar way. Trust me, I am not proselytizing on behalf of the Buddha, especially when it comes to you. If you are remotely intrigued, by all means look into it. Invariably, at some point during my talk with Eiju, I will break down in tears because we have mined a delicate place within. I always feel enriched and grounded after all our conversations.

Sometime around Noon, I got on the Tangerine Dream and grabbed a beer and took it down to the little harbor I frequently visit. Cracked the beer and looked out at the indescribable expanse of the Pacific Ocean. After a few sips into the bottle, I called Ken H. and we had one of our typical conversations, which are always great fun. He will do some of the show business stuff, along with political observations and I provide the Kauai color, with stories of whatever I happen to be up to. He loves to hear my lady stories, no matter how brief or unsatisfying, which is not necessarily that fair. The various brief adventures I have had during the past year, which I have shared with you, have never been disappointing. You know, as long as you are as straight ahead as you can be and in the moment, nothing is lost. I wouldn't trade any of these mini-episodes for anything else with that woman because it is a mental exercise I try not to engage in. Ken and I had a ball and I slowly wheeled home after it.

In the afternoon, I headed north for a scheduled date with Jessica. On the way, I made my ritual stop at my friend, Ken S's tree house perched above the street level with parking underneath. We had a dark version of a White Russian cocktail, which was very tasty. In addition, I will have to confess to getting high, God forgive me. As usual, the conversation was far more complicated and esoteric than my usual fare, but that is what Ken does and it is totally fine with me. Conversations from his side always seem to focus on sustainability and an idealistic view of how we can cure what I believe is an incurable disease. It is the human disease of ego, denial, selfishness and a level of suffering that handcuffs us to the whipping post, whether we are conscious of it or not. I love him dearly, but I am always alert to his limited attention span for others and will cut short talk in order to return the spotlight to him. I always enjoy my visits and when his wife is around, I have great sidebar conversations. Susan has had an incredible life in journalism, a male dominated business and she more than held her own. She was on the mainland this time, so it was just the two of us. Both of them are very special to me.

I gathered up my lubricated faculties and smokehouse perceptions, continuing on my journey to fair Jessica. Before hitting my destination, I pulled off the road and had a good talk with my friend, Michael, which brings us to number four. We talk weekly and are fairly current regarding each other's lives. Jessica was a new addition, so it was fun telling that tale and the fact that I was headed up to her place for our second get together.

After our brief repartee, I wheeled out and headed for my next destination, which turned out be my Gourmet Meals for Single Dummies pick up. My friends, Marta and Dan, were house sitting close by to Lady J and I stopped off to pick up my ten entrees. After learning they would be staying in a place called Princeville, it made sense to grab the meals and share a couple of gourmet entrees with Jessica, just a few minutes away. They are good people and I always have fun engaging them.

Headed out to my final destination, Jessica's Princeville condo. Told you a little about her already and no need to go backwards. She had a lovely space and good taste was everywhere to be seen. I am a hard pill to swallow for most ladies and that is just how it goes. I don't mean to do anything, other than being honest and seeing what happens. We had a lovely evening and she was clearly touched, but not a match that would ever work. I am a bare bones kind of guy, who is interested in the basics and not the trimmings. Women even remotely close to my age seem to have a clipboard full of pre-requisites and they are pretty specific. It is like I am going in one direction and everyone

I have met seems to be going elsewhere. The baggage is too much for me to carry. In her case, she is a recovering alcoholic in AA and told me she couldn't be with a man who drinks. I wouldn't give up my pleasures for Cleopatra or Marilyn Monroe and don't see why that would be even remotely necessary.

To me, it always starts with the heart and then you look around and see what else matters. Had a great gourmet meal, snuggled a bit and then headed for home, certain we would not speak or see each other again. It would be very cool to meet a lady who didn't have it together and made no apologies. So, my boy, after four conversations and a date, Saturday came to a close.

The Sunday ride was wonderful as usual. Pretty good turnout with around 20 some odd bikes, which is a lot when they are stretched out on the highway. Home this afternoon and reflecting on the past few days. If anything should ever happen to me with a woman, I don't think it will be some calculated endeavor on my part, rather a pre-ordained accident, which I won't see coming. I know I keep threatening to resign from the hormonal race and I think I have actually hung up my jersey and can now just relax. Optimism has not been vanquished by pessimism, it is neither one, hopefully only an openness to whatever may come. We will see if I am a man of my word or if I simply go back over and trample my present intention.

Food for Thought

One of my recurring themes has been the state of affairs at the time I am writing to you. It seems like something is going to happen, sooner rather than later. The powerful, the rich and influential, either as individuals or bearing a corporate name, have seemingly taken over the fate of all of us and our planet. On many levels, it feels so surreal to me that it could be a science fiction tale that I am sharing with you. Recently, the Supreme Court ruled that corporations have the same rights as individuals and can therefore throw as much money as needed into the pocket of any politician. Our governmental agencies continually rule on the side of big business, with farmers, small business owners, retirees, those less fortunate, not to mention people with serious illnesses getting fucked, plain and simple. Oh, pardon me for leaving out Mother Earth which has no seat at the table and a voice that power is deaf to acknowledge. Heroes are gone and replaced by idols, symbols of lives none of us have any access to. Fame is cheap, fleeting and insignificant. Everyday, someone is famous, downright ubiquitous and then they are gone without a trace.

It seems to me we are on an inexorable march to an oblivion of the spirit and with clipped wings we will trudge on in our lives, the ones we are allowed to live by those far, far more fortunate than ourselves. When I look ahead, the landscape looks incredibly bleak. You know, once people and institutions have a choke hold grasp on power and control, they will not willingly give it up.

In case our secret police are reading this, I am not advocating revolution, I repeat, I am not advocating revolution. Now, leave me the fuck alone!

There is a decadence married to this opulence and it will eventually swallow its own enlarged tongue and make horrible gagging noises as it collapses on to the very earth that has been forced to host this abuse. You may think I am being negative, but I am not. I just don't see anything changing on a significant enough level that it would steer the course of this civilization in a different direction.

I was joking with my friend Beth about a title for my next mythical book and it would be called something like, *"An Optimist Who Has No Faith in the Future."* I get up every damn day, thinking I can make a difference. It can be a couple of sentences with a friend or stranger, it could be attempting to influence policy on this island, it could be creating a successful business that leads by example or it could be whatever I choose to write to you after this opus.

In this country, the entire focus is on our differences from one and other. As long as we are divided, fractionated by manipulation, we are no threat to power. While it stills feels invisible, these fractions are quietly beginning to take action. More and more people are growing much of their own food and feeling a greater sense of responsibility for how they live their lives. There are people with differences quietly finding common ground. The noise around this effort is deaf like and it is difficult to pick up. My Quixote Order of the Windmill, a group I have put together, is an example of this. You have people from the so called Left and the so called Right and the common themes are endless. The Quixote business is a cool story and I will tell it soon enough.

This thing I am sensing doesn't have a name and feels incredibly delicate, meaning it could take flight or just as easily end up in a prison cell with no escape. This is likely a movement that has not been organized, but it has been organic. The Occupy people had a message in mind, but these other folks are just quietly walking the walk as best they can.

You should have a front row seat for all this, as I suspect it will break down eventually. It could be calamitous or subtlle like air seeping from a punctured tire that goes flat down the road aways. Honestly, I don't know how much we can take and by we I mean the vast majority of earth's sentient beings and the resources that sustain them. The plight of people in poor countries is so horrid it is beyond my ability to comprehend. These people suffer unspeakable crimes and very often their resources are plundered by the same faceless names that champion the corporate good.These countries are no more than pawns for the wealthy countries to play with, swearing allegiance one day and shunning them the next. Character is virtually extent in this deadly game and its rare appearances often results in harsh penalties for those who dare speak truth to power.

Honestly, I keep coming back to this as one of the central themes because the momentum of today will birth your world of tomorrow. There is no way for me to like where it is going, but there are just enough people around to make the ride well worth the price of admission.

The following is brought to you courtesy of a piece of journalism, true journalism. I have been reading an incredible writer by the name of Chris Hedges. Whether one agrees with his politics of the Left, this son of a bitch can put some fine words together.

I rarely bring in anything from the outside, but a closing paragraph from his recent work caused me to immediately copy and insert it in our story. I figured I would paste it in and then build around it when I was ready for another entry. Ending this little piece with his potent paragraph seemed like the direction to follow and here it is:

"And here is the dilemma we face as a civilization. We march collectively toward self-annihilation. Corporate capitalism, if left unchecked, will kill us. Yet we refuse, because we cannot think and no longer listen to those who do think, to see what is about to happen to us. We have created entertaining mechanisms to obscure and silence the harsh truths, from climate change to the collapse of globalization to our enslavement by corporate power that will mean our self-destruction. If we can do nothing else we must, even as individuals, nurture the private dialogue and the solitude that make thought possible. It is better to be an outcast, a stranger in one's own country, than an outcast from one's self. It is better to see what is about to befall us and to resist than to retreat into the fantasies embraced by a nation of the blind."

Eleven and Al

Right now, I am going to take a leap and draw a connection between your parents' eleventh wedding anniversary and yet another quote from a very special being, Big Al.

The suede "yarmulke", which I just had to spell check because it is not a word I ever have to spell, is sitting comfortably on a photograph that needs a little explaining. On the left side of the plastic holder is a photo of your Dad and Uncle and myself. They are standing, with your Father showing a little bicep flexion and I am kneeling and trying to hold on to a schizophrenic dalmatian I briefly owned with Gail in New Mexico. We were about to embark on a weekend camping trip in my red truck, which I still happen to own after nearly 20 years. Gail took the photograph prior to our four wheeled launch into the wilderness of southern Colorado. They were young men and your Father had to be somewhere at least around twenty. Danny rode in the back of the open pick up truck all the way to our camp site that had to be at least a four hour drive up some scenic roads and then on to serious back country, eventually ending up on old logging roads. By that time, I was a reasonably experienced car camper, especially with Gail packing everything that anyone could possibly need for a weekend in the middle of nowhere.

I think some of those kinds of experiences with me, including several summers at the PA farm house, impacted on both my boys in ways they would not have had without me. I like that very much. We camped a couple of times while I lived in New Mexico with Gail. She was a good lady when it came to the boys and the few other women throughout my life I hope left each of them with a special feeling for ladies. I think Andy is a fine husband to your mother. I would be lying if I said I didn't care whether his experiences with me helped to make him feel a bit more secure about being with a woman. His mother and I were not a shining example of how it is done. In a perfect world, wouldn't it be great if you could look at this side of your family and see a loving couple, thrilled to call you Shane? Sorry buddy, you will have to take it anyway you can get it. As you have hopefully gathered by now, I am a huge fan of women and I think my sons know that.

Where the fuck were we? Right, the photo on the right of the plastic holder is the official wedding picture of Andy and Andrea, your Mommy and Daddy. I guess it is a typical smiling groom delicately posed with his smiling bride. This is a photograph from eleven years ago tomorrow, July 14th. They were with each other for a number of years before that and they were together for most of their college time at Rutgers University. As I have told you, your Dad had a rough go of it for a while at the beginning of college and your mother was fuckin' Aces to the Max, staying with him and loving him throughout. I sincerely hope they are able to weather all the shit coming at them for the next bunch of years and still be very together when you read this for the first time.

As the captain of the Cyrano Team, I am always rooting for love to conquer all and I just think they may have the right shit to stay close, as the landscape continues to change, sometimes pulling them away from each other. The passage of time puts all of us into some unpredictable places and we can only deal with them as they happen, no way to plan for it.

Now, what does any of this have to deal with Albert Einstein, one of my sidekicks on this word adventure? The answer is likely not a damn thing, but I saw another one of his stellar quotes and I wanted to include it, adding one more of his priceless discoveries for you and I to ponder. For all of his immeasurable scientific/mathematical intellect, he seemed to have an even greater understanding of life's secrets and mysteries, with a brilliant instinct for hitting the proverbial nail on the head.

Whether we are open to it or not, our decisions are based upon our intuition and/or heart, whatever you want to call it. The one thing it is not is the orderly process of the mind or intellect, whatever you want to call that beast of diversion. For all of the important stuff, we have some kind of pre-conscious moment that is just barely detectable, but I am one who believes that our lives depend upon our ability to pick up those feint signals and put them right in front of us. It is has to be tough to be a younger person and willingly give up the reins on your life and just let that stallion of chance take you for a hell of a ride. Christ, it took me around 42 years to get my shit in gear and that is a long time...................

Took no more than a half hour break from the machine, but I am a changed man. I had one of my Single Meals and it was simply spectacular. OK, so I am sitting in my shorts, got some serious Blues in the background and I sit down to a BBQ Pork Chop with Sauteed Apples and Baked Beans. I reheated it in my wok and ate it right out of that wok, something likely unthinkable around most any woman at all.

Our senses are pretty interesting antennas to what is going on around us and it is those moments between the sensory registration and the mental awareness that all the magic of life occurs. The closer you get to that pre-cognitive moment, the fuller your life. Believe me, I am no angel, but I have been doing the best I could to live from the gut. It ain't all that bad either. You indulge in yourself and others don't add to your weight, so you are actually more available as a result.

Here is the quote from Al and I couldn't agree with him more. Life is a magical thing and it can't take a back seat to any effort to explain the invisible. OK, Al, it is your turn now:

> *"The intuitive mind is a sacred gift and the rational mind is a faithful servant. We have created a society that honors the servant and has forgotten the gift."*
> Albert Einstein

Now, there is a tough act to follow, but I don't feel like shutting down just yet. However, I can't follow a rare spirit and mind such as his either. We will let his two sentences stand for themselves and quietly move along.

We do seem to have this need to understand everything, continually encroaching upon the sacred and it has taken its toll on civilization. Nearly all of us have built our lives on the shoulders of the indigenous peoples that were here before. Most everywhere you look in the world, progress has devoured those societies. They're still around, but their numbers are not all that great and the centuries of abuse have beaten them down terribly. While far from perfect, the First People put great stock in Big Al's intuitive mind, long before he came along to give it voice.

Be a renegade if you have to be one, but make sure your heart beats strongly and you listen for it and to it. Shit, your parents are likely to read this before you and I don't want them to think I am preaching a life of rebellion and shame. I am feeling very comfortable with anything I have written and everything I've shared to this point, with more to come. I simply want you to have the fullest life you are capable of having at any point from this first reading forward. Certainly, I am not interested in you living my life and I can't imagine why you would want to do that anyway. My life continues to be a great ride, but it has got a single seat, just like everyone else's.

You're In Luck

Well, aren't you the lucky one? I've got nothing pressing to do and some time on my hands. It is a Wednesday evening, whatever the hell that is supposed to mean. Took a quick peek at what I wrote a number of days ago and I think I miraculously understand it and more importantly, I am not inclined to change any of it. When I went back on the first one hundred pages, it never dawned me to change anything at all, beyond a typo or a loose end of some kind. When this is all done, I want to comfortably be able to say that I meant everything I wrote, regardless of what I might think of it in a day or a year or a decade.

Got the Blues in the background, which is such a perfect soundtrack for a life story. If you really give yourself an opportunity to live your life fully, the Blues is the soundtrack, at least over the long haul. Keep in mind, there is nothing sad about the Blues; it is the music that attempts to explain our ordinary lives. I love it, but it was an acquired taste. You add the seasoning of life experience to the passage of time and you've got the Blues ready to serve.

Most every night, at least for the past eight months, I generally end up in my private space, sitting in my shorts and writing you or thinking about writing you. In between, we sprinkle things like Gourmet Meals for Single Dummies or an occasional TV show I enjoy watching. I sit quietly or occasionally move to whatever music may be permeating the atmosphere. Sometimes, it feels incredibly boring and repetitive and other times it feels incredibly personal and connected. Living this life is a weird state of mind. If you think everything is terrific, not sure it matters whatever the "reality" might be and also not sure who holds the tape measure for that slippery measurement anyway. I know it ain't me, my boy.

Because of choices I have made over the past twenty-five, some odd years, I have had plenty of time to stew in the pot of life. I like to think of myself as a gourmet stew because gourmet implies quality and stew is an everyman recipe. I am just a regular guy trying to make the best of his life and employing a bar that has gotten continually higher for me to top. Shane, if one thing is clear to me, you have to keep growing until you stop breathing and I am not shitting you on that score, believe me.

It is amazing to feel passionate about things and how that passion affects your life. It is incredibly energizing and downright mind blowing at times. If you get me going on issues relating to the future of the world or more importantly, the future of my inherited island home, watch out! Giving your self the freedom to feel is the most liberating path imaginable and I am not sure if anyone claims to have achieved this state, but I am out there trying.

Gratitude, baby, that's the ticket. If you stopped to think about it and we never would, what if a rock was offered the opportunity to be a feeling human being for just a year? Sadly, many of us go through our years imitating rocks. For years now, I have easily gotten to a place of being both incredulous and grateful for this amazing experience. It is truly an indescribable, collage of moments and moves far faster than we could ever imagine. I know I have told you to enjoy the ride before, but it is worth repeating ad nauseam. It is your turn now and the world will let you know what it expects of you. If you are an asshole, you will never get the message, no matter if someone screams it at you. Selfishly, I am counting on your not being an asshole because that would be very depressing for me. Based on what little I have observed, I don't think you will have anal proclivities. I will give you an update after my September visit. There is probably not too much to worry about because I am thrilled with what I have witnessed so far and I think you have the ability to be a special being. Now, don't shit yourself because there is nothing you need to do about it. You make your heart your compass and your actions compassionate and you simply live your life. This is such a terribly primal sensibility and yet our society demands a more exacting price for our so-called civility.

Over the course of my years, I have thought of so many things I should have written down because I liked how they sounded between my ears. The search for the vocabulary to define life is never ending and it has had an attraction to me for too many decades. This is some unimaginable catharsis for me and it never crossed my mind those eight months ago when I had the inspiration to find my voice. You couldn't convince me in a million years that I am a good writer, but I like what I have to say about all sorts of shit and that is what matters to me. Describing who you are is about the most elusive chore one could undertake and putting some words together in an effort to shine the light in that direction is what I enjoy. After all is said and done, it will be a failed effort because it is simply impossible to have anyone else get inside you, but you can get pretty close if you try hard enough and that is what we are doing with all these words.

Rodeos and Gun Control

I spent this entire Friday at the CJM Rodeo Grounds because they are hosting a rodeo this weekend that draws a lot of people, which is part of something called Koloa

Plantation Days. The feed company I have been involved with for quite a while now, The Paniolo Feed Company, is one of the event sponsors. We have a banner up in the arena and a small tent with another banner and that houses yours truly. The location is predictably hot, dry and windy. It is a fabulous spot that overlooks Maha'ulepu Beach, which is a pretty long stretch of beach and one of the better ones on the island. My job is to get to know many of the cowboys and cowgirls because they are my prospective feed customers. Most of the activity during the day was qualifying teams in the steer roping competition. The first rider lassos the animal around the neck and the second person drops a rope to try and catch their hind feet, which does tend to stretch them rather unpleasantly when it happens to work.

Later in the day, there was women's barrel racing (look it up), which was followed by guys wrestling a steer to the ground and tying all four legs. One guy ropes the steer and the second comes running up and tries to wrestle the animal to the ground with the help of his riding partner, who dismounts in order to make it a fair fight because the steers are very strong.

The event was capped off with bull riding, which blows my mind. You sit on the back of a pissed off bull and try and hold on with some rope tie and he is just bucking like a son of a bitch. I think they do something to make it uncomfortable for the beast and it causes him to kick his rear legs in the air. Eight seconds is the time to hit and you are judged for form, etc. On a good day, very few cowboys manage to take the full ride.

You might ask yourself, what the fuck is the purpose of the rodeo story and what does it have to do with gun control? Well, once again, I am glad you asked. The rodeo has nothing whatsoever to do with gun control. These are two separate subjects that are on my mind, based on what happened today and what I did today. I will get to the gun thing in a minute, but the rodeo episode is personal and the other is merely opinion.

I suspect your own experience to this point has not included cowboys, horses, cattle or any part of that way of life. You probably wouldn't know that there were cowboys and cattle roping in Hawaii, long before the American West. Around 1800 or so, King Kamehameha acquired some cattle, some horses and one real Mexican cowboy, a vaquero He was the first of many, who came here to spread their cowboy culture and it has been an integral of these islands since then. It is really a fascinating story and worth exploring. Most people probably assume the Hawaiian Islands were this idyllic cluster out in the Pacific, pretty much isolated for years and years. The harbors of these islands were filled with whaling ships back in the 1600's and a lot of trading was done.

There I go again, off on a verbal safari, taking us far away from today's rodeo experience. The strangest part of the rodeo day was the fact that I was there and in the middle of it. I don't know, maybe I am exaggerating my varied life experience, but I don't think so. I think it would be hard to find any predictable pattern, especially after leaving the City. You could probably rightly conclude that my professional time in NYC was pretty jumpy. With the exception of one ad agency, I never lasted more than two years at nearly all my gigs back in the Apple.

Finding myself at a rodeo on Kauai and in the horse and cattle feed business is a pretty decent turn in the road for me, yet again. I started writing this to you because I thought there was a remote possibility that my life might be interesting and worth your while to have some record of it. I am very far into this excursion and it is going to go the distance and you will do with it as you may.

Today, some guy, decked out in body armor and a gas mask, opened fire during a midnight showing of one of the Batman films in a Colorado town. This prick killed at least a dozen people, wounding more than double that amount. This murderer had tear gas canisters and automatic weapons, whose sole purpose is to kill people. I am totally good with hunting and the licensing of firearms to anyone who passes a background check. The gun lobby in this country uses the "right to bear arms" clause in the Constitution as a justification for concealed pistols being carried into bars and churches, etc. We are not a Clint Eastwood movie (terrific actor and director worth checking out). What the gun thing will be like when you read this is another one of the incalculable differences between now and whenever. Many people opine that the fore fathers meant for all of us to have the right bear arms to fight the tyranny of government should it go astray. These extraordinarily brave visionaries, which I firmly believe they were, also kept slaves and fucked the slave women anytime it moved them. I suspect there were economic factors that impacted on their respective choices as well. Those powdered wig dudes were no saints and not clairvoyant. My issue is simply with violence, regardless of the instrument of delivery and it doesn't understand politics.

These days, excess would appear to be the norm. There is now a class of people that doesn't even breathe the same air the rest of us do. No home is too big in America because it is simply testifying on behalf of our gluttony and gluttony is king. The gun gorging has gone too far in this country, but it is impossible to find common ground between the two sides. Some of these weapons might as well be old school Gatling guns that swallow a belt load of bullets and spit em out pretty damn quick, cutting people in half with the lead separating top from bottom.

You know, I am not a schmuck. I understand violence and our limitless capacity to commit it for every conceivable reason imaginable. I am not sure the last time anyone bothered to check, but it is the worst fucken solution to any problem. When there are winners and losers, there are only losers. Far better minds than mine have agonized and masturbated over this absolutely awful way of treating one and other.

When we were very hairy and cave bound, our predecessors attacked intruders because they felt the need to protect their food and property from those that were different from them. They probably started by throwing rocks at them and evolved to the level of efficiency I am now living with. We are sending into the air something called drones, which are just pilotless planes "flown" by computer pilots somewhere in the middle of America. The targets are any ones determined to be a threat to our country. Let me tell you, it is amazing what we have come to consider as viable threats to our national security. We celebrated the murder of Osama ben Laden by a bunch of Navy Seals. He could have and should have been captured alive and put on trial for his crimes because that is what a civilized society does. If retribution is not sought in a court of law, we stoop to the level of the perpetrators of violence. Sadly, this is what we do and what we have always done.

Killing has always been a way of life. It would be rather lame to lobby for a world free from violence because our past is our pattern as a species. It is engrained in our genes at this point. Opting out of the cycle has put many brave individuals at risk for advocating another way. Trust me, I am not shaving my head, putting on purple robes and disappearing into the mountains of Tibet, assuming that country even exists years from now. The Chinese have been slowly devouring this peaceful society and the world has stood by, helpless to stand up to a goddamn bully because they are holding the world's currencies in their banks and we have become a mindless junky, hooked on the Chinese financial needle.

I know that several times I have promised not to project what your world will be like, but it is tempting sometimes, especially when dealing with such contemporary issues like the abuse of power, wanton violence, greed gone mad, environmental degradation, climate catastrophes, loss of privacy, control of information and a host of other equally pleasant goodies. The pendulum is not finished swinging and am not sure its arc will make it back in time. The few have sold the many on the idea of freedom, a freedom that only works if you have lots of green. Never mind that stark reality because we don't ever want to be in the nightmare where we might actually need something and have nowhere to turn. According to many, if you just let things take their natural course without government intervention, we will all be much better off. If you leave people to their own devices long enough, they will ultimately cannibalize each other and the carcass will not be a pinup. Societies need rules and controls, but there are ways to balance these necessities with personal freedom. Unfortunately for us all, it is simply not in our nature to share and this has nothing to do with socialism, which I could give a shit about.

We are living in a very strange time, indeed. Many of the technological advances have actually made us more primitive, more isolated and our souls pay the price for these horrible transgressions. I just don't know if there will be a true tipping point somewhere down the road at an undisclosed location. We are a pretty docile lot and I am wondering, which will break first, the system or its victims.

Then, there was the balance of the rodeo this weekend, a dramatic departure from solving the world's jigsaw puzzle, with its many missing pieces. A good time to mug the philosopher with a lasso and a dramatic steer take down. It went very well for me on any number of levels, business and personal. Got a chance to talk about my business to a bunch of cowboys and cowgirls and I was honest and sincere and believe it was appreciated. It is great to put my professional education to use and to do it in a manner that reflects who I am. Being honest and open is the easiest thing in the world because you don't even think about it.

Rodeos have been the same for decades and decades. The cowboy shirt, jeans, boots, big buckle and cowboy hat have been the uniform for a long time. Many of the events have been around even longer than this one in Koloa. Loads of these guys and ladies travel from island to island in order to compete and none of them are professionals. It is just in the genes here. Some of the families have been ranchers and riders for generations and to one degree or another, you become part of that history when you are born into it.

In its own way, it is inspiring to witness gatherings like this because these are the things that bring us together. My riding with the Sons is sort of like this, although the cowboys commit much more time to it. We all share a love of riding and this feeling is contagious and makes our gatherings very uplifting. I spent my time around the rodeo participants and not out in the audience. They live in this cowboy world and it may only be for an afternoon or their everyday world. As an outsider, it was just amazing to try and absorb.

Getting ready to pack it in and the rodeo is where we will move on from. This past burst represents a couple of days of verbal visitation, but there didn't seem to be any reason to make a big deal of it. Catch you later, Shane.

My Mistress

There is this uncontrollable need to give voice to my internal world and this tale is made up of all that I have not been able to share with anyone else because she has been absent. We are not talking about having a good buddy or a best friend, whatever the fuck that means. To me, this other person fulfills the desire for intimacy and knowing what to do when it hugs your heart and won't let go. It has definitely been since hitting my sixties that this need to share has become one that can't go unfulfilled. Certainly, one of the chemicals in the test tube that created this whole experiment with you relates to the need I now seem to have. This has more than foot the bill and that is a major understatement if there ever was one.

I would fess up to a dose of mortality reality, which has had its own impact in the bubbling test tube. I have had an incredibly good time with myself for many, many years. I want you to know it is definitely possible, no matter where the hell you are when you masticate your way through this personal pie of my mind and place it in your own baking oven, so it comes out just right. I would bet that last sentence is a grammatical nightmare, but what do we care?

As one who increasingly appreciates times rapid rate of attrition while the calendar marches on, I needed an insurance policy and this is it.

Listen, I hope I have a couple of more decades of inhabiting a reasonably responsive body and mind. In spite of that hope, I can't afford to take a chance that all this goes when I go and I want to make sure that at least you have the keys to my kingdom. It is a treasure because of its ordinary nature. If you think about it, all of our lives are both ordinary and extraordinary, but you never let the latter go to your head.

At the risk of offending, which I feel is worth the chance, every one of us takes a shit and wipes their respective ass. When we are naked in front of a mirror, we are simply naked and that is who we are at that moment. This idea quickly levels the playing field; at least it certainly does it for me.

Now, I look through the prism and see endless possibilities and countless images, blurring into one moment and then gone. I try hard to see things that way, but there is no one to talk about it with and I can't keep it inside, which is obvious by now. I did a lot of this stuff with Laura and I know she appreciated it, but I wanted more and her primary focus was elsewhere, which is not meant to be damning on my part, it is just how it happened to unfold and then refold into two disconnected lives.

There is no question that my desire for connection is often blinding and I end up walking full tilt into a brick wall. As far as I can tell, none of these collisions proved to be fatal because here I am. This purge of my mind and heart has the sole intention of cheering you on as you hit the inevitable brick walls that lay ahead on your very own highway.

You know, I always visit the last few paragraphs of whatever I have written last, but go back no further. Sometimes, I find incredibly nonsensical things and I change them to make at least an ounce of sense. One of the reasons I don't like rereading what I have written is that I don't want to identify any style and carry it forward. This is also one of the reasons why certain things appear repeatedly and I know I have mentioned that at least several times. I vaguely recall that as being one of the rules I laid out in the beginning. There are rules I have been very careful not to read again, because I hate rules. Working this way maximizes my creative freedom, but I know what I would have said in the beginning without having to read it again.

Speaking of creative freedom, today is Mick Jagger's 69th birthday and that is worth some mention. I was in my late teens when the Stones broke into the US. They were a mainstay in the jukeboxes of the Upper East Side singles bars that I had the pleasure of visiting repeatedly in my early twenties. Believe me, I never gave a moment's thought to being at this point in my life and still enjoying The Rolling Stones new music. They are celebrating their 50th anniversary some time soon and I am sure there will be a fresh recording to be supported by a global tour. Back in the day, Rock and Roll was something of a juggernaut, fostering an unbridled energy that was incredibly vibrant and it engulfed most of the earth.

As us early rockers have aged, the musicians of our time have carved paths to rapid oblivion and others have simply continued to evolve and everything in between. Every art has its clowns, but most of the folks who are still at it in rock 'n roll after decades of work must have hit a chord that cuts across time.

When the bicycle was still my main means of transportation way back in the day, I don't think I could have comprehended what my sixties would be like. It isn't something you would ever think about. I never thought about myself getting older or imagined any of the rock icons as elders. Now, here I am and all these living rock 'n roll legends are getting older and older and dead. I do hope that many of them survive over time and continue to be a voice for youth; no matter how old they are, knowing the majority will be gone before you get to this. The music of the Sixties and Seventies was something special and I suspect it will only increase in significance, especially with the dearth of talent I see around. The music I am talking about was part of a social phenomenon that began around fifty years ago and started flaming out after around ten years or so. It happened so quickly back then that it took a while for the fat cats to get their claws in it and turn it into a money machine.

Since the wild times of the Sixties, the course has settled down considerably and the vast majority of us have been on an upward consumption trajectory, leaving tremendous destruction in its path. Music is much more manufactured and access to the machine is tightly controlled. At the same time, great artists will always find their audience, at least I believe that. Creativity will never die, but it is always vulnerable to contrivance. Big business can stultify creativity and they have been strangling music for quite a while now, but it will never die. Mick Jagger is a true icon of that era and he has handled himself just like a rock star should, even as the decades passed. Go find Exile and Main Street and give it a listen.

The Plan of the Moment

We have around three months until this saga comes to a close. I will likely keep slinging it in August and then spend September attentively reading what I have written up to that point. Any noteworthy events will certainly find their way into the September regimen. October gives us a full month to bring it all together, tie it with a bow and leave it on your doorstep.

I have gotten a little stuck recently because there really isn't anything out of the ordinary happening. I will try and not write any more about music because I am starting to get tired of it myself and God only knows how boring you may find it. Unfortunately, this thing has become quite addictive and even if I have nothing of any consequence to share, I come up with whatever I can, enabling me to continue this wonderful inner dance. I like looking for words to fill in the blank until the next one inevitably pops up. The absence of any real drama recently has definitely curtailed my penchant for flying on a word carpet, but what can you do?

After a very wet start to my Sunday bike ride, the few of us brave souls ended up on the west side of the island, where it is usually dry and the sun shines. I called your Dad and he put you on the phone. You stayed on much longer than usual, although it was close to impossible to decipher what you were so excitedly talking about. You did your imitation of a beat box (check it out) and it was incredibly cute. You were extremely animated and running from one topic to another, which left me completely in the dust. Of course, the truth is, just hearing your voice is all I care about anyway. You are this little being; opening to the world around you and it must be incredibly exciting for you and definitely years beyond your ability to understand. It is incredible for me to witness, albeit at a distance, how you are gradually becoming the true Shane.

Rhonda Fleming and Margie Grossman

Been laying low for a couple of days. At this point, we have plenty of material and I absolutely don't feel any pressing need to pile on. Have already described the rhythm of most of my days for now and it is hard to pull anything out worth sharing. The bad news is many people live their entire lives that way and I am periodically forced into it that mode, but there is always something coming along to rock my world.

As I am sure I've mentioned, I allowed myself to get sucked into the world of computer dating and keep swearing off it, sort of a like a junky saying he'll only do one more needle, an exaggeration simply for affect.

So, I shot myself in the ass with one more computer dating needle and saw a photograph of a woman that I thought was incredibly attractive. Most noteworthy was her red hair. Rhonda Fleming was a striking redhead who starred in many films in the 40's and 50's. Margie Grossman was a freckled redhead, who was my girlfriend in the 7th grade and I really liked her. The woman in the photograph offered virtually no information about herself, so if I wanted to communicate, I was stuck with writing to a photograph. I suppose it is no different than seeing a photograph of any complete stranger and then concocting some kind of semi-benign overture that will elicit any response. All I could work with is what I had in my memory and it was Rhonda and Margie.

When I started thinking about writing to the photograph, I thought of our adventure and figured that it would get incorporated, one way or another. Then, it dawned on me that I would write to her with the idea of including it and whatever transpired in our story. Needless to say, should I be fortunate enough to have her privacy trump my need to share, we will quietly shut it down. At the moment, we are dealing with my initial message to her, which follows, along with her response and a brief phone conversation. Here you go:

> *"I am going to take an incredible risk and assume you are not going to get in touch with me and I will proceed on that basis, lest you think I am trying to win over your good graces. First, there was an incredibly vivacious actress in the 40's and 50's by the name of Rhonda Fleming and this photo reminds me of her, so in the absence of a name, I shall refer to you as Rhonda.*
>
> *Dear Rhonda*
>
> *I have been working on a singularly personal project since October of last year. While stuck in Portland, OR on Halloween, I decided to write a book to my three-year-old grandson, Shane. Now, mind you, this is anything but a sweet, children's*

book. It is an honest recollection of the most important things from my history, heavily seasoned with observations, impulses and anything at all I feel like sharing at the moment. The style would be closest to a clone between Hunter S. Thompson and the Buddha. Actually, I think it is a fairly unique style, especially when it regards sharing my life experience with my grandson.

I would tell you more about it all, but I would only do that in person and that is simply a statement of fact and not intended as a strange enticement.

This evening, I decided that rather than sitting down and writing to him, I would write this note to you and include it in my story to Shane. So, I am writing to the both of you. You will likely read it in the next twenty-four hours and he will read it in about fifteen years. I did something similar in the two hundred pages or so written to date. However, this is different because we have never met, which means I have the luxury of imagining you the way I would like you to be.

It would be lovely to be around a woman who could be described as lithe. You have an incredible smile and you carry yourself with a subtle grace. You are extremely confidant in who you are and not threatened by someone who feels the same. You are a sensual woman, who enjoys touching and being touched. You enjoy being around someone who has not been cut from the same cloth as you. Actually, you find it incredibly entertaining and wonderfully challenging to be around.

Rhonda, I have no idea what you're supposed to say to a photograph, accompanied by a handful of semi-personal tidbits and little else. I basically have a picture to go on and that's it. When I was in junior high school, my girlfriend, Margie Grossman, was a freckle faced red head and I liked her a lot. I am working with a dead actress and a puppy love redhead experience. It ain't much, but I don't need all that much to go off on a personal journey.

This is a one of kind transmission and there is no need to be concerned about any further semi-literary intrusions."

The following is "Rhonda's" response, which ain't half bad.

"I am just about all the things that you summarized, very fun, slim, full of grace. Have been on stage in Utah. My birth state, then Calif. for High school and College. Always a swimmer but fell in love with surfing and water that could move! I am a Healing Touch provider and have worked at Hospital.

I have always been with younger men; so don't worry about that aspect at all.

Did Yoga, but no Zen. Have had some very fun out-of-body trips while doing Yoga and then got into going out when I needed to. I have a photo for my business cards. Woman of Vision."

The lady in question, who will keep nameless, and I spoke after this exchange and it felt a little strained, as it should. We agreed I would call and we would get together in a few days. In my woman discussions, I likely mentioned I have at least one more love affair left within me, but no promises after that. This affair could last a week, a year or the rest of my life. There is more to come, but it is also probably safe to say the odds are pretty slim, mainly because life has moved me into a space with very little room for others, but there is a good front row seat always reserved for a special lady.

I was going to wait until after she and I met before reporting in because the suspense will doubtless be unbearable. We're a little ahead of schedule because of a very recent conversation, our second. I called to make arrangements for a get together on Saturday afternoon. she answered the phone in a business manner, which is to be expected, considering she is in the real estate business. I said something incredibly provocative, " Hi XXX, its Larry." She then said, "How can I help you?" It is this last line that had me immediately looking over my shoulder, wondering if she was talking to someone in the room with me, because it sure as shit didn't fit the nature of the call. That line is now immortalized forever and it is a beauty. "How can I help you?" Believe me that will not go without mention when the two of us meet. It will be interesting to match the photograph and the voice with the actual gut read I get the moment I see her.

My sense is we are dealing with galactic influences that will repel our planets from each other. In some ways, that is a very liberating place for me because I can't say I care terribly what she thinks of me. So, fair XXX shall get the full treatment. The other side of the coin is the ease at which we can create a scenario of negativity and it is something to be attentive to as well. I will try and remember this for Saturday upcoming. However I feel is who I will be.

Abort! Abort!

The next debriefing was scheduled to be the post XXX wrap up, but we have a last minute bulletin that dramatically impacts on the entire situation. I know I have already told you about Fran, my friend and phone therapist. She is a terribly good lady and I respect and enjoy the shit out of her. Well, I called to tell her about an art opening close to her that I was going attend. My friend, Marta, who cooks my meals, is married to Dan, who I must have spoken about in the past few months, but I really don't want to wade through all this stuff to find out if I have. After all, who really gives a shit? Dan is one of those very talented visual people and one of his talents is photography.

The conversation quickly segued to my date with XXX prior to Dan's show. Fran knows her very well and her reaction was lightening quick and a gigantic red stop sign. You know, I am definitely driven by humor and I could make this story about XXX incredibly funny, but it would be at her expense and I don't feel comfortable doing that. I will make fun of myself at the drop of a hat because I can take it, but I have no right to make judgments about others. Fran has spent time in my head and that is a very dangerous place, so I respect her advice.

Fran has been a great friend for years and she has never, ever issued a cease and desist order, so I had to take heed. According to Fran, my first sighting of her would likely take my breath away and quite possibly my life. The adventure ends right here because there is no burning need to risk it all and go against the very strong advice of my most trustworthy friend in these matters. Believe me, I kept her on her toes with Laura. I have deleted the woman's first name because she actually died somewhere between my writing her name for the first time and now. Keep in mind there are time lapses in all this and whenever I am writing this sentence and the one before, it could be anytime at all.

I am a goddamn hippy of some kind and believe me, it was never a way of being I actively sought out. The edge is my friend and it is a very dull blade when opposed by a strong will and a heavy dose of faith. I am simply living my life in a way that makes some sense to me. People anywhere near my age get into computer dating with a completely different mindset than my own. A bunch of years ago, I began to think about stuff that most folks don't and that is just how it was and how it is.

I quit smoking cigarettes well over forty years ago and it did not come easy. I had tried to stop a number of times in the years I was smoking. When I finally stopped, I knew it was over and part of me stopped out of spite. I am a pretty willful person and that is how it is. It might take me a while to get there, but when I do, it is a done deal. The computer is no place for me to find a companion and the line has finally been crossed, time to dig a hole and bury it. We dodged a bullet this time, buddy boy. Even an idiot can get the message, eventually.

You were pretty sick two nights ago and your parents were worried about you, partially because your temp spiked at 104. Turns out, you had some kind of virus and were already feeling much better when I spoke with your Dad. It is a terribly helpless feeling when your little one is suffering and you can't do a damn thing about it. I would really worry about Andy and Danny, when either one was sick, especially as little guys. Not sure fathers get the credit they deserve. Believe me, I am not campaigning for Father of the Year, but there are some wonderful guys out there, like your Dad.

I just got a great picture of the both of you. I think it was taken on a cellphone and you and your Father are squeezed into a photo. I am increasingly excited about seeing you and I have a feeling we will have a terrific time.

This disjointed opus is running on because I really don't feel like making a statement and then amplifying it the way I have in many places before now. We are still operating under the heading of Abort! Abort!, but I for one have dropped from memory the circumstance that elicited the double exclamation mark. It was only yesterday, but it is gone. I have had close calls on the road, both in a car and on a motorcycle and once they pass, there has never been anything to hold on to. The excitement of getting together with XXX completely dissipated the moment Fran ordered me to stop dead ass in my tracks.

Today, I was at the job site and we spent from 7:30AM until around 4PM cutting up trees and chipping them. All of the logs were incredibly muddy and difficult to handle. I guess I am in pretty good shape for an old man. With my not weighing more than 150 lbs., the wood could get real heavy, real fast. When I got home, I was a ball of mud, a very tired one at that. My forearms have little cuts all over them because the weight of some of the wood rested directly on my forearms and I am temporarily the worse for wear. I sank into the couch and disappeared from view for Sunday evening.

On Monday morning, following the daylong logging ordeal, I was dragging my self around the house. I felt tired doing yoga and that is a clear sign that something happened the day before, which completely drained my energy. The daily run followed and it was also harder than usual and I worked to finish. I've been painting several large metal containers that will be used for drying and cooling the feed. The paint is rust red and I end up wearing large amounts at the end of each day. My work jeans are slowly beginning to show red markings all over and a handful of shirts have been donated to the process as well.

It is Monday evening of the very same day and here I am. When I got the picture of you and Andy, I returned one of myself that had been taken the night before at the art opening I went to. First, I do not like having my picture taken and never did. Dan is a good photographer and the shot was casual and not posed. He sent it to me the next day and that is what I sent to you guys. I look pretty fucken old and I can't say that is a feeling I like very much. My forehead is a horizontal thruway of lines and the crow's feet at the corners of my eyes are a flock full. My eyebrows are slowly taking on the Scrooge effect. Worst of all is the goddamn chicken neck and I am definitely roostering out in this pic.

It is certainly an interesting place to be, at least for me. When I was talking with Fran on the Abort! Abort! call, we also talked about the difference between being hopeful and being optimistic. I am a very hopeful person and have always believed that anything is possible. However, I am definitely not an optimist because that brings an element of certainty of outcome, which is definitely not my world. My Zen thing has led me to believe that anything is possible at any time, so I hope, knowing there are no guarantees.

Speaking of Fran, during that call I read her a little bit of what I had written relating to XXX. No one has ever read anything in here up to this point. I actually felt reluctant to read it to her because this has become such an incredibly personal thing to me and I didn't really get that until I actually read a little to her. I know she was touched by it, but I am going to keep a good grip on what we are doing and hold to the mission.

I want to get back to the hopeful thing because it is something for you. Everyone has disappointments in their lives and it starts pretty damn young. Obviously, I am clueless where you will be when you get this and what your life will have been like up to that moment. As I have mentioned repeatedly, it would be beyond my wildest dreams to actually share this story with you while I am alive and you are old enough to at least get some of it. We will have to wait and see about that one.

Hope and faith are interchangeable in my vocabulary and all religions take a back seat. Yeah, I know I am not supposed to be trying to influence your behavior, but put a wad of hope in your pocket and you don't hesitate to pull it out. If you are always trying to be genuine, regardless of what that means, at every point in your life from now forward, it's all good. The faith thing comes in to play here because it backs up hope, making sure nothing happens to it.

I remember I made a big deal out of hitting one hundred pages and that was quite a while ago. After whipping out the A material, our production has slowed down some. Keeping up the pace was never in the plan because that isn't what we are doing at all. Get ready for this, according to this particular iteration of the Word program, we are well into page 199 and 200 is just a couple of paragraphs away. I honestly don't know which story is where and if there is even a semblance of order. I think the employment legend and places lived followed a pretty decent order, albeit with the inevitable interruption that couldn't seem to wait their turn. Just between us, I am very proud of having pulled this off. We kind of lived together for this year and there was also enough history to take us back a bunch of years as well.

You know the plan. I will keep filling in the blanks between now and the end of August, a little over three weeks from now. Aside from visiting you in September, I will spend much of that month rereading the first 100 pages and reading the second hundred for the first time. There are around 3 months left in this rhythmic inhalation and exhalation of my mind breath, with an occasional word or two thrown in for good measure.

200

I can see page two hundred from here and I think it will hit pretty quick now. While thinking about this really incredible, personal milestone, I crossed it with the most personal question imaginable. Why are we here?

I am pretty sure the Zen practice keeps this question very focused on the individual practitioner, or cushion sitter. Frankly, there isn't much difference between "Why am I here?" and "Why are we here?" However, each one conjures up very different answers. If the individual is merely a microcosm of the world around him, then maybe the answer to the larger question lies in the smaller one.

Based upon our history to date, global societies have never been able to live in balance with each other and all that surrounded them. It takes enough individual humans committed to a common path of compassion to affect any real change on the life stage. My boy, at no time in my life have I ever heard and witnessed the levels of stridency and corruption that are everyday now. The wealthier you are and the larger the corporation, the less likelihood there is of being punished for any wrongdoing. We too quickly sanctify and/or demonize anyone, anywhere, anytime.

I know there is no answer to the question that is at core of all our lives and that has to do with wondering if there is any purpose to our being here. The answer lies in the non-verbal, internal and indiscernible language of the spirit. I may be close to understanding it, but don't have any words to express it.

It is so easy to buy into any series of answers as you grow up. I think it is best to be an observant student, slowly tilling the fields until the first harvest begins to yield some slim, dim sense of understanding. It takes decades to truly bear fruit, but you stay close to the hope and faith thing. Personally, I don't think there is any earth shattering reason why any of us are here. Beyond making the best of everything that comes at us, not sure what else is worth a damn.

We freakin' did it! We are on 200. The preceding brief ditty is a perfect bridge through into the second century. I am not writing this to answer anything other than, "Who am I?" Good luck with that one.

It is the next day and it is necessary to issue a precaution. The honest to God reason why I am writing any of this to you is because I have absolutely no choice. It is not being done to mine any deeper than deep veins of life's truth. I have known for quite some time that I have a good story to tell, and I have actually been occasionally impressed by what I had to say to myself. It is good to live a life that has to invent adjectives to describe it. Given that each one of us is so totally unique, it is rather incredible to see how easy it is for us to forego individuality for the sake of homogeneity. I have just had this nauseating flash that I may have used the homogeneity thing before.

Now, this takes me to another side road in the spider highway of my being. My actor friend, Ken, called me toward the end of this afternoon while I was at work in the field. For reasons only he can ascribe, he is my biggest fan, in terms of my humor and writing ability. We talked about our book, yours and mine. I told him that I would never allow anyone to touch this manuscript. I will likely "publish" it on the web and have a hard cover book available. Books can now go directly to your technical outlet, or whatever the fuck you want to call it. By the time you get this, they may have created book suppositories that allow you to download a book by just bending over.

When you write anything that anyone else might read and vaguely misconstrue as writing, it is important to fix it before it actually gets read. Today, anyone can write anything about anything and simply make it available to the connected Universe. At the same time, there is this judgment about things like syntax and run on sentences and abused pronouns, etc. which are part of the rules of being a writer. To me, it's like shaving or wearing a tie. Are the ideas of a casually dressed, unshaven guy any less worthy because of his "disrespectful" appearance? I would prefer your being moved by my writing and not being concerned about my adherence to someone else's rules.

My life is a life of imperfection and that is an important part of this whole story. If something could have been stated more effectively or not at all, why would I possibly care? I told Ken this was an extremely personal venture for me and long ago began to feel like a mantle I was called upon to carry for a full year. Be clear, a mantle is not a burden and is more like a crown. Life laid a silver blade on each shoulder and gently upon my head and I temporarily became Lawrence of Flushing, Queens.

My mission is the one we are on and I think we are doing a helluva job. I suppose one of the things that sucks is that this narration is coming from someone so much older than you. It wouldn't be mathematically FEASIBLE for me to be your age AND a grandfather. Don't even think about it because you will get a headache. Trust me, the numbers absolutely do not work.

This is such a cool thing to do. At the same time, I apologize for spending too much time on self-congratulatory mentions like the prior sentence, because I honestly don't mean it that way. I know it has come up before and my intention is unchanged. *"Ladies and Gentlemen, we would like to introduce you to Larry Feinstein. He has asked for a bit of your time to share a year and a lifetime with you. He has promised not to cosmetify this story with any pre-determined formulas and it will include the use of make believe words and terrible grammar. He'll simply share where he happens to be at any given time, always keeping in mind this entire undertaking is being done for the sole benefit of his grandson, Shane Feinstein."*

I also have to be honest and tell you that I have approached every fucken word as a writer and not as a grandfather blabbering to his son's son. None of this stuff falls out of my mind and onto the keys. Again, I know I have mentioned this before, but some of this shit is meant to have a continuous thread throughout. I want you to understand this is a balls to the wall commitment from me and I am enjoying the shit out of it. At the same time, I am disciplined to be completely present whenever I am talking to you. I am trying real hard not to cheat my intention and so far we are kicking ass in that regard. I started out true and I remain steadfastly true. I own it all.

I am thinking about more stories to tell before we hit the September wall, but not sure any of the good stuff has been left out by now. We will see what happens. It is like opening the doors to the theatre and wondering if anyone will come and if there is anything worth coming in for. It is my party and I sure as shit hope it is worth the price of admission. Not to worry, you get a free copy and probably even more than that. Everyone else has to pay because I didn't write with him or her in mind at all, ever. Now, I am not seriously talking about others literally paying, but for you it is a gift, the gift of my life. I can't imagine profiting in anyway from this, primarily because I have already gotten an incredible return on my investment.

Next week, you are going to Bermuda, your second trip there. I know you vividly remember the first time when you were six months old. Somewhere, there is a photo of you being held in the air by your Dad and you look very young, which kind of makes sense. Apparently, you are quite excited about going. I must credit your parents for exposing you to a wide variety of experiences at such a young age. While you are incapable of truly appreciating it at the time, I hope you are left with a rich palette of memory hues from your childhood.

Speaking of memories, you will find they change with time. Anger can dissipate into empathy and sadness can expand into joy. When the spark is initially ignited, you think it will burn with the same color flame forever. It is amazing what a remedy time and distance are for any pain you are holding on to. The sooner you can hit the bulls eye of peace within, the better off you are going forward.

Thinking about this today because Harold, riding in the front of the Sons, decided to detour onto a road that passed Laura's home, a place where I spent a good deal of time and a couple of bucks to make sure she could keep her place back a number of years ago.

I am sure I will find the following writing somewhere prior to this because it is one of my favorites. The mind and the heart do not speak the same language. When you are in love, you are not sensible, not even close. I knew early on that the relationship with Laura would leave both of us coming up short for completely different reasons. Personally, the clear understanding didn't seem to help a helluva lot and I would excitedly get back together time after time. She was a dream to me, but the damn problem was we are supposed to be awake in our lives and not asleep. Enough buttons got pushed from beginning to end that kept my foot on the accelerator, even after hitting the brick wall more than once.

Living with the purpose of doing so with a full heart is bound to subject you to incalculable pain throughout your life. Paying the price is a deeply personal choice and I definitely got my ticket punched for this ride. Up to this point in the ride, I regret nothing. At the same time, I accept and embrace the consequences.

Imagine if I unloaded all this shit on a woman in the course of this nearly completed year? By now, she would be long gone; having vaporized under the pressure of all this honesty, at least that is what I think. Soon, I will be safe because I have gotten most everything down already, then this quasi-literate catharsis will have been completed. Honestly, I don't think I have the strength to hold on to a true partner, but this doesn't mean I have turned away from the dream. I have not.

38

Today is August 13th and as you are undoubtedly aware, it is your Father's birthday. He was born at North Shore Hospital when we were already living in Glen Cove. Don't know if I mentioned this or not, but I had nothing to do with the decision regarding both of my sons coming into existence. Yes, I am responsible because I did impregnate your grandmother, but it was never something discussed on either occasion. Should you find yourself in a similar situation, be very clear with your partner about having a child. Women have this uncanny ability to make up their minds about all sorts of things and we find out about it after the fact. Men have been terrified of giving women any more power than they already have because the guys know they are incredibly spirited beings from the get go. They make phenomenal partners and very worthy adversaries and as long as you religiously keep that in mind, you should be in good shape. Plus, after all is said and done, they rule, whether we like or not.

Andy and I talked a couple of days ago when he was on his way back from some kind of grueling cross training program that he got into last month Personally, I am glad he wants to stay in condition because it is a great habit to have and one to take with you for your entire life. It sounds like it is a rotating series of exercises that also involves weights and gives you the cardio workout at the same time. Actually, that is when he told me about your second sojourn to Bermuda. Let me tell you, if you like it there, you are going to love my Kauai. This place is no multi-colored postcard for the sole benefit of rich tourists. It is far subtler here because you have to go passed all the activity and people living their lives in order to be with a kind of magic that is mutedly experiential. The views alone take your breath away, time and time again. What a fucken place!

I sent him a short note this morning and left a Sweet Daddy birthday wish for my son, whom I love with all my heart and soul. He called me back without even listening to the message and we spoke briefly, wishing him a happy birthday and telling him I love him. He is truly a good man and you lucked out big time. I hope he gives you the freedom you need in order to come into your own. He can be a tad conservative, simply out of concern for your well-being. It's a bitch to let go and leave it to the Gods, but he will likely have come around or will have come around by the time you sneak a peek at this.

I just got up to swallow my pills. Have I told you about them? I only take one for medicinal purposes and that is a little helper to keep my blood pressure in check, but I think it is OK. No need to worry, especially when you get to read this, if you get my drift. Let me tell you what else I take and I will return to the cabinet to bring the arsenal over to the machine. One to lower BAD cholesterol, Niacin for blood flow, garlic for the heart and overall health, an elephant dose of Vitamin C, Fish Oil for heart, some kind of herbal stress relief pill, a male herbal insurance policy pill, a multi-vitamin and a prostate placebo. I take them at night and in the morning I do it all over again, but in the AM it is with a powdered drink that promises to do most everything. I have no idea if any of this does shit for me, but I like that I care enough to be healthy and swallow all these goddamn little darlings in order to stay well. This is one of the many things that would never come up in conversation with anyone, but if there is an actual witness or an eventual witness like you, I've got no stuff around it. It is one of those many things I simply do because I choose to. It is funny, when you live on your own, there is no one to say something is weird, hence no frame of reference. Much of what I do around my space could easily be perceived as modern cave man, but as long as I don't offend myself, what can happen?

Anyway, today is your Dad's birthday and you make sure to always give him a gift, material or otherwise. It is incredibly cool to hear one of your children tell you they love you and to do so when they are old enough to have a clue about you and themself. I love my sons and I am pretty sure they both love me in return. Just as mine is different for each, I would safely bet each has his own unique connection to me.

Flyin' Time

Your Father's birthday was this past Monday and somehow it has gotten to be Thursday. Time zooms by with interstellar travel speed and I am certain it was never something on my mind when I was your age, assuming this is the young Shane and not the "Let Me Reread Halloween in Portland" Shane. I am writing to a young man, but much of what has been written wouldn't have made a great deal of sense to a young Larry, so I don't know if it will to you either.

Back then; I did so many things because that is what others expected of me. When the childlike idea of pleasing your parents very slowly morphs into pleasing yourself, you are doing the "Individuation Dance"; one that never stops once it begins. The rhythm seems to speed up with age; at least it does for me. You know, it is like dancing with a ravishingly, beautiful woman that you have just met and you know you only have this dance to say whatever it is you want to say. You are concentrating on keeping the beat and maintaining a sense of control, while you dread repeats of the chorus because that signals the song is ending.

Our lives are like that dance. We are really drawn to it, but we are not sure what to say or do, aware the song is not really all that long to begin with. At the end of the tune, you want to feel you made your mark on her life, whether you ever see her again or not. Your tattoo is your intention.

The week is nearly over and I could swear it was last week.

Sabrina

This thing is less about the facts and dates of a life as it is about the in the moment thoughts of my mind. I remember writing early on that this was not intended to be some kind of one dimensional diary, dry heaving the precise dates and times of various occurrences in my life.

Today, we shall talk about someone we will call Sabrina and that is not her name because I have never had the presence of mind to remember it. She works on a food truck that appears at various markets and events I happen to be involved with. She has an extraordinary body, with legs that would take your breath away.

As I got briefly into the Sabrina story, knowing before hand where I was going to take it, I thought of a similar circumstance that has been left out until now. It was not terribly earth shattering, although the Sabrina story isn't either. A couple of years ago, I saw this beautiful, voluptuous blonde woman. She was way younger than me, but at the very least, I needed to tell her how magnificent looking she was, which I did. Helle is from Denmark and she belonged on their national stamp. We spoke for a while and ended up going out for a couple of dinners, one with her thirteen year old daughter. It went nowhere pretty quickly, but my imagination had a grand old time.

Getting back to the subject of this entry, I have respectfully ogled Sabrina for at least two years and have held back saying anything that would cross over the imaginary line of the impersonal. My sole reluctance has been her age, which is considerably less than mine. I would be shocked if she was more than forty and you do the math with my sixty-seven on the other end.

The Helle mention has to do with the age difference thing, which is only an issue if it is an issue. Sabrina doesn't react to me as if I am her friend's father, even though I could easily fit the bill. This is being brought up because of a run in today. The Farm Bureau, of which I continue to be an extremely important person, puts on an annual County Fair; an incredible amount of work for those of us who help make it happen. She stopped at the fair grounds today and looked spectacular. I was within inches of saying something, but I didn't, primarily because of my own age hang up. Trust me, I am not some schmuck guy looking for a woman half his age so he can make fucking references to his locker room buddies.

When I make up my mind to do something, there is every reason to believe I will muster the courage to do it. I am going to tell Sabrina when I see her she literally takes my breath away, which is the honest truth. Understand, I am not dealing with a woman who has no mileage and that is something you can see by the creases around the eyes and some other life markings. The cradle and heisting a virgin from it is not what this is about.

We will follow this episode closely because I am right there and a conversation will take place within the week. I guarantee it. While it might be days until it happens, it will only be a couple of pages at the most for you. The Fair eats up my life for about five days or so and that is coming up toward the end of next week. I get home late and I am exhausted, so we will see what kind of juice I have for this effort during that span. A Sabrina bulletin will come shortly after it occurs, regardless of the hour.

Listen kid, if I can do this shit at my age, you better have the energy and mindset whenever you read this for the first, second or third time. I have no idea whatsoever ever why we are here and have recounted that throughout. However, the quest for intimacy is incredibly high on the list, at least on my own list.

This will be the last opportunity before you fly to Bermuda sometime tomorrow. Well, aren't you a lucky dog? I am looking forward to some pictures and then talking with your Dad about your adventures. I will let you know what I find out, albeit quite a bit after the fact for you.

Bermuda

Got a picture this morning of you sitting in your First Class seat, binky in mouth, which we need to talk about, while concentrating on your computer screen with earphones in place. You are living the life, my boy. You have doting parents with sufficient income to make sure your needs are met and that is as good as it gets. What happens between now and then is up for grabs, but I hope your good fortune continues. I also hope you are sensitive enough to appreciate how lucky you are, which is not intended to engender any guilt whatsoever, just a dose of gratitude.

Not sure what it is about kids and beaches, but it is an incredible baby sitter for most. I don't know if it is the sand or the large expanse of water or both, but it seems to tweak a little one's imagination. My childhood memory sucks, but you may be one of those who has an outstanding ability to remember special experiences, regardless of time's distance. You might actually remember this trip.

Without the privilege of being able to read this backwards, I feel a modest obligation to explain the blatant insanity on display here. The Mind is incredibly powerful and the best you can do is get a well made saddle, a comfortable grip on the reins and take a ride, trying not to look like an asshole in the process. In addition, you can't separate yourself from your Mind because it is you. I am talking about awareness and not impulse. The longer you stay in the saddle without being bucked, the better the ride. It's all gonna come at you no matter what and grace in the saddle is a lifesaver. There is also something about surviving painful times in your life and learning from them along the way. While I am no more confident now than you are at your age, I have decades of experience on my side. Trust me, it doesn't mean I am any smarter, just more familiar with the forever seesaw of highs and lows.

I am not crazy talking about Sabrina, nor am I certifiable because I have never been able to get Laura out of my mind. This is how it is for me and I am passed the judgment thing. Daydreaming about women is a past time that roots the first time you see That

Girl and hopefully never lets up. Sabrina is a fun fantasy, at least for now. Laura is a far more complicated situation and there is not a single reason in the world for me to hold on to anything at all, but you tell that to my Heart. She was my last substantial relationship and regardless of the facts, something has repeatedly drawn me to her and now it is only in my mind. This is a space that hasn't been replaced yet and until it is, I only have to go back to her to fulfill the fantasy and aspects of it were truly a dream come true. I would periodically wake up from the dream and realize it really wasn't working out all that well, followed by an excruciatingly painful break up, followed by getting back together and so on. It had its own shortcomings for Laura, but this is not the venue for that stuff, plus they were hers and not mine. After all, this is about me and we have talked about her plenty before this.

Well, you are still in Bermuda playing in the sand and hopefully having the time of your life. Pictures and gloating parental stories are likely to follow your return home this coming weekend. I will let you know if you had a good time and what you did to make Andy and Andrea swell to the point of explosion with your unadulterated cuteness. It does sound like you are somewhat fearless when it comes to engaging complete strangers and that is an extremely wonderful quality and I hope you keep it going forward.

I know I have these awful tendencies to go off on a wide variety of philosophical tangents, if you could even call them that. Truly, no harm is meant in any of it, nor is there any intention of having you ingest it and become it either. I am not cooking any Soylent Green (yet, another thing to check out) for you to swallow. Remember, this is my story, which is the filter for everything else that comes up within. In the very beginning, we are dealt a hand and we do have opportunities along the way to draw new cards and reshuffle the deck just enough to keep it interesting.

I was pretty excited to go back and read the first one hundred pages a number of months ago. After that, I moved ahead, feeling a bit more like a veteran of this first time experience. In a couple of weeks, I will revisit the whole enchilada and there is definitely a part of me that is not looking forward to it, for fear that this second piece is repetitive and worthless. Initially, I was simply amazed at the accomplishment of writing one hundred pages and it carried me through that virgin reread.

Honestly, it doesn't matter to me what you do with this, but I hope you at least find it informative and entertaining. Valuable is a world purposely left out because that solely depends on the degree to which this resonates deep within you. Appreciation would be extremely cool, while emulation is absent from any intention of mine.

I will get sucked into the County Fair beginning tomorrow afternoon. Beyond the thought of looking forward to the sight of Sabrina's muscular legs, there is nothing at all that works for me. Crowds are one of my least favorite environments, plus there are tons of stupid teenagers in a hurry to be grown up and copying some fairly shitty role models. Yes, this is a judgment on my part, but there are plenty of kids living in lousy conditions, something likely foreign to you and that's OK. The event doesn't shut down until midnight for each of its four nights and I am wiped out at the end of each evening.

For the past five years, I have been the sanitation engineer, which means garbage is my game for the Fair. Fortunately, it has gotten to a point where I serve as an inspiration to others and my hands rarely if ever touch a garbage bag.

The Rights of the Individual

I really didn't think I would be able to write until the Fair is over and that will likely go into effect tomorrow night, when I get home too late to do anything other than instantly crash.

There I was, sitting at my little glass topped table and having Teriyaki Chicken and Kauai Pineapple Stirfry from my special gourmet chef. This is an election year, with Barack Obama running for re-election against Mitt Romney. You will notice there is likely no mention at all about this in any prior writing. The specifics of this contest are reviling to me and any political rhetoric, mine or anyone else's are of absolutely no interest to me.

I don't know if it was the wine, the teriyaki or the inhaled cocktail, but it hit me that the entire national dialogue is about the rights of the individual. None of these professional assholes ever address the rights of others with whom we share this country and the entire globe. Do we have any responsibility for the wellbeing of others? It is no stretch to ask whether we have any responsibility for this place we inhabit and all the other sentient beings who call this planet home. All the nauseating dialogue is simply about the rights of that selfish individual because that is synonymous with freedom, America's favorite buzz word. Truthfully, I am not sure true freedom is possible without compassion, both for self and other.

The inmates are running this country and the rest of the world. Whatever is expedient is right and consequences are even less than irrelevant. In good old Zen, it is not possible to split the one and the many because they are the same. Without embracing everything, you can't embrace the one and visa versa. Yes, life is a bitch, but don't look at me.

Things have really run amuck and I know it can easily be traced back to 9/11, but it goes back much further than that. It is like the American Trajectory, an inevitable curve that ultimately swapped out the many for the few. We have this righteous manifesto about the American Dream, so sacrosanct that we think nothing of burning cultures and countries that are not in lock step with us. It is all wrong, Shane. If we are all brothers and sisters, sharing the same primal seed, what the fuck are we doing brutalizing each other the way we do?

I hope some of this crap is not too heavy for you. Personally, I can't imagine getting a message in a bottle like this from my mother, saying that her father wanted me to have his stories. I guess it would depend upon how it was written, which is why I have tried incredibly hard to speak from my heart, without any concern for how you might perceive me. Frankly, I don't give a shit because that is obviously not the purpose of any of this. This is simply a secret passage way into my mind that only those who read this can enter. Again, this was always for you and it still is. You and I are the only invited audience to this show.

Sabrina is in the cross hairs of my radar and a report will be forthcoming.

Survived

Last week, around this same time, I made the last entry into our tome. The County Fair was grueling, emotionally and physically. There are probably as many as 15,000 people on the grounds during peak hours and that is just too many people for me to be around. While the majority are reasonably civilized, there are large numbers who behave like animals, dropping their shit wherever they happen to be. When your focus is garbage, you get to see how incredibly inconsiderate many people are. These kinds of things help to set your perspective straight, especially when it comes to hearing people spout out incredibly naïve, high principled predictions about how we will all come together and overcome the manmade catastrophes that have been set upon us. All you need to do is spend four days at the Kauai County Farm Bureau County Fair and you will lower your expectations dramatically.

The Fair is lost time for me and it is like life stops days before and picks up again a few days after. Happy to report that I am back on track.

The code name Sabrina story is a short one, but I at least did what was promised. The first evening of the Fair, I took her aside and told her that her figure was absolutely spectacular and it turned my brain to complete mush. She was extremely flattered and never saw it coming, especially from me. I am like the ambassador of the Farm Bureau, always charming and considerate. Talking about getting turned on by her body definitely caught her off guard. While nothing happened over the next days of the Fair, at least it is out there and one never knows, does one?

Your Dad sent me a slew of pictures from Bermuda. The three of you looked so incredibly happy. Your parents are both very busy and weekends are the only time they really get to spend with you. To have a full week with you was a real gift for them. You were having a ball whatever you were doing. According to Andy, you are a very engaging young boy and your light shines. I really can't wait to see you in a few weeks. Then, I will have my own opportunity to check you out and see what all the fuss is about.

Can't really write too much now because it is still early in my recovery, but I wanted to pick up our story as soon as possible. I am still feeling a bit drained and energetically flat.

+24

Pretty much back on track now and not at all sure where to take this as we begin looking at closing time. Honestly, I have pretty much accomplished what I set out to do in the beginning. It would have been easy to run on longer about most anything that has been written, but I didn't want to run the risk of sounding too bombastic, allowing for the possibility of lines unintentionally getting crossed. Sitting down here and now, I am not overtaken by any burning need to get something written that has been left out, some gaping hole in the narrative.

When I go back for the final reread in a couple of weeks, it will be a fairly time consuming exercise and that is the way it ought to be. Crooked stories will get straightened out and some of the pontificating will get deflated and filled in and flushed out a bit more. I think I will make notes to myself for things to look for further along and do my best to make this a well written piece. This is my story and it is very important to me to do it justice. My life has been and continues to be priceless and no way this is going to be some bargain basement bullshit.

This coming weekend, which happens to be the Labor Day holiday, is the time for the gears to change and for me to begin looking backward into this incredible narrative to you. Believe me, it is coming right on time because of this feeling that we have done what we set out to do back in Portland.

This is all some kind of dream, but we are in a waking state instead of fast asleep. None of what has been written is true, it is simply how I felt at the moment of writing. If

I decided to write this story from the very beginning right now, it wouldn't be anything like this. The beginning of this entire undertaking occurred at a very specific time in my life and the path of its launch and arc are singular. Our time is spent looking for irrefutable truths and never changing facts, but these are serious illusions.

We are not comfortable standing on a magic carpet because we need certainty, otherwise chaos ensues. Living in a world of constant change with no handles to grab on to is simply unacceptable to most everyone. There is no greater meaning to your life other than the life you live, probably yet another repeated reference. It is the likelihood of these repetitious things happening more frequently that leads me to believe we are in the last act of this word theatre.

Writing all of this has a fair dose of ego in the mix and that is a cautionary spice. What could possibly make me think there is anything remotely worthwhile that I can write to you, now or ever? I have tried not tp make any of this have a grand feeling because that has not been my intention. This is simply me sharing some stories and opinions with you, never meant to be taken as important. Our lives are not important or unimportant, they are our lives.

Here is something I have no problem repeating and that is you enjoy your life, live it like it is only the one you will ever have, an undeniable truth and likely the only one of any lasting merit. Whether I am here or somewhere in the ether, there will never be any judgement at all from my corner. My sharing all this with you is only intended to encourage you to be your own person and live your life in a uniquely individual manner. Compassion is an oft repeated word from me and if you can keep it close, you will soar like a bird.

Well, I have just made myself cry again. The tight face, the teary eyes and the cotton throat spontaneously erupt when I nip my heart and strike a major life artery. I hope you get to all this stuff decades before I did because it is enriching beyond your wildest dreams.

There you go, I am beating the shit out of the same old stuff. It is funny, this was started with a beginning and an end in mind and now I am feeling the end and winding down creatively. Oh, I will not preoccupy the balance of the fresh writing with too much of this stuff. It needs to feel alive before it hits the keys.

Breaking a Years Old Routine

Ever since moving to Kauai and likely before that, I do my Zen sit right after getting up and then go on the computer while I drink my coffee, followed by my Iyengar Yoga practice, capped off by the run. The change, which will go into effect tomorrow morning, throws the computer part under the bus and makes it last on my list. Of course, the absolute last thing I do is have breakfast and the thousands of natural, healthy placebos I swallow religiously every morning and evening.

This could be a watershed moment or just another neurotic glitch on the highway. I know this is a lot for you take it in all at once, so let me set your mind at ease and provide some context. I actually think it is possible I no longer give a shit what happens outside of my immediate universe, in this case, a small island in the Pacific. You know that my co-workers are rabid Conservatives, with air tight justification for feeling no obligation to their less fortunate brothers and sisters and sons and daughters. The Left isn't much better because they are supposedly too intelligent to get in the mud and prefer to do it from a distance and it is just as reprehensible and inhumane.

The table setting for our present political banquet has seats at the table for the wealthy and influential, while being served by those who are worth less in their eyes and therefore entitled to less from their same Mother County, America.

Our first half black President, Barack Hussein Obama, has been a disappointment of unparalleled proportion. He has continued our useless wars and added mechanized flying assassins called drones. These little puppies travel the world and take out anyone at all the White House wants them to. There are so many secret departments within the federal government that there are likely more sinister citizens than ever before and I am talking about people who are a danger to us. He has his lips wrapped around the organ of BIG MONEY and in many ways is reminiscent of the absolutely repugnant Black slave, who saw after himself and cared nothing about his people. Yes, I know this is a terribly racist thing to say, or it could be easily be taken that way. It is a goddamn methaphor or something like that. I think he was so concerned about being perceived as a Black President that he became a transparent human being. This country has never had a better shot of having someone in charge who knows in his gut what it is like to speak truth to power, but power became his truth. He is running for re-election and assuming he wins, maybe he will take the opportunity to right his horribly, compromised wrongs.

The farther I spread my horizon from here and the more global my view, the less enthusiastic I am. There were many reasons for coming here and for adapting as naturally as I have. Maybe, it is time to pretend I am living on an island in the middle of nowhere and whatever goes on thousands of miles away is of no consequence to me at all. Hence, the strategy of putting off the computer time and completely nurturing my inner world before getting more details about the shit storm to the East, which would be Amerika.

Maybe I was not ready for the intensity of this adjustment until now. Trust me, back to backing a Zen meditation, a yoga practice and a run drills in pretty deep to the core. Breaking this up by getting lost in the pollution of the world around is a great way of dulling the full experience of that intra-personal trio of practices.

The plan for tomorrow is to get up and fall on my cushion for about twenty five minutes. This is followed by a couple of quick prayers and a trio of bows. We will then brew the cup of coffee and NOT turn on the computer. I will relax and drink the cup of hot black java. Yoga practice will follow and hopefully be a good one. Barely looking at the dormant computer, I will get into my minimal running gear and head out for my half hour, balls of the feet run. By the way, still pretty challenging to run in those new shoes after three plus months, but I am definitely committed to this style. I will then come up the stairs, sweating and breathing heavy. I will immediately take off my shirt, shoes and shorts. I will grab the towel and a bottle of water and that is when I will see what kind of horse shit has plopped out on all of us yet again.

This has everything to do with not really caring anymore about all of that stuff. Believe me, I am anything but a passive citizen of Kauai, getting myself into the middle of all sorts of pretty basic issues. In my mind, there is nothing more important for this island than becoming a self-sufficient little country. When it comes down it, absolutely no one else will consider this island of any value. In the world of the uber Rich, every other being outside their circle is invisible to them and they're completely oblivious to those with less. I am looking for some real small triumphs in this effort, beyond the value of undertaking it in the first place.

I love my little island Country and feel a strong patriotism for her. Living in a heavenly place is certainly a state of mind, but you get a superb head start in the race for paradise when you are actually there already. I guess this could happen anytime one is open to it, but I don't know the answers to the big things around it all. Personally, I am looking to wrap my life in a ribbon of some kind of loose mosaic of integrity and that is why I will open my computer only after I have finished taking care of myself. I just don't know what the actual value is of knowing what is going on. For the most part, there is nothing at all I can do about any of it whatsoever. If it is for purposes of being able to have intelligent conversations, I can do that without having any information at all.

Well, it is now the evening of the morning after irreparably rupturing my years long, sunrise routine. It was a very quiet beginning and continued silently through the sit, the cup of coffee, the yoga practice and the run. What a screwy precedent of getting up and immediately engaging the world outside, without paying an ounce of attention to the most important person in my life. This change might stick, at least for now. It is a little more challenging and less appealing when you share your bed with another, but I am in no immediate danger of having to make my bed when I leave my place. I feel a little like a high quality grape , ripening in the sun until harvest time, increasing in richness with each new day until the quality is sufficiently high to permit inclusion in a very rare bottle of priceless wine.

I am sure I have told you way more than once that getting old totally sucks. The only thing worth a shit is the reservoir of lessons learned along the way. There is something about appreciating beauty from this side of the clock. It is really an unfathomable miracle, this life of ours. Every sight, sound, taste, touch, smell, etc. is incomprehensible and I bequeath rationality to my chronological heirs because it is of no real value to me anymore.

Let me tell you something else about the incredibly valuable, personal return by my undertaking this story. The deeper I dig into the veins of my illusory core for you, the more grounded I have become in the process. I have enjoyed my story telling very much and it has had and continues to have a profound influence on me. It is pretty much all here, minus a couple of secret, personal hygiene practices, which are private, but not even remotely consequential in relation to any of this. I never really thought about what effect this writing would have on me over time, because it was really unimaginable to actually think I was going to write over two hundreds pages in the experiment. As you may sense by now, I am even feeling somewhat overwhelmed by the power of all this. Metaphorically, I shrink to a microscopic speck and get absorbed into my mind, where I am free to roam. There are no gates or dead end roads or railroad tracks to cross.

Selfishly, I hope this is something that is very hard for most every one else to do. Sitting here, in this place, in this time and writing to you in another time is not your average work. In a typical movie, Grandpa Larry would gracefully kick the bucket in his bed and underneath it is a time tattered book, entitled Halloween in Portland. You discover it and your face takes up the full screen and then we fade to black because the next movie is yours. Knowing someone's history is not even close to knowing the person. You have to talk with him and find out his story. Unfortunately, in our case, I must be the conversationalist and/or protagonist, comfortably living in between my ears. As I have repeatedly said, I certainly hope I am around for at least your first reading. Let me tell you something else that will hopefully be alluded to very rarely by me , we have hit it out of the park, my boy. This I will only write once and should it appear anywhere else further on, I will yank it. I got the chops, Shane. I do have a gift and this is it. I will ring your fucken neck if you don't like it.

Déjà vu Plus One Hundred Or So

This is another one of our mini-milestones, hitting September 1st, when we shut it down and go back to the beginning. Somewhere back there, we already went through my stopping and reviewing the first one hundred pages, which we have spoken about plenty already. Reading over two hundred pages of intensely personal material is going to be fairly challenging for me.

When we have time to catch up after the completion of that task, I will tell you about it. Right now, I can't imagine what it is going to feel like to read what I have written from the perspective of someone who doesn't know me at all. As luck would have it, that universe includes anybody who reads this, other than myself. I am sort of a stranger to anyone else who reads this because it's a private side that only I have known to this very moment. I am not quite sure how you leave yourself behind when the time comes. This sure as shit is one of those ways and we are already pretty clear on that. This is my mark.

For what it's worth, we should not misconstrue this undertaking as a Last Will and Testament by yours truly, some overly long obituary. Truthfully, I have to catch myself more than I would like about this very thing. This is something I have needed to do and for the most part, it has written itself. We are celebrating my life to this very moment, a moment that I hope keeps getting stretched farther and farther into the future. The one thing that is certain is I could not have written this if I was already dead, so the best time to do this is while I am alive. On balance, I look forward to each new day, simply because it is a new day.

Tonight, I get my ticket punched on the two hundred plus page ride back in time, all the way back to Halloween of last year, flying home from Portland. Honestly, I really hope it is anything, but a shitty read. So you know, that sentiment has nothing to do with anything remotely commercial; I want to like it or I will change it along the way so I do like it. As long as I feel good about it, nothing else matters and nothing will get in between this finding its way to you completely intact. I am sure I was a little sloppy about other people and I need to make sure they would never be upset about anything I have written. I know I tried to do this in the reread of the first one hundred pages. I have no concerns about exposing myself, but I prefer to respect the privacy of others. I suspect there is some sloppy shit and it is in no one's best interest to let it stay.

As I did upon reaching the first century marker in pagedom, I will dive back into the muddy morass of my demented mind and see what we've got. Beyond an extended and elegant closing, we are pretty much at the station already. Forgive me, listening to a

Blues tune, inspired by freight train metaphor(s). Not sure how many pages I will be able to absorb in a sitting, but I will not push it. My investment in this is huge and I will return to our past in the same way I have worked at providing this text in the first place, with complete honesty.

Bear with me for a while, but I have to see a man about a horse....... I hope I am not too rough on myself because this is like composing an orchestral symphony and until it is finished, you need to wait for the final notes. There is more to come and if it is really important, I will break from my sworn allegiance to the code and simply right it forward, like coming up for air, in the midst of shoveling through previously written pages. I think we are in good shape because it is what I feel inclined to do at this point anyway.

Listen, I will see you on the other side of this process, unless I have to lay something down that cannot wait.

You take ‘er easy Shane.

One More Thing

I’m sorry, it is the day after the above and I just wanted to say one more thing before I go back to page one. The rhythm of that process is going to be a tough adjustment. I have to do a very good job of presenting everything with some sense of clarity about it. Some aimless horseshit will not do and we will need to be on the lookout for that as well. I will have to keep some kind of handwritten notes to let me know how many times I have sung the same tune or not sung it at all. Up to this point, we have looked into my unmade room and maybe the cleaning lady could make it all feel just that much better. I am going to take the night off before tackling the retro flow of this endless spouting. Blessings to you, blood of my blood.

What I am about to write is going to sound like serious waffling because I am off the game plan. In the midst of reading backwards, my time to see you is upon us.

In The Air

Somewhere before this entry, I have talked about coming to see you and your Mother and Father and your uncle Danny. I am now in the air on the second leg of my flight to Newark. The first flight from Kauai to Phoenix was an overnight. Much to my pleasant surprise, I met a friend at the Kauai airport and we were on the same flight. His name is

Lelan and the stories he shared were really interesting and unusual, but I first want to let you know where we are in the revisitation process.

I have reread about 25% of my stories to you to this point. Some changes were necessary for the sake of clarity. As you already know by now, I broke the self-imposed code of not tampering with anything already written. My initial comments about the cross country ride and the homosexual encounters troubled me and while I simply could have changed them without your knowledge, I wanted to let you know that I was revisiting my writing, something I ended up sharing with you much later in this tale. These time warps are sometimes confusing to write about and I hope the time travel doesn't drive you mad.

For the moment, I am just going to build on the back end and write about this trip to see you. Once I return home, I will get back to page 60 or so and continue the house cleaning job before figuring out how the hell I am going to draw all this to a close.

Lelan has been living in Hawaii for around 50 years, which gives him a long history here. He runs a very successful nursery and landscape business and happens to be an investor in the company I am working with and that is how we met. Lelan is originally from cowboy country in Idaho. He is an avid rodeo participant and travels all over the States, competing in calf roping events. On this trip, he was headed to Ft. Collins, CO, where he keeps a horse, along with a trailer and all of the necessary gear. He has had this same horse for nearly 20 years and has moved it around to various locations throughout the west, competing in rodeos in these different places. I thought about how fascinating that must be, being part of a true American tradition. I know I have already told you that Hawaii's cowboys are called paniolos. They learned their craft from the vacqueros of California, when it was still part of Mexico, at least 50 years before cowboys appeared in the American West.

Lelan and I went to the airport bar, where he was very well known and for obvious reasons. We each had a double Bloody Mary. Before you know it, we hear our names being called on the PA because the plane is waiting for us. We hustled to the plane and had to walk past all the stares of the waiting passengers. It was an overnight, so we had breakfast together the next morning in Phoenix. A colorful, traveling buddy made the entire travel that much more pleasant.

Before leaving home, I found out that Andy and Andrea lost a long time friend just a few days ago. Andy knew Rob from the time they were both eleven years old, more than 25 years ago. They were part of a tight knit group of guys and Frankie is one of them as well. I am hoping Frankie is still in your life when you get to this. He has been a successful model for most of his adult life and has this terrific charm that brings women to their knees. He is quite a character. Anyway, there is a wake and funeral for Rob this weekend and it will add an element of sadness and that is just the nature of life I suppose.

When you lose people that are close to you, it hurts terribly. Beyond wishing them well on their next journey, if there actually is one, all we can do is live our lives with a little bit more appreciation for our own limited time here. As you know, mortality is one of my favorite themes throughout.

Uncle Danny, freshly arrived from Israel, will be picking me up at the airport and taking me to your home. Your parents will likely still be at the wake and Dan is going there after dropping me off. I am incredibly curious to see who you are and am very much looking forward to visiting with you.

You know, while I have the machine on and some time to kill, I think I will burrow back into the story now. I will be making periodic entries during the weekend to keep us both up to date on this visit and will be adding them right below this entry. Talk with you soon, but now it is time to stroll down memory lane yet again.

Life in Hoboken

I have now been at your house for a little over 24 hours, having arrived late Thursday afternoon and it is now Friday evening. Everyone, including you, have gone to sleep, so it is a perfect time to catch up a little.

Uncle Danny picked me up at the airport and we went straight to your house yesterday. You were very happy to see us and you didn't hesitate in knowing that I was Grandpa Larry. You are a very sweet child and very affectionate. Your language skills have exploded and you are constantly talking.

It is hard to figure out who is older, you or your uncle Danny. Frankly, I honestly think he gets hyper absorbed with you because in your eyes, he can do no wrong. I don't think certain areas of his life have been a cake walk and I am thrilled to see the two of you connecting so beautifully. I love him dearly, but sometimes wonder what is going on between his ears. I have kept my cards face up on the table for a long time now, but that is just my nature and everyone plays their own hand by their own rules. Regardless of what motivates your uncle, you worship the ground he walks on and the connection is delightful. I don't know, maybe he just loves you so much he can't help himself. Believe me, I am no shrink and my only job here is to tell you some stories, primarily about my life through my eyes. Dan is a good guy and I love him dearly. He has a very keen eye, but does not share it all that much.

Tell you what I am going to do, he wrote an incredibly witty piece celebrating your birth and I want to make sure you have it. It blew me away when I read it because it was unbelievably imaginative. I will slap it on to the end of the story.

Last night, we ordered in some food because your Mother and Father were very tired from a day of mourning the loss of their good friend, Rob, which I will share with you in a bit. This morning, your Father and I took you to school and it was great to see you fit so comfortably into that environment. I met you and Emmy later in the day because your class went for pizza and I walked over to the restaurant, so we could walk home together.

The loss of Mommy and Daddy's friend, Rob, has been very upsetting for them and it is completely understandable. They came home a little bit after we arrived because they were at his funeral. Uncle Danny arrived before they did. Later on this afternoon, all of us went to a local bar, where friend's of Rob's had gathered. Uncle Frankie was there and it was great to see him. He is supposedly sleeping over here tonight, but he is one of those guys who enjoys being single and women really seem to like him. I know for sure that he loves you and your Mother and Father because he can rely on all of you to be his family. Frankie is one of those guys you might think has it knocked, but he doesn't and nobody really does. I am not sure he has great experience when it comes to receiving affection or giving it back out. He hovers on the surface quite a bit, but your family gives him something that he has never really had in his own life. He is an extremely good looking guy, who carries himself with a certain panache and it has been a magnet for women for the many years I have known him. He is a successful model and lives in a world different from more conventional lifestyles.

You, my boy, are a sheer delight and it is great fun watching you as you navigate through your world. I think the love you receive from your parents and Emmy and others in the family has made you feel pretty secure for a little guy. At the beer hall this afternoon you were very much at home around all of the grown ups and it was a joy for me to watch you.

Tomorrow is Saturday and I am not quite sure what is in store for you and me. There has been talk of going to some kind of dinosaur park or maybe into Manhattan and Central Park. We will see what happens and I will let you know.
I am still very tired and jet lagged from my flying, so I will go to sleep now and write you tomorrow.

Through the magic of imagination, we are now at the end of the next day here in Hoboken. Saturday was a great day, although the plans detoured from the night before.

I got up early in the morning and did my meditation sit. Everyone was already up when I finished and I went downstairs for some coffee. I had to get a move on it because every Saturday morning you do Tae Kwon Do and we needed to get in our yoga practice and run before taking off for your martial arts instruction. You and I did my yoga practice, which was very entertaining, at least for me. You did some of the poses with me and some of the others were only for grown ups, at least according to you. Your Father came home from that insane basic training physical work out that he has gotten into recently. As soon as he arrived, I bolted in order to get my run in before we had to leave for your self-defense, training regimen. Dad and I drove you there and we waited for Danny to arrive.

After Tae Kwon Do, we all went back to the house and met up with Mommy. All of us went to a restaurant for a late breakfast and/or early lunch. You were terrific at the restaurant. I had a good meal with a couple of Bloody Mary's to ease me into the day. We came back to the house and I know I fell onto my bed and had a good nap, which is what you nearly always do in the afternoon these days.

Later in the afternoon, everyone went to a nearby park and you ran your Uncle Danny into the ground, which is something you unquestionably enjoy and do whenever you are together We hung out for a while and then walked back to your house, which is when we saw your Mother's recently painted blue toenails. Anyway, you had your dinner and then we had ours a couple of hours later. Your uncle Frankie, who had slept over the night before, returned for dinner and all of us had a great time.

Watching you is a thrill beyond compare for me. You are very animated and imaginative and seem to be quite comfortable in adult settings, which is much to your credit. During dinner, the wine flowed and the conversation was equally as comfortable. Uncle Frank is a good soul and he is incredibly fond of your parents.

This visit was a little different than my other ones because of the death of their very close friend. Shane, loss is an absolute bitch to deal with and it is never something you can somehow resolve. It is raw, unfair and unforgiving and there is nothing anyone can do about it. It is hard for me to see your parents and their friends suffer with this kind of loss. At this point in my life, I understand loss in a different context than they do, but at the same time, there is nothing I can do to alleviate their pain. The game of life has no rules and winners and losers neither earn or deserve their outcome. You do the best you can to embrace it with an open heart and try to accept all that comes your way with some modest sense of grace.

We all had a terrific dinner and it helped to comfort your parents and Frankie, who were really hit hard by the death. Needless to say, Uncle Danny was always available to you and you didn't miss a single opportunity. Your Mom took you up to bed after our dinner and then your Dad and Frankie went out to drink with some mutual friends of Rob. I guess Danny was going to join them at some point.

Here I am, sitting on the bed in what you call the office and jotting down some notes to you. I really like where you appear to be going and it is exhilarating to watch you inhabit your world. Every now and then, you exhibit spoiled brat characteristics, but they pass pretty quickly, especially when your Mother very quietly reads you the riot act. I like you very much and believe me when I say that if I didn't, I wouldn't hesitate to share it with you.

Tomorrow, we are going to Steve and Brenda's house for Rosh Hashanah dinner and there are going to be lots of relatives there. Tomorrow is my last day with you for this trip and it is has been a treat beyond compare. You're a good kid and your parents have been doing a kick ass job bringing you up. You are showing promise, my man.

You probably think we are seamlessly going to read about Rosh Hashonah dinner, but you are wrong. We have undergone some time travel. It is the day after and I am presently squeezed into my seat on a flight to Phoenix, the first of three legs in my return trip. I didn't really have any time to write yesterday, so it will get recounted at 30,000 feet in the air. In addition, I have spent the past couple of hours cleaning up what I had written from the beginning of the trip until now. This bumpy flight will be ending shortly and then it will be followed by a short ride to Los Angeles and I think I will keep the computer stashed for that leg of the return trip. The flight from LA to Kauai is around five and a half hours and there will again be more time to wrap up the visit.

I am back now, on the final flight from LA to Kauai. Sunday started slowly, partially because your Father went out drinking with Frankie Saturday night and they both got back very late and very intoxicated. Mourning takes many forms and inebriation is one of the ways to try and make sense of loss, especially when you are fairly young. You had your breakfast and then we did our yoga practice again, followed by my run along the Hudson River. Your Dad finally woke up and we drove to Steve and Brenda, who go by the name of Poppy and Meema, respectively. The gathering consisted of your Mother's relatives. These kinds of things don't rank terribly high on my list. I have been on my own since before my New Mexico days and am quite unaccustomed to large gatherings of blood kin. There were plenty of kids for you to play with, many of whom you have gotten to know at similar functions during your short life. Once again, the highlight for me was simply being able to watch you. As for me, I did the best I could, trying to shield my discomfort and probably not doing a very good job of it.

I sat in the back of the car with you on the drive home. You were up for some the time, making music requests to hear an awfully vapid teen sensation by the name of Justin Bieber and fortunately your parents were able to hold you off until twirling your hair and sucking on the pacifier gave way to a fitful sleep for the balance of the ride. Every now and then, I would gently grab hold of your little bare foot and enjoy the indefinable pleasure of being close to you.

Aside from your rapidly developing language skills, music continues to draw your attention. In a couple of weeks, you will be starting guitar lessons. The electric guitar that I got for your last birthday finally came out of the box during this visit. You seem to have a genuine affinity for the instrument and it will be curious to see what happens. In addition to the music lessons, you are also going to start taking cooking classes, something you seem to enjoy doing with your Mother. Both your parents are very attentive to your development and so far, so good. Emmy's skillful and loving presence is the icing on the cake for you at home. She is very special. Of course, your grandparents, including Ira, shower you with tremendous affection.

When we got home last night, everyone went immediately to sleep, but I waited for Uncle Danny to show up for our last visit together. We talked for about an hour or so, much of it about the sorry state of world affairs. I really hope I haven't given you the wrong idea regarding your uncle. It is just hard to tell what he is really thinking some times because he doesn't communicate all that openly about what is going on in his life. He definitely loves you to pieces and that is all you need know.

It is Monday and I am still in the air. I am now just a couple of hours from home and then it is back into my own world. The just finished journal of my time with you guys feels a little flat and equally as forced, somehow like an obligation I was required to share with you. The feelings mean more to me than the facts and they are pretty simple. I really love your Dad and the man he has become. Spending these brief times with him is a highlight of my life. I love Andrea with all my heart and am so indebted to her for how she has embraced me as part of your family. I know your Uncle values our time together very much and so do I. As for you, my little prince, the gods have smiled on you and made you a blessing for all who come in contact with you. I have already told you I think you are an unusual person and I hope the future is kind to you and you return the kindness in spades.

My friend, Ken H. did not come down from Amherst, where he is teaching one semester on Acting of some kind. Only mentioning this now because I recall making a big deal about that before I started the trip.

My assignment upon my return is to finish making adjustments to the text already completed. It will definitely take a couple of weeks to get back to where we are now. Of course, the process will likely be interrupted by one thing or another, requiring me to explain yet again where I have been and where I am going and why. What can you do? We can only hope that we get interrupted by the scent of a woman, although it is an unlikely occurrence in the next six weeks or so.

While we are on the subject of world affairs, I continue to find strength in my resolve to essentially not give a shit about what is allegedly reported to be going on. Being uninformed definitely has its virtues and I am only beginning to appreciate them. The less you know, the less there is to be concerned about, plus there is nothing we can do to alter the global course of the power and money juggernaut.

Home Stretch

Wow. It is Friday evening, October 5th and I am on my familiar perch at home. A little over a month ago, I began dipping backwards into this crocktail and it has taken quite a bit of time and much effort. At the beginning of the reread, I jumped over the pond to visit with you and your family, dutifully recorded in the prior handful of pages. I have been home nearly three weeks and instead of my writing time, it became my reading time until last night, when I finally finished and got right up to "Home Stretch". Truthfully, it is a mixed bag of stories and opinions. It actually feels like I spent too much time on Zen affairs and the Ladies. On the other hand, I sincerely try to mirror my life in what I believe is the path of Buddha and other than my blood family, being in love with a woman is blood passion.

I really had to change gears and read all of this as if I didn't write it. Things might make absolute sense to me when I share it and some time later, it turns to shit and I have no idea what I meant at the time. Fortunately, that didn't occur all that many times, but it sure did happen more than once. I took some notes where I felt there might be a loose end, but I haven't figured out exactly what to do about it...............

Well, I just dove back in and plugged a couple of holes somewhere back there because I really don't want to waste words trying to explain why I did what I did. The only event that deserves more attention is the story around my ending up in the NYC Marathon and I will make sure to draw it in before we tie the ribbon on this package to you.

For better or worse, the highlight of these past few weeks would have to be my imminent purchase of another motorcycle. Tomorrow, I will be buying a 2007 Honda Shadow Sabre. It has an 1100 cc engine, considerably larger than the Tangerine Dream.

Been feeling antsy on my bike for a while now and this new bike will give me a boost and that's for sure. It has more than enough power to get me into trouble if I am stupid, a road I will avoid traveling. Actually, I am thinking we might want to make the back cover me posing with my new bike because you get the front. I think I will enjoy the availability of power and gradually acclimate to having it under me. I will let you know how it feels, as soon as I have had a chance to take her out by myself, something I would definitely want to do before riding with the guys. We sometimes ride in close quarters and it is important to know your bike, which takes a bit of time.

Feeling a little out of writing shape because there hasn't been any need to drive our bus down the highway for a while. During this break from contemporary recording, I have come to terms with the idea that this is a story without end and it is pointless to try and trap it between two covers. There will always be something I haven't written about or a memory that has changed. I still haven't thought about what I will do with this discipline once we are at the end of this discordant life opera.

Maybe, we should just keep on keeping on and on the last day I will think of something special to share. I don't like multiple toasting at any event. The idea is that one person makes a special toast and everyone drinks to it and that is that. We will try and live one day at a time, just like we've been doing until now.

I felt it would be tough for this first time back on line and it has been. I will do what I can to keep the same rhythm we have been dancing to since the beginning. Each day will bring whatever it wants and we will take note of it or let it slide by. The discipline to keep this front and center for a year in my life is a very powerful force and I have attempted to be respectful of it. Anybody fool enough to do something like this has to feel it is important for whatever reason they hold close. This is so cool.

Flaming Lips

I rode into town on the Tangerine Dream this morning and bought the new bike, riding it only far enough to the local mechanic, where I left it for a once over. This one has considerably more power. I will lower it a little and have to change the handle bars, but everything is just fine the way it is. I will pick it up early next week and spend some time putting it through its paces, so I am sufficiently comfortable to ride in a large group.

Based on all my stories and the various adventures, you would likely be surprised to hear that I don't like change all that much. Keeping large parts of my life very stable has afforded me the opportunity to spend a fair amount of time simply thinking about many of the things I have shared with you until now. Much of what I have shared comes from years and years of honing a feeling or a thought into a relatively small package. The style is spontaneous, but many of the comments have been stewing until they are hopefully soft enough to ingest without excessive mastication.

While I will likely handle the motorcycle switch with aplomb, the yurt and the dislocation and acclimation that come with it is likely going to be a pretty big deal. I have been comfortably habitating in the same space for around seven years. Virtually everything I do around here is done without thinking because of the entrenched habits that provide an automatic pilot of sorts.

Recently, I walked out on the land where the yurt will go. It is a huge tract of land and the nearest home is likely a half mile away. The nights out there will be very special. I hope I stay with my plan of creating a private, spiritual haven that puts any visitor at ease. Along with who knows what else, our time will have run out before the yurt move. There was a good reason for putting this in the framework of a year. No matter what I write and no matter how long I write, this story will always be incomplete.

In the beginning, the only thing I had decided on was a style of communicating to you. However, I never thought it would chronicle forever. The idea of a year is not terribly original, but it locked in pretty early in this workout. While it would be easy to keep this going, easy is not always best. I am curious to see how this urge will give birth to itself and where it will take me subseqently. As for you, this incomplete story will give you enough to chew on for a whole bunch of decades, not to mention the generations to come, wherever the family tree grows!

In the split second it has taken you to move from the prior paragraph to this, a day has transpired. Can you believe that? Once again, it is Sunday afternoon and I am home from a ride with the bruddahs. Told everyone about the bike deal and I am good to go with what little I want to do to it. Someone is giving me small shocks, so I can lower the bike a few inches. Another rider is giving me handlebars that will be comfortable and he is going to install both the shocks and bars. If all goes well, I will be good to go next weekend.

Other than getting the bike together this week, I have a couple of other highlights. Getting together with the Mayor for one of our talk stories, a local phrase for shooting the shit. That is on Tuesday morning and in the evening, I have dinner with Yvette, whose name has not come up yet. I met her early in my time here. She was editing a magazine called Zento, a kind of upscale, new age, Hawaii glossy. I actually wrote my first thing ever for her and it was a story about the Zen temple in Hanapepe, where I actually sat for a while.

Before I moved here, I went on line to check on Zen temples, where I might continue my practice. There was only one and I spoke with the priest, Kosho, prior to coming over. I probably sat with him and several other haoles (Hawaiian slang for white people) for a couple of years. It was kind of startling to see how the Japanese observed the practice. When it is taught in the West, daily sitting or zazen is a given, in addition to participating in a variety of rituals. Here, nobody sits and they only go to the Temple for weddings and funerals. I was part of a small pocket of practitioners from the mainland and we tried to become a part of the congregation, an effort met with limited success. I did meet Eiju there and that is more than enough for me, plus several years of practicing with a priest, who was always very helpful to me. When I was unable to get out because of my big time leg infection, Kosho would often come by and take me to the hospital for an examination. We were reasonably friendly, but he moved on to Seattle and we have not really kept in contact.

So, when I first met Yvette it was in the role of writer. We became friends and she is a wonderful character. Another woman from Texas, but has been over on Maui and here for many years. I haven't seen her in well over a year and she is coming in for a visit and we are meeting for dinner. She knows all sorts of women and I have asked her to see if she can pimp me out, a challenge she will undertake with delight. It is always great fun to see her and catch up.

There are a couple of people coming in from the mainland on business that relates to some of what I am doing. At the moment, it feels incredibly boring and we will simply limit the mention to the visit. It does change the rhythm, which is always more fun for me. Next Saturday is the Kauai County Farm Bureau thank you dinner for volunteers who worked the recent Fair. Always great to have a free meal and so many of these people are acquaintances, which makes for a relaxing evening for me. Once we get into the week, I have no idea what I will write about in relation to any of the above.

Christ, I have spent huge amounts of time by myself. It really did start with the night I was alone in my shared bedroom with Mo, which is what I have always called my brother, Marty. The night my father died was the true beginning of my internal journey and I have been at this sucker for a hell of a long time. There are an awful lot of people who are fixated on the externals, while my fixation has been on my inner world. I can stare off into the distance and still be with whatever is going on inside. This entire effort comes from within, the only place it could possibly come from. Whatever I end up writing about after our time together, it would not be possible to change the approach. I don't want to tell a story unless I am somehow part of it.

I always kind of wonder what people are thinking, especially when they do something incredibly fucken stupid. Most of us are very adept at justifying virtually anything. If compassion is the engine, the road is pretty straight and there are no side streets for close mindedness. I seem to have an affinity for internal monologues, which is partially how we ended up here in the first place.

Shane, try and not to be one of those stupid people and the stupidity I am referring to has nothing to do with intelligence, it has to do with insensitivity. Yes, I know I am not supposed to impose myself on you, but the aforementioned plea is absolutely for your benefit and not mine.

Last night was interrupted by The Wild Bunch, a classic Peckinpah western with William Holden and others. I was up and wandering about and not feeling terribly inspired about journaling any more. The movie was to start in about ten minutes and I decided I was in the mood for a kick ass, bloody Western. It was a ball to watch one more time. This brief explanation would likely be better suited up above, but I didn't think about writing it until this very moment and there you have it.

Oh, Hell, I Don't Know

Just looked at the calendar and counted around three weeks before we wrap, a theatrical expression I think we can use under the circumstances. Everyone's life is a play of some kind. The vast majority have no idea they are on a stage and the entire world is the audience. Your life is always in front of you and my most loyal audience throughout my countless performances has been myself. I have tried really hard in recent decades to be true, absent any façade. While you are likely somewhere in your teens, I have difficulty remembering the details of that time in my life. If it were possible to write to you from that time, I would and then it would be like two friends, sharing some unimaginable blood bond.

I want to knowingly repeat something written once before and I hope no more than that. This year long process has been a labor of pure, unadulterated love and it is a kind of love that comes from so deep within my internal world, my spirit being. Every time I sit down, I am in the machine that will bring this to you without even a gram of distortion or pretense. My mind hardly ever wanders during my time with you because I want to deliver the full voltage of who I am right at that very moment. It has been hard work, which makes me feel more relieved than tired when I finish a piece. I am getting it out there to you, laddy..

If you play your cards right, life kind of comes full circle on you. I would like to think I am recapturing the beautiful innocence of my young childhood. All of the colors are there and most of us never get to paint our lives using the rainbow of feelings and insights we have been gifted. True, there are things that now make me weary and it goes beyond a hard day of manual labor. I am just so tired with the way things are in the world. Religions are weapons used to kill lesser Gods. This planet is considered a resource to be plundered. Science is fighting for its very existence and often considered blasphemy. Wars are tolerated, frequently justified by fictional assessments of their necessity. Our industrial food supply is filled with chemicals and genetically altered ingredients. We have never learned and we never will, because it is our fate. One arrogant individual is bad enough, but an entire society is doomed. It will rise and fall just like those before it.They never last because the are engorged with arrogance and starved for compassion.

Wandering around in my mind, as you can plainly tell. It is a habit that has been with me a long time. Being a gemini, we are supposed to be kind of two-sided and an internal dialogue slips in there, too. Personally, I believe in everything because when you discount even one thing, you discount everything. My God, or lack thereof, can't possibly be better than whatever another person believes in. Hell, I don't know.

Hello Dalai

Picked up Flaming Lips today and I am stoked. It is in great shape and the difference in power is very serious. Nine years on the same ride is long enough and this switch will enliven my two wheel touring considerably. I will make some minor adjustments, but not too much.

My dinner with Yvette last night was wonderful. We spent several hours talking about everything from relationships to work to life in general. We will see if she pimps me out to anyone at all. Sent her a picture of you because I am so incredibly happy to have you in my life and I love showing you off to people I care about.

You know what would be incredible? It would be you knocking on my door right now and crossing the threshold as an eighteen year old young man. Of course, you would have somehow already read this entire volume and felt instantly compelled to get on a plane and come to visit. You would have long hair, a genuine smile on your face and ready to surf. Yes, I know we are doing big time Twilight Zone (absolutely check out Rod Serling), but it is easy for me because it is simply whatever I happen to imagine. I can tell you right now I am sharp as a mother fucken tack and there ain't all that much that gets passed me. Assuming I even have the good fortune to be around here in fifteen years or so, I have know idea what my body and/or mind will be capable of pulling off. At sixty seven, we are doing pretty well, but who knows what the Creator has in store for me down the road. It sure would be cool to enjoy you as a young man and I would be happy to get that far and make whatever peace I need to make with whomever I need to make it with after that moment.

Well, isn't this a perfect segue? In my normal early morning E messages, there was a quote from the Dalai Lama and I really liked it. Remember when I told you this undertaking has required tremendous focus? When I read the quote, it was automatically going to be the anchor of the next entry into this pseudo-diary of ours. Sitting down this evening, it was already copied into our text and what I do is write my way to that quote and go beyond. I remember doing it several times with Big Al. A good word to use is crafted. I have tried with every ounce of Larry I could muster whenever this process began again and again. All of this is who I am.

Let's take a look at the quote and while you think about it, I am going to heat up some Portuguese Bean Soup and Corn Bread.

"You see, the past is past, and the future is yet to come. That means the future is in your hands-the future entirely depends on the present. That realization gives you a great responsibility." H.H. the Dalai Lama

Sorry, it is still heating, but it will be ready soon. Keep thinking about it.

The soup was terrific and so was the corn bread. If you need more time, you can always connect back in and catch up, which won't be real difficult. Before Dancing With Dalai, thought to tell you also listen to The Who and Led Zeppelin. When they first hit, I was never really connected to their music, but I now totally appreciate their respective legacies. I tell you, it is really hard to imagine another era comparable to the 60's and 70's because it was incredibly special.

You know, I might want to change the last sentence in his quote to read, "That realization gives you a great freedom." If you can somehow manage to be present in the present, the future is now. There is some kind of nexus where the past, present and future are one. It comes from within and asks a lot of you. It's like betting on a long shot and never thinking about losing, not for one minute.

The present is this very brief, gone up in smoke time, while the past and future are under no pressure at all. In its own way, it is the razor thin fulcrum on the seesaw of before and after. There are so many ways to define that moment and me weighing in is like a broke down fighter who can't possibly beat the champ, heading into the slaughter house and defiant until a few seconds into the fight when it all goes black.

If anything in here smells of platitude, feel free to completely disregard. I think there are ways to communicate that cut through nearly all differences and that is the stuff that comes from the heart. It is a language spoken by all forever. It is the language of liberation that also accepts responsibility into its vocabulary.

Believe me, I am not being smarter than His Holiness, who would likely have a way of accepting my feelings anyway. For those who attempt to walk on the path of great men like the Dalai Lama, I wish them good luck on their journey. As for me, I will avoid the crowd and take the scenic route. Yes, there is judgement sliming in and I must take responsibility for that unexpected slip in my perfection rating. It all comes from within and whatever it takes to mine it is fine with me. This part time venture of ours has really helped me to anchor myself and to refine my world.

Go To Your Left, Go To Your Right

I got angry today and that is a true rarity for me. It was made even worse because it was over a comment about a movie, if you can believe that. As you know, I work with a group of politically conservative people and I can't say that it resonates with me, but I have also lost any attraction to the folks on the other side, which can be just as strident. I commented about being ineterested in a movie that was about to open, called Argo. It has to do with creating a brilliant ruse that followed the kidnapping of Americans in Iran in November 1979 and dragged on painfully for well over a year. I am looking forward to seeing the film, which opens tomorrow. When I recounted the plot and the actors involved, the immediate response from the Right was that its release was timed to give Obama a boost, as evidenced by all of the liberal actors in the film. It felt like getting hit on the side of my head with a shovel, metaphorically speaking. When I took exception, it was relegated to naivete on my part. I stopped dead in my tracks and immediately said I was very angry and didn't want to talk all. I was very pissed off and that pissed me off all the more.

Without an ounce of paranoia, I swear, there is something in there about the rich Jews who "control" the entertainment business. All the actors are liberal and would never consider taking on a role that disagreed with their politics, which is truly a horse shit idea. The capper is that all of those greedy Jews are less concerned about box office and more concerned with "their" President. Now, if you want to talk about naïve, that industry is all about the money and you either make it or lose it. Causes take a back seat to commerce in this notoriously greedy industry. Don't get me wrong, I love movies, but I am anything but naïve in terms of how it breathes.

I am living in a world of extremes. You are either a liberal or a conservative, unless you are lost in between these poles, a vacillating fool. It is a dream to think this will ever change. I could run for President on the Compassion party and definitely count on my vote. A society is no different than a single person, if you put shit in and you get shit. We are complex organisms and more subtle than one extreme or another. Personally, I would be hard pressed to share my agenda because I don't have one that I am aware of. Being as genuine as possible is one terrific way to energize your agenda, assuming you give a rat's ass about agenda related issues in the first place.

I am feeling wisdom tendencies and that gets my attention. Wisdom, if there is such a thing, is only worth a shit if it comes absent of ego. Personally, I have an immeasurable wealth of experiences over the decades and that is all I lay claim to.

The anger incident is still with me and the only way is for me is to disengage, which I will do. Arrogance is so low on my list that I can't even see the letter "a" under my feet.

A Short Break and a Return

Took a couple of nights off because I felt like slowing down a little. Friday evening, I decided to indulge and take a break from anything remotely thought provoking. Saturday, I got Flaming Lips taken care of by having a riding friend lower it a few inches. Later in the day, I stopped off at Ken and Susan's for a to die for mojito that Susan conjurs up during many of my visits. I spin my yarns and Susan definitely enjoys listening to them. Ken, God Bless him, is rather consumed by his mission in the world, but that's OK and I love him for it. Left their place walking on air and I then proceeded to a 100+ person thank you dinner for all of the County Fair volunteers. It is interesting to walk into a roomful of people all by yourself and then gradually weave your way into a comfortable hammock for the evening. I know so many of these people and like a good number of them and I enjoy spreading the love. I particularly like to say endearing things because most of us don't speak the language and everyone wants to hear something like that at least once a day.

Earlier today, Sunday, I mounted Flaming Lips and whipped her into Lihue for my ride with the Sons of Kauai. When I pulled into the 7/11 in Lihue at 9A, it was impossible for any of the boys not to notice the change in my two wheel transport. I may have mentioned this already, but from the first time I rode with these guys around nine years ago, I park in exactly the same place in the parking lot. Everyone pulls in and positions their bikes so they are facing out and can leave with out effort. Yours truly, is so happy to arrive that I just pull straight in and face every other bike. I guess on some level it is also a statement regarding my being dramatically different than all the guys I ride with. After all these years, I would likely have to confess to enjoy being different from most everyone around me.

We rode up the mountain at Kokee to the end of road, featuring a heartstopping view of the Kalalau Valley. The new bike was a revelation. She handled very nimbly on the turns and there was never a shortage of power. This is a ride we take very often and the road is familiar to me by now. The new bike handles so much better than its predescessor. This was one of the most exciting rides I have had since getting here because of the new wheels. Making today even sweeter, I came home and a guy showed up to buy the Tangerine Dream, no questions asked. He pulled into the driveway in his truck and didn't even start the bike. He gave me a check and I gave him the title. Then, I rode the bike to his house and he drove me home. I am not sure if it could be easier to sell a bike, but I am very happy with the ease of this transaction. Basically, I have dramatically upgraded the quality of my ride and it only cost me $1,500. Not knowing what your currency will be like, there is really no other choice, but to use the Yankee Dollar in 2012 as the benchmark. I have no fucken idea what will pass for currency in the future because what we are using right now is smoke and mirrors and an empty pocket backs it all up.

Oh, you're gonna love this, I spoke with your Dad yesterday when he was walking back from his Superman work out and we had a fair amount of time to talk. I always want to hear about him first and I always save you for last. Whatever happens in between is usually up to my orchestration, which is fine. He talked a little about work and some upcoming travel. I talked about Flaming Lips and some of my own business stuff. I always save you for last because it is what I want to be left with at the end of a conversation with Andy. Apparently, you are actively soliciting pizza dates with some of the girls in your class. You are way too young to understand how totally cool this is. You don't even have any stinkin' hormones and you actually prefer the company of women, which is very interesting. We had a good time talking about your nascent proclivities. Just for the record, beyond hoping you don't get into beastiality, I really don't give a shit where your hormones take you.

This probably gets us to where I am right now. It is 5:31P and I am in my space, wearing my blue rayon shorts. Have just begun slurping my third "short" wine glass of merlot. Small is emphasized because it is true and not said to mask a bottle swigging wino. Yes, I have done the other as well, but pretty infrequently. Good music filling the room. Tonight's gourmet meal is Green Chili with Kalua Pork, Cheddar and Brown Rice, which I will likely have once we have finished our current insertion, so to speak. Sunday has been such a favorite day for writing, partially because I can get at it early in the afternoon, as opposed to the evening after a day of humping stuff around. There is a part of the motorcycle ride that is very primal and it carries over into my time after at home. I have good, strong energy and especially after a special day like today with Flaming Lips showing me what she can do out there.

Feeling done for a Sunday. I have never sat down here for less than an hour and in most every case it is at least two hours or more to get enough down to feel like a bona fide effort. It is feeling like time to leave the planet for a couple of hours and not have some obligation to report in. Over and out.

Totally Beat

A couple of days have gone by and I am back at it. The funny thing is this is never far from my consciousness, especially now that we are within weeks of the finish line. I know I have already leapfrogged to the end before this moment and I have no interest in really ending this effort with any finality because both of our lives will continue beyond our pulling this plug. This may not be a bad time for some house cleaning and after that, I will tell you why I am totally beat to shit.

Running in the NYC Marathon back in 1982 was an otherworldly experience for me. I had started my running regimen out in Glen Cove, Long Island around six years before that. My routine was pretty much unvaried from day one of my running. I would always run a minimum of a half hour and sometimes longer, but rarely if ever for a full hour. Literally a week before the marathon, a business friend told me his buddy up in Boston, who had qualified for the NYC Marathon, was unable to run. He offerred me the credentials and I immediately accepted. Now, keep in mind, my running pattern was not even close to marathon training and the race was in a week.

I was living in Park Slope and driving something called a Gremlin, one of the ugliest and shittiest cars ever built. I parked my car near the finish line over on the west side, adjoining Central Park, where the race has always ended and will likely be in the same place when you read this. The night before, I stayed over at Buzzy's apartment, a lunatic, red haired friend from my college days. Back then, we actually stole a headstone from a cemetary and brought it to our fraternity house, where absolutely everyone shit a brick when they discovered it. Yes, I know it is terrible thing to have done and we did return it under the cover of darkness. Sacred is a tough concept to grasp, regardless of age.

I am not quite sure how we connected after at least fifteen years, but we did. We had the requisite carbo-loading dishi of pasta, plus alcohol and mary jane, which set us off fo early morning bus ride over the Verrazano Bridge to Staten island, where the race is staged.

If you know anything about running, you will understand that I was nowhere near the proper training level to run a marathon. I could have trained for it, because I was at least a mediocre runner. The idea of actually running twenty six miles, accompanied by around 15,000 others, was not something I was prepared for, physically or emotionally. The experience for me was unimaginable and without peer. Your grandmother was kind enough to bring one of the boys to greet me as I ran over a little bridge, somewhere in Queens. For the life of me, I can't remember if it was Andy or Danny, but they know and you can ask them who was there to witness my triumph. When I first saw the finish line in Central Park, I began to cry and felt my legs losing power. At that moment, I gutted out the last couple of hundred yards and made it the finish line. When you cross, there is someone to see if you are OK and offer to put a foil blanket over your shoulders in order to control body temperature.

After completing this unbelievable trial, without ever walking or stopping, I was on another planet. Now, I had to get in the beshitten Gremlin and drive back to Park Slope. I shivered all the way home. I immediately went to bed and briefly left the bed to get some takeout from a nearby restaurant. The race is always on a Sunday and going to work the next morning was pretty painful. I remember hanging on for dear life as I walked down the cement stairs of the subway and walking gingerly for quite a few days. After that experience, it was crystal clear to me that repeatedly running in marathons and putting your body at risk is incredibly fucken dumb. Anyway, I did it and the experience is very, very special for me.

The only other thing I made a note about was to give some kind of follow up to the nearly year old Occupy movement. You know, I am not quite sure about it at this time. Going up against the power structure is almost like a science fiction tale at this point. Occupy appeared to be a somewhat organic and spontaneous coming together of a very diverse group of people, all opposed to the rapacious ways of those with the power. I don't think they were crazy and actually believe they were on to something. I thought they would come back to life after the winter and make their mark once again this past summer, but nothing happened.

Frankly, I have no idea what's to come with the looming Obama- Romney election. I don't know if America was smarter before these past decades, but it seems so incredibly dumb to me now. This was a place that really valued intellect and independence and forward thinking. Innovation is one of this country's strengths and it has been lost through the dumbing down of discourse, a purposeful effort by those with the juice.

I don't think we are even close to through with people taking to the streets to protest the cancers of greed, hatred and ignorance.

This day was spent with either a machete in hand or a sickle bar cutter, in an effort to cut down foliage around our reservoirs. We have several of them on the land and we are responsible for a certain level of maintenance. Today was absolutely exhausting. Don't you think it is cool for a guy sixty seven years old to be recounting stories like this? I do. The funny thing is I never think it is even remotely weird to be doing whatever I am doing. However, I can step away with time and be at least a little surprised. At this moment, I am seriously tired and longingly eyeing my dinner to be, Green Chili with Kalua Pork, Cheddar and Brown Rice, a dish I have had before.

Glad we had this time to talk. We will keep on keeping on until next time.

Next Time

I really didn't need a heading for this new entry because I find myself in exactly the same circumstance as yesterday. Spent the day cutting thick, tall guinea grass around another of the reservoirs on the land. The Kauai sun can really cook and you tend to turn to toast after a full day of strenuous work under its powerful stare. The muscle memories are particularly strong up and down my arms, from shoulders to fingers. Energetically, I am a day before do over. Yesterday, I latched on to two loose ends in the narrative and that made the effort much less taxing than it could have been.

I have been thinking about figuring out a way to do the same tonight. I wasn't sure if I told you about the Quixote Order of the Windmill, so I confess to checking back in the text. There was only some stupid mention and I didn't want to mess with what I had written and simply indicated it was a story worth telling, so I could elaborate on it now.

Around eighteen months ago, I had this flash that it would be very cool if I could bring some of my good friends together. I have an exceptionally eclectic collection of buddies. I came up with the idea of the Quixote Order of the Windmill because all of these guys were fighting the good fight in their own unique way. They became Knights and I began peppering them with correspondence. My sign off was always something like:

The Dude
Minister of Ideas
Founding Member
Quixote Order of the Windmill

We have gotten together at least six times since then and everyone of the guys looks forward to the evening. We've got about ten at this point and it is wonderful for me to see how my friends really like each other. There are ranchers, farmers, entrepreneurs, Univ. of HI people and other loose cannons. We now have a permanent home at the soon to open Kauai Brewery. One of the Knights, Jimmy G., is a really good friend and he makes the best beer I have ever had. He is opening a microbrewery in downtown Lihue and we have been meeting there for a while now. Once it finally opens, we will definitely want to continue using it as our HQ.

I remember writing to you that you could probably figure out a person by the music he/she really enjoys and it would apply to movies, etc. However, if each one of your friends was some ingredient on a whole pizza, what would it taste like and who are you anyway?

The Quixote Order of the Windmill actually had a predecessor in Santa Fe, years before. It was myself and another guy, who I cannot nail at the moment and we thought it would be entertaining to get a small group of guys together. We called ourselves the Usual Suspects, a film classic you must see, if you haven't already. Most of the time, we met up in the foothills of the Sangre de Cristo mountains, where one of the fellas had land and the makings of a homestead. We talked, listened to music, played cards and once or twice we watched a movie. One woman joined up pretty early in its short life and she was a great addition.

Connection is a wonderful thing for us humans. It provides some comfort in having to deal with the reality of our circumstance. I hate to keep harping on the Zen thing and was very surprised in the last big reread to see how many times I went off on some Zen side road, only to return to the story after the diversion. If you are able to be there for another without feeling some unmet internal need, you are in a fine place. This Windmill thing has been an effort well worth the results. I am a very, very low key Maitre D' at the gatherings and I often find myself looking around the room and marveling at the easy connection between everyone.

Have just come up for air and moved my body around, only to be met by resistance due to the earlier abuse of the day. In a few minutes, I will quietly fade off the page and tend to my dinner, to be followed by some serious mental dialysis on the tube, watching something called the Daily Show with John Stewart. I will then look for a classic movie or something totally banal. Just looked out and saw a crescent moon, which is a very quieting image, at least for me.

Well, glad I told you about the Knights. It is actually a gathering that has no agenda and no pretense. We just enjoy ourselves and that is the only rule. The guys really appreciate the opportunity and I am very, very pleased to have provided it for my friends. What a world. What a world.

I must say it feels very strange to have put all of this down during the past year. I am not sure if anyone has gotten closer to me than you will be, even after your first read. This has afforded me the opportunity to tell my story without any interruption and without correction or feedback. It is hard for me to imagine the experience for you or anyone else reading this from page one through to the end. I really don't know if I will want to hide this from everyone other than you because that is a judgement to be made after the deadline passes.

One More Sunday

Most of our quality time has been spent on Sunday afternoons, following my ride with the bruddahs. Here I am once again, but this time there is only one more Sunday left for us in this particular word incarnation. Today was one of those perfect rides on a motorcycle, especially considering the freshness of Flaming Llips. It is a stone cold gas to be on this bike and I am taking bucket loads of pleasure from these early rides. She pretty much does whatever I want her to do and that is a very centering feeling on a bike. Relaxing on a cycle has a raw elegance about it and today was another one of those experiences.

Most of the aches and pains from last week are pretty dull by now, but they are still making themselves known. Like it or not, resilience is one of those characteristics that gets thrown under the bus as you roll on down the road. After around two days away from the grass hacking, I am still pretty tired from it all.

I just got slapped in the head with the word eloquence. If you are able to talk about your life with eloquence, you are likely on to something worth pursuing. Our time here is all there is and it behooves us to make the most of that allocation. I know it is very early in your own ongoing metamorphosis, but what stories do you want to be able to tell those whom you love? Be the person you want to be and don't settle for second best. The eloquence is in the effort.

On a good day, I could be a life salesman. As fucked up as everything is right now, I have hope there are just enough people all around the world to move in a history defying way and then we might have a chance to preserve what is best about us. On the other hand, it is exhausting to try and be a fake, brilliant observer of all that goes on, personally I don't have the mind, the eye, the ear or the voice for it. Big wields the stick, but there are countless little things that can be done and they could possibly make a difference. We don't have to reach any further than the small world right around us. I don't know if any of that works, but there is a nobility in trying. My idea for Knighthood in the Quixote Order of the Windmill is how I often feel, primarily due to the lingering romanticism of possibility I can't seem to shake.

Let me tell you, it is a very weird feeling to know that I have far less time ahead of me then I have behind me and it is tough to feel gracious under the circumstance. Amongst other things, that reality is definitely part of the engine driving these stories and my commitment to share them with you. Mind you, I would love to have years and years ahead of me and that is my plan, but I have no idea what is in the True Plan. In between now and then, the person I have been kind of describing to you will continue to experience many new things, but never losing sight of the fragility of it all. Up to this point, I can't say I have a single complaint or regret. I would change nothing in my past because that would alter my present state and there is nothing I want to alter about who I am right now. Trust me, it is the antithesis of perfection and very simply about being present.

Somewhere in the last few paragraphs, two days have gone and it is now Tuesday evening. When a couple of days go by it is a big deal to me, but you will likely be gliding from one paragraph to the next, oblivious to the gut wrenching pain this passage of time visits upon me. Not sure if I still have to tell you I'm kidding, because I sure hope you've got it by now. This is no pained confessional.

This is has been such a time twister to write for me. You can't possibly imagine how weird it actually is from over here on the inside of the page, long before you get to read it. After the Halloween shutdown, eight days from now, I will go back through the entire muck and mire splattered on these pages and finish it out, but never going passed our end date. There is the possibility that something could occur before Halloween and I could write about it within that time frame. Due to our limited budget, I am forced to referee all decisions, but ethics will always have a hand on the wheel for this ride.

One Week And Counting

I signed a mythical contract to complete this thing within a year and we have actually done it. This next time will be the third and final time I go back to the beginning for the grand reread. Hopefully, when you have gotten this far along in the story, you won't have bumped into too many change explanations. There is still only one I know of and that involves my misstating something involving homosexuality and it was much too important to me to not do something honest regarding it. So, there is the possibility that some of what you have already read as gospel, may have been tampered with during one of the rereads. It's all part of the time warp we find ourselves diddling in. Obviously, you will read this as a whole, which is what you are supposed to do. On my side, I have been creating this, one small slice at a time and each is uniquely flavored to reflect when it came out of my oven of a mind. In addition, I have gone back to tamper with some of the initial writing because of the Mickey Spillane syndrome.

Trust me, this is all about spontaneity, but every now and then you got to make sure the wheels are on the road. Working free hand is a challenge that doesn't work for the writer in me. The only reason to write is to clearly communicate and it really doesn't matter to whom or why. There is a little of the Mickey Spillane in my approach to all this. He wrote boiler plate private eye, murder mysteries. Allegedy, his style was to stay up all night with a bottle of booze and have a book in the morning. I can guarantee you someone had to edit his excesses before it got published. I certainly have indulged along the way because it absolutely helps to unleash any constraints. I know I do a damn good job of capturing my flight pattern each time I read, think and write about where I happen to be at any given moment.

Every time I start an entry, I look back a few paragraphs, which I think I may have already mentioned. Sometimes, I get stuck in those last few paragraphs for an hour or more before I get going on a new addition. Usually, at the end of any piece, there is a tendency for sloppiness and disconnection to appear, hence the quick re-entry check.

A week from tonight it will be Halloween and I am already feeling nostalgic about drawing this to a close. Tonight, I had the idea of occasionally writing essays to you about what is going on in the world around me. This story will definitely end in seven days, but my future continues beyond that. My first priority will be to wrap this puppy up and put it down. As I have told you, I might self-publish, but I am not sure why anyone other than you would give a shit about all this. Well, that is not completely accurate because this has meant a great deal to me. Now, saying something like, "meant a great deal to me"' doesn't even live in the same galaxy because there are no earthly words I can think of that would even lick the boots of this journey for me.

The Future

I just finished cleaning up the couple of final paragraphs above us, which took about a half hour. Just as I was putting it aside, the future made itself felt. I can speculate about my own years with little hope for accuracy, but thinking of your world is absolutely beyond my capability.

Being a lazy bastard, I will start with the easiest future to lay out and that would happen to be mine. My longevity wish is to at least get to a point where you and I can communicate with few concessions to the age difference. I want to move into the yurt and create a special place for myself and anyone else who shares my heart. Paniolo Feed Company becomes successful and gives back big time to the community. I want to feel the Qi as long as the Gods will allow. My body will continue to age with grace, primarily because of my mania over yoga and running, not to even try and factor in years of Zen sitting. Dreams for the future will remain alive and well for as long as possible. The best for last is the hope of having at least one more interlude with a woman that makes me go insane during our time together, whether for a day or the rest of my life.

Fifteen years from now would have me clocking in at eighty two fucken years old, if you can believe that! Frankly, I hope my world on Kauai is pretty stable and removed from the roller coaster ride ahead. It will be very, very expensive to fly around, but I will always come to see you, no matter what. Best of all is if you can come here on your own and be with me in my world. It really doesn't have to be fifteen years because if you are a smart, together kid, the sooner the better. It is safe to say you will likely be here a few times before reading all this.

Believe me, I have no idea what your world will be like in a bunch of years. The only certainty is that you are being handed a very teinted gift and whether you guys can do anything at all about it is beyond my piss poor clairvoyant ability. At this time, October 25, 2012, the world is in a state of total balls to the wall, clusterfuck and I am certain it is going to get even worse for a while. The well endowed inmates in this global insane asylum are likely insatiable, so they will push until the system finally breaks down.

In all of time, there has never been an empire that promoted peace and non-violence at its core. A sense of responsibility has always been very much a part of the exercise of power, but it is always power gone terribly astray and predictably perverted to violence. It is that damn violence thing that has fucked us up for millennia. Seriously, it is likely possible not to do harm to others and get along just fine in the world. Oh yeah, most people don't give a shit about any of this stuff and much of what I have shared from the beginning. My opinions are completely my own concoctions, but that is what happens as you distill and ferment your experiences over the course of your life.

Most important, when you read this for the first time, you will know what kind of world you are living in. Therefore, there is no need for me to herniate my mind trying to conjure up your world in advance of your reading this. I know where I am at and what I think is coming in the near term. When I use "near term", I mean less than the arbitrary fifteen year mark continually referred to here. Shit is going to happen between now and then, I just know it.

When you continue to escalate violence between people, you can rest assured that backwards is the march. Think about it, how can you expect any people to relish being taken advantage of, either by their own or the US, more than likely? We have invested our citizens and our resources in a fiendish effort to destroy or establish regimes, which ever suits our purpose at the time. I think power has always manifested that way, a club over a hug. You know, it is amazing how much better people react to being respected and cared about. It applies to one person, a hundred people, a country and even the entire planet, which feels just a tad over zealous, but that's one of my jobs here. If I wasn't a zealous spirit, there is no way I would give a shit about leaving some tracks behind.

So much happens everyday, no matter what you are actually doing. It is not remotely possible to monitor the pace of the stimuli that zap you every fraction of a second. If our basic focus narrows until measurement is totally impossible, we begin to live in a world that makes less and less sense. We live one instant after another, between yesterday and tomorrow. I sure hope you have our genetically transmitted sense of humor, because you are going to need it, my boy. I know for a fact that I have it and so does your uncle. I think your Dad is too good to be too funny. The best humor comes from darkness and Andy might be just a little to good a person to whip out the machete and cut up anyone in the way, including himself. Your uncle has been fairly repressed and in some ways his humor is like the molten lava, bubbling up to the surface. I can feel the comic force whenever we talk or visit with each other. My oldest has some blockage in the heart area and I love him all the more for it. I mentioned a bit earlier that I will include Danny's ode to your birth, as it is priceless. It will follow the Epilogue.

We get whatever fucken hand we are dealt and the rest is up to us. If you try real hard to imagine the world you want to be in, there is at least a possibility it will manifest.

We just took a short break. I had one of my gourmet treats, Forbidden Rice Pilaf. The rice was black, which was very strange, but the taste was over the moon. Marta stopped putting detailed information on my packaged rations, so I am not always sure of what I am eating and this dish is a perfect example.

When it comes to eating, you should try and really enjoy the experience and everything after that is gravy, so to speak. I'll tell you something else, it is a bitch to be a farmer or a rancher and it helps to appreciate the hard work that makes all of this possible. In my years living here, I have grown to appreciate the people who work the land and it could be the farmer growing rambutan or the cattle rancher or the papaya grower. These are special people and I don't even mind if I have already said this. You can't do that kind of stuff without a strong spirit because you are always battling Mother Nature, a mismatch to say the least.

During the dinner break and for a while before that, the local public radio station was playing loads of Bob Dylan. I hope you can appreciate the idea of public radio, on top of taking in the magnitude of Dylan's importance for decades. I know his name has come up before, but he is entitled to at least two mentions in this narrative of mine. His library of work is phenomenal and I would be surprised if you didn't know who he was before reading any of this. If you know about Dylan, there is still hope for the planet.

This is our last weekend together, at least in this exercise. Friday evening began several paragraphs ago, which was also about two hours on the clock. Time to go, likely check in tomorrow.

Surprise, it is now tomorrow and some time in the afternoon. Spiffed up the ride a little this morning and took her out for a wheeling to town. Visited the farmer's market, something I frequently do on Saturday morning, primarily because I had a good deal to do with it being established and I think that is another repeater. Grabbed a cup of coffee and talked story with several people. Then, it was off to a matinee of a film called Argo, which you might enjoy. I brought this film up before because of my getting angry about stupid politics. Back in the 1970's, we continued supporting a harsh Iranian dictator, the Shah of Iran. His regime was incredibly oppressive and finally a groundswell of energy, backed by growing anger from the Islamic community, overthrew his rule. Americans were taken hostage at the US embassy and held for well over a year, before a negotiated release. This film deals with a half dozen Americans, who took refuge in the Canadian ambassador's residents, an act of unbeiievable bravery. This is the story of how these six Americans managed to slip through the Iranian hurdles. We have somehow managed to ultimately create hostility with every country's people that we have supported, solely for our own aggrandizement, without an ounce of consideration for the lifelong residents.

The sun was shining Kauai bright after the movie and the ride home was very sweet. I figured I would likely get a head start on our project when I got home and here we are.

I have a short story on the woman business for you. When I met with my friend, Yvette, not quite three weeks ago, we spent a fair amount of time talking about a woman for me, any woman. About two thirds of the way through the conversation, she had a matchmaker epiphany. Her friend on Maui, Susan, would be perfect for me. Through the magic of modern technology, she proceeded to pull up several pictures of the chef, which is what she does and one was her, standing rather statuesque in a bikini.

For better or worse, men think with their dicks and that is just how it goes. I didn't need any other information about her after viewing the bikini delight. If you are turned on by a woman before you ever meet her, you are starting off on strong personal footing.

Needless to say, I strongly encouraged Yvette to find out what Susan's personal story was about. Several weeks went by, peppered with gentle reminders from me and I finally heard from her. It gets interesting here because dick thinking is completely one dimensional, while woman fly with much more depth in their choices. Yvette called yesterday to say she had spoken with Susan. It seems she had a long term, committed relationship that ended a number of years ago. She is actually my age, which is very unusual for me. I have never been terribly interested in being around women in their late sixties, primarily because the majority believe they are old. A vivacious, sexy woman with the same number of years would be a real treat. There is just a whole bunch of shit you can't possibly know until you start flipping the years on your customized calendar.

Women are never in a hurry and tend to be more cautious and thoughtful than our gender. True to form, Yvette informed me in her last call that Susan is available, but with an emotional parachute. She feels she has had the love of her life and is very comfortable living in balance with that. As the illegitimate child of the literary marriage between Don Quixote and Cyrano de Bergerac, there is always possibility for me. You climb the mountain of life, clearing one peak after another and each time you barely clear a peak, another lies off in the distance.

What are the first things a woman will want to know? What is his sign? Are his cards compatible with yours? These humans are witches and there is nothing we grizzlies can do about it.

Apparently, the initial research indicates certain elements of compatiblity and Susan will let Yvette know what she thinks. I approach every one of these damn stumblings of the heart with the same enthusiasm, even after countless count outs. If this forever dynamic was a ballet, the woman would be the swan and the man would be the frog, awaiting his princely liberation provided by her attention. Got to be honest here, I don't know how frogs and swans get along. My guess is that they don't give a shit about each other, which is not exactly what I have in mind for the fairy tale. The chick swans have powerful maternal powers and their stare will freeze a frog in his tracks. Now, what happens after the encounter is something best left to your imagination.

I will get a message from Yvette that it is OK to call Susan or I won't. Aside from the bikini pose, she is doing some interesting stuff on Maui. I don't like to think of myself as influential, so it is challenging to talk about all that I do here. If I suddenly had any idea what I was doing, there is no doubt in my mind that I would be some snapped human spirit, wandering around aimlessly. It comes up on occasion when I read what someone is doing on these islands. I could write a story about what I am doing here, but that is not the motivation for anything I do. It seems Susan has great credentials in the increasingly popular, locavore movement with a nice little empire built on her chef skills and food knowledge. There is way more to her story, but this is not her story after all, is it? I would say that between now and this coming Wednesay, the 31st, not a damn thing will transpire between us.

What a pain in the ass? Susan will give the go ahead or she won't. As you must know by now, it is the story that counts most. We are presently in between not ever communicating or spending the rest of our lives together. If I was a bookie, I'd go with the odds of nothing at all ever happening.

Calibrating the distinction between fantasy and reality in any relationship is a tricky business. I want to be a human radio station, selecting any music I like and finding a female listener who has all the moves and plenty of her own. There is a blues song in there, but I am only able to feel it and giving it musical life is way beyond my limited talent.

I tell you what I am going to do. I am going to send what I have written in relation to Yvette and Susan and ask Yvette it she would please share with Susan. I think it would be great to slip in just one more reference before you and I part company in a couple of days. I am going to do that now and then we will move on to something yet to be discovered.

Well, the deed is done. It is a grenade of honesty and we will read the casualty list pretty quick. I do feel a little like the gun slinger in these matters. Let me tell you, if a sixty seven year old woman is offended by anything I have written, we will both have saved a lot of time and effort. I think the handful of women I have been privileged to be with have always left with me more than before the interlude and that applies to your grandmother as well. In many ways, I owe your grandmother my life, but that is a story we will still leave untold, primarily because it has nothing at all to do with your life. God only knows, if we did everything right, what the fuck would we learn?

This thing is the only insurance policy I can think of that might connect with your own Qi and maybe infuse an indetectable amount of my own within yours. This has been like trying to put the shot glass down on the bar top and capturing all the air in the room, an exercise in futility if ever there was one. I hope you know this has nothing to do with being special in anyway. On the contrary, it is how remarkably ordinary we all are. I would never want you to think that I have given you the Star Wars blessing to let the Force be with you. Until more people speak like the Daili Lama or Bishop Tutu, we are kind of screwed. You know, I am not sure whose job it is to do that kind of work either. I am pretty certain it is our job, each and everyone of us, but it is so much easier to leave it to others.

It has been Sunday afternoon for a while because I needed to go up above and do some repair work on the Susan entry and what briefly followed. Our last motorcycle ride together happened today and it couldn't have been better. Today is the tenth anniversary celebration of the Sons of Kauai being formed by three guys, Harold, Jack and Rudy. I hope I have mentioned Bruddah Rudy before. He was this wonderfully, dignified man, who didn't have to say much. He passed away around four years ago and he is always celebrated by the boys. These guys decided to meet at the 7/11 in Lihue on Sunday morning and if anyone else showed up, they would ride together. At the bash today, there were fifty bikes, which doesn't sound like a big number, but that is a lot of bikes, believe me. The vibe was maximum Aloha, from start to finish.

Today, we had a poker run, along with raffle sales and a paid meal at a local bar that opened its room for our group. Poker runs are popular in the biking community as a way of raising money, with winners keeping most of the money, if not all of it. You start with a piece of paper and it has five blank boxes and under each box is a location. At each stop, you pull a chip with a letter and a number, which are coded for the cards in the deck. The top three winning hands take the cash in ascending order.

Everybody hangs out with everybody and it is real fluid to see how connections slip and slide during the day. I will talk with anyone at this point, partially cause I have creds in the group, which I know we got into in some earlier biker babble. Don't think I told you about my wearing a sheriff's badge on my leather vest. One day, years ago, I showed up wearing a badge on my vest and I don't even recall how I came into its possession. Since then, I have been referred to as The Sheriff and have already replaced the original badge once and will likely have to do it again. I collect tickets and/or money at these big events because of my stature within the hierarchy, coupled with virtually everyone being terrified by the mere sight of my star.

My friend, Michael, recently reminded me about my story of the Indian Motorcycle when I was still living in Santa Fe. First of all, the story of the Indian should be studied by every M.B.A. class in the world. Indian was a motorcycle manufactured at the turn of the 1900's in MA. They literally had the motorcycle world by the balls and they completely blew it. You have got to read about them and see how you can take an incredible opportunity and flush it down the toilet. Anyway, I briefly hooked up with a charlatan out of Albuquerque, who claimed he had the elusive rights to manufacture the Indian Motorcycle once again. Well, surprise, he turned out to be full of shit, but I had some fun with it for a while.

Not that you will remember, but a gargantuan storm is supposed to be whacking the east coast any time now. It is being referred to as a Perfect Storm, a coming together of diverse weather patterns that can create the phenomenon of 1 + 1= 3. The date is October 29, 2012 and Sandy, the name of the villain, will likely be easy for you to find and that is unfortunate because it will mean a great deal of damage was done. This is looking like a meteorological shit kicking and I have asked your Dad to let me know how it is going. You might experience some flooding close to you, but I hope I am wrong. I will keep you posted on developments and you can figure out the time travel tripping in it all. Everything I have written has an immediacy about it, even though you will end up discovering it as part of this archeological dig into a time a decades before your first breath, with a little spill over into your single digits.

Oh, that reminds me, I spoke to you yesterday for approximately 2 ½ seconds. Andy was in Atlanta and scrambling to get back before the storn, which he did. I wanted to call Andrea and say hello and to see where she was at regarding the approaching calamity. Your Mom has her shit together, so I knew she would be all over getting exactly what you needed, in order to endure minimal inconvenience and that is what she was doing. The both of you were in the store getting survival supplies and she put you on the phone and you said something or other to Grandpa Larry. It was just great fun to hear your voice on the other end of the phone. For a man to have a grandson is something special and there is no preparation for it. It would seem like the right thing to do would be to share your story with him, kind of like Genetic Geritol. I think most tribal cultures honor the transfer of wisdom and insight from the elders to the youth.

You will be relieved to know that so far all is well in Hoboken regarding Sandy. I spoke with your Dad late in the day on east coast time and he was relaxed. To be clear, we are talking about Monday, October 29th. I wrote last night about the hurricane, but used today's date in terms of its impact on you guys. The storm is doing huge damage all along the coastal northeast and lower Manhattan is taking a beating from the surge of the ocean, which feeds into the East River and Hudson River. This storm is so huge that it will take several days to run its course and it is beating up everything directly in its path. I can't really tell you not to worry because why the hell would you be worried when you read this? You would have to be unbelievably neurotic to let something that had no effect on you as a child, suddenly become an incredible psychological issue to be resolved at great personal expense. Like most everything else in here, it isn't going to mean much of anything in your world. Of course, this Holy Grail will always have immeasurable value for you and all those who even merely touch the gold bound text.

I have finally heard from Eiju, my Zen priest friend from Mendoza, Argentina. As you know, he promised to write something for the book because I had a feeling it would belong. Presently, he is at a US west coast Zen center because those who know him have a sense about his unique nature and he is often invited to participate. It has been difficult to communicate with him for the past month and change. I finally got a rushed, broken English email from him. Computer access for him is tricky, but he is going to write something for you, which will likely be in Spanish. I don't give a shit exactly what he writes to you because it will be the unedited epilogue. When I finish off on the 31st, I really hope I don't write anything else within this format and I don't think I will. After all this time, why fuck up what feels like a miracle accomplishment for both of us?

Two more nights and we are pau, local Hawaiian pidgin for finished and done. I think I will write whatever I do on the 31st and that will be that. As long as we continue to be mortal, we will always come up short at the end. Life and death are really not a perfect circle, seamlessly joined and making one indistinguishable from the other. They just are what they are and at the very least, we should make it interesting between the open and the close of our show. What else is there? Most everyone could do well with a humility suppository on a fairly regular basis.

I sure as shit hope you find all of this to be very entertaining. Now that I think of it, this is actually intended to simply entertain you and not inform you. Treat this like a gourmet meal that you have every now and then, aware that the taste and texture will change with time. Gourmet has nothing to do with the purity of the ingredients, it has to do with the care in the preparation, presentation of the dish and getting your senses dancing. You work with what you got and you try and make it look and feel good. Seriously, there is nothing out of the ordinary about my life and I never think of my life in those terms anyway.

One More

Well, I will figure out a way to say ciao tomorrow, so the heat is off for tonight. The previous series of entries that began under The Future heading have run for a quite a few days by now. It was kind of like meandering toward the end of this tale, but we might as well start to get ready for Halloween. It is definitely going to take me some time to read through the two hundred fifty some odd pages I have written to you. It could take up to a month to get it right for the last time. Not writing for a month is not in the cards for me. I am accustomed to doing this at least every other evening and I will not be able to cut it off for that long. We shall see what happens on Nov 1st and go from there. At the very least, I will be forced to write essays to you that are stand alone pieces and I remember already bringing this up. Who knows, if I get into the essay thing the way I have with this, maybe we can pull off Volume II and call it Essays for Shane?

My writing muse is totally satisfied doing this stuff. Hopefully, I write slightly more literate emails, etc. than most people, but it is this singular, solitary thing we are doing that brings me the greatest, writing joy imaginable. If I can completely understand what I am writing about at any given moment, I am home free, baby.

If there are things you don't understand in here, it's OK and you sure don't have to agree with any of it either. You might likely take issue with any number of statements in here, but I wouldn't put a lot of energy into such an effort. If you happen to reread this one last time when you sneak up on your own sixty seventh birthday, it will have a dramatically different meaning for you than the first. We can have a metaphorical handshake and hug at that time. I know this is a tremendous legacy for you because of what is in here and how it is written to you. This is not immodest, it is simply honest.

We Made It

Happy Halloween, Shane! I'll be damned if we didn't pull this one off. This is cause for celebrating and I am. Do you have even the vaguest idea how deeply personal everything in here actually is to me? We got to hang out together for a year, during which time I told you about my life and my loves and my longings and what might have happened on any given day during this year of ours. I would like to think at this time that there are just two people who truly appreciate the gifting and the receiving. Lest you think the receiving is only on your end, be advised it has been an incredibly rich experience for me.

A year ago is not all that long in my mind and I remember everything about the weekend in Portland and Josette. We would not be here right now if I hadn't gone to Portland, pursuing a matter of the heart. When it clicked for me back then, I really wasn't sure I had it in me to do the full deal, but it was clear that it would be all or nothing. If there was anything half-hearted in this work, I'd be done in a flash. Believe me, not looking for any trophies, but this is a big fucken deal to pull off and I am feeling incredibly fine about it all.

You are now my best friend because no one else knows all of this stuff, but me. You will likely hear throughout your life people saying that you really didn't know who they were. More often than not, folks don't truly share themselves with others and while I can completely understand the mental mechanism behind it, people only know what we show them. As always, it starts and ends with us and no one else.

You know, I am trying to think of what to say. I certainly have no interest in pretending to be profound and I have tried to keep an eye on that particular tendency. This is not some old guy telling a young man what life is all about, God forbid. All of this is simply about my own life and nothing more. Just in case this whole thing has any value at all to yourself and possibly a few others, it is based on a true story, but should never be confused with the truth.

I am still amazed and in shock that we have finished out the year doing this. No matter what I write tonight, the only thing I give a shit about is that we done it. When I actually crossed the finish line of the New York City Marathon in 1982, it was a sensation impossible to convey. Let me tell you, it took some serious tenacity for me to finish that run without ever stopping or walking. Doing this has that same drive about it and I was committed to not walking in this race either.

I am terribly sad to bring this to a close, but it is not goodbye. Still, the story has been told and there is no backwards anymore.

Again, I look for something incredible to say and it isn't there for me. After all this time, if I haven't said it already, not sure it is worth saying.

Just as I was getting to the end of this tale, it dawned on me to write an introduction of some kind because I think most books start with something that allows you to eaves drop on what's come and the like. Even though our story has officially ended at this point, the introduction will be written after all is complete. I hope this is not confusing. I will now go backwards to the beginning and end up in this exact same place when the work is done.

Thanks for letting me tell my story. God bless you, Shane.

PS: The possibility with Susan slid into the shitter, just in case you thought I would leave it out of the ending. Happy now?

Epilogue by Eiju

The manifestation of human life, the life of all sentient beings, is the result of the same law of causation, everything is impermanent and everything changes. Only the human being is imbued with the capacity of reaching what is called, the Supreme Wisdom, the complete understanding of the truth of the existence, of life and death. In life, we find suffering, but we can be liberated from the causes that produce the suffering. Finding the keys for this liberation should be the most important matter that we undertake in our life. Our lives are very short and we must do whatever we can to free ourselves from continued suffering.

In about fifteen years, the manifestation of suffering for you maybe will be very strong or maybe not. With each passing generation, the changes are more remarkable. You will inherit the fruits of our actions and in my modest understanding of things it won't be as flavorful as those we received from our ancestors. We don't seem to learn from our past and that is enough to taint the flavor we pass along.

Look for the truth, the truth that can give you the reality of the meaning of birth, old age, sickness, and death. One of my teachers, Harada Tangen Roshi Sama, said to us, "You are the truth." This truth is revealed in a particular way to each of us, and even this is the unique Truth that pervades the entire Universe, but nobody can give it to us, show it to us, we must realize it for ourselves. It is the Supreme Truth, and I dare to say that the same one is always in front of our noses.

Truly, nothing is separated from us. The whole universe is oneself, only the illusory thoughts, the cultural baggage, the language, has formed in us that idea that we are somehow independent. We believe we are separate, something we identify as me, my. This has always been our identity, but that identity doesn't exist. How would we point out our identity? Is it you or is it you talking about your self. The perceiver, the medium and the perceived are not separate. We don't exist the way we think we do.

To wake up to the reality of our essence is to reach harmony and supreme happiness, where suffering doesn't take place and everything is in its fullness. We exist moment by moment in the eternity of each instant, where everything is perfect just as it is, nothing lacking and nothing in excess. Our essence is the truth that we call Buddha or God or whatever name we choose.

"Marvel of marvels, me, the great earth, the grasses, the stars, rivers, mountains, the whole universe, everything is Buddha nature". It is impossible to translate into English the Buddha's first words on being enlightened because he spoke in a language called Sanskrit.

There is a sutra or teaching called the Heart Sutra. It is something you can read your entire life and never feel you completely understand. The reason for this is simple, the awareness the Buddha talks about is not an intellectual process, rather it is something for which there are no words to adequately describe. It is like a secret you tell yourself and there is no language to explain it. Shane, read this sutra for the rest of your life and don't attempt to make sense of it, just allow yourself to feel it.

MAHA PRAJNA PARAMITA HEART SUTRA

(Hannya Shingyo)

Avalokitesvara Bodhisattva, doing deep Prajna Paramita,
Clearly saw emptiness of all the five conditions,
Thus completely relieving misfortune and pain,
O Shariputra, form is no other than emptiness; emptiness is no other than form;
Form is exactly emptiness, emptiness exactly form;
Sensation, conception, discrimination, awareness are likewise like this.
O Shariputra, all dharmas are forms of emptiness, not born, not destroyed;
Not stained, not pure, without loss, without gain;
So in emptiness there is no form, no sensation, conception, discrimination, awareness;
No eye, ear, nose, tongue, body, mind;
No color, sound, smell, taste, touch, phenomena;
No realm of sight . . . no realm of consciousness;
No ignorance and no end to ignorance . . .
No old age and death, and no end to old age and death;
No suffering, no cause of suffering, no extinguishing, no path;
No wisdom and no gain. No gain and thus
The bodhisattva lives Prajna Paramita
With no hindrance in the mind, no hindrance, therefore no fear,
Far beyond deluded thoughts, this is nirvana.
All past, present, and future Buddhas live Prajna Paramita,
And therefore attain Anuttara-samyak-sambodhi.
Therefore know, Prajna Paramita is
The great mantra, the vivid mantra,
The best mantra, the unsurpassable mantra;
It completely clears all pain, this is the truth, not a lie.
So set forth the Prajna Paramita Mantra,

Set forth this mantra and say:
Gate! Gate! Paragate! Parasamgate!
Bodhi Svaha. Prajna Heart Sutra.

My teacher, Tenshin Roshi, in a talk that he gave the other day, said to change the name of Avalokitesvara (great compassionate bodhisattva), for the name of each one of us. It is true, each one of us is this compassionate being, and in this case, I allowed myself to change the name for the one of **Shane.**

This is my only appearance in the epilogue. The following is lifted verbatim from the initial email I received from Eiju. The whole first Spanish paragraph is missing from the translation above and I am simply going to leave it to you to sort out. I have a feeling his original Spanish version is likely richer than the forced conversion to our language. I know I am supposed to have stopped writing on October 31st and I promise my story to you is complete. Just been killing some time on the front end while I wait for Eiju, but you know that from having read the introduction. Apologies to anyone else reading this paragraph, but I think you can appreciate that my responsibiity is to be truthful and heartfelt and always remember I am writing to my grandson.

Message to Larry´s grandson, Shane

Mi estimado amigo Larry, mi hermano del dharma, me ha honrado pidiéndome que escriba un mensaje que incorporará a un libro para que su nieto Shame, lea cuando cumpla los 18 años, antes que nada, es de tener en cuenta que la escritura no es mi fuerte, no soy bueno para ello, pero habiendo tomado la decisión de hacerlo, puedo ahora encontrar algo de tiempo para ello, estoy recién llegado a Yokoji, Zen Mountain Center, de Los Ángeles, y esta semana pasada me uní, a una sesshin o practica zen de entrenamiento intensiva, de una semana de duración, inserta en un periodo de tres meses llamado Ango, donde hay tres de esas semanas más intensas y el resto del tiempo es de acuerdo a un régimen que tiende a profundizar la práctica....

........La vida humana se presenta de diferentes maneras a través de los tiempos, pero me atrevo a decir que es solo en apariencia, porque la existencia de los seres sintientes es el resultado siempre de la misma ley de causalidad, todo es impermanente, todo cambia, en un devenir constante, y es quizás, solo el ser humano, quien esta imbuido de la capacidad de alcanzar lo que se da por llamar, la sabiduría suprema, la comprensión de la verdad de la existencia, de la vida y la muerte, es quien puede alcanzar la liberación de las causas que producen el sufrimiento, lo que en definitiva es el más importante asunto que deberíamos comprender y para lo cual solo contamos con un periodo de tiempo muy, pero muy corto, el desarrollo de una vida.

Para un joven de alrededor de 20 años, en el futuro cercano, quizás la intensidad de la manifestación del sufrimiento en su propia vida no sea muy fuerte, o quizás no, generación tras generación los cambios son más notables, para quienes hereden, los frutos de nuestras acciones, en mi modesto entender, los mismo no serán tan sabrosos, como los que recibimos nosotros de nuestros antepasados.

De todas maneras, todos en algún momento buscamos la verdad, mi maestro Harada Tangen Roshi Sama, suele decirnos, "Tu eres la verdad" y aunque ella sea algo propio de cada uno en particular, nadie puede dárnosla, mostrárnosla, sino que debemos alcanzarla, por nosotros mismos, pero aun que particular a cada ser, es parte del todo, de la verdad suprema, y me atrevo a decir que la misma está siempre frente a nuestras narices, porque somos esa verdad, nada está separado de nosotros, el universo entero es uno mismo, solo la mente, los pensamientos ilusorios, todo el bagaje cultural, el lenguaje, nos ha formado en la ilusión de que somos algo independiente, separado, algo que identificamos como yo, mi, mío, ha sido siempre nuestra identidad, pero esa identidad no existe, es aparente, no hay nada que podamos señalar como eso, no hay quien perciba y que este separado de lo percibido, y en esa misma identidad de la impermanencia de todas las cosas, somos uno con todo, despertar a esa realidad de nuestra esencia, en la propia experiencia, eso es alcanzar la armonía y felicidad suprema, donde el sufrimiento no tiene lugar, y todo es en su plenitud, simplemente eso, la existencia momento a momento del todo, del cual somos parte, sin importar el estado de esa manifestación, solo el cambio, vida y muerte se inter penetran mutuamente, no hay una sin la otra, todo es perfecto tal como es, nada falta, nada sobra, se es parte del todo, momento a momento en la eternidad de cada instante, y aunque esa vivencia es personal, imposible de compartir, la diversidad de las mismas, están dentro de la misma y única verdad, todo es la misma naturaleza de Buddha, Dios, o como quiera llamarse.

Maravillas de maravillas, yo, la gran tierra, las hierbas, las estrellas, ríos, montañas, el universo entero, todo es naturaleza de buddha, **¡Gate! ¡Gate! ¡Paragate! ¡Parasamgate! ¡Bodhi Svaha!**

The Shane Chronicles by Uncle Danny

Late that dark and chilly night in December
That was a day I will always remember.
In the waiting room of Mt. Sinai it is true,
We did wait for the latest member to the Feinstein crew.
Nine months in the company of Angels he did spend,
In conversation learning and all of his needs they did tend,
With the Angel Harriet, the Angel Ida and the Angel Betty his time did pass,
Until the Lord felt it was his time alas.
Onto the hands the of Andrew and Andrea the angels did deliver,
The hero of this story, the beautiful little Shane all a 'quiver.
From his mommy's tummy he came out,
With a cacophonous and mighty shout.
And all that looked upon him will never frown,
One glance at his little face and his full red crown.
And from the elevator to the waiting room his father did erupt,
With the news that no evil could corrupt.
Later to bed we all went that night,
Without an idea that awaited an aweful fright.
Daddy Andrew found himself on the basketball court,
With Frankie, Matt, Rob and his whole Leonia cohort.
A mad pick-up game it certainly was,
The whole crowd was raucous and abuzz.
He jooked left he jooked right, daddy was great,
For his diminutive size he had an impressive gait.
From the depths of the Overpeck swamp there appeared giant adders,
Poor Frankie, Matt and Rob nearly lost control of their bladders.
Only daddy Andrew stood true,
Somehow he knew the Mighty Shane would come to his rescue.
Suddenly from the reeds appeared the Mighty Shane,

In his hand there was a diamond gilded cane.
To the ground the cane the Mighty Shane did throw,
Into a giant king cobra it changed wouldn't you know.
Everyone watched with great wonder,
As the Mighty Shane's cobra tore the giant adders asunder.
Everyone with happiness did weep,
And the Mighty Shane disappeared with one mighty leap.
Daddy Andrew awoke eyes a'gleam,
As real as it felt he thought it but a dream.
Then surprised he saw there did hang,
From his bedroom ceiling one enormous fang.
Grandpa Ira stared at his monitor blue,
Watching the Dow Jones go up just as he knew.
Then suddenly catching him unaware,
Busted through the wall a giant bull and bear.
Getting up he ran without looking back,
Thinking poor Jimmy must be having a heart attack.
Onto Lexington avenue he did turn,
Moving so fast every sinew a'burn.
Just when he thought the Lord would take him away,
He spotted the Mighty Shane riding in a Hummer Limousine Cabriolet.
In his right hand an enormous dish
Of horseradish and gefilte fish.
The dish with ferocity the Mighty Shane threw,
And drowned the giant bull and bear in a reddish gelatinous goo.
Thankful it was a dream Ira woke with three great huffs,
Until he saw on his bed giant bull and bear ear muffs.
In Mah Jongg Grandma Ingrid had no border,
As she fleeced her friends of every last quarter.
Amassing an enormous bag of money,
Grandma Ingrid was thinking of what she would buy Shane, her little honey.
Suddenly crashing through the glass living room door,
A bunch of samurai and ninja from Japanese lore.
The ladies ran to the back except Grandma Ingrid,
Somehow she knew the Mighty Shane would come and bust their lid.
Looking out the window over the Hudson she did see,

The Mighty Shane alight a golden dragon, his face full of glee.
With armor, shield and sword he looked like a centurion,
And arms with the strength of Conan the Barbarian.
Crashing through the roof the Mighty Shane came,
For their mistake the warriors had none but themselves to blame.
For the warriors it all went awry,
Have you ever seen a samurai cry?
With a heave he struck left and right,
Oh my goodness, what an awesome sight.
The Mighty Shane on his golden dragon flew up in the sky blue,
Grandma Ingrid and her friends didn't even have time to say thank you.
Realizing it was a dream Grandma Ingrid woke with a smile,
Then she noticed a hundred nunchucks lying in a pile.
Grandpa Larry and some friends were aboard a canoe,
Singing, laughing and drinking some strange brew.
From the ocean their appeared explosively quick,
A whale a hundred times the size of Moby Dick.
Eyes black as death and each tooth a lance,
One of Granpa Larry's friends soiled their underpants.
But Granpa Larry's countenance remained strong,
Somehow he knew things wouldn't go wrong.
Just before everything went awry,
There came from above a thunderous eagle's cry.
Grandpa Larry looked up startled and nearly deaf
He spied alight a giant eagle the Mighty Shane dressed as a Benihana chef.
The Mighty Shane leapt from the giant eagle's back,
Straight into the whale's eye he dove on the attack.
With knives in his hands and ginger in his pocket,
The Mighty Shane disappeared into the whale's eye socket.
Before Grandpa Larry could strike a chord,
All that remained of the whale was a huge Sashimi board.
Suddenly Granpa Larry awoke,
"Oh my," he thought "What a Joke!"
His tune changed when he spied on his stoop,
An enormous pile of whale poop.
In the desert were Jen, Lauren and I,

The sun so hot on my head an egg could fry.
Laughing, joking and playing a game,
Riding through the desert on a giant horse with no name.
From over the horizon charging without discipline,
Came an army of angry urologists, geishas and Bedouin.
We thought it crazy we thought it strange,
But the fear we felt none of that did change.
Then from no where we saw the Mighty Shane,
In his hand an enormous candy cane.
Riding a chariot looking from out of the embattlements,
Of the pharaoh Ramses from The Ten Commandments.
Before the army had time to retreat back,
The Mighty Shane snarled and went on the attack.
An enormous sandstorm ensued,
All that escaped my lips was "dude."
Jen woke up and in denial,
Found in her bedroom myriad stethoscopes in a pile.
Lauren found looking like clam chowder,
Her wall caked with a thick white makeup powder.
I awoke but nothing could see,
There were hundreds of kafias piled all over me.
Aunt Allison and uncle Carey hitting a couple of holes at the club,
Were thinking about finishing up and getting some grub.
Then from the midst of the fairway did appear,
A monstrous alligator with a terrible sneer.
Riding a winged horse the Mighty Shane looked down without stress,
He thought he'd let big cousin Zack take care of this mess.
With a crash Zack came busting through the trees,
In disbelief Allison and Carey fell to their knees.
With a giant Big Bertha cousin Zack attacks and attacks,
Driving the alligator high up into the Adirondacks.
Allison and Carey woke spying in the middle of their abode,
Zack decked out in a stylish fitted alligator wardrobe.
Grandma Brenda was at a game of poker and winning,
Making so much money her head was spinning.
The chips were piled high, she was making a ton,

All she could think was what she would buy her grandson.
At the table were Brooklyn Fred and Hoboken Tad,
At the game too many scary characters she had.
When it was over the meanies said with a belch,
On Grandma Brenda they were going to welch.
Before Grandma Brenda could say a toot,
The Mighty Shane appeared in a Fadora and shark skin suit.
Shane had his Tommy gun in tow,
Where to turn the meanies did not know.
As the Mighty Shane pulled the trigger, the gun did hum,
And fired a million pieces of chewing gum.
When the dust cleared gone was the trouble,
They disappeared into space in a big giant bubble.
Waking Grandma Brenda could not get a grip,
On her night table was a million dollar casino chip.
And in her closet in place of her scarf of agora,
Was The Mighty Shane's purple fedora.
Grandpa Steven walked out the door
Whistling a tune on the way to the toy store.
For his grandchildren he was to buy,
Whatever nice things that caught his eye.
From out of the sky came to the attack
A great cockatoo with eyes of black.
In his giant taloned feet,
He carried an enormous bottle of Baron de Rothschilde Chateau Lefite.
Grandpa Steven tried to run but did stumble,
The entire neighborhood began to rumble.
Busting through the street like the Incredible Hulk,
Was the Mighty Shane in all of his bulk.
Wearing a insulated suit and in his hand a flame gun,
He looked like a character from Farrenheit 451.
High The Mighty Shane's gun was heave'n,
Because he knew it was time to save his Granpa Steven.
Then from the gun came an enormous flame to the sky,
The giant cockatoo felt his time was nigh.
Granpa Steven woke with a "huh,"

For on his dresser was a beautifully garnished plate of Coco Van.
Mommy Andrea was busy making a Stew,
On Sunday evening as was her custom to do.
It was a recipe from some panel,
That she saw earlier that day on the Food Channel
Stirring and stirring and feeling great,
Awaiting Daddy Andrew was a savory plate.
From nowhere erupted from the pot of stew,
An enormous threatening monstrous Ragu.
It came at mommy at a heck of a pace,
Dripping peppers and tomatoes all over the place.
But mommy didn't show any fear,
Because in her heart she felt the Mighty Shane was near.
Then jumped down the stairs with a loud thud,
Was the Mighty Shane, mommies little spud.
Around his neck he wore a golden bib,
In his hand a giant spoon he fashioned from his crib.
To the Mighty Shane the Ragu did appeal,
But no mercy for monsters did the Mighty Shane feel.
Half way the Mighty Shane did halt,
Turning to his mommy he said, "it could use a little salt."
Waking mommy Andrea nearly did swoon,
All that was left of her kitchen was a mess and a huge dirty spoon.
It was with neither force nor power,
That The Lord created from his mighty tower.
Rather, fashioned and sculpted is the world with love,
As he showed Father Noah with a white turtle-dove.
Looking into his crib I no longer feel sad,
For in Shane's eyes I see the child I long ago should have had.
Now when I am tucked into bed at night,
I shed no tear and feel no fright.
For me as with you abolished should be fear,
In the knowledge that the Mighty Shane is near.
Written this song is by his number one fan,
It is I, his chronicler, Shane's uncle Dan.

Made in the USA
San Bernardino, CA
08 May 2014